The Lawyer's Guide to Strategic Practice Management

2nd edition

EDITED BY LAURA SLATER

Head of legal publishing
Fiona Fleming

Publisher
Helen Donegan

Editor
Laura Slater

Published by
Globe Law and Business Ltd
3 Mylor Close
Horsell
Woking
Surrey GU21 4DD
United Kingdom
Tel: +44 20 3745 4770
www.globelawandbusiness.com

ISBN: 978-1-78358-223-5
A catalogue record for this book is available from the British Library

Contents

Executive summary

The legal profession continues to experience change, and law firms must continue to adapt. While the economy has improved, and businesses are recovering from the global economic downturn, the recession that was undergone introduced new challenges in the form of greater client demands, increased competition, internal cost cutting, and a greater focus on operational efficiency – to name but a few. And these are here to stay. Law firms that recognized and responded to these changes have survived. The leaders of these firms are aware that they must continually seek to improve and refine their management strategies in order to compete and thrive in an increasingly challenging market.

The Lawyer's Guide to Strategic Practice Management, 2nd edition, has been fully updated with new material providing expert advice for law firm leaders on key management areas. This edition has been expanded to contain 33 chapters, covering six crucial areas of law firm management: strategy; market and client development; people and talent management; finance and pricing; and optimization and technology.

Section One (Chapters 1–5), in recognition of the fact that law firms need to have clear and coherent plans in place in order to continue to prosper, is devoted to law firm strategy. It begins with chapters on defining law firm strategy and the steps in a strategic planning process, and moves on to provide expert guidance on how to analyze strategic trends in order to determine how your firm could be affected, and what plans are needed to prepare for them. This section also covers mergers as a strategic option, as well as the importance of innovation in legal services and how to cultivate a culture of innovation within your firm.

Chapter 6 is the first to appear in Section Two (Chapters 6–11), and this chapter bridges the gap between law firm strategy and the next area of focus – market and client development. This chapter identifies methods for looking to the future to identify and capitalize on growth opportunities. Continuing on from this, the remaining five chapters in this section explore how a firm needs to constantly evolve its business development and client strategies in order to remain competitive in today's market. Expert advice is provided from renowned business development coach David H. Freeman who outlines the steps a firm can take to identify market niches and develop business development strategies that will differentiate your practice. David's experience and expertise is also shared in another chapter in which he provides practical advice on how to motivate lawyers to cross-sell within your firm.

Section Two also contains a chapter on key relationship programs, with information on how to assess your firm's need for such a program, along with a key relationship management self-diagnostic. Heidi K. Gardner (Harvard Business School) and Rebecca Normand-Hochman (Venturis Consulting and the IBA) discuss how culture can assist you in giving clients a true one-firm global service. The section concludes with an important chapter on how to unlock value through collaboration with outside counsel.

According to the Altman Weil "Law Firms in Transition Survey" 2015: "Law firms that have changed their strategic approach to lawyer staffing, efficiency of legal service delivery and pricing are consistently more likely to see increases in gross revenue, revenue per lawyer (RPL) and profits per equity partner (PPEP) than those firms that have not embraced strategic change."[1] In recognition of this need for strategic direction in the areas of staffing, legal service delivery/optimization, and pricing, these are the areas of focus for Sections 3–5 of this book.

Section Three (Chapters 12–18) covers one of the most crucial components of a law firm's success: its people. This section focuses on lawyers of all levels and a firm's talent management strategy in acknowledgement of the fact that, without having the right recruitment, professional development, compensation, and leadership practices in place, nothing else in your law firm will work. The section begins with a focus on diversity and the importance of building inclusiveness into the talent development function for the benefit of the business. In particular, this chapter provides practical advice on how to align women's initiative efforts with your firm's talent management strategies.

Chapters 13 and 14 cover the crucial topics of law firm compensation systems and measuring the performance of your partners, with advice on integrating incentives with firm goals and how to link performance to rewards. Following on from this, Section Three also contains a chapter on the roles of partners and leaders. It outlines the future partner roles that will exist in law firms, along with the use of competency frameworks and Balanced Scorecards. Chapter 16 continues the leadership debate with advice on law firm leadership development. It outlines a plan for practice group leadership development, with guidance on leadership styles. Patrick McKenna's chapter explores the topic of leadership succession, and it provides tips for the succession process for both the outgoing and the incoming leaders. This section ends with a chapter on the hugely important topic of how law firms can get the best from the new generations of lawyers entering the profession.

Section Four (Chapters 19–22) focuses on finance and pricing, and it opens with a chapter on cash and lock-up profiles for law firm teams and departments. This is accompanied by a practical chapter on improving cash flow. Fee expert Patrick Lamb shares his advice on alternatives to the billable hour in Chapter 21. He explains the link between fee structures and behavior, and outlines the options in different fee arrangements. In a joint chapter by Toby Brown (Akin Gump) and Vincent Cordo Jr (Reed Smith), the authors advise on developing the right pricing model for your firm, based on data.

Section Five then moves on to the subjects of law firm optimization and technology. The section begins with two chapters on optimization and Lean strategies for law firms. Chapter 23 explains the importance of optimization for law firms, with detailed information on what optimization looks like in a law firm and the difference between a strategic and operational focus on optimization. Legal Lean Sigma Black Belt and certified Six Sigma Green Belt Catherine Alman MacDonagh provides insight into what legal process improvement is in practice and how Lean and Six Sigma can be applied in a law firm context. The fundamentals of technological advances in law firms are covered in Chapter 25, with a focus on concepts such as bring your own device (BYOD), big data, and cloud technology. Next, Chapter 26 explains how to align your firm's IT and business strategies, and this is followed by a chapter focusing on how to ensure greater value from your firm's IT investments.

The increasingly recognized and accepted topics of AI and "robot law" are discussed in Chapters 28 and 29. Advice is shared on the future of law in this technological age, with examples from practice, and guidance on the need for preparation to deal with these changes and use them for the benefit of your firm.

Finally, the book ends with Section Six (Chapters 30–33) and covers some important legal and business development skills for lawyers. With all of the work done to get prospective clients interested (based on the advice shared in Section Two) comes the hard part – the pitch. Having a bullet-proof pitching process in place dramatically improves your chances of winning new business and Chapter 30 looks at the pitch planning process, with advice on how to decide on your pitch team, pricing and fee reviews, meeting plans, and the overall pitch strategy. Next, expert tips on social media strategies are shared in two chapters. Practical advice on building a social law firm is discussed in Chapter 31, which outlines how a firm can develop a strategic social media plan and put governance in place to monitor this. This chapter also highlights how a firm can build social advocacy into its culture, and go on to measure and adapt its social media strategy to suit the firm. Tailored advice is then shared on how to optimize a LinkedIn profile in order to be found by and attract your ideal clients. Step-by-step advice is provided on building your profile, with information on how to make your profile stand out. Finally, to conclude Section Six, in the final chapter of the book, cognitive interviewing expert Geoff Coughlin shares advice on how to manage a witness interview and the skills required to ensure that your interviews elicit as much accurate information as possible, in order to save time and ensure success for your case.

Within the pages of this book is the expertise and practical advice of some of the best minds in the legal and business consulting industries. The second edition of *The Lawyer's Guide to Strategic Practice Management* gives you the advice you need in order to ensure the future success of your law firm.

Reference

1. Clay, T. and Seeger, T., "Law Firms in Transition: An Altman Weill Flash Survey", by Altman Weill, 2015. See: www.altmanweil.com/dir_docs/resource/1c789ef2–5cff-463a-863a-2248d23882a7_document.pdf.

Part 1:
Law firm strategy

Chapter 1:
Defining your strategy

By Viv Williams, chief executive officer of 360 Legal Group

Defining a law firm's strategy should be something that all firm partners have already considered and implemented. However, when most lawyers become partners they continue to work "in their practice" rather than "on their practice" and never seem to have a clearly defined strategy to enable them to see where the growth might come from. When fee earning dominates the agenda, and collecting cash also preoccupies partners, there is little wonder that there becomes no time for strategy.

Without a clearly defined strategy law firms are doomed to fail. The strategy is not a huge document that might sit in a bottom drawer for years to come, but instead it should be a living practical plan that moves as conditions and circumstances change. It should define the key salient points required in managing a firm's practice as a business and in developing its strategy for future growth.

The strategy should include:

- The firm's business structure – Separating ownership from management;
- The services offered – Pricing each department for profitability;
- The skill set of people to deliver agreed services – By utilizing work flows and other cloud-based solutions a number of services could be delivered by de-skilled people; and
- Managing the firm's finances – Access to working capital.

Knowing who the firm's clients actually are and what services they want is an exercise that should be undertaken. Understand what type of clients the firm serves and what they can afford to pay for the firm's services. In other words firms should not build their strategy around high net worth clients when their current client base has a very different make-up. As new competitors enter the market offering a diverse range of legal services, firms must accept that, as this is becoming the "new norm" it will become more relevant to know who the firm's clients really are.

Strategic planning for law firms has been on the agenda for years, but sadly most practices have ignored this essential tool in defining their future. Before firms can even consider growth and competing with the new entrants for market share they have to recognize who their clients actually are.

Defining what the firm wants

Well before contemplating what services to offer and to whom, firms need to agree the fundamental issues concerning their corporate structure. Developing a simple model for explaining what the firm wants both collectively as a business and individually as owners or partners is an essential tool in defining the firm's future.

The partnership model, although not completely obsolete, is not fit for purpose in the current era for most firms. The collegiate approach simply does not work and managing any business by committee leads to a lack of decision making and inertia. Hence the move of many forward thinking practices to convert into a corporate structure and to seek professional management advice, invariably from a person who has not trained to be a lawyer but must understand the nuances of the profession. Now 37 percent of practices trading in the UK are limited companies.

If the firm's strategy is to retain independence and develop a business model that is both fit for purpose and in line with current corporate thinking, then this seems to be the only realistic option.

If a firm is thinking realistically about future strategy, then corporate governance and legal entity should be one of the first items on the agenda. It will solve numerous fundamental issues such as:

- Buying the firm's own goodwill – It may be the only buyer for the foreseeable future;
- Succession issues – Younger owners do not want traditional equity but may take a directorship;
- Exit strategies for partners who wish to retire;
- Corporate governance – Planning to manage the business not letting the business manage you; and

- The potential of private equity funding to grow and develop the business.

Additionally there are significant tax advantages in becoming a corporate; however, one of the most significant changes when a firm converts to a corporate is the management. Corporate governance drives performance in law firms; it fundamentally changes the culture. Lawyers are simply not trained to be good managers and not many make the transition from good lawyer to good manager (there are of course obvious exceptions).

When a practice converts, invariably the questions are posed as to what happens to existing partners who remain stakeholders in the new business but tend not to be involved in the day to day management. In any corporate body there is a managing director (managing partner), a finance director, and perhaps some strategic appointments as directors from the existing partners. This means that the new board of directors are responsible for running the business in a day to day capacity. They produce targets and cash flows and report to the shareholders and stakeholders in the business on the performance. Directors can be removed from the board for non-performance and failure to reach adequate targets.

This does not sound like the traditional law firm with some partners performing well above their billing targets and others underperforming, yet no one is ever removed from the partnership despite a falling out of the partners over individual performance. The number of partnerships where this is true is staggering – partners who carry other dysfunctional partners who should have been removed from the partnership many years ago.

Whilst this does not happen in every practice, partners should honestly assess whether this rings true for their own law firm. Problems to identify are as follows: no succession and exit strategies; no marketing or business development ideas; and no idea how to compete against the new brands currently winning clients and taking away core business.

What should be at the core of the strategy?

Once a firm has decided to retain independence as a practice and compete in this new world for existing and new clients they need to consider what the next step is.

The fundamental answer to this question is to know who the firm is serving. While the firm and its lawyers may not have been proficient in cross selling in the past or even in communicating with clients, it is still likely that the firm has a number of loyal clients who value the work done for them by the firm and who value the firm's services. They may offer work more frequently if they are told about the firm's various offerings!

Decisive actions

New and innovative ways of delivering legal services are increasingly in the spotlight – witness the creation of the ABA Commission on the Future of Legal Services. In the UK and Australia, the arrival of "alternative business structures", which allow non-lawyer investment in law firms, have really shaken up the market. In this context, it is imperative that law firms decide now what direction their firm is planning to take.

The profession can be categorized into three areas: the well managed strong national and regional firms; the firms who are seriously financially challenged; and the vast majority – probably as much as 75 percent of the remainder – who do not have a clear direction and plan. These firms are not under severe financial pressure but have no succession or exit strategies for the existing partners. Do they continue to practice for several years? Do they try to sell up, and at what value and to whom?

The new dawn of legal services offers considerable opportunity to those prepared to plan their future. Unquestionably there will be challenges along the way, but the poorly marketed brand of "lawyer" will still have a significant role to play in the new era.

Many lawyers are often so preoccupied with immediate issues that they lose sight of their ultimate objectives. That is why a business review or preparation of a strategic plan is a virtual necessity. This may not be a recipe for success, but without it a practice is much more likely to fail. A sound plan should:

- Become a framework for decisions;
- Provide a basis for more detailed thinking and planning;
- Explain the business to others in order to inform, motivate, and involve;
- Assist benchmarking and performance monitoring; and
- Stimulate change and become a building block for future plans.

A strategic plan should not be confused with a business plan. A strategic plan is designed to be a short working document whereas a business plan is usually a much more substantial and detailed document. A strategic plan can provide the foundation and framework for a business.

The starting point must be to determine if there is an existing vision, mission, objectives, and strategies. Then judge these against actual performance along the following lines:

- Is there a current vision and is this being achieved?
- How has the firm's mission and objectives changed over the past three years? Why have the changes occurred or why have no changes occurred? Identify primary reasons and categorize them as either internal or external.
- Describe the actual strategies followed over the past few years in respect of products/services, operations, finance, marketing, IT, management etc.
- Critically examine each strategy statement by reference to activities and actions in key functional areas covering such matters as:
  - How has the firm been managed?
  - How has the firm been funded?
  - How has the firm sought to increase turnover?
  - How have overheads increased?
  - How have redundancies affected the business?

Take each of the above and try to reference this against actual performance. Continue to ask why and establish the reasons for differences between the actual and desired performance.

A firm rarely succeeds or fails for minor or trivial reasons. The causes are usually substantial and are often self-evident, at least to an outsider. For example, the firm completely over-borrowed, management was weak, badly implemented mergers, client care and cross selling of services are ignored, or exiting former partners expect capital account repayments in an unreasonable way.

It should be possible in the course of a few pages to set down the main elements of a business's vision, mission, values, objectives, goals, strategies, SWOTs etc. The compilation of a short report along these lines is likely to prove much more difficult than a lengthy dissertation which mixes up details and principles, and confuses the broad picture.

Partner retreats

In many cases, partners in law firms cannot agree to even writing the most basic strategic plan and at this time of extreme change it is more important than ever that law firms have a clear vision as to what the future holds for them.

Law firms have traditionally grown by succession and have never needed to consider why they are in practice in a traditional partnership or what services they should offer and how they charge for these services – it has been passed on over decades. Many younger partners are now questioning why they deliver certain services. More importantly, they are questioning their very existence in this new legal landscape.

A partner retreat will focus partners on these fundamental and important issues rather than the urgent ones that crop up every day. Partnerships that are not in full agreement as to the key issues should consider taking time away from their day to day fee earning activity to gain the advantage of a formal meeting away from the office.

It is essential that all firms have a shared strategic vision and all the partners must agree to that vision. How many partnerships continue to operate with one or more dysfunctional partner who has a different agenda to the remaining partners?

This lack of a common vision with a dysfunctional partner (or more) creates the poor performing practices seen today – many of which will be poorly managed and have profitability and cash flow issues. It is these practices that will be among the thousands of law firms that are predicated not to be in business within the next few years.

Partners find it difficult to share their views with each other if there is dissatisfaction within the partnership, whether it be due to lack of profitability or more fundamental issues. The average age of an equity partner in a law firm is now 60 years of age and it is when those partners realize that there are no younger potential partners willing to become equity partners in their firm that their exit strategy becomes a real concern. The traditional exit route for an equity partner was for younger people with potential to become partners to raise the necessary capital to buy into the existing partnership and therefore provide the repayment of the capital account of the partner looking to retire.

All partners will benefit from a partner retreat. The aim of the retreat is to establish the correct outcome for the law firm as a going concern, and not the individual partners. To date it has generally been the mid to larger firms that have taken time to stand back from the daily routine and fee earning. In his book *The E-myth Revisited*,[1] Michael Gerber encourages all businesses to spend time working on the business and not in it.

What is in the best interests of the firm has to take priority over the interests of the senior partner. An outside facilitator can force the partners to vote on this type of fundamental issue. It is essential that the retreat has an outside facilitator who is aware of the firm's issues. Partners will open up when challenged and an outcome for the benefit of the firm can generally be achieved.

It is always advisable to hold a retreat away from the office, avoiding the obvious distractions, and it will take one or possibly two days. Many firms hold their retreat over the weekend to avoid the loss of fee income. Other firms will take a day away from the office to complete their retreat. Spring and autumn seem to be the most popular times but avoiding key holiday times or when work flow is at its most demanding time. The facilitator will write the agenda with the assistance of the partner/ partners who have organized the retreat.

In a recent example, a 10 partner practice with a turnover of £3.5 million ($5.3 million) agreed, following a day's retreat, to become incorporated and to have five directors, the youngest female partner becoming managing director of the newly formed business – now that's a result.

Each retreat is very different and the outcomes vary but there are examples of outcomes that can be achieved as follows:

- Decision to seek a merger partner;
- Decision to sell the practice;
- Decision to acquire other practices and develop a strategy for growth by acquisition;
- Split up of partnership – Partners responsible for publicly funded work leave partnership to join other publicly funded partners;
- Agreed exit strategy for dysfunctional partner(s);
- Partner agreement to drop unprofitable legal services – Some partners agree to re-train;
- Partnership agreeing that they need help and assistance to develop the firm;
- Partners agree to appoint non-lawyer to effectively run the practice; and
- Agreement to change the partnership to either LLP status or limited company status. (This greatly assists with succession planning.)

As more firms begin to realize they will need to change the way they deliver services and become more business-orientated there is an increasing demand for partner retreats. These are serious fundamental strategy sessions to ensure the firm is addressing the fundamental issues facing the legal profession.

In many cases the day is split into two sessions: the relevant team members (accounts, practice manager, heads of departments etc.) would attend the morning session but only the equity partners would stay for the remainder. If tough decisions have to be made then that has to be the responsibility of those that own the firm.

All aspects of the firm should be discussed, however, there are usually one or two burning issues that become paramount.

A written report is provided by the facilitator to the partners and this is the basis of a strategic plan. The plan will have action points some of which will require outside assistance. This is then converted into a growth plan.

The implementation process behind change management will assist those firms who wish to embrace change to realize their true objectives.

How to ensure clients value the firm's services and how that becomes part of the strategy

Many law firms have failed to recognize the importance of client care and how, by taking care of their clients, they will encourage clients to take care of the firm. A firm cannot develop a strategy for growth without knowledge of the market they serve. As mentioned above, there is no point whatsoever in stating the firm's intention to drop entirely a type of work that makes up its core business. Every firm should know the cost of obtaining a new client – it actually costs six times as much to find a new client as it does to retain an existing one.

How can a traditional law firm compete with new market entrants offering fixed fees for commoditized services? Many years ago a traditional law firm could open up a new practice on a busy high street and be relatively assured of a decent footfall to encourage new clients – this is no longer the case. It is no longer sufficient for firms to claim that they have been established for many years and expect that to bring in clients. Clients have changed and therefore the firm must change; both the services offered and the way they are delivered.

How many law firms actually take the time to ask their clients what they want and how they could improve their service? Surely at every file closure it is appropriate to write to the client and ask a number of pertinent questions:

- How would you rate the service you received?
- Is there anything we could do to improve our service?
- Would you recommend us to another potential client?

The clients of most law firms do trust their lawyer and in a survey of 12,000 commercial and private clients of law firms in the UK who have responded to a satisfaction survey, over 96.4 percent would recommend their lawyer to another potential client.[2] Unfortunately over 99 percent of those asked "would they refer others?" claim never to have been asked. Is this a missed opportunity?

Client satisfaction surveys also indicate the differences between how a client rated a firm in comparison to the client's expectations. The three key areas for concern are:

- Higher fees than expected;
- Poor timeliness in both delivery of service and, even worse, the failure to return telephone calls; and
- A lack of pro-activity.

Clients are demanding that lawyers become more pro-active with advice and guidance. More "want" rather than "need" driven services are being offered by progressive law firms and it is these firms who will attract the clients from the firm who is not being pro-active.

Giving clients what they want, and offering a delivery mechanism to ensure the services delivered are on time, is the way of the future. A simple message to all partners and fee earners is to "always under promise and over deliver". If this simple philosophy is adopted clients will not only remain as clients to the firm, but will undoubtedly tell others about the excellent service they receive.

Clients should be at the core of every practice – a people-focused client centric practice is essential to maintain and grow the client base. It is recommended that a program of 10 contacts per annum be introduced, avoiding holiday months of both August and December. These contacts should consist of a variety of contacts and those firms who had the foresight to gather the email addresses of clients when opening a file should find this an economical and rewarding exercise. Ten years ago very few of us had an email address; now most of us have at least two, if not more. This logic can be applied to your own clients, whatever their age, and they actually prefer to be contacted by email.

Of course, this assumes the firm has a decent client relationship management (CRM) system to enable it to take advantage of this idea. Those law firms who do have a CRM system can contact both existing and potential clients by the following: a quarterly newsletter, a series of news alerts, an invitation to a seminar, or any other item or event that is relevant to the client.

It is essential that a law firm becomes an information centric organization; profiling the existing client base will give the base information needed. Once the firm has established the mix of clients, i.e. a breakdown of the percentages between private client and commercial, profiling what type of client the firm is most successful with will give the core information required to create a marketing process.

The term cross selling is often used, and by profiling the client base the firm can create practice-wide opportunities. The simple acronym AIDA (attention, interest, desire, and action) can be applied to all marketing processes. Not surprisingly, offering the right service to the right client at the right time, and with the right offer, produces outstanding results.

Relationship marketing is the basis for creating a "loyalty ladder" for clients. On the first rung are potential clients who are merely "suspects" at this stage; the second rung identifies these as potential "prospects", potential clients who match the firm's profile; the third rung is when they actually become "clients"; and the fourth rung is when they are so pleased with the service they receive that they "advocate" the firm to others.

A useful exercise to undertake is to evaluate the potential lifetime value of clients. Once the firm's best clients have been identified, the database model will track each client and update all their activity with the firm. This will give a forecast of client value to the firm over time and is invaluable when identifying new clients. Once the firm has established what type of client gives the greatest lifetime value, firms can focus the bulk of marketing activity to the same type of client profile. This has the effect of focused marketing and is both cost effective and targeted.

In conclusion, it has been found that the highest return on investment comes not from new clients but from existing "best and valued clients". Adhere to the following steps to ensure clients look after the firm:

- Identify the most valued clients;
- Improve the firm's CRM system to enable it to measure their value;
- Try a pilot program to deal with the firm's best clients on a one to one basis;

- Try a client advisory group and gather ideas from them;
- Profile the firm's best clients and target similar groups;
- Ask clients to nominate a non-client for a special offer;
- Ensure that all staff realize the importance of client loyalty;
- Calculate the lifetime value of a loyal client;
- Develop a number of client "rewards" for the firm's best clients; and
- Create a plan (with a deadline) on how the firm can create greater client loyalty.

The firm's services

What services are currently being offered by the firm and how do they fit with the client base? For example if the firm has a large number of a particular type of client, why should they suddenly change what they buy from the firm? Packaging and bundling of fixed price services is already becoming the norm and these services will have to match the demands of the client base. It may well be that some of the services a firm has traditionally offered to clients are no longer profitable – so how should the firm's strategy deal with this issue? Should the firm simply tell the client that they no longer provide that type of service and recommend another firm?

These are difficult questions when deciding on the future growth of a firm and some partners may no longer be required for the sake of the future of the firm. Hence the collegiate attitude will have to change when deciding the future strategy of the firm.

Who will do the work?

Fixed price services delivered and given the undivided attention of a partner are a recipe to lose money on every file. A number of practices still believe that giving partner-led services at a commoditized price will make them money and these firms are losing money. If a firm is to deliver a commoditized service then who should be doing the work?

The Co-op, who employ the largest number of paralegals in the UK, have a model based on the "pile them high sell them cheap" principal, although the Co-op may argue that point. Value for money services delivered ethically will compete favorably and head to head with independent law firms.

Defining the difference between a client and customer has an important bearing on future strategy. If a firm chooses to deliver fixed price commoditized services that are price sensitive then they have to de-skill the staff and utilize cloud-based work flows that will ensure the quality of the work is not compromised.

The counter argument is to change the firm's strategy so as not to deliver these types of services. For many firms this is a big question to answer.

Dropping services, staff, and even partners will be one of the biggest decisions facing many partnerships, but that all forms part of defining the future strategy. Tough decisions have to be taken if the firm wishes to ensure survival. Are there departments and parts of the firm that are simply unprofitable? Could growth be improved by reducing overheads and releasing unprofitable partners and their departments?

This first appeared as Chapter 3 in Williams, V., Growth Strategies for Law Firms, *ARK Group, 2013.*

References

1. Gerber, M. *The E-myth Revisited*, Harper Collins, 2009.
2. Independent survey carried out by 360 Legal Group of 12,000 law firms.

Chapter 2:
Introduction to the strategic planning process

By John Sterling, co-founder and partner at Smock Sterling Strategic Management Consultants

The purpose of strategy in any for-profit organization is to position the firm to achieve better and more sustainable returns than the competition – in essence, to capture a sustainable competitive advantage. Doing so requires the firm to satisfy major stakeholders (primarily customers, but also knowledge workers, shareholders, and others) over both the near and longer term. Ultimately, business strategy is about winning in competitive markets.

The origins of business strategy can be directly traced to the immediate post-WWII era and Peter Drucker's 1946 book *Concepts of the Corporation*.[1] Drucker gets to the heart of the issue making the following point: "A company's primary responsibility is to serve its customers. Profit is not the primary goal, but rather an essential condition for the company's continued existence. There is only one valid definition of business purpose: to create a customer."

In other words, if an organization cannot satisfy its clients in a superior manner over a sustained period, the rest of its mission is doomed – there will be no profits for the shareholders, no wages for the workforce, and no future for the firm.

Business strategy really began to flower in the 1960s, when Bruce Henderson founded the Boston Consulting Group (BCG).[2] While consultancies existed, BCG cemented the idea of business strategy. The premise that tools and models could directly influence business performance gained legitimacy during this period. Firms like BCG, Bain & Company, McKinsey & Company, and Arthur D. Little all contributed to the proliferation of useful models and tools. Today, most managers understand things such as economies of scale and the experience curve, product life cycles, and the various matrices that consultants trot out to analyze markets and businesses.

More than perhaps any consultant, academic, or management guru, Michael Porter[3] has provided the central definitions for what we know today as business strategy and strategic planning. In his seminal 1985 book *Competitive Advantage: Creating and Sustaining Superior Performance*, Porter began with the supposition that: "Competition is at the core of the success or failure of firms… Competitive strategy aims to establish a profitable and sustainable position against the forces that determine industry competition." Porter highlighted three so-called generic strategies in *Competitive Advantage*:

- Cost leadership – Capturing customers on the basis of price;
- Differentiation – Capturing customers on the basis of offering unique value; and
- Focus – Targeting narrow markets in which your firm has an advantage.

A decade or so later, Porter refined this thinking, specifically sharpening the definition in his landmark *Harvard Business Review* article,[4] "What is Strategy?", by explaining that: "Competitive strategy is about being different. It means deliberately choosing a different set of activities to deliver a unique mix of value."

Porter makes the further point that simply pursuing the low cost position is not a source of sustainable advantage – someone is always willing to go lower. In the legal marketplace we see this manifest in many ways – the continual erosion of rates and margins in insurance defense, the increased outsourcing of document review to low cost alternatives (for example, contract attorneys, off-shore operations, etc.), and the standardization of transactional and other documents (for example, simple wills, loan documents, etc.).

This chapter describes the four-phase roadmap for creating a strategic plan at the firm or practice group level, assuming one is starting essentially with a blank sheet of paper. Most of today's firms are not starting with a totally blank slate – many firms will start the planning process with a well considered and widely embraced mission and/or with a clearly understood set of shared cultural values. In general, the process works from the bigger picture and the longer term and moves gradually toward more specific decisions and the nearer term.

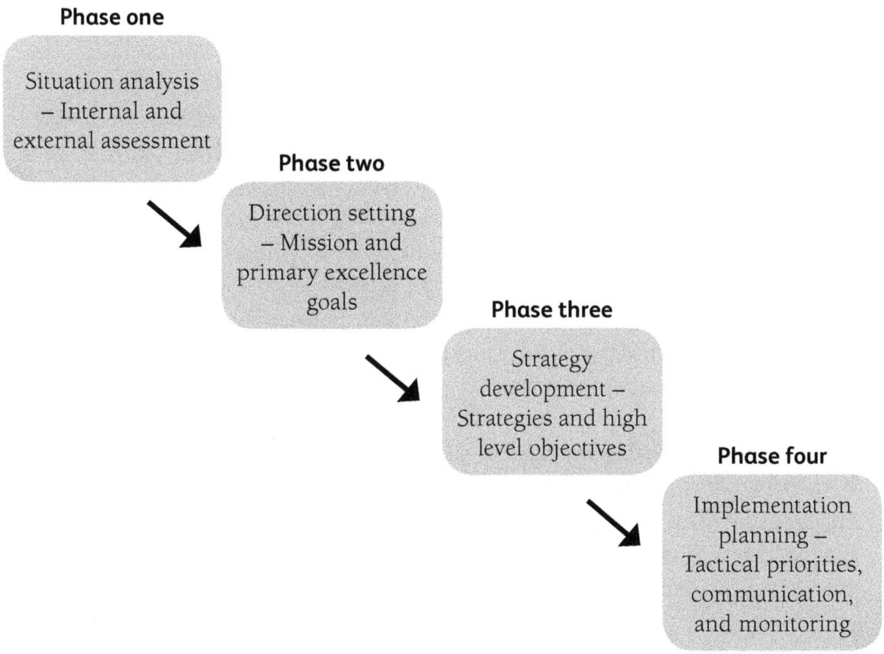

Figure 1: The schematic phased process for creating a strategic plan

Phase one – Situation analysis

The situation analysis phase is designed to ensure strategy development is built on a foundation of facts. The intent is not to create analysis paralysis, but rather to establish a shared understanding of the internal state of the firm (or practice) and the external, competitive market environment it faces. Ideally, work during this phase is driven by a principle of information sufficiency (i.e. gathering enough information and performing enough analysis to understand the situation). Frankly, there is always one more data point that could be gathered, but ultimately continual fact gathering will result in diminishing returns.

Phase two – Direction setting

The direction setting phase focuses on reaching agreement on the big picture questions. What does the firm (or practice) aspire to become? What areas will it focus resources on to gain a sustained competitive advantage? The end product is generally some combination of a well articulated vision and mission for the firm (or practice) and a related set of primary goals. The time horizon in the direction setting phase is longer term – three to five years (often longer with regard to the vision).

Phase three – Strategy and objective development

The strategy development phase focuses on making strategic trade-offs among rational alternatives. Since resources are necessarily limited – in a law firm environment, time is the most finite resource – choices need to be made. The strategy development phase enables the firm (or practice) to answer the question: "What do we intend to do to achieve our primary goals?" The issue of how (in the very near term) the firm will implement those decisions is dealt with in phase four. This phase also positions the firm to identify high level measurable objectives that will enable management to assess progress against the primary goals – answering the fundamental question: "Are the strategies working/ helping us to achieve our goals?"

Phase four – Implementation planning

This final phase puts the strategic plan into action in the near term. At the firm level, it should enable the practices, firm leadership, and firm administration to align activities with the strategic direction of the firm. Further, it prioritizes action, so that efforts are not wasted or dissipated. At the practice group level, it creates clear roles and responsibilities for every member of the group – so that everyone is engaged in some meaningful way in the implementation of the strategy.

There has been considerable debate in strategy literature and among strategy professionals surrounding the subject of "top down versus bottom up" approaches to strategic planning. The process detailed in the following sections explains why, on the contrary, the process needs to be both top down *and* bottom up.

Critically, people need to be engaged early in the process to think (and opine) on the state of the law firm (or practice) and the opportunities and threats apparent in the external market. Further, people should be engaged from the outset in thinking about and talking about the long-term direction and vision the firm should pursue.

Likewise, people need to be clear on what the resulting strategic plan means for them on both a short- and long-term basis. Ideally, they should have some direct role in moving the firm (or at least their practice group or team) in the direction the partners have agreed to go.

To further aid bottom-up engagement, process checkpoints can be created to share working drafts with all but the largest partnerships as the planning process unfolds. Thus, the process should have a bottom-up nature both at the beginning and the end of the process and can include even more involvement if necessary.

That said, with the exception of very small firms, a smaller group will need to do some of the heavier lifting associated with articulating the strategic direction, working through strategic trade-offs and choices, and setting high level objectives. There are many ways to engage a broader (or large) partnership in adjusting and affirming those decisions. However, some smaller groups will need to take the lead – and there are many ways to make that work effectively. Some alternatives include:

- Working directly through the governance structure of the firm – using the firm's management committee, board of directors, or executive committee (or their counterparts) to act as a de facto strategic planning committee.
- Creating an ad hoc strategic planning committee broadly representative of the partnership vis-à-vis areas of practice and thought leadership. With highly capable process facilitation, an ad hoc committee of this nature can be relatively large (roughly 25 members). While that may not satisfy every political consideration in the partnership, it should enable even fairly large partnerships to be well represented.
- Engaging in a hybrid approach, where a small governance body (for example, an executive committee) develops draft work products at each stage of the process and a larger committee engages in debate and discussion to improve upon those drafts – freeing the large group from getting bogged down in wordsmithing, while enabling that large group to be directly involved in strategy development.

This overview underscores the need for good process design, management, and facilitation. That in turn raises a recurring question: Does a firm need an outside consultant in order to develop a strategic plan? The short answer is no. Many firms develop strategic plans without outside assistance and that includes some of the most successful law firms in the world.

A broader question is: How and where can consultants add value to a firm's efforts? A good consultant should be able to tailor a planning process so that it fits the firm well – leveraging the right analytical models and applying the right strategic principles to the issues facing the firm. A good consultant should bring strong facilitation (and listening) skills to the process – to ensure partners' time is used efficiently and effectively throughout the process. Finally, a good consultant should balance industry expertise and knowledge with creativity and an open mind – ensuring the firm avoids pitfalls and blind alleys, while encouraging the firm to find its strategic differences (rather than forcing law firm management dogma on a firm's leadership team).

This first appeared as Chapter 1 in Sterling, J., Strategic Planning for Law Firms: A Practical Roadmap, *ARK Group, 2012.*

References

1. Drucker, P., *Concepts of the Corporation*, John Day, New York, 1946.
2. Boston Consulting Group, visit: http://www.cg.com.
3. Porter, M., *Competitive Advantage: Creating and Sustaining Superior Performance*, The Free Press (Simon & Schuster), New York, 1985.
4. Porter, M., "What Is Strategy?", *Harvard Business Review*, November-December 1996.

Chapter 3: Seeing the future first – Analyzing strategic trends

By Patrick J. McKenna, author, lecturer, strategist, and advisor to the leaders of premier law firms

In many of the most northern regions of the world, there is an old tradition whereby hunters construct blankets made of animal skins. These blankets are not for shelter, but are intended as a crudely improvised form of trampoline. The blanket is spread across the ground and one of the hunters steps into the middle. The remaining members of the group grab the edges, heave the blanket upward, and propel the hunter high into the air. The purpose of physically hurling the hunter into the sky is for him to see if any caribou are in the area.

While we have evolved from those humble techniques, there remains a need to look toward the horizon to see what kind of future might potentially unfold. Behind every new trend and its ensuing ramifications there is either a potential marketplace threat or a window of opportunity. Those keen enough to perceive the trends early are in a prime position to pilot their firms into a more promising future. The obvious challenge is to be the first to predict or identify that future and then to devise appropriate action plans to take full advantage of subsequent circumstances. And isn't this precisely what engaging in strategic planning is supposed to do?

In my work, I have been exposed to dozens of different law firms' strategic plans. What I have discovered is behind different firm names there are fairly similar plans – at least from the way in which most firms over-obsess about internal issues, such as associate retention, timely billing processes, or the latest cost savings initiatives. In my experience, very few firms give anywhere near enough attention to what is going on outside of their own walls – in their external business environment.

Now, admittedly, almost every firm that goes through the conventional strategic planning process does use some form of SWOT analysis. Which means, quite simply, that as part of a strategic planning exercise, partners briefly look at the various internal strengths and weaknesses of the firm, and then assess what particular opportunities or threats there are. That sounds sensible enough, and it is. But the process, as it is most often executed, is a complete waste of time.

The greatest handicap with the conventional SWOT process is that it implicitly assumes, whatever assertions are made to the contrary, that the future will be more or less like the present. Leading firms know that their future will not be an echo of the present. In fact, I believe your firm's executive committee needs to regularly engage in some very deep strategic thinking about trends that are currently shaping the profession.

Getting to the future first requires firms to be deliberately farsighted. Why is this important? By investing some serious time in examining trends, it can enable you to see what competitors may not, thereby allowing you to get a serious jump on exploiting new opportunities or preparing contingency plans for the possibility of any disruptive events unfolding.

I am not talking about navel-gazing or trying to predict the future. Rather, that tomorrow's potential threats and explosive opportunities are already being hinted at today. If you look closely enough, you can see the beginning of trends – often years before they become common knowledge. Seeing the future requires that you understand the potential of what is already happening. The essence of winning in a competitive marketplace is to be at the right place *before* the right time.

Scanning the future

My central premise is that there is no proprietary data about the future. Whatever you need to know about tomorrow is, to some extent, already visible. The data is there for everyone to see, but there is an enormous difference in firms' abilities to construct new opportunities out of that understanding.

Interestingly, the sophistication of professional services firms varies considerably in the discipline with which they direct consideration to their external environment. The largest and most sophisticated of the accounting and consulting firms have long devoted serious attention to what is happening outside their doors. Many law firms, however, are populated with professionals that are so preoccupied with their particular area of specialty that they are remarkably out of touch with the wider world.

Not all partners are equally up to date on what is happening. Many will be fully aware of issues that affect their particular practice area, but it is not at all uncommon for an entire practice group to lack a coherent concept of those macro-trends affecting some of the client industries they serve, or the firm as a whole.

As our overall business environment becomes ever more complex and fluid, it becomes more critical that every member of firm management maintains a running dialogue on the meaning of significant events and trends, and that they use their understanding of those trends to develop consensus on refining the direction and strategy of the firm.

Realistically, can anyone who devotes time to exploring "what's going on out there", ever fully understand all of the dimensions and interpret all of the signals? Not likely! But by thinking of your business environment in terms of its major components, we can at least make the challenge less daunting. We need to start, therefore, by dividing the external environment into more manageable categorical components so we can begin to organize our knowledge of it.

External strategic components

I have identified a number of different environmental components. The importance of each may be quite different depending upon the practice composition of your firm. By studying the goings-on in these areas and connecting the trends in all of them, you can build a reasonable basis of fact (and speculation) about what is going to happen over the foreseeable next few years:

- Client needs and wants – This refers to the changing, unmet, and emerging needs of key existing and prospective clients (e.g. clients demanding more discounts and flat fee arrangements);
- Technological changes – The degree to which technology is provoking new ways to practice and deliver services (e.g. IBM investing $1 billion in its cognitive decision support tools, "Watson", to target the legal sector);
- Relative costs – The relationship of a firm's key cost elements relative to those of competitors (e.g. more firms going to the cloud);
- Market barriers – Various factors which help keep potential competitors out of the market or profession (e.g. procurement departments now looking favorably at "NewLaw" service providers);
- Economic volatility – The health of your marketplace with respect to consumer and business confidence (e.g. the prospect of a prolonged period of flat demand for legal services);

- Integrity – The basic trust that clients place in the profession, your firm, and your services (e.g. the impact of enhanced transparency);
- Special abilities – The competency of any one firm to significantly outperform its competitors in ways important to clients (e.g. specialist teams using social media or online resources to exploit ever-narrower market niches);
- Market values – That cluster of marketplace values that creates demand for specific new services (e.g. the continuing attractiveness of outsourcing); and
- Resources – Refers to all professionals, physical assets, and materials employed in running your practice (e.g. challenges in dealing with leverage, under-productive attorneys, and generational differences).

While this list of nine components may not be comprehensive, and you may wish to add your own factors to the list, it can serve as a starting point to begin to examine some of the myriad trends and developments now emerging in each of these areas.

The process of analyzing trends

If we had known in 2015 what we will know in 2020 (only five foreseeable years into the future), how would we have changed our attitudes, actions, and the way in which we practiced law; the services we offered, the clients we targeted, and the ways in which we chose to deliver our services? That is what this process is really all about: observing the present trends to determine how we might interpret the future.

There are a number of different steps involved in going through a process of identifying and interpreting external trends. The most sophisticated firms might make this a regular quarterly review item on the agenda of their management meetings. If your firm is not yet at that point, you might want to start with making this the process you engage in leading up to the next annual partner's retreat.

STEP 1: Identify the relevant trends

Your first step is simply to scan the external environment for early warning signs, and for areas of new opportunity. It is my contention that the members of your firm's management or strategic planning committee are the ones who should engage in this activity. Many larger firms assign this as one of the responsibilities of their office heads. The process of identifying trends and transforming the data into valuable insights about the future of their markets/practices is an inseparable part of the intellectual leadership that this committee needs to provide the overall partnership. While consultants might help, they should not supplant the committee's work. If the members of your committee do the job, they will own it. It will form a key part of their thinking process, and it will guide the decisions they make.

Some firms approach this by simply having each member of the committee volunteer to take one of the nine categories and devote a bit of time to researching, reading various publications (both within the profession as well as across related professions), browsing the internet, and speaking with consultants, clients, and so forth.

The question to ask each committee member is: "In your opinion, what would be the 10 most important trends capable of impacting, both positively and negatively, the overall profession and our firm's operations over the next five years?" In general, it helps to keep each identified trend reasonably concise – otherwise reading and reviewing it becomes a chore. Drowning your colleagues in facts, figures, charts, graphs, and detailed analysis makes it difficult for busy practitioners to find the critical insights that can help them shape their direction. Therefore, document and distill each trend into a carefully prepared, thoughtfully written, one-page statement of "what's going on out there". Also, the act of distilling the information can often lead to valuable insights. Explaining something in very concise terms forces you to get to the core of the concept.

Beware of incomplete or defective data

In one of those classic *Pink Panther* films, Peter Sellers is seen checking in to a quaint hotel. In a corner of the lobby, he notices a small dog. Thinking he might go over and pet this cute little animal, he inquires of the innkeeper, "Does your dog bite?" Hearing the elderly gentleman say "no", Sellers reaches down only to have the dog snap ferociously at him. Sellers turns to the innkeeper and says, "You said your dog didn't bite!" To which the gentleman calmly responds, "That's not my dog."

In identifying relevant trends, you must remain keenly aware of the problem of incomplete or defective data. What you ask, whom you ask, and how you ask can be critical to getting valid and useful information. Here are a few guidelines to consider:

- Censor incoming bits of information at their source – Be constantly vigilant to the impartiality and agendas of reporters, journalists, commentators, and anyone supposedly "in the know", reporting their take on some new development;

- Get as many different perspectives as possible – If you are hearing the very same predictions from a number of sources, try to find a contrarian's view;
- Distrust your own biases – If you are hoping to find the research to support a strategic decision you have already made, it is very likely that you will find the support you are looking for;
- Be willing to contradict prevailing beliefs – The majority is not always right, the conventional wisdom not always wise, and the accepted doctrine could very well be flawed (breakthrough thinking depends on it); and
- Be careful of jumping to conclusions – Are you betting your future on the assumption that a particular market will materialize, grow, or disappear? Do you have enough real evidence to support your conclusions?

STEP 2: Discuss and evaluate each trend

A special meeting of either the firm's management committee or strategic planning group should provide the means for focusing attention on the business environment and building consensus about what the signals are telling us. An effective way to tackle this is for your committee to divide into small working groups of about three or four partners. These participants share their thinking about the issues at hand and thereby can help to uncover important differences in the ways each might perceive the impact of any given trend.

Each group is first assigned one of the trend categories (i.e., technological changes, market barriers, etc.) and prepares its interpretation of the data. Each group can then be given their choice of one other trend category to review. During the process, debates or differences will emerge about various aspects of these trends. Although these discussions can sometimes become rather animated, they tend to be very useful.

To see the future first, you may need to deconstruct some old notions and ideas. It is important during this step to keep a watchful eye on a few natural tendencies that do occur:

- **Denial** – When a trend suggests a potentially negative consequence, some suffer from the ostrich syndrome. They would prefer to bury their heads, deny the validity of the trend they are observing, and ignore any danger signals.

For example, in the billing arena, some firms do not (want to) see the trend for providing clients with complete transparency as it relates to who is working on what matter, when, and at what internal billing rate. These partners often act as though they would like to believe that the provision of a one-liner invoice at the conclusion of the client's matter should still suffice. In other words, the firm's billing processes will take place in the future just as they once did in the past; or other partners will continue to believe that the traditional hourly rate system will continue to be the mainstay of compensation from clients, despite its well-known inefficiencies, misplaced incentives, and perceived unfairness relative to the value of the work produced.

- **Blindness** – What we know (or think we know) determines what we see. Unfortunately, the more experienced and the smarter we are in our particular area, the more myopic we may become. Often trends present themselves, but firm leaders do not see them. Not knowing how to look for them, or simply missing them, is the primary factor. What we see determines our destination.
- **Arrogance** – The late management theorist, Peter Drucker, once commented dryly, "Whom the gods would destroy, they first grant 40 years of business success." Drucker believed that, sooner or later, time will turn your most precious assets into liabilities, and that the most powerful competitive advantage may eventually be neutralized by the shifting sands of the external environment. Intel's past chairman, Andy Grove, agreed with his now famous remark, "Only the paranoid survive." Ironically, one of the reasons why leaders miss trends is from what I call "success arrogance": the firm is doing so well that firm leaders fail to see the danger signals.

The key point here is to make sure that all members of your committee participate on a personal and intellectual level in forming a consensus about what is going on. One of the critically important by-products of this process is that, through active participation, they will also be much better equipped to communicate any particular trend's meaning to other partners in the firm.

STEP 3: Determine the impact potential of each trend

Each of the trends that have been identified can be evaluated within the context of the *probability* of occurrence and *impact* (negative and positive) on your firm. The diagram in Figure 1 is designed to help with your analytical efforts. You can use this graph to assess the overall pattern of the trends identified.

Impact on firm

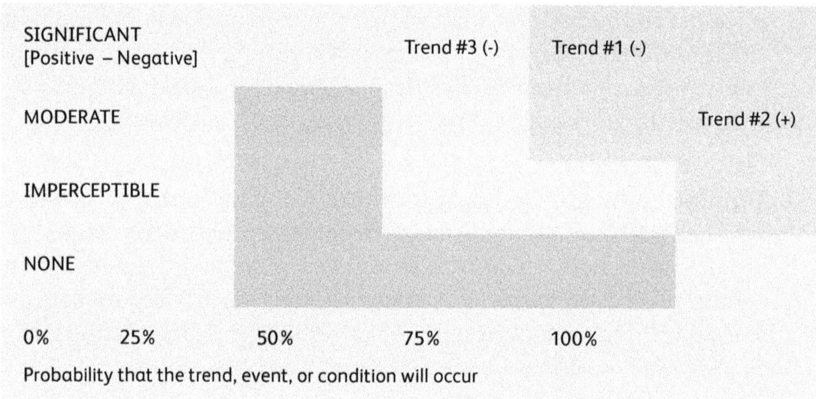

Figure 1: Trends analysis assessment diagram

Obviously, those trends judged to have a very high probability of occurrence and a very harmful impact, or that portend huge opportunities should they occur, become your top priority. Clusters of trends falling into the top-right-hand corner of this diagram are the ones I tend to label "mission critical" and are the ones that require your *urgent attention*. In those instances, I have found this assessment diagram serves as a great tool to help explain to other partners the need for urgency.

The secondary band, running diagonally through the graph, represents those trends that are likely further away time-wise, but which should nevertheless be considered *important* and needing executive committee attention by way of ongoing monitoring.

Finally, the cluster of trends that will tend to occupy the bottom-left-hand corner of the graph fall into the area best labeled as *postponable*. These trends should also be periodically monitored for changes which could cause them to shift to a higher priority.

In spite of the graph presented here to help with your analysis, let me not create the impression that this processes is scientific, systematic, or precise. If anything, sometimes seeing the future is guesswork at best. The events, trends, issues, and opportunities in the external environment are ultimately whatever we interpret them to be. Intelligent professionals may disagree completely about what a particular trend's impact may suggest.

The most valuable aspect of this process is how it can enable members of your firm to discuss, debate, interpret, and assimilate the lessons the external trends have to teach us. Out of this understanding, which must be continually updated and refreshed, they can commit energy, attention, talent, and resources for the greatest strategic value. This assessment diagram is merely intended as a practical tool that I have used with countless firms in our strategic planning endeavors, to help them make sense out of and prioritize those external issues deserving of some attention in their efforts to determine their best strategic direction.

STEP 4: Develop your action plans

Finally, it is necessary to transform the discoveries that come from your discussions into actions. There is little point in knowing that you are heading for an iceberg if you do not determine how to course-correct and steer around it!

Your action-planning session should draw upon and involve partners from various different practice areas. I have often observed that partners not normally involved with any particular issue can have very creative and useful insights relevant to that issue. I often find that the insight has never been tapped because that partner was never asked to share views outside of their particular area.

In order to be effective, some portion of your firm's strategy must concern itself with what we must be doing right now in order to be well positioned to capitalize on our future. Among other considerations, your strategic plan therefore should identify:

- What skills your firm should be developing (or hiring) *right now*;
- What you must do to anticipate and better serve unmet client needs *right now*;
- What new practices you should be pursuing *right now*; and
- What new experiments and field tests your firm should be engaging in *right now* in order to intercept the future.

A necessary part of your strategy process, but also an ongoing exercise

When partners sit down to think about their firm's strategy, too often they take 90 percent of "the way things have been done in the past" as a given, and it then becomes the major constraint. Monitoring and analyzing trends should be a continuing process of observation, reflection, and learning. Even where it is formalized as a critical ingredient of the strategic planning process, the best firms will still need to be attuned to their external environments all year round. It is not as if you can activate this exercise once every few years, scan the environment, and then shut it down until the next planning period. We need to have an ongoing format for staying constantly alert for the first signs of important new developments.

The American writer and humorist Mark Twain advised: "When everybody is out digging for gold, the business to be in is selling shovels!" And there is actually a grain of wisdom in his wisecrack. So, what foreseeable trend do you think may represent the figurative "shovel" that every client will need tomorrow?

This first appeared as Chapter 1 in Slater, L. (ed.), 2020 Vision: The Future of Legal Services, *ARK Group, 2015.*

Chapter 4:
Why law firms might consider a merger as a strategic option

By Andrew Hedley, director of Hedley Consulting

Why a merger might make sense

In the most straightforward of terms, a merger makes sense when the combined business is in a better position to compete compared to when each firm is operating alone. There are a number of reasons why a merger might be appropriate for a firm.

While the theorist would argue along academic lines only, the pragmatist recognizes that mergers are often pursued because a host of factors come together, some objective and others emotional, some concerned with a desire to develop, and others with an urge to reduce risk. It is the interplay of these factors which will often persuade partners that a merger, albeit with perhaps unpalatable aspects, is the best option to secure the future viability and success of their firm.

Across the range of mergers, drivers will typically include:

- A desire to extend into new markets: These may be geographically or sectorally defined, and the direct demands of significant clients may be a motivator in some cases;
- A merger may provide an opportunity to access new skills: These could be lawyer capabilities – increasing the scope or depth of resources of the firm – or center on management capabilities;
- Providing access to new clients and putting in place the capabilities needed to serve existing ones better is another strategic driver which leads firms to consider merger;
- A well-executed merger will result in the new entity having an enhanced brand: What this means in practice is that there will be fewer constraints on the quality and scale of work for which the firm is considered. The bigger firm will generally attract better work and clients;

- An improvement in bench strength: In both depth and breadth of resources, in order to appeal to the more sophisticated purchaser and to better manage the inherent risks associated with small teams and an over-reliance on a small partner pool;
- Any merger by definition reduces competition: How material this is in a very fragmented legal sector is a moot point. It will be the case, however, that in some highly specialized or niche areas, such an effect will be experienced. However, client conflicts and the need to have a number of advisors engaged in a typical large-scale commercial transaction mean that the likelihood of any merger taking place which impacts significantly on a client's choice, to the point where a pricing advantage may be enjoyed, is limited;
- When boiled down to their essence a number of mergers, in a market where supply far outstrips demand, are about reducing the combined cost base, improving overhead efficiency and squeezing the combined middle line: By holding the top line and reducing the middle, margins are improved (or at least the rate of erosion is reduced). The economic drivers in the current business environment mean that such cost-reduction exercises will also generally be accompanied by a reshaping of the equity base – a reduction in the number of equity partners in order to prop up profit per equity partner figures; and
- A merger can give the perception of creating a safe harbor for the firm, reducing risks for both the business and partners individually: Of course, the wrong deal can have the effect of doing the reverse – the creation of a larger, more complex business with all of the underlying issues and challenges of its antecedent firms' risks could simply exacerbate historic problems and risks. (In short, it is likely that the combination of two small underperforming firms will only create a larger underperforming firm unless a merger is accompanied by far-reaching changes in working practices and behaviors.)

Synergy, or the much debated "2 + 2 = 5" factor, is often talked about as a driver for merger. Just what constitutes this elusive, magical factor is somewhat harder to define. In reality, any synergistic effect is a combination of the elements listed above which, when taken in their entirety, propel a firm to a level beyond that which was anticipated.

A merger can also be a Trojan horse for the management team, a disruptive event which provides an environment in which changes to working practices and initiatives to modernize the firm can be pursued more easily. A merger should be a means of achieving a strategic objective; a valid question for many firms centers on how much real strategic freedom they enjoy. The vast majority of firms are constrained by their geographies, skills base, client franchise, access to capital, and appetite for risk. How easily can they break out of existing markets and practices? They have neither the capacity nor the capability to make "big, strategic moves".

Many firms being driven to consider merger options will, in truth, be doing so not out of any grand strategic plan (no matter how they dress it up), but rather as a means of reducing personal risk for partners and in an attempt to ensure the viability of the business. In this context, the merger may initially be more about short-term survival rather than long-term strategy, but longer term objectives should also feature. If a merger, de facto, simply buys time for the management team to deal with longer term strategy, then it is crucial that this window of opportunity is seized.

A framework for understanding the nature of a merger

In considering the nature of any merger, it can be helpful to think of four components. These are illustrated in Figure 1 on the next page and are explored in more detail in the explanation which follows.

All mergers will have characteristics which fall into each quadrant, but the overall shape and intent of the firm that is subsequently created will be defined by the weighting or emphasis attributed to each area.

Consolidatory and complementary mergers

A consolidatory merger takes two firms that are broadly similar in their nature, skills, and client base. By combining the firms, squeezing the middle line, and improving productivity, a larger, more efficient organization is created.

There will be some element of duplication in any merger and so an opportunity exists to improve the overhead ratios, which should be grasped.

There is also generally the potential to consolidate the combined partner numbers, whether through a formal restructuring or because a number of historic partners, for personal reasons, do not wish to continue in the new firm. Some may seek an alternative relationship

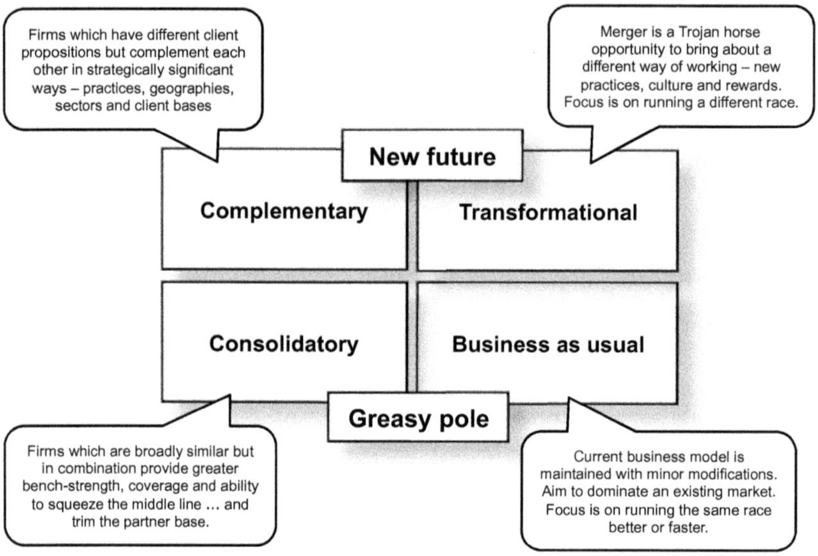

Figure 1: Four components which interplay in every merger situation

with the business, perhaps a salaried or consultancy arrangement, while others will retire or join a different firm.

Taken to an extreme, a merger which is almost wholly consolidatory in nature simply creates a larger version of its antecedents, with better overhead utilization and fewer profit sharing partners, but little else changes. This larger firm, with greater strength in depth, may find itself more attractive to clients who see the larger and more focused resource as attractive, reducing risks and increasing the volumes of business which are directed to it by very large purchasers.

This increased brand strength will also enhance the firm in the recruitment market, making it easier to attract skilled staff in its core areas. One would also expect a consolidatory merger to focus future investment with clear priorities and to therefore make it possible to drive through further efficiencies. It may also mean that more peripheral practices recognize that they are no longer central to the firm's strategic focus and seek to relocate elsewhere or to form their own niche practices.

A complementary merger, by contrast, is founded on the premise that two firms which are dissimilar can combine to create new opportunities (both from within their respective client bases and with new clients) that neither could do alone. While there will be elements of cost saving, this is not the strategic driver for the deal. Instead, this type of merger is all about a broader spread of offer – whether that breadth is based on geography, practice areas, or client types. The complementary deal brings new approaches and cross-fertilization to the table and offers an opportunity to define a different approach, both internally and externally, which neither antecedent could have achieved alone. A more diverse business may be better able to service the wider needs of a certain cadre of client but will also need to ensure that it does not spread itself so thin as to lack true strength in depth. Consequently, mergers which have a strong complementary driver will also generally have a consolidatory component too.

Moving then to the operating model employed by the new firm, depending on the relative sizes of the firms, it would be possible to adopt a business as usual approach. This is particularly the case when one firm is much bigger than the other, with the larger organization's systems, policies, and procedures simply being adopted across the new enterprise wholesale.

In other cases, a variant will be implemented in which best practice from whichever antecedent firm is considered to have the most appropriate approach is adopted. This may be more commonly found where firms are of a similar size, but can also be manipulated as a political construct, to appease one side or other of the deal, which should be avoided where possible.

A merger also presents an excellent opportunity to adopt a new approach which allows a more transformational model to be implemented. The new firm seizes the opportunity to start with a relatively clean sheet of paper and introduce practices which are the best-of-breed from the wider market. The over-riding objective is to create a business model which is fit for the future rather than one founded on increasingly redundant operating models.

While the overall approach adopted in every merger will draw from all four quadrants, it should be clear that a deal which is principally about consolidation and business as usual runs the risk of being a greasy pole solution to long-term structural changes in the profession.

Such a move will undoubtedly provide opportunities to resolve short-term issues for the merged business, but without any more strategic realignment there is a danger that the firm incrementally slips so that, over a period of time, it finds itself back in a position which is commercially untenable.

A merger which has an emphasis on the building of complementary business streams and which is prepared to contemplate more radical changes to working practices stands a better chance of redefining the firm and positioning it for a new future which neither antecedent firm could have achieved by itself. This long-term view is vital since, to be considered a success, any merger must improve profitability and sustainability for the future.

This first appeared as Chapter 3 in Hedley, A., The Law Firm Merger: A Leader's Guide to Strategy and Realisation, *ARK Group, 2014.*

Chapter 5:
Building a culture of innovation in legal services

By Adam Billing, partner, and Abigail Hunt, associate, at Møller PSF Group

The innovation imperative

The trends that are driving change in the legal sector are well known: clients demanding more for less, the billable hour under fire, shifting workforce demographics, the growing need for global reach. These trends are all exacerbated by new technologies that enable, among other things, greater legal process outsourcing, e-discovery, and virtual working. All of these factors, combined with new client needs and regulatory changes, create an environment ripe for disruption in terms of how legal services are delivered, what those services might include, as well as who is delivering them.

At the present time, the greatest impetus for change in legal services is coming from in-house legal teams. These teams are under pressure to deliver both more and different strategic value to their own changing businesses.

Des Woods, chairman and a founding partner of the Møller PSF Group at Cambridge University, said "Clients complain constantly that their legal suppliers are behind the game in terms of innovating around service delivery and pricing. Their view is that most innovation is in the in-house lawyer community, as they face direct budget pressure from their boards. Having said that, the market has definitely woken up and many, but not all, firm leaders are gearing up for major change."

How long will it take to reach a tipping point when some law firms will be forced to change their model? And how long before innovation is at the top of the agenda for more than just the most forward-looking firms?

Greg Bott, head of the Client Development Centre for Addleshaw Goddard LLP, commented: "The improving economy might have been detrimental to the rise of innovation – hiding some of the issues and cracks. A slight cooling may help unearth those things that need to be addressed."

Exactly how the legal services landscape will evolve over the coming years is far from certain. What is definite, however, is that innovation will play a central role in this evolution.

Legal sector innovation

Over the last few years, legal sector innovation has received increasing attention in the media and from a growing number of awards bodies. New service, product, strategy, and process innovations have in many cases been driven by advances in technology that are transforming the way work is managed and delivered, both externally and internally.

A culture of innovation

With some notable exceptions, much of the innovation that has taken place in the legal sector has been what can be described as "spot innovation". These are innovations that occur in response to a particular client request, regulatory change, or internal business challenge – not the result of a strategic and coordinated effort to drive growth and profitability through innovation.

While these successes should not be undervalued, innovation in legal services is still rarely taking place at the level required to take full advantage of the opportunities ahead and to cope with the magnitude of change and uncertainty building within the sector. This requires a more systemic and intentional approach than currently exists in most firms today. It requires a "culture of innovation".

CASE STUDY

Legal sector innovation in action: External strategies

Externally focused innovations include new legal strategies, such as Simmons & Simmons' creation of a cost and time saving strategy to redirect PPI litigation away from the courts, and instead into its clients' internal complaint-handling functions. Or novel service offerings such as Hogan Lovells' creation of the Privacy Innovation Assessment, a tool that helps clients assess the privacy implications of new business developments and recommends practical steps to address them.

In recent years, "creating a culture of innovation" has become a frequently cited strategic objective for businesses of all kinds. But what does that really mean? We define a culture of innovation as the collective practices, mindsets, policies, and norms that enable an organization to make innovation part of business as usual. In this type of culture, innovation is a core, constant activity of the organization – as opposed to something that is done in addition to the "real" work of the firm.

When a culture of innovation is in place, the firm is inherently better able to identify new opportunities as they emerge, think creatively about how to respond, and mobilize resources to rapidly develop and implement solutions. Specifically, this results in:

- Greater agility and responsiveness to change;
- Improved collaboration across the firm, with clients and other parties;
- Profitable new revenue streams and internal cost savings;
- Improved employee engagement and productivity; and
- Increased growth potential and competitive advantage.

CASE STUDY

Legal sector innovation in action: Alternative service providers

AdventBalance, a young Australian firm offering fixed rates, lawyer pools, and a unique staffing arrangement, whereby top-tier experienced lawyers work directly in client businesses on a secondment basis has enjoyed double and even triple digit growth rates in the last five years. Schillings reorganized itself entirely when it moved to alternative business structure (ABS) status and repositioned itself as a multi-disciplinary firm offering a comprehensive reputation defense package made up of consultancy services, cyber security services, and legal assistance. Since the change, the firm's revenue has climbed by 30 percent.

How this manifests will vary widely from firm to firm. There is no one-size-fits-all solution – nor are there transferrable templates to follow. Organizational strategy, structure, history, and innovation objectives all have a profound effect on the shape a firm's culture of innovation needs to take to be effective.

However, from our experience of working in the professional services and corporate sectors, a number of lessons learned and key success factors have emerged that can help law firms create an innovation culture that produces the desired results, while avoiding some of the most common pitfalls.

Create the foundation – Building skills and awareness

The bedrock of a strong innovation culture is a shared understanding of how innovation works and the business case for doing it. This requires a common framework that everyone can easily grasp, apply, and practice – forming the basis for a common language and approach for how innovation happens in the firm.

Creating this foundation requires an investment in developing people from across the firm – not just fee earners or senior leaders.

CASE STUDY

Legal sector innovation in action: Internal strategies

In the realm of internal innovation, there is a move towards more flexible time arrangements, as well as the provision of more structured training in areas beyond law, such as wider commercial skills for junior associates. Allen & Overy made the move to flexible working in 2010 and Linklaters allows lawyers to work from home one day per week as of 2015. Simmons & Simmons has been recognized for its internal innovations, including the launch of its own MBA course in partnership with BPP business school, designed to prepare a new generation of lawyers with a range of legal and business skills.

Design thinking – A unifying framework for innovation

In recent years, a growing number of law schools and firms have looked to "design thinking" to equip lawyers and law students with the process, tools, and mindsets required to successfully innovate for their clients and within their firms.

Design thinking, an innovation framework used by some of the world's most consistently cutting edge companies, gives people a straightforward, practical approach to creative problem solving that can be applied to virtually any challenge (see Figure 1).

It starts by seeking to deeply understand what people (e.g. clients or internal customers) really value, need, and care about, and it applies a creative process and toolset to arrive at more innovative solutions for the challenges they face. Individuals trained in this approach learn how to use techniques such as effective questioning and empathy building,

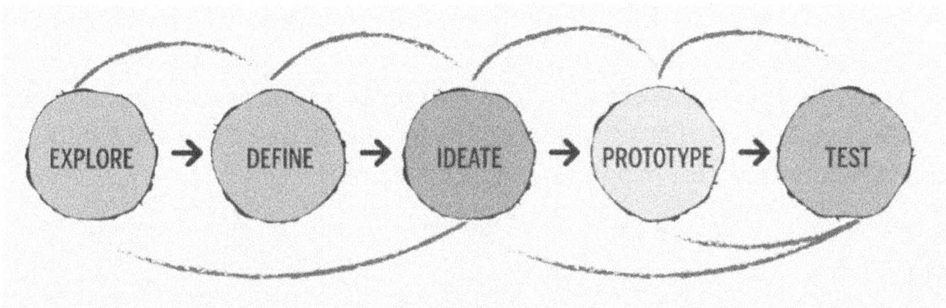

Figure 1: Design thinking – An innovation framework

opportunity framing, brainstorming, and lateral thinking, as well as rapid prototyping and experimentation.

With these core skills and mindsets instilled, every individual in the firm can be part of the innovation process. They become "listening posts" for opportunities to innovate both for clients and internal stakeholders. They also become more confident in suggesting new ideas, secure in the knowledge that others understand the importance of deferring judgment and building on the ideas of others. Meetings tend to become more focused on action and rapid iteration, rather than endless updates, and discussion and collaboration between disciplines become more fluid due to a shared toolset and approach to problem solving.

For many organizations, the most immediate benefits of equipping people with an innovative framework and toolkit like design thinking come from the way these techniques are applied in day-to-day work. Small changes to the way individuals and teams organize and manage themselves can have a profound effect on the quality of work and the speed at which it is accomplished.

Making innovation skills development count

Leadership development and structured training can be powerful tools in building a culture of innovation, but there are several common pitfalls to avoid.

1. Don't just develop senior people

What often happens is that a small cohort of senior leaders will go away for a day or so of innovation training and return to an organization that is not only oblivious to the concepts that they have learned, but in some cases geared to stamp them out. This makes applying and disseminating any of these new ideas very difficult, and despite best intentions, organizational inertia takes over and the status quo prevails.

Another problem with rolling these skills out to only a small group of senior leaders is that while their buy-in is required to establish a culture of innovation, it is not enough. The real work of innovation takes place on the front lines. These individuals also need to be engaged and on board before any real progress can be expected.

CASE STUDY

Legal sector innovation in action: IT-driven innovation

In terms of IT-driven innovation, firms have used technology not only to reduce time and costs though automation, but also to enhance communication and facilitate collaboration, especially across offices. For example, Berwin Leighton Paisner has been able to assume responsibility for all the legal needs of some of its clients under multi-year, fixed-price agreements because it has built a multi-sourcing platform that supports BLP onsite teams. Technological innovations are also helping firms to provide longer term, more predictable fee estimates. Paul Hastings was recognized in 2015 for its development and deployment of a matter management system that improves efficiency and helps to give predictable fee estimates to clients.

2. Don't just develop a small group of front-line innovators

For many organizations, there is a temptation to invest heavily in developing the innovative capabilities of just a small group who will be tasked with driving innovation in the firm. These are frequently those people who are deemed to be "the innovative ones" – and could be partners or associates who have been flagged as future leaders or high potentials.

These groups are often tasked with projects, which when launched have strong top leadership support. But as projects continue, team members often face pressure from direct line managers to spend more time on their "real jobs" and are pulled away, resulting in stalled projects and disheartened would-be innovators.

Another danger of only developing small cohorts is that the way they will be working often won't make sense to their colleagues, and will therefore be rejected. Worse still, they may seek to involve senior people who haven't bought in to the value of seemingly counter-intuitive concepts like fast failure and rapid prototyping, and so end up getting criticized or "marked down" as a result.

Development initiatives are absolutely key to building a culture of innovation, but making them count takes real commitment. Not everyone in the firm needs to become an "innovation expert", but virtually everyone needs to possess basic awareness of a shared framework, understand how innovation aligns with the business strategy, and be ready to support and encourage others.

What kind of innovation do you want?

Knowing what kind of innovation will be most important for your firm can help inform the type of culture you need to achieve it, and the practical steps you need to take to build and sustain it. One simple way to look at different types of innovation is to divide them into incremental, evolutionary, and revolutionary (see Figure 2).

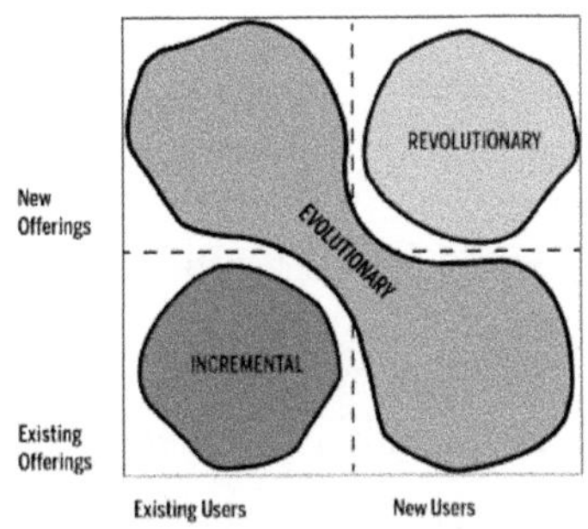

Figure 2: Categorizing innovation – Incremental, evolutionary, or revolutionary?

Incremental innovations involve making changes to an existing service that is being delivered to an existing client. Examples of this might be a change in the way a service is priced or an added feature on an existing product. These innovations tend to be relatively low risk, and with little disruptive potential.

Evolutionary innovations involve diving into a new market or new product or service type. The firm might be entering adjacent markets, combining elements where the firm has existing expertise or relationships with others that are entirely new to it. Here, the risks as well as the potential for rewards are increased. Examples from the legal sector include Bird & Bird's Baseline and DLA Piper's Noble Street, where the firms offer non-legal advisory services in familiar markets.

Finally, there is the top-right quadrant: revolutionary innovation. Here, the firm might be making a radical move into an entirely new service sector where the firm has no real experience. Innovations of this type are extremely high risk (often associated with greater than 90 percent failure rates), but have the highest potential for market disruption if they are successful.

Depending on your strategy and risk appetite, your firm may tend towards one end of this spectrum more than another.

Provide the right time, space, and funding

David Halliwell, director of knowledge, risk, and legal services for Pinsent Masons LLP, commented: "Partners get out of bed to solve clients' problems, and those go beyond the specific transaction or need for advice in front of them. Where partners have time and space to think – and a client-led incentive to deliver – then innovation flies."

Without making time to innovate, innovation is not likely to happen – at least not in any deliberate, reliable way. But what is the best way to do this in the time-starved environments of most law firms? Strategies such as allowing a certain percentage of time per week to innovate have gained popularity, following examples from companies like Google and others of that ilk. However, our experience working with organizations that have implemented similar policies tells us that this approach often fails because:

a) It is never fully implemented;

b) Top leadership support isn't sustained;

c) People lack the skills and tools to use the time in a useful way; or

d) It is slowly eroded away by other projects that inevitably take higher priority.

Allowing time to innovate means allowing time to reflect – which in turn means removing high-priority tasks from the already overflowing plates of most fee earners and support staff. Perhaps, one day, time spent on innovation will carry the same weight as meeting ambitious billing targets and deadlines for urgent client work. Until this happens, most law firms, and most corporates for that matter, are going to need to find other ways to make innovation happen.

Making innovation teams work

From our experience, even in organizations where innovation is widely encouraged at the individual level, there is no substitute for dedicated innovation teams when it comes to delivering on the full promise of innovation.

Innovation teams might be formed of members drawn from across the firm on a rotation basis. The innovation project might, but does not need to be, the sole priority of members for a period of several weeks to multiple months. At the most basic level, successful innovation teams require:

1. **A clear brief** – A well-framed opportunity and definition of what is in scope, what is not, and under what conditions the project should be extended or dropped.
2. **Sufficient funding** – There is also no better way to demonstrate the firm's commitment to innovation than to visibly put real resources behind it. At the outset, make a budget available that is commensurate with the potential upside of the project, but encourage teams to develop the project through frequent low cost experiments that lead to more developed pilots as learning is incorporated in each iteration.
3. **Diverse membership** – The best teams are comprised of a people with wide and varied skill sets from across practices, sectors, and offices – and not just lawyers. They might include business services people, administrators, and managers, as well as clients and other contacts from outside the firm.
4. **A process to guide them** – Innovation teams will struggle to make real progress using their traditional ways of working. Having a structured process to guide their thinking and working will improve outcomes and the ability for diverse teams to quickly and fluidly collaborate.
5. **A dedicated space for the project to live** – Even if it is a space as humble as a single conference room or the corner of an office space, innovation projects tend to be more successful when teams have a fixed physical space to go to where they can be immersed in the project.
6. **A hands-off management approach** – Innovation teams need to be managed and rewarded differently than teams focused on the core business of the firm. This requires a good deal of trust, empowerment, and permission to fail as long as the learning from that failure is captured and applied to ensuring the next iteration is closer to success.
7. **Measurement that fits the task** – A team working on a "revolutionary" innovation project (see Figure 2) shouldn't be measured in the same way as a team working on an incremental innovation, which has a far higher chance of success and is much closer to the firm's core business. Teams on high-risk projects could be rewarded, for example, not only for the success achieved, but also for the valuable lessons captured and shared with teams working on less risky projects.

Perhaps most importantly, successful innovation teams require the rest of the firm, especially senior leadership, to be on board with the team's purpose and the process they are using. This is the best way to ensure that the required time will be made available and respected in spite of competing priorities. Broad awareness and buy-in can also greatly reduce the risk of teams' interim work products and methods being evaluated by traditional measures and potentially getting quashed before they get off the ground.

Recognize common barriers to innovation

Innovation is not easy for anyone. It can create a fear of change and a resulting pulling up of the drawbridge. Actively or passively resisting change is, for some people, much more comfortable than managing the uncertainty that comes with something new.

Innovation can be especially hard for law firms with their business model still largely based on partner ownership, the billable hour, often strict hierarchies, and a long history of practicing law and running their business in a certain way. While there are no easy fixes, and change in most of these areas will be slow at best, it is vital to actively anticipate these roadblocks to innovation and use levers such as incentives, performance measurement systems, remuneration policy, and inspiring leadership to address them over time.

The billable hour

Innovation requires an "outside-in" mentality where the client is at the heart of the firm's strategy and service delivery model. The billable hour model is an example of "inside-out" thinking that is driven by what the firm is providing to the client as opposed to what they are creating for them or helping them achieve.

Andrew Giverin, sales director at Radiant Law, commented: "From the client's point of view the legal sector is crying out for innovation. Everything pegged to billable hours encourages inefficiency. The billable hour is based on input not output or the value of what is generated. This makes it difficult to generate innovative ideas."

From this perspective, as well as in terms of measuring and rewarding innovation activities, the billable hour model presents significant challenges. A fee-earner's performance is primarily measured by billing levels, and innovation work is most often non-billable. In a delivery-focused culture, this creates a major hurdle for securing the time, resources, and support required to make innovation happen.

Hierarchies and power pockets

As well as the pressure of billable hours on lawyers, there is almost always an entrenched hierarchy in place, based on title, expertise, billing power, and years of post-qualification experience. Sometimes, as is the case within many groups of people, alliances and pockets of power can be partly hidden. For example, close colleagues who have moved en masse from other firms, friendships based on decades of working together, and cliques cemented by, say, godchildren or golf.

Innovation requires, if not a flat structure, a flat mentality that sets aside rank, role, and history. With partners at the top of the decision-making tree, it may take real effort to create an environment, even if just a temporary one, where the ideas of a junior lawyer or business services manager have equal weight to those of a senior partner. It is, after all, not always the most senior people in the firm that will have the most revealing insights into emerging client needs or where internal process or cost efficiencies might be found.

Short-termism

Law firm leaders have to balance partner pressure for maximum short-term profit share against longer-term investment in innovation. Convincing partners exactly why they should care about and invest in innovation requires a compelling vision and strategy for success in both the short and long term.

Client feedback, client requests, and a changing share of the client purse add weight here. In addition, regular competitive analysis, working to stay attuned to likely future market shifts, and monitoring trends in other sectors that might impact on longer-term service demand can help to reinforce the link between current innovation initiatives and future competitive advantage.

Bias for precision

Almost everything about the training and professional standing of lawyers encourages "getting things right", a fear of failure, and an aversion to making mistakes. Innovation requires most lawyers to change their mind-set or, metaphorically, to put on a different hat. Being able to flex between cautious, detail-oriented legal thinking and more risk-friendly and "bigger picture", innovation-related thinking requires self-awareness, sustained effort, and encouragement. Failure, when it inevitably happens, must not be seen as an "end", but rather a necessary step in an iterative process, and it must be recognized as a means of ultimately achieving success sooner.

Organizational structure

Here, structure is not only the central partnership model but also the systems and levers that make the business work – the groups, the hierarchy, reporting structure, information and decision making channels, reward and promotion systems.

Innovation requires collaboration – and lots of it. Collaboration can be especially powerful when teams are drawn from diverse backgrounds, allowing for fresh perspectives and solutions to emerge. Not all firms are structured in a way that enables great collaboration. In fact, some seem to be set up to almost deliberately encourage silos and internal competition, and collaborating across practice area or offices is often both difficult and frustrating. Such barriers may exist due to implicit norms around sharing of information, cross-practice tension, cultural differences, a by-product of the reward system, or the "not invented here" mentality.

However, structure can also play to a firm's advantage. Cross-disciplinary collaboration is one of the benefits that can come from taking a sector-based approach – something claimed by many firms yet achieved by just a few.

Christian Bartsch, Partner at Bird & Bird LLP, said: "The culture at Bird & Bird is underpinned by a shared sense of natural curiosity. Our deep sector focus means that our lawyers are truly passionate about their sectors, sector-based budgeting encourages strong collaboration, and our clients tend to be highly innovative themselves."

Lead by example and others will follow

Without leadership support, any effort to build a robust culture of innovation is very likely to fail. Influencing something as hard to pin down and measure as law firm culture requires committed and consistent leadership action in deeds as well as declarations. It takes a willingness to empower people across all levels of the firm, take risks, and accept and even embrace the ambiguity that comes with venturing into uncharted territory.

While there are many attributes that a strong leader of innovation needs to possess, in our experience, there is none more powerful, or indispensable, than being a clear and visible role model. Creating and maintaining a culture of innovation requires unequivocal leadership modeling by law firm leadership and management teams on a day-to-day basis. This is a universe away from well-intentioned lip service and an annual innovation awards event. Innovation has to become a visible and integral part of business as usual from the top down.

Being a role model for innovation involves sharing regular and credible evidence of your commitment to promoting the best thinking of your people, to support them when they try in earnest and sometimes fail, and to publically recognize them when their efforts bear fruit as learning or progress in whatever form.

Without trust that their innovation-related mindsets and behaviors will be welcomed rather than penalized, your talented workforce will likely:

- Continue to sit on potentially valuable ideas;
- Hold back their strong views and insights;
- Feel under-confident about discussing innovation with clients (leaving space for competitors to do so);
- Become frustrated and weaker ambassadors for your brand; and
- Be less inclined to collaborate internally and with clients towards creative and more innovative solutions.

This all adds up to a significant loss of competitive advantage. By showing, through body language, words, and deeds, and on a day-to-day basis, exactly how vital innovation is to the business, senior leaders can model the message a thousand times more effectively than any number of board papers, emails, or glossy brochures ever could.

Successful innovation necessitates a "do as I do", not a "do as I say" leadership style.

Conclusion: Building a culture of innovation

If you and your firm are already building a culture of innovation, be sure to do it well. This is no subject for a shiny veneer or superficial commitment. Culture change is never fast or painless. However, creating an environment where innovation happens in a continuous, strategically aligned way can have a profound impact on a firm's long-term profitability and growth potential – especially in times of accelerating change.

From our experience, this requires funding and actively supporting both firm-wide development initiatives and dedicated team-based innovation projects simultaneously. Omitting one dramatically limits the effectiveness of the other. When done together, they are mutually reinforcing. It also compels firms to take a close and honest look at those aspects of their existing culture, structure, and leadership style that might help or hinder a culture of innovation – and take meaningful steps to address them. Finally, law firms need to be open to learning from other sectors, and willing to adopt and adapt the right practices and frameworks in a way that is compatible with their uniquely delivery-focused and standards-driven environments.

David Halliwell, director of knowledge, risk, and legal services for Pinsent Masons LLP, said "... law firms are the last businesses in the supply chain to be transformed. But being last is not such a bad thing. Law firms can learn quickly from other sectors and bring mainstream concepts newly to law to make business-changing progress quickly."

The time is now. Don't procrastinate. Take small steps right now and fast – the advantages are enormous.

The ripple effect: Broader implications of an innovation culture

Innovation is relevant to every aspect of the business – not just to the development of new products and services or IT systems. As a culture of innovation grows within a firm, many of the practices and norms that we take for granted are likely to evolve along the way. Changes you might expect include, but are not limited to:

- The way you inspire, develop, empower, and reward your people;
- Greater likelihood of involving colleagues and clients in the very early stages of designing new products and services;
- The way people in the firm ask questions, actively listen and observe, and provide feedback;
- Communicating value, scope, and pricing options clearly and in a way that meets agreed rather than assumed client needs;
- Your style of leadership and management approach;
- Greater attention paid to the innovations of competitors, including new entrants who have based their entire model on technology, client service, and innovation;
- The way you collaborate internally and externally, including investing time in building diverse networks and listening to different perspectives;
- The way you encourage ideas, manage expectations about how they will be used, develop prototypes, and respond to "failure";
- Greater appetite to learn from other sectors about trends and different ways of doing things;

- Overcoming the tendency to hold on to work that can, over time, be more profitably and efficiently done elsewhere or in a different way;
- Having greater leadership support or authority to move at speed to capitalize on small-window opportunities to meet client needs ahead of competitors; and
- Ensuring that everyone in the firm understands their part in the bigger picture – the link between their work and the specific client benefit.

What changes might you expect to see in your firm?

This first appeared as Chapter 2 in Slater, L. (ed.), Law Firm Innovation: Insights and Practice, *ARK Group, 2015.*

Part 2:
Market and client development

Chapter 6: Horizon scanning to identify and capitalize on new growth opportunities

By Andrew Hedley, director of Hedley Consulting

Ted Levitt, the economist and business thinker who penned the game-changing *Marketing Myopia*[1] in 1960, commented that "the future belongs to people who see possibilities before they become obvious". His words capture the essence of the challenge faced by many legal professionals. In a world where the pace of change is quickening and the future appears uncertain, how can firms identify the new markets that will define their sustainability and success?

A significant area of strategic focus should be detecting markets and clients that are in the early stages of their growth curve and into which firms can invest their finite resources. The firm should be strategically positioned to take advantage of new business paradigms, both with current and future clients. Investments should be targeted at building the skills, competencies, and resources that the firm will need to exploit opportunities.

One observed strategy, which has been both simple and successful for many firms, could be summarized as "grab newly-emerging markets by the coattails and hang on tight". This pragmatic approach may not win awards in the strategy classroom, but in the final reckoning, what matters is the result rather than the theoretical model. The strategic question is how much of this (apparently effective) Remora-like activity should be left to chance as opposed to being part of a deliberate plan?

Prioritizing investments

To create a business that is fit for the future, firms must work hard to build a good understanding of where current clients or markets are headed and where new opportunities (at both a sector and client level) are emerging. Without a clear picture of the most appropriate prioritization of current and new resources, the firm runs the risk of squandering its investments (at best) or sending itself into a strategic cul-de-sac (at worst).

To create competitive advantage in this environment, three things are needed:

1. An assessment of the commercial catalysts and their impact on clients;
2. An awareness of what the firm's competitors are doing to move into these spaces; and
3. The ability to speedily reconfigure structures and acquire new resources to take advantage of new opportunities.

Choosing the right horses to back will be the major determinant of success. Strategic thinking needs to be employed in deciding how such opportunities are identified at an early stage and thereafter developed so that the firm creates strong capabilities and a defendable market position.

Adapting classical marketing strategy can be useful here. By conducting analysis through the eyes of the client (rather than the usual firm-centric approach), insights can be gleaned about macro- and micro-environmental opportunities, the competitive context, and the forces that are impacting on client performance and prospects. Analysis should focus on the nexus between industries of predicted high growth, the way in which these industries use law firms, and the relevant skills or experience that the firm can offer immediately, develop quickly, or acquire soon.

Positioning offerings

Having articulated market growth potential and a sensible resource fit with the firm, it is important to identify potential clients with high relative market share, unique capabilities, or strong market positions. This analysis will provide a focus for sales and client-development activity in fast-growth markets, where there will often be myriad players, many of whom will fall away as consolidation and maturation sets in. Winning a significant share of these clients will allow the firm to achieve a leadership position as the market matures.

Client feedback systems can give the firm access to a broad base of knowledge, opinion, and strategic intelligence. Important insights can be gained by encouraging clients to discuss how they see the future (in terms of opportunities and threats), as well as their own plans and the broader environment that their sector faces. These perspectives can then be the subject of further, more analytical, scrutiny as the firm decides where to invest for growth.

Some firms have established advisory boards or client panels which meet on a regular basis to share views and opinions on strategic responses to market changes. Such meetings can provide an excellent mental breakout space, giving the firm's leaders the opportunity to reflect on long-term strategy in a setting that is both challenging and supportive of their overall ambitions.

Law firms that recognize the importance of creating competitive advantage by identifying and acting upon growth opportunities will ensure they develop good long-term scanning capabilities. Coupled with excellent acuity to act on the most compelling opportunities identified, they will be the ones that see the future early and put themselves in the best position to capitalize on the openings that they have unearthed.

A version of this article appeared in Managing Partner *magazine in September 2015.*

Reference

1. Levitt, T., *Marketing Myopia*, Harvard Business School Publishing, 2008.

Chapter 7:
Finding niches and developing your strategy

"I skate to where the puck is going to be, not where it has been."

Wayne Gretzky, 9-time National Hockey League MVP

By David H. Freeman, J.D., chief executive officer of David Freeman Consulting Group

In firms of all sizes, lawyers' careers are often determined by the type of work they're given. A young associate is assigned to a client and works on the same matter for years. A partner retires and their book of business is handed to a younger lawyer. An industry becomes hot, and lawyers in slower practices are encouraged to retool in the higher demand area. In all, many careers unfold more by default than design, resulting in lawyers who are unfulfilled and lack the motivation to enthusiastically build a great practice. The question you must answer is: do you truly want the practice you already have? And if your answer is no, what are you willing to do to change it?

Over the years, I've trained and coached thousands of lawyers, and I've found that those with the greatest passion, who love to meet new clients and hustle to get more work, are very often those who truly enjoy the type of work they're doing. To unleash this energy, however, lawyers must take proactive control over their career arc. They must be clear about the type of work they want to do, articulate the type of clients they want to work with, and define the type of firm that can best support them on their journey. In all, they must develop a plan and, more importantly, consistently implement that plan.

In this chapter, we will share best practices for refining your thinking around developing a sound plan. Expert insight is included from Ross H. Fishman, CEO, Fishman Marketing Inc.; Mary Kimber, regional director of marketing and business development, Bryan Cave HRO; and James (Jim) Stapleton, former chief marketing officer, Littler Mendelson PC and Fenwick & West LLP.

Defining and differentiating yourself – Who are you and what do you enjoy?

Clients can choose between many lawyers. Why should they select you over someone else? What distinguishes you in a way that makes you stand out from the crowd? One characteristic is your level of engagement. People generally want to work with others who are passionate about what they do. Think about it: would you rather hire a professional who is highly motivated and eager to do the work, or one who is virtually sleepwalking through their day? While the world may not be so black and white, experienced buyers of legal services can tell the difference. "Clients can feel the passion you have for their business. You can't fake that energy and excitement. If you have it, clients see it immediately and find it very enticing", explains Ross Fishman.

"We also don't often talk about fun in terms of marketing in law firms", he continues. "Lawyers are smart, they work hard, they look after their clients – they're good people. But as a general rule, they aren't having fun. Many don't enjoy the practice of law and have lost their energy. They need to step back and ask themselves: What do I like doing? What case did I enjoy handling and why? What industries am I interested in that can be built into my legal practice? What knowledge do I have that other lawyers don't possess? What hobbies, special interests, and lifetime experiences do I have – what job did I do before law school?"

A balanced approach

Can a lawyer build an entire practice solely around their personal interests? For some, the answer is yes, but for many others, their interests, strengths, and experiences may represent just a portion of their practice. It doesn't have to be an all or nothing proposition, according to Ross.

"A lot of lawyers don't want that full-on specialization – they find it demotivating and they prefer the intellectual challenge that comes with variety. Remember, you don't have to focus on a single practice; you're just sharpening your marketing attention and energy on certain people or groups for efficiency. Perhaps specialize a portion of your practice in areas you're comfortable with. To get a feel for where you should spend your limited marketing time, answer these questions:

- What do I love to do?
- What kind of people do I like to be around?
- How can I spend more time doing what I like?"

Build on your strengths

There is no "one size fits all" approach to building a practice. Different personality styles lend themselves to using different techniques, so it's important to build on your strengths when reaching out to the marketplace. Jim Stapleton shares his thoughts: "In the early part of an attorney's career, we put them through a number of training classes to find approaches to suit their individual strengths. We often ask the firm's top rainmakers to talk about how they found approaches that fit their strengths; they all have very different tactics and yet are equally successful.

When I think of all the brands and strengths I have come across I can fit them into five subsets. Most of the attorneys who speak at our sessions align with one or more of these categories:

- Quality;
- Client service;
- Industry and expertise;
- Business acumen; and
- Cost effectiveness and value."

The following examples from Jim Stapleton illustrate ways rainmakers have built on their personal strengths to develop their practices.

CASE STUDY

Case study 1: Service

"One attorney on the panel was a master at client service. He deeply understood the mind of the client. This attorney gives presentations on client satisfaction and feedback – the title of his presentation is '11 Steps to Significant Client Satisfaction'. In fact, it totaled 55 discrete steps, and by the end of his presentation, I absolutely understood why clients followed him like puppies!"

Case study 2: Public speaking

"There's an attorney who is absolutely the best public speaker I know. He's a tax partner; he speaks at tax conferences all around the world. He's not headquartered in New York but his billing rate is roughly equivalent to the New York City tax partner level. He's nationally and internationally recognized, and because he has this ability to connect with people through public speaking, he's been extraordinarily successful."

Case study 3: Business acumen

"We have an individual who has been an attorney for many years, but he spent about five years in the business world, first as general counsel and second as head of corporate development. He has an excellent capacity for speaking about business issues – not just as they relate to legal, but business issues in general. The time he spent in the boardroom allows him to give invaluable expert advice to his clients. An attorney who knows business adds tremendous value to a client in a way most others can't."

Case study 4: Writing and media relations

"Another way to engage with prospective clients and referral sources is through writing and media relations. We have an attorney who knows and works with journalists and who has a writing style that is different from most other lawyers. He once received a $2 million piece of business from a quote of his that appeared in the *New York Times*. A CEO saw it and saved it for two years before contacting him. The attorney is particularly knowledgeable in his area of expertise, which happens to be employment, but the fact that he has an affinity for writing – and the interest in pursuing it – is what separated him from the pack."

Ross Fishman adds additional insights into ways to efficiently use writing as a business development tool. "Lawyers all know they should write. For many, however, it is a painful, time-consuming process, they dread (and avoid) opportunities that could add to their credentials and gain them greater visibility. The kind of writing I'm suggesting is perhaps 500 words on a topic you already know intimately and on which you don't need to do additional research – colloquial subjects and business-oriented topics linked to your practice.

The hard part for most lawyers is getting the information out of their head and turning it into an article because they're so busy. I advise lawyers to dictate the content for the article and send it to a writer – there are a lot of great writers out there who are relatively inexpensive. They can do 95 percent of the writing and it is up to the lawyer to do only the last five percent. With this kind of strategic delegation, the project gets started, most of the work is done by someone else, and having another person involved keeps momentum going."

CASE STUDY

Case study 5: Legal process and efficiency expert

Jim Stapleton continues: "Many years ago, when we were all committed to time and expense billing, one attorney's large client asked for more predictability around expenses. The client did not want him to be unprofitable, but pointed out that some things could be more efficient. The attorney responded to the client's request, and marketed his newfound approaches to managing M&A deals to become top of class in alternative fee arrangements and designing efficient processes."

Narrow your focus

In today's world, lawyers are competing for a limited amount of high quality business. To stand out from the crowd, you need a laser approach to marketing. By concentrating your business development energy toward a clearly defined population, you can build deeper and stronger relationships and cut through the clutter of other lawyers who are flailing around trying to capture their attention.

While some may need to reinvent themselves, most others can build on their strengths, utilizing the resources they already possess to enhance their opportunities. One approach is to identify where the bulk of your revenue comes from – this may be a particular area of law, an industry, or a specific set of referrers – and target those sources.

Develop your niche(s)

According to Ross Fishman, "Too often, the fundamental problem lawyers have with business development is they don't know who they're marketing to. There's little focus; they market opportunistically to anyone they happen to bump into wherever they happen to go. There's little structure or strategy behind it, so it becomes paralyzing and often overwhelming. They end up feeling like they are marketing to 'all of America'. Trying to be all things to all people hinders your ability to get noticed and remembered.

Developing a niche allows lawyers to focus on a more manageable portion of the market to display their skills in places where they are most likely to be noticed. You need to target and nurture a solid network of hundreds of people if you want to become an effective rainmaker."

Building a large personal network takes a significant commitment of time and energy. Given your limited capacity for both, you can't afford to engage in a time-consuming and wasteful scattershot approach.

Stand out to be outstanding

Unless you have something outstanding to say, you will just be seen (or not seen at all) as "yet another lawyer". According to various studies, you need to meet people seven or more times before they are likely to consider giving you their business. "It's just too hard to do that if those people don't go to the same places and do the same things," observes Ross. "You can't see 'America' seven to 20 times – where does 'America' go? Where do 'business people' go? Without some sort of strategy to target the right subset of people on a regular, ongoing basis, your efforts will be extremely inefficient."

By choosing a niche, you can zero in on the right people, send consistent messages over time, be seen as an expert, and thus be remembered when clients have those issues. By focusing on one or a small number of niches, you can better "own" that legal space in a prospect's mind. According to Ross, one effective technique to gain repeated exposure to a targeted group is to join a trade association that is populated with the kind of people you want to meet.

Groups and trade associations

A trade association is a great way to start networking with a particular group of people. The beauty of joining the right association is they do all the work of attracting and communicating with the kind people you need to know. By using their marketing and educational vehicles, you can hit hundreds, and perhaps thousands of current and future prospects through articles, newsletters, webinars, speaking, advertising, leadership positions, and attending periodic meetings and conferences.

Whether you are more comfortable speaking, writing, or joining subgroups, you can find a strategy that fits your strengths. Ross describes trade associations as the "silver bullet" that exists for law firm marketing. You can find them in the Encyclopedia of Associations, published by Gale, and the best for you may be smaller ones where other law firms do not have a strong presence. You can then work toward leadership positions within those organizations. With the right finesse, you can become *the* lawyer they think of when they have legal problems.

Develop a personal scorecard

In any sporting event, there are two levels of scorekeeping. One is the final score – the eventual win or loss numbers. The other is the game within the game – the personal statistics that show whether the players are on track toward the eventual "win".

Similarly, there are two ways to keep score in a law firm. Success measures – such as hours billed, revenue collected, and profitability – are our final score. While these are critically important measures, a deeper analysis of progress measures will allow you to see how well you're doing on your path toward winning. To that end, you should develop your own set of personal sub-goals and measures, and Mary Kimber shares her approaches in this area.

"Keeping score is one of the most critical factors of any business development or marketing plan, whether you're a large organization or an individual practitioner. Setting personal metrics can be the single most important difference between whether you will be successful or not. We should use the lessons of the Hawthorne principle: 'That which is measured will improve.' Once you define your goals, develop a system for measuring those goals and make this a part of your daily routine. By making measurement a top priority, you will be much more likely to achieve your personal goals.

Set your goals and create measures that are within your reach, but put some stretch into it. Some preliminary questions to ask include:

- Where am I right now, and where do I want to be?
- What must I do to build my practice?
- What am I currently doing, and how can I improve on that?
- What am I trying to change or improve?

- How will that change or improvement impact me?
- Can I break my goals into sub-steps to measure my progress toward my goals?
- How will I measure my progress?"

Examples of progress measures

I can't stress enough that one of the great secrets to developing a solid, consistent practice is to develop and track specific "progress" measures. Good measures provide better focus, they increase motivation over the long haul, and they keep business development top of mind. The key is to find the right measures that will lead you to your goals, and that also fit your personal strengths and interests. Examples of some effective progress measures include:

- Client feedback meetings – which can result in greater loyalty, more of the same work, increased cross-selling opportunities, and possible referrals.
- Extraordinary service delivered – measure yourself on the number of "wows" you receive, the number of times clients praise you for doing more than expected.
- Business development discussions with others in your firm – which can result in identifying opportunities, holding each other accountable for action, and cross-selling.
- Leadership positions in targeted outside organizations – which can lead to meeting more targeted prospects and greater visibility in your niche markets.
- Contacts made with high priority targets – which can lead to greater top-of-mind awareness and being in the right place at the right time when opportunities arise.
- Size of key networks – the more people you know, the better chance you have of getting work. Collect a lot of the right people, and cluster them into similar categories to help you communicate with them efficiently.
- Referrals given and received – the more referrals you give, the more likely it is that people will feel obligated to give referrals back to you.
- New relationships built on both sides – meeting more people inside a client, and getting more of your clients to meet others in your firm, can

increase client retention and lead to more cross-selling opportunities.

- Meals with clients, prospects, and referral sources – there is something magical about sharing food with another person. Increased face time and sustained conversations create deeper personal connections and more opportunities to explore their needs.
- On-going communication – given that we've learned it can take seven to 20 contacts to get work, you need to develop many creative and value-laden methods for staying in touch.
- Presentations – this can get you on-site at a client's location, allowing you to demonstrate your capabilities, deepen existing relationships, and meet new decision-makers.
- On-site visits – whether for presentations, general visits, delivering documents, holding meetings, grabbing lunch, or conducting "office hours", getting on-site opens worlds of opportunities to meet new people and find more work.
- Practice groups used – the more the client uses the firm in areas other than yours, the tighter the connection to the firm, and the less likely they are to leave.
- Time invested in business development – nothing takes the place of good, old-fashioned effort. Put in the time, in the right ways, and good things will come.

You should allow yourself to acknowledge and celebrate your progress. Whether it's a new prospect lunch, a meeting with a new referral source, a new leadership position, or an in-house presentation to a client that gets you in front of other decision-makers, give yourself credit for doing the right things that will help you to build a bigger, better client base.

Create personal deadlines

It's not enough to just measure – you must also set deadlines for when you will achieve those measures. Four lunches with prospective clients are good, but by when? What is a stretch, but reasonable number of activities you can complete? Push yourself, because in most cases you can do more than you are now. Organize yourself so that it becomes part of your routine on a daily, weekly, or monthly basis.

This first appeared as Chapter 1 in Freeman, D.H., Secrets of the Masters: The Business Development Guide for Lawyers, *ARK Group, 2013.*

ACTION PLAN

Action planning worksheet

Which of my current practices do I enjoy most?

What particular strengths can I build on (e.g., quality, client service, industry and expertise, business acumen, cost effectiveness and value, etc.)?

In the practices I most enjoy, where can I find a niche group of decision-makers?

What group or trade association can I join, and get better known in, that is filled with targeted prospects?

What should I do within that group or trade group to get noticed by more targeted people?

Which measures can I use to chart my progress toward achieving my goals?

How frequently will I check-in on my progress to see how well I'm doing?

Chapter 8: Increase motivation to act on cross-serving

By David H. Freeman, J.D., chief executive officer of David Freeman Consulting Group

At its core, maximizing cross-serving, like anything else, boils down to two simple rules: (1) doing the right things; and (2) doing them more often. This chapter will focus on how to get more effort from those who work in your firm.

If you have ever tried to implement a major cross-serving effort in the past, you have probably run into a laundry list of roadblocks such as low motivation, siloed practices, dysfunctional groups, lack of trust, inefficient teams, ineffective leaders, poor communication, misaligned compensation, weak selling skills, unclear goals and measures, inconsistent client service, minimal accountability, and inadequate follow-through. In addition, law firms are usually not places where leaders can give orders and lawyers dutifully follow. Firms are filled with people who are skeptical about change, and who are also highly skilled in the art of finding holes in new ideas. By their very nature, lawyers are trained to analyze, dissect, challenge, and explore other approaches before they are comfortable moving forward.

In the ongoing tug-of-war between investing time in billable versus non-billable activities, most lawyers naturally choose billable hours. While that's fine for keeping the lights on today, it does not help to build the necessary foundation for addressing tomorrow's needs. This goes to the heart of one of the major challenges of leadership: getting people to invest their non-billable time now in ways that may benefit them sometime in the future.

Another related issue is that many lawyers and staff just show up and do their time. They are not truly connected to the enterprise, and they do not possess a sense of ownership that inspires them to dedicate non-billable time in service to the firm. They just hover, believing it is someone else's job to care about the current and future health of the firm. This disassociation means you lose out on their creativity, energy, and passion.

Overcoming these formidable challenges requires exquisite skill. When vying for your lawyers' time and attention, your initial focus must be on how to set the stage to maximize their acceptance. Removing these obstacles often requires taking two steps back to make the larger leap forward. As Abraham Lincoln once said: "If I had eight hours to cut down a tree, I'd take six sharpening my saw." "Sharpening" in a law firm context means getting people to buy-in, to feel a sense of ownership toward the new approaches. Simply stated, you must find ways to get them to care. Leaders need to reach into their change management toolkits to create higher levels of individual engagement throughout the firm. Leaders need approaches that get others to see the line-of-sight between firm needs and how it will benefit them personally. Once firm members understand "what's in it for me", it can translate into a higher level of internal motivation.

To tap into the potential energy that exists within each person – entrepreneurial energy, team-based energy, and service-oriented energy – leaders must internally promote, communicate, teach, cheerlead, measure, manage, reward, and provide ongoing recognition. By pushing the right buttons, you can access more of what people have to give, which helps them, and the firm, achieve higher levels of performance.

The good news is that you have a running start when implementing a cross-serving initiative, because service in itself is a source of motivation. According to studies cited in the book *Give and Take*, when people act for the benefit of others it activates the reward and meaning centers in the brain.[1] In effect, encouraging a cross-serving culture creates a self-fueling loop that inspires people to give more of themselves to the organization and to their clients.

Build the business case

Activating the service loop is just one approach of many leaders can use to redirect a culture. Another tactic is getting lawyers to understand why cross-serving is so vitally important to the well-being of the firm, as well as to them personally. Providing ongoing education can go a long way toward convincing them of the need and the value of actively engaging in these behaviors. Allison Karp, strategic accounts marketing manager at Grant Thornton, says: "Firms should try to teach their lawyers that a bigger pie means larger slices for everyone." Some educational sources can include:

- Industry and firm data showing how cross-serving supports growth and longevity;
- Success stories from your firm, as well as other firms;
- Stories of clients who were poached by other firms, and an explanation of how a more effective cross-serving effort might have kept them from leaving;
- The voice of the client – collect and communicate stories where clients articulate why cross-serving is important to them;
- Examples of how cross-serving behavior is rewarded in the compensation system;
- Internal training on the key components that make up a highly functional cross-serving effort; and
- Internal surveys to identify which approaches for overcoming cross-serving obstacles and raising performance need improvement.

Focus on the "coalition of the willing"

To paraphrase an old Head & Shoulders commercial, you won't get a second chance to make a first impression. If you plan to roll out a serious cross-serving initiative, you must get it right the first time or you risk poisoning the well for future efforts. Since we know all lawyers are not created equal, you need to find your pioneers – those with passion who are willing to invest the time and energy to make it work. Their early success can breed ongoing success, so to get your firm's flywheel moving, start with your "coalition of the willing". Another way to look at this is expressed by Mark Karkazis, director of marketing at Nixon Peabody, who says: "Work primarily with lawyers who are not impacted by the obstacles".

According to Douglas Spiker, employment services group leader at Roetzel & Andress, leaders should "seek out like-minded personalities to pursue cross-selling". To build greater momentum, you need to encourage faster action, instill accountability, and bring these early adopters together in small teams. Cross-connecting people who possess a true desire to help each other can create self-energizing pods that can act as role models for other parts of the firm.

Access the inner entrepreneur

"Law firms are incubators of great lawyers, but not incubators of entrepreneurs", says Michael Droke, partner at Dorsey & Whitney. Too many lawyers suffer from the "large firm syndrome" – a belief that it's someone else's job to get things done. If each lawyer was solely responsible for the fortunes of the firm, you can bet they would act very differently. To increase engagement, leaders need to get their lawyers to act more like owners.

Setting the stage for greater engagement means leaders must develop an environment that nurtures entrepreneurial energy. It must encourage dreaming, risk-taking, planning, mentoring, coaching, supporting, and teamwork. Through training, practice, and proper rewards, firms can unlock and direct more of the ownership and entrepreneurial energy that fuels cross-serving success.

Collaborative planning

Another way to increase engagement is to include people in a collaborative planning process. By incorporating them into decision-making, they will develop a greater sense of ownership around achieving outcomes they agree are important. With the right approach, they can come together to understand the need for taking action, analyze their problems, develop consensus on solutions, create a common language, and establish roles and responsibilities for implementation.

Aligned personal planning

In the book *Aligning the Stars*, authors Jay Lorsch and Thomas Tierney argue that professional services firms need to align the needs of the organization with the goals and desires of the individual "stars" that make up that organization.[2] Therefore, another level in the engagement cascade is to have your lawyers create personal plans that support the group/firmwide cross-serving plans they had a hand in crafting. To be effective, this may require interaction with leaders and marketing/business development professionals who can help them build individual plans that serve both personal and organizational interests. Such mentoring and coaching can deliver a number of benefits, such as:

- Balancing personal and group goals;
- Developing approaches that serve short- and long-term goals;
- Building on personal strengths and improving areas of weakness;
- Drilling down to specific action plans with deadlines; and
- Maintaining ongoing accountability and action.

Compensation

In most conversations about cross-serving, the elephant in the room is the money. Firms need to clearly align their compensation system to reward desired cross-serving behaviors. Marijane Benner Browne, director of lateral partner recruitment at Ropes & Gray, says firms "need compensation systems that fully support teaming and cross-selling". Stephen Brewer, owner of Brewer Business Research LLC, agrees: "In my experience, most problems in any law firm result directly or indirectly from the compensation system. If cross-selling is rewarded, there will be more of it; if it is not, there will be less of it. In many firms, the compensation systems still encourage hoarding by the partners to protect their incomes."

In addition to developing the system, firms must also do a better job communicating the cross-serving factors that are used in compensation formula, since lawyers often do not realize, or believe, these behaviors are considered. One approach is to regularly tout examples where lawyers who cross-serve receive additional compensation based on the rewarded behaviors.

This first appeared as Chapter 2 in Freeman, D.H., Creating a Cross-Serving CultureShift: Mastering Cross-Selling for Lawyers and Leaders, *ARK Group, 2015.*

References

1. Grant, A., *Give and Take: A Revolutionary Approach to Success*, Weidenfeld & Nicolson, London, 2013.
2. Lorsch, J.W. and Tierney, T.J., *Aligning the Stars: How to Succeed When Professionals Drive Results*, Harvard Business School Press, Boston, 2002.

Chapter 9:
Does your firm need a key relationship program?

"I do not seek to close a sale; I want to open a relationship..."

Anonymous American saying

By Robert Pay, global services business development director at Alvarez & Marsal North America LLC

The purpose of this chapter is to familiarize you with the core concepts of relationship management and to help you decide if a key relationship program (KRP) is right for your firm or practice area. We start by giving you an overview of:

- What is meant by a key relationship program and the main elements;
- The reasons why professional services firms use KRPs; and
- Current levels of uptake of KRPs by professional services firms.

One word I will avoid using is "account". We are dealing with people, not a financial instrument, so the word "relationship" seems more appropriate. (This is despite having started my career in an advertising agency where the concept of an account manager started and is still deeply embedded.) The book's focus is what in general business language would be termed key account management and how to establish the process in a professional services firm.

Key relationship program: A definition

It is an incontrovertible fact that a strong relationship between an adviser and a client is a valuable commercial asset, even though it may be difficult to put a precise value on a relationship. Losing a good relationship can be very costly. Relationship capital is real but hard to define; you know when you do not have it or have lost it. The core elements are ease of communication and mutual respect for the value an adviser brings, and these are based on experience of working together.

A key relationship program is the technique used to bring a systematic approach to managing a clutch of major relationships for a firm, a practice area, a region, or an industry group, in order to build the quality and financial value of client and referral relationships. It comprises a set of processes, tools, and techniques through which client relationships are systematically analyzed, nurtured, and grown. An effective program will have the following core features:

- A small number (relative to the total client base) of relationships selected against specific criteria;
- A process that provides some core disciplines for managing the relationship, such as the monitoring of:
    - Activity levels, frequency and quality of touches;
    - The health of the relationship; and
    - The financial performance;
- Documented analysis of the relationship and action plans;
- Well-defined roles and responsibilities for those charged with managing specific relationships;
- Skills programs to support relationship building and client service; and
- Accountability for specific clients.

There are some optional elements; for example, the KRP may or may not be supported by a client relationship management (CRM) system. The excellent technology now available facilitates a key relationship program, but it is possible to have an effective program without much technology (although the larger and more complex a relationship, the more difficult this becomes).

Some features will almost certainly make your KRP more effective, such as having third party client satisfaction interviews and reward systems linked to goals for a specific client relationship or batch of client relationships. However, it is possible to have a program without such features, and it may be easier to gradually add elements as the program gains traction.

Of course, all firms serve clients and manage relationships, and you may be asking yourself the degree to which your firm has a recognizable client relationship program. Table 1 highlights the differences between a traditional partnership approach and the approach that this book follows.

Traditional client approach	Client relationship management approach
Intuitive	Intuition plus process, learning, and technology
Service levels at individual partner's discretion	Firm service levels, plus clients' individual service objectives clearly defined
Client relationships proprietary	Client relationships belong to the partnership
Role of partners vis-à-vis client relationship undefined	Roles of partners and lawyers defined; performance measured and rewarded
Little focus on individual client relationships by firm management	Firm management monitors the progress of important relationships

Table 1: Traditional versus professional client management approach

Relationship management approach ≠ selling

While a primary aim of a relationship management program is to increase sales, it achieves this by focusing on the client's needs, not yours. The relationship management approach demands putting the clients first. To quote Charles Green of Trusted Adviser Associates LLC, the co-author of *The Trusted Advisor,* "A seller with low self-orientation is free to completely and honestly focus on the client – not for his own sake, but for the sake of the client. You succeed more at sales when you stop trying to sell. When all you focus on is helping prospects, they trust you more and buy from you more as well."[1]

The advantage with this approach is that it suits the way professionals think about themselves and their general dislike of selling. It is easier said than done, however. The process set out here aims to make that approach systematic.

Reasons to implement a key relationship program

There are many commercial reasons for a introducing a key relationship program. Any one of the factors listed in Table 2 could be a trigger for the decision, but normally it is a combination of issues. Let's consider each category in turn.

Possible reasons for implementing a key relationship program

Category	**Details**
Financial	• Focus best resource on the best opportunities (scale/profitability) • Reducing cost of sales, reducing need to pitch for new work • Improve the nature of work undertaken • Increase the volume of work undertaken
Competitor advantage	• Become better placed for opportunities than competition • Improved chances of winning new business
Risk management	• Stem attrition by focusing on valuable relationships at risk • Institutionalize relationships against defections and competitors • Reduce exposure to large clients or single industry • Decrease dependence on few key rainmaker client partners
Cultural	• Improve transparency and accountability for precious assets • Develop a client-centered, business development culture
Insurance	• Protection against downward fee-pressure • Mitigate impact of service shortfalls

Financial

Best opportunities for growth

Big tends to be beautiful when it comes to client billing and contribution to a firm's revenues and profits. The 80/20 rule normally understates the importance of the top 20 percent of clients. In some firms it is 20

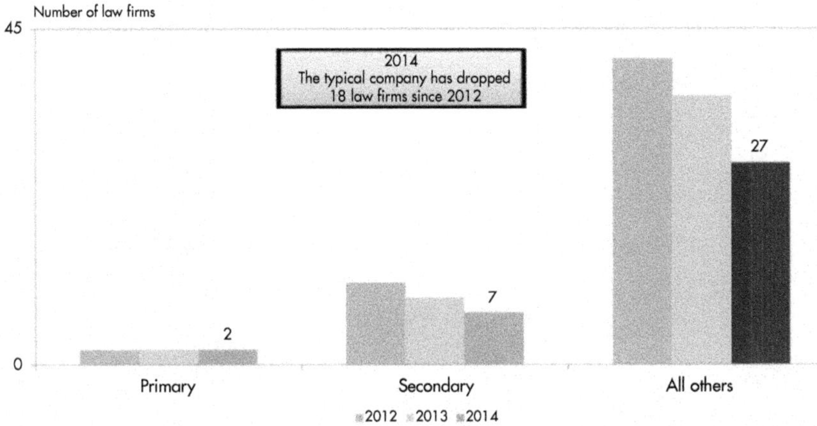

Figure 1: Fewer firms, bigger opportunities for the survivors. Source: "The BTI Market Outlook And Client Service Review 2015". Copyright by The BTI Consulting Group (Wellesley, MA), 2015

clients that produce 80 percent of revenue and profits. Whatever the precise figures, the chances are that a very small number of your firm's largest clients generate a disproportionate amount of revenue and profit. (Scale of revenue does not guarantee profitability; at one firm, we parted company with the third biggest client because it was not profitable.)

If a small group of clients generates a disproportionate volume of revenue each year, then consider how much impact getting 10 percent more from that group will have on the bottom line. Getting the equivalent revenue from new or smaller clients would entail a great deal more effort in terms of time and money spent.

Benefit from roster or panel shrinkage

Being a small player on a big-spending client's roster can be a perilous position. A recent study by leading US professional services market researchers BTI Consulting showed that, for big-spending clients with a roster of law firms, on average, 11 core firms account for 80 percent of outside legal spend, while a further 36 compete for smaller work. Within that group of 11 firms, there were normally two firms that got the lion's share of plum projects. The number of firms used by the average respondent had decreased by 18 since 2007.

The study also showed that the amount of dollars going to law firms was not increasing, with more revenues being diverted to the in-house team. In terms of relationship building, the job just got more complex, while the prizes for those who succeed have gotten bigger. This underlines

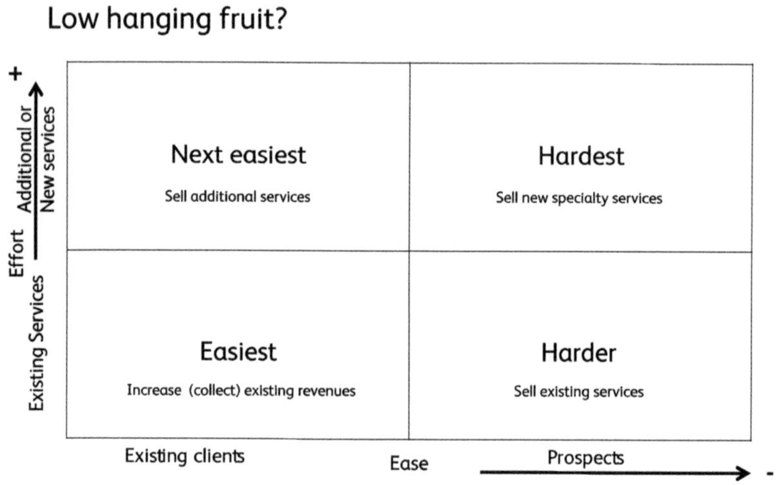

Figure 2: Current relationships – Easiest targets for growth

the benefits of focusing on growing relationships and staying away from the fringe of the roster where you may be the next firm to be eliminated.

Value and volume of work

It is also probable that your largest clients offer some of the best opportunities for you to develop valuable service capabilities. These may well benefit both your general ability to compete and your market profile, and may also boost your firm's professional skills. In a marketplace that craves innovation, winning and keeping an innovative client can help you generally.

Reducing the cost of sales

It is commonly acknowledged that it is far easier to grow revenues from existing relationships than to sell to new clients, although some new relationships are essential to most firms. For years, professional services firms have been frustrated in their desire to cross-sell. Cross-selling failed largely because it was internally driven, rather than driven by client needs. If you put the client first, as the relationship management process envisages, then selling no longer feels like "selling", rather it becomes meeting client needs. That means spending time to understand the client and build trust. In short, a KRP is the only way to achieve professional services firms' universal, and largely unmet, ambition to cross-sell. This approach also falls within the comfort zone of most professionals.

Risk management

Institutionalization of clients

Recent research by LexisNexis Redwood Analytics[2] has shown three factors that reduce attrition rates and contribute to building stronger, more loyal client relationships:

- Breadth of relationship contact – The involvement of more than one partner;
- Range of services consumed – Working with the client across more than one service line; and
- Longevity – The age of the client relationship.

In other words, the more points of contact and services rendered, the greater the client loyalty. Also, the longer you maintain that status, the more it becomes self-fulfilling. While this research was undertaken for law firms, there are similar findings in other professions.

This has implications for the tightly held client relationship. The "bow tie" relationship format, based on a single partner and key decision-maker (Figure 3), is not a good model for larger, more complex organizations, although it still has validity in smaller simpler relationships.

Institutional relationships are secured at all levels; the middle management of today is tomorrow's board. Contact with the client beyond those

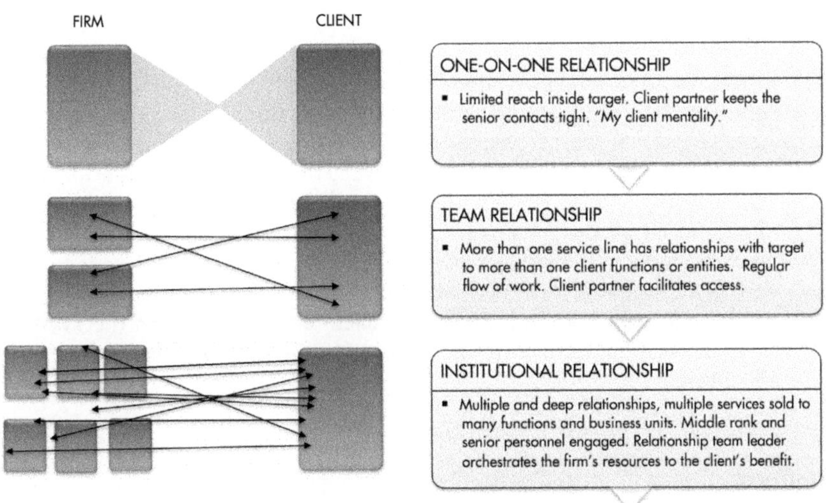

Figure 3: Institutionalization of relationships – Bow ties going out of fashion?

client executives actually involved in the work can also be useful in improving loyalty.

Diversification

Actively managing your client portfolio is essential. Firms may go through a period of defections caused by partners leaving or retiring. Quality is not always scalable; sometimes a merger or rapid growth means that quality suffers. Sometimes the unexpected loss of a major client through acquisition or sale has a major impact on the bottom line and prompts a desire to diversify.

This "client churn" is sometimes made worse because management often look only at aggregate figures, so it is possible for relationships to quietly slip away unnoticed – a phenomenon referred to as "client leakage". It is very rare, except in the case of audit firms, for a client to demonstrably fire a firm. They simply stop using you, sometimes slowly over a long period as they quietly transfer work to a rival. Unlike new business where partners are likely to be very vocal about their successes, few raise their hands to say a client has left them or that they are having problems and need help to save the relationship. In many firms, partners do not feel it is safe speaking up, or they may be ignorant of (or in denial about) the problems.

CASE STUDY

A regional US accounting firm had undertaken a string of mergers and was suffering a high degree of churn amongst frontline professionals. It had placed a strong emphasis on client acquisition, possibly to the detriment of existing clients and client service. Although one year, they increased new business revenue by 15 percent, another year they lost 16 percent through client attrition. As a result, the firm introduced a KRP with a strong service element that was intended to reduce client loss. The emphasis for the client partner was to flag issues so as to be able to scramble support from senior personnel to ensure additional resources were made available when necessary, or to call upon senior diplomats to smooth out problems. Critically, management made it safe for partners to say there was a problem with a relationship, and rather less safe to ignore a problem.

Cultural

Transparency and accountability

An asset as valuable as a major client relationship should be actively managed. As a managing partner, CEO, or practice area head, a KRP gives you a tool to manage a commercially critical part of your client portfolio. The process of developing a KRP will encourage you to become more client-focused and make partners responsible for the health of the relationship and the growth of business beyond their own account.

In some partnerships, firm and practice area management meetings still continue to focus largely on historic financials without looking at the underlying business in terms of individual relationships. This is like driving by looking in the rear-view mirror. In a growing number of firms, the KRP is also a vital part of the forecasting process. A KRP will give you some vision of the future and a way of measuring how well your key assets are being managed. In order to grow what you have, you need to understand the potential for growth and the risk of loss. Careful listening to and understanding of client needs, combined with the ability to spot opportunities for your skill set, is key to the growth of the relationship. This needs to be documented and the information shared with the client team, and occasionally with practice or firm management.

Finally, appearances can be deceptive. Longstanding relationships between individual partners and regularly high-billing clients actually may be in terminal decline while retaining the appearance of being in good shape: a regular flow of matters, steady revenue, nothing that would ring an alarm bell. Indeed, such dying legacy relationships may persist for a long time while other firms carry off the real prizes.

The following anecdote is a good illustration of the advantage of having transparency around relationships, rather than just focusing on partner performance in financial terms. In this case, a relationship plan might have prompted questions about the need for a wider range of services and the composition of the team. There was work that the firm would have struggled to deliver, but with greater insight and management, there would also have been a chance to manage the decline in the firm's share of purse, or to direct the work to a friendly third party. The relationship worked for that partner, but clearly did not work for the client or the firm.

CASE STUDY

I was once undertaking a client satisfaction review on behalf of a UK law firm. The client, a well-endowed college of a major university, told me they were staying with the firm only until their relationship team leader retired. In this case, the college had sometimes been sending substantive work elsewhere for some time. The team leader had rarely introduced others to the client and, as a result, the client had a view of the firm that had not kept pace with its capabilities. However, the relationship team leader continued to regularly receive healthy amounts of work and to make his numbers. The billing figures had remained substantially stable with the result that, up to that point, no one in management at this firm seemed to be aware of the decline in the overall relationship. Not surprisingly, the relationship team leader never raised the issue of seepage of work, and not all consultancy work or lawyering is in the public domain.

Building a client-centered business development culture

A well-designed KRP can act as a beacon of best practice for both client service and building relationships. Mobilizing frontline professionals to manage relationships systematically can help to spread good practice across the client base, especially if backed up by training and documentation that makes it easy to transfer techniques and procedures. It is not unusual to see teams using client plans for relationships not formally in the program or adopting client satisfaction procedures that were designed for top tier clients.

It has long been the case that many firms are over-dependent on a few rainmakers and struggle to replace them as they near retirement. A KRP will help to spread good practice and develop a business development culture to sustain the firm's growth if younger professionals are involved in the client teams. At the heart of effective relationship management lies consultative selling. This approach is best suited to professional services because solutions always have to be tailored to client needs. The ability to transfer this skill to the next generation is best learned by watching and listening, as many of us have done, supplemented with training and process. Being part of a client relationship team is a critical way of passing on the DNA for building sustainable client relationships.

Of course, some partners are intuitively good at developing relationships without any training or processes, and some younger professionals may be lucky enough to work with them and learn by osmosis. However, a KRP gives a real life context for BD-related training and sharing ideas, and it is a useful vehicle to help join up a number of disparate elements firms spend time and effort on, including:

- Learning and development around sales and networking;
- Performance metrics; and

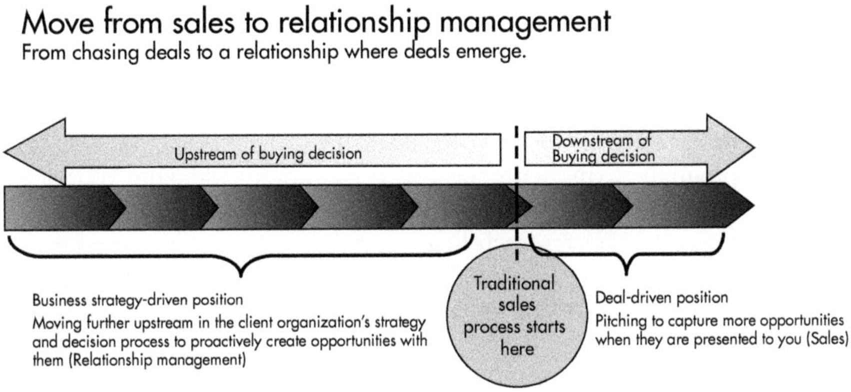

Figure 4: The benefits of moving "upstream" in a relationship. Source: The Forum Corporation

- Mentoring.

Another reason for involving non-partners is that, before a firm can institutionalize a major client relationship, it helps to secure the relationship at every level.

Competitor advantage

A major characteristic of a successful adviser relationship is the partner's closeness to their clients and to any major new developments. This means that they often get sight of opportunities ahead of their competitors, before it goes to pitch. Often, such firms pre-empt a tender being issued. In account management jargon, this is known as being "upstream", close to the other enviable position of being a "trusted adviser".

Relationships are often shared; larger clients are rarely totally monogamous. The chances are that someone else is competing for your relationship, and complacency is unlikely to be a sustainable strategy. The client has a choice around its relationships; you don't have a choice about managing them.

Insurance

Mitigation of service problems and fee pressure

One benefit of a strong client relationship that should not be tested too often is the ability to both mitigate service problems and to deflect downward pressure on price. Delivery issues are a part of all professional services; every time you disappoint, your store of relationship capital depletes. The market will ultimately dictate general fee levels, but great service both strengthens a relationship and can increase the perceived value of services delivered. Procurement departments can be held at bay by a powerful champion at senior level.

Evidence for success of the KRP concept

Not surprisingly, firms with "best in class" key relationship programs are coy about releasing information about their KRPs. According to BTI Consulting, a market research firm specializing in the legal market for over 25 years, the law firms with the absolute best client relationships included in its 2014 survey enjoyed:

- 19.5 percent rate premiums; and
- 35.6 percent greater revenue.

Whether this is based on formal key relationship programs is not clear, but it is likely that these firms are systematically client focused and listening hard to what their clients say. In programs in which I have been involved where we have benchmarked against clients not in a program, I have seen figures similar to those quoted being achieved. Over time, the figures diverge further from the generality of clients. In part, this because these relationships were already significant, but also because of the management focus they were given.

In the face of the relentless focus of smart competition, it is inadequate to hope that an innate, general good client service and intuitive partners will be sufficient for your firm. The fact that almost every major professional firm has some sort of KRP is also a powerful recommendation. Kevin Wheeler Associates undertook a global survey of key relationship programs in professional services. His findings on uptake and longevity are revealing.

Uptake

Asked whether their firm had a formal KRP program in place – and by "formal" the survey specified that it had to be a documented program with responsibilities, deliverables, and timescales – just over half (59 percent) said that they did. 41 percent of respondents reported that their firm does not currently have a KRP in place. This figure rises to two thirds (67 percent) among the smaller (<$100 million) firms. Not surprisingly, a formal program was more likely among the largest firms with nearly three-quarters (73 percent) of the firms with an annual fee income in excess of $500 million having such a program. A quarter of respondents said that their firms are currently putting a KRP program in place, and 16 percent said they did not have one. The smaller firms (<$100 million) are more likely not to have a KRP program; 37 percent do not.

Longevity

Nearly three-quarters (72 percent) of those with a KRP have had it in place for less than five years. On average, law firms have had their programs in place for the shortest time, with 34 percent having had a KRP for less than two years. The accountancy firms have had KRPs in place for the longest, with 43 percent having had one for more than five years. The larger the firm, the more likely that a KRP has been in place for more than five years.

Generally, the accountancy-based firms emerged ahead of the others, while the law firms, particularly in the US, have been late coming to the party. It might be argued that the larger, global firms have most to gain from a KRP, and many are clearly making progress in adopting these practices to service their international clients. The North American, predominantly US, firms appear to be the most hindered by a lack of willingness to share clients and appoint partner/director "account managers" for these, which is often put down to their "eat what you kill" cultures.

The "ownership" of a client, highlighted above, is perhaps the biggest issue for partnership to address when considering introducing a KRP.

Client relationships: Personal or partnership asset?

In a true partnership, meaning an entity where partners share risk and reward, there is strong case for a client relationship to be treated more as an institutional asset than as the exclusive property of an individual partner. As partners are mainly responsible for bringing in and developing clients, there are clearly advantages to a partner feeling responsible for the "ownership" of a client, particularly if this sense of ownership is combined with a healthy inclination to grow and broaden the relationship. An overly proprietorial nature of the "ownership" may result in relationships being stunted, placing the overall relationship at risk from competitors. The risk is particularly acute where a partner has a narrow relationship with one or two contacts at the client. This mindset is also a major barrier to adoption of relationship programs by professional firms.

To counter this traditional "my client" approach, the intention of many firm's KRPs is the institutionalization of client relationships, which will be the theme of the second half of the book. These firms view client relationships as a firm asset for which individual partners have responsibilities rather than a proprietorial role. They are rewarded for carrying out the role of nurturing the relationship rather than for "ownership". Indeed, the aim of institutionalizing the client is to secure the relationship for the firm in the event of a key partner leaving or retiring, or conversely an important member of the client team leaving. As the recession following the financial crisis has proven, C-suite people at clients who seemed permanent and immoveable can disappear overnight.

Where is your firm?

By now, you may be wondering where your firm or practice stands relative to the market. Before designing your KRP, you may wish to take the survey that follows to see to what extent your firm already has a genuine relationship management program, and how readily your firm might accept one.

Key relationship management self-diagnostic

Introduction

This questionnaire has been designed to gauge the extent to which your firm can be said to have a key relationship management program. There are three sections:

1. About you;
2. On your firm's current program; and
3. On your firm's culture and its suitability for a program.

This will take you no more than ten minutes to complete. Please check only one box.

About you: Where do you work?	
Accounting and advisory firm	
Architect	
Consulting firm	
Law firm	
Realtor/Property advisory firm	
Tax consulting	
Other consulting business	
Consultant or supplier professional services firm	
Your role	
Frontline professional	
Business development or marketing professional	
Other support staff	
Your position	
Firm management	
Practice management	
In charge of BD marketing	
Line partner/MD or equivalent	
BD/Marketing director or manager	
Which CRM system do you use	
Interaction	
Salesforce.com	
SAP	
Other commercial system	
CRM built in house	
Excel spreadsheets	

For each of the following questions please use a cross to indicate the statement that best describes your view. Please choose only one statement from each question (except Question 6).

Current status	
1. Which of the following statements best describes your firm's approach to a key relationship program?	
a. Individual partners are assumed to be responsible for developing their clients. There is no formal key relationship program.	
b. We have a program with a list of member organizations and teams, but not much else is written down or measured.	
c. We have a program with teams, live plans, and roles and responsibilities clearly laid out.	
d. In addition to (c), we measure the results of our program internally and validate the status of our relationships with the clients/referral sources.	
2. If you have a KRP, what is the level of adherence?	
a. People ignore it or pay lip service...	
b. Uptake is patchy, but there are some areas of the firm that really get it.	
c. There are a few naysayers, but by and large everyone gets it and follows the disciplines.	
d. It is the way things get done; it is part of the culture; it dictates what gets measured and how individual performance is evaluated.	

Suitability for a KRP	
3. Which statement best reflects the current culture of your firm regarding a client partner involving others?	
a. Some people cross-refer and team because it is the right thing to do, though the reward system encourages a proprietorial approach to clients.	
b. There is a patchy level of cooperation between many partners, dependent on personal goodwill.	
c. We have a few barriers to cooperation on major client relationships and the management supports and incentivizes sharing of relationships.	
d. We have analyzed and removed barriers to cooperation on client work and ensured that our reward system incentivizes teamwork.	

Your BD/Marketing function	
4. Which statement best describes the role of your current marketing/ BD team?	
a. Our BD/marketing function is very centralized and focuses mainly on marketing communications and writing proposals; it has little involvement with specific client relationships.	
b. BD managers sit in each division/service line and support a wide range of general BD/marketing.	
c. Our BD function plays a support role to client teams organizing internal meetings, events, updating client action plans, and inputting data into the CRM system.	
d. Our BD function has significant involvement in meetings and planning around key relationships and makes a significant contribution to strategy.	
Appetite for/attitudes towards a KRP	
5. Which statement best reflects the culture of your firm?	
a. Our firm does really well through the innate skills and historic structural capital (brand name, client base). We don't need a special program; client relationship management is in our DNA.	
b. We think what we are doing currently is fine, but we need more rigor or process.	
c. The focus on relationship management and client focus in general needs to improve as our competitors are getting better at this.	
d. The management team is committed to driving client focus though client relationship and service initiatives.	
e. We use or would trust third parties to interview our clients to measure the strength of relationship/client satisfaction etc.	
Your most senior BD/marketing officer	
6. Which statement best reflects the culture of your firm? (Check every box that applies.)	
a. Is focused mainly on marketing communications (website/PR etc.).	
b. Designed and/or runs our key relationship program.	
c. We have another professional who is responsible on a day-to-day basis for our relationship program (head of business development).	
d. Is a member of our profession or a journalist who moved into marketing/BD.	
e. Is someone who would be credible in person meeting our most important clients.	
f. Has extensive marketing/BD experience in business and/or multiple professions (other than this one).	

Scoring

Questions 1–4: (a=1, b=2, c=3, d=4)

Question 5: (a=0, b=1, c=2, d=3, e=4)

Question 6: (a=0, b=3, c=2, d=0, e=3, f=2)

Maximum score: 30

What your score means:

Your score is 25 plus: You are part of a small, elite group of professional services firms. You probably only need to tighten up the process – for example, by undertaking more third party interviews or getting better support for the front lines.

Your score is 15–25: You are on the road to getting serious about a key relationship program. Make sure you do not fall into the group of professional services firms that delude themselves that they have done enough.

Your score is below 15: This is the danger zone, unless you checked box 5a, in which case you are probably a seemingly bulletproof firm likely to be in a decline that does not worry the management team enough to make any changes, or for whom change is more threatening than missed opportunities and eroding competitiveness. This is the graceful decline zone. The likelihood is you will also have checked boxes 4a, 6a, and 6d.

This first appeared as Chapter 1 in Pay, R., Designing a Key Relationship Program: Building Strong Client Relationships, *ARK Group, 2014.*

References

1. Maister, D.H., Galford, R., and Green, C.W., *The Trusted Advisor*, Simon & Schuster, London, 2002.
2. Satkunas, K., "Client Attrition Analytics: Firms Can Control Whether Clients Stay or Go", Accounting and Financial Planning for Law Firms®, January 2007, see: www.lexisnexis.com/redwood-analytics/pdf/client_attrition_analytics.pdf.

Chapter 10:
Competing via culture – How to give clients a true one-firm global service

By Heidi K. Gardner, fellow of Harvard Law School's Program on the Legal Profession, and Rebecca Normand-Hochman, founder of the Institute of Mentoring

Law firm leaders are increasingly fighting a war on two fronts: the battle for talent and the battle for clients. Many are struggling to explain what distinguishes their firms in a crowded legal marketplace. Those that can offer a compelling proposition to both lawyers and clients will undoubtedly take the lead in these dual, interlinked campaigns.

The ability for professionals across the globe to work together in a productive way has, over the years, become a critical factor of law firm performance and success. Much has been researched and written about teams in professional services firms, raising the level of knowledge and awareness about the dynamics and value of collective work.

This chapter looks at two other angles of how lawyers work together to win the war for talent and clients: mentoring and collaboration. It is based on two research projects: one led by Harvard Law School's Center on the Legal Profession and the other by the Institute of Mentoring. By collecting and analyzing hard data, supplemented by interviews and other qualitative evidence, we have been able to uncover fresh insights about the types of professional relationships that allow lawyers to work most productively. Our research, combined with hands-on work with law firms around the globe, has helped us to develop an approach which hinges on lawyers teaming up to share their experience, expertise, and wisdom to increase performance and productivity.

Mentoring is increasingly recognized in the legal profession as a business driver and one of the essential competitive advantages to win the war for talent. Although other professional service industries started to address the talent issues that the increasingly complex and hypercompetitive business environment stimulated about 15 years ago, the legal profession has only more recently woken up to the talent and leadership challenges.

Mentoring is increasingly recognized as a critical success factor to attract, integrate, develop, and retain the best talent. The distinction between mentoring and coaching matters because, although mentoring and coaching have common tools and techniques, mentoring, in its European definition, has a broader focus on long-term development.[1] By enabling a significant increase in the number and quality of mentoring relationships, law firms can use one of the most effective ways to invest in talent.

Collaboration between partners in law firms has also become essential for developing and maintaining competitive advantage. As clients' problems become increasingly complex, firms have been responding by creating more narrow practice areas and encouraging their partners to specialize. As a result, professionals' expertise is now dispersed across different practice groups and offices. Yet, the only way to address these complex problems in a world of narrow expertise is to get experts to integrate their highly specialized knowledge into a joint solution that is superior to any single contributor's potential. Our research shows that, when professionals do successfully collaborate, their clients are stickier and more profitable.

Neither mentoring nor collaboration is an end in itself. Rather, both of these processes are essential to developing high caliber, committed lawyers who are more capable of providing exceptional client service. Further, our research shows the type of unified law firm culture that supports both of these critical approaches.

This chapter explains how law firms can integrate mentoring and collaboration into their working practices to most effectively develop talent and win clients. The first part explains the importance of culture in creating a competitive advantage through mentoring and collaboration and describes the values and behaviors which create a culture that actively encourages and supports both crucial activities.

The second part explores the outcomes that introducing or increasing mentoring and collaboration have both on the individuals and the firms. It focuses on two critical stages of the lifecycle of lawyers: the integration of lateral hires and the client succession process. The latter takes place when a senior lawyer hands over a client to a junior partner, such as when preparing for retirement.

Both lateral hire integrations and transitions out of firms combine elements of mentoring and collaboration. We offer examples to illustrate how the best firms successfully integrate the two processes and derive from them superior business outcomes.

How mentoring and collaboration work in law firms

Mentoring

Mentoring in its modern approach has significantly moved away from its traditional usage. Traditionally, mentoring involved a senior member of the profession providing advice, guidance, and protection to young lawyers so that they could then become established and reputable in their own right.

Over the past two decades, mentoring has evolved to be much less directive and more developmental. Mentees are now the ones who drive and manage the mentoring relationship according to their needs. Peer mentoring, reverse mentoring, and group mentoring have also broken the traditional assumption that only senior people can support the development of others in a significant way. They have put the onus of talent development on a much wider number of people across organizations.

In the legal profession, the traditional aspects of mentoring are taking longer to be replaced by the more progressive elements, but there are some indications that this is about to change.

Collaboration

Collaboration involves expert lawyers working together to integrate their specialized knowledge in order to tackle complex, sophisticated legal problems that none of them could sufficiently resolve alone.

The increasing demand for collaboration as a business driver stems from two competing forces. On the one hand, lawyers need to increasingly specialize in narrow areas of their profession in order to claim true expertise over a domain. On the other hand, as clients have globalized and confronted more sophisticated technological, regulatory, economic, and environmental demands, they've sought help on increasingly complex problems. The only way for narrow experts to solve broad client problems is by collaborating.

But, don't confuse collaboration with cohesion or cross-selling. Cohesion involves a broad set of "play nice in the sandbox" sorts of behaviors that provide glue for a firm's partners to act like a true partnership. There are plenty of firms where lawyers are friendly and genuinely like each other, where they play golf and even socialize with each other's families outside work, but nevertheless lack a single instance of true collaboration on client service. Cohesion eases collaboration, and collaboration can help to build a more cohesive firm, yet they are distinct.

Further, collaboration is absolutely not cross-selling. Firm leaders often push partners to cross-sell, but partners have surely heard what general counsel uniformly report to me: clients hate to be cross-sold.

Specifically, they hate when their adviser who handles one domain "offers" introductions to other partners in the firm who can provide service in their own narrow domain (for instance, the tax expert who proposes his real estate colleague to do strictly real estate work).

This sort of traditional cross-selling risks appearing more self-serving that value-add for the client. Instead, what clients want is for their advisers to understand their issues deeply enough to offer sophisticated advice and to line up the right team to deliver it – no matter where in the firm the needed experts reside.

1. Culture and values

First, let's consider the importance of culture in creating competitive advantage through mentoring and collaboration. Any lawyer who walks into a new law firm quickly perceives the level of formality, support, or competition that exists between people in that environment. It is an instinctive sense that we develop though experience because we have to adapt to a particular culture in order to be able to work within it.

Our research shows that it is culture that enables, encourages, or prevents mentoring and collaboration to happen more than processes; processes only support culture when they are aligned to that particular culture.

"Within a few days of having integrated my new firm", recalls a senior associate at a Magic Circle firm, "I knew that the types of professional relationships in that firm didn't foster the support and collegiality that their values proclaimed to. It was obvious that I would have to walk my way through that environment and create my own circle of support and guidance in order to develop well."

Surprisingly to some lawyers, clients care deeply about the degree to which their external counsel collaborate with colleagues in their own firm.[2] Jennifer Daniels, chief legal officer of Colgate-Palmolive Company, recently explained her point of view at a conference in New York: "Colgate is a huge business, and nearly every problem I have is multidimensional. So I'm always thinking, how do I manage the complexity in solving that problem in the most efficient way?"

She continued: "I've found that the most productive and efficient way to solve a very complex problem is to have deep collaboration between a team of my outside lawyers with my in-house team and the business team so everyone understands the problem. Having those teams and all those people engaged together, we get to a better result than if it's a bunch of specialists each doing their piece of the problem."

Key attributes

There is no need to make a choice between mentoring and collaboration because they mutually support each other and, when well embedded within the firm's values, create one culture.

Mentoring promotes collaboration by building relationships, increasing trust, and encouraging the transfer and sharing of insights, knowledge, and experience. Collaboration promotes mentoring by sharing knowledge, facilitating communication processes, and reinforcing the value of benefiting from a strong network.

The elements involved for both mentoring and collaboration create one type of culture which is built on the lived values of responsiveness, citizenship, and trust.

Responsiveness

In the most successful firms, people feel comfortable reaching out to others within their organization for assistance or advice, regardless of rank. They feel assured that their colleagues will get back to them promptly and with care for their problem as it if were their own.

"In my years as a junior consultant at McKinsey", said a former management consultant, "I recall that my supervisor told me to reach out to someone in Texas. That partner got back to me immediately and followed up our phone call by sending me some sanitized documents so that I could see their analytic approach. Only many years later did I realize he was one of McKinsey's biggest billers, a 30-year veteran of the firm, and a world-renowned expert on the topic. But, he treated me and my very basic questions with respect."

Some conversations are difficult to have for a pressured mentor who is prone to filter incoming ideas through the lens of his own experience (because that is his comfort zone and helps to lower his own anxiety). In order to be responsive, lawyers need to be supported and comfortable in their own professional development.

Citizenship

Professionals with this value typically believe "what goes around comes around". In other words, they are willing to contribute – their time, contacts, and knowledge – generously, without calculating direct returns. They act with faith that building up their colleagues' capabilities is the right thing to do and trust that they may ultimately benefit from this in an indirect way. They don't keep score or mentally track reciprocity.

In mentoring, this means that lawyers who feel that they can contribute to someone's progress in a certain context naturally reach out to that person without expecting that it will promote their own career or advancement. Professionals in that type of culture know that, by involving colleagues from other departments/offices in a client's matter or providing guidance to a colleague, it will ultimately best serve their clients' or their firm's interests, without calculating whether it will benefit their own interests or career.

Trust

Both collaboration and mentoring hinge on trust between partners. Competence trust means that partners have faith in their colleagues' capabilities so that the knowledge they employ with clients or pass on to mentees is consistently high quality.

Relational trust implies that people have faith in each other's characters and motives – reducing fears that a fellow partner will take advantage of an invitation to join a client by trying to take over the account or, worse, take the credit but do no work at all. Relational trust is also critical to people being willing to reveal their true concerns or seek advice on sensitive issues, free from concerns about how their mentor will use that information.

In one law firm, a partner agreed to do a big cross-border M&A transaction and realized that she couldn't do it alone. To help her with the workload, she went to a partner she trusted. His personality and work style was similar to hers and, first and foremost, he didn't have a sizeable ego. The original partner wasn't worried that the new partner would try to steal her client.

"I thought he'd do his part very well to the full satisfaction of the client, but also interact in that he wouldn't take away the project from me. I trusted that he'd be working in the client's interest", she reflected.

The two ended up working together seamlessly, each individually doing what they could do best, interacting closely the whole time.

For mentoring in the law firm context, the trust element is, to a large extent, linked to confidentiality and how sensitive career or personal information is treated. In firms that have a culture which enables productive mentoring relationships to be built, there is a common definition of mentoring and of its rules around confidentiality; it allows mentees to feel comfortable in reaching out for guidance across the firm and beyond.

2. Business benefits

In this section, we first discuss some of the general benefits that a culture which supports mentoring and collaboration can provide both firms and individuals. We then focus on two areas in which such a culture can have the most impact on a firm's ability to align talent and clients' needs to significantly increase its competitive advantage: the integration of new talent and the transfer of experience and clients when a partner leaves the firm or the profession.

General benefits

For law firms

Firms that have mentoring embedded in their culture and performance management processes can:

- Improve performance;
- Reinforce values and culture;
- Significantly reduce turnover;
- Build leadership skills;
- Increase the number of women and minority-group lawyers achieving partnership; and
- Achieve greater success in change management processes.

As shown in the empirical work conducted at Harvard Law School, the financial benefits to firms of multidisciplinary collaboration are unambiguous.[3] These include:

- Higher revenues and profits;
- Greater client loyalty;
- More complex work – with less risk of commoditization;
- Better ability to weather a financial downturn;
- Faster and more reliable integration of lateral hires; and
- A distinctive value proposition for attracting and retaining millennials.

The more practices that are involved in serving a client, the greater the annual average revenue the client generates (see Figure 1). Clients might

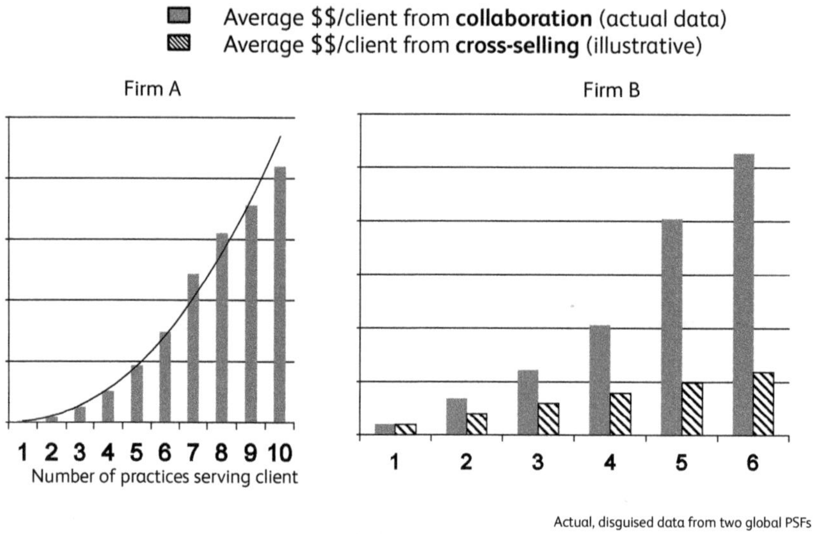

Figure 1: Effects of cross-practice collaboration on revenues

view any given lawyer as fairly fungible (except for those with uniquely specialized expertise – but how many can really claim this?). But, they will find it difficult to find substitutes for entire cross-practice teams.

Further, cross-specialty work is likely to be less subject to price-based market competition. Whereas clients view single-specialty legal expertise as a commodity that can be bid out and sourced based on price, they know that cross-specialty work is more sophisticated and harder to accomplish effectively. They're willing to pay for it. As the CFO of a major multinational told us, "margins rise with complexity".

For individuals

Research shows that the most successful people across industries refer to the influence of one or more mentor(s) the most; there is no contradictory evidence that this is not the case for lawyers too. Mentoring enables lawyers to take responsibility for their own professional development, as well as to feel engaged and included in the firm's development. Lawyers with mentors feel closer to the firm's culture and values, as well as more nurtured and supported in their own career progression.

Our research shows that lawyers who collaborate by sharing the work they originate end up with significantly bigger books of business than those who tend to hoard work. Analyzing millions of data records that span outcomes over a decade showed a clear causal pattern. We found that rainmakers who systematically involved other partners in their work grew their books of business in subsequent years far more than their colleagues, on average. This pattern held even after controlling for other factors that are likely to affect individual billings, such as one's office, practice group, organizational tenure, and previous year's billings.

We've now replicated these findings using data from multiple law firms that vary in size, geographic scope, and compensation system. Law firm leaders might be interested to know that these results are similar in other professional sectors that we've studied, including accounting and consulting.

Integration of lateral hires

Several law firms have introduced a formal mentoring program as an integration tool in their onboarding process for lateral partner hires. But, a very small percentage of partners have actually taken up the offer and benefited from the guidance and experience of a mentor when they have arrived at a new firm.

This low take-up could be due to a number of reasons; one is that the firm's culture may not allow trust, citizenship, and responsiveness behaviors to be shaped. Another possible reason is that mentees and mentors have not developed the skills required for productive mentoring relationships to be built.

Given the high rate of unsuccessful lateral hires movements in law firms (20 percent of laterally hired lawyers are no longer with the firm a year after joining and 50 percent have left within five years[4]) as well as the cost (the average cost of a failed lateral hire is £100,000[5] for just the recruitment costs and resources, which doesn't take into account other negative effects which are difficult to quantify, such as the impact on the firm's image and market credibility, strategic drift, or morale problems), it is surprising that more attention is not paid to supporting the creation of mentoring relationships. These are a cost-effective way to provide a new partner with the intangible knowledge and skills that they need to navigate the firm's culture, politics, and unspoken rules and values.

"The message we send to the market", said one managing partner about the firm's mentoring program for lateral hires, "is 'look at the support we give you to make you successful upon joining'. And, since laterals value that, we've been able to attract higher-caliber candidates."

At Harvard, our analyses of firms' client and personnel records demonstrate that collaboration is essential to ensuring that lateral hires become successful and productive post-move – or else their flight risk is radically higher. For laterally hired partners to be successful at their new firm, the evidence shows that they have to be sufficiently integrated with incumbent partners and clients within the first 18 months, if not sooner.

Of course, the exact number varies by firm and practice. But, our data confirms that if a partner reaches the year-plus stage and hasn't convinced at least a couple of the incumbent partners to work on clients they brought with them, and if they haven't also been invited to join the account team for a couple of the firm's existing clients, there's a very, very high chance that they will leave within the next year or so. Collaborating brings lateral hires up to speed with firm practices, allows them to get to know their colleagues, and most importantly, builds trust between lateral hires, their colleagues, and new clients.

Combining mentoring with a collaborative environment creates the highest chances of a lateral hire being successfully integrated (see box: "Best practice for integrating lateral hires").

TOP TIP

Best practice for integrating lateral hires

- Assign a skilled mentor to every lateral partner to foster responsiveness, citizenship, and trust.
- Hold formal roadshows for laterals to present their client work to offices, practice groups, and sectors.
- Provide a budget for laterals to visit colleagues (even for exploratory conversations) and set the expectation that they will use the full budget (appropriately) within the first six to eight months. Then, follow up.
- Immediately upon their entry to the firm, work with laterals to develop a strategic client service plan that identifies specific opportunities for them to involve incumbent partners. Leaders should facilitate those introductions and make it clear to incumbents that they are expected to participate.
- Invite lateral partners to mentor strong associates.
- When the lateral partner has settled into the firm (after 12 or 18 months), assign them to a committee or a role.

Client succession processes

What happens to the wealth of experience and to the client relationship when a partner leaves a firm or retires? Experienced partners' transition out of firms is a topic that law firms have recently started to pay more attention to. Although mandatory retirement is increasingly seen as ageist and unacceptable, some firms still require partners to retire as early as in their fifties.

The transition process (either when partners are asked to leave in downturn periods or have reached the firm's retirement age) is often a painful phase that they have to go through with hardly any support from their firm. Some partners are lucky enough to be offered a role as consultants, but all the others have to navigate on their own.

Beyond the psychological turbulences that their partners go through, firms are also becoming conscious of the huge experience and knowledge that leaves the business when partners walk out the door. They take with them often decades of skills and wisdom that they have rarely been able to successfully pass on to their firm's next generation of partners.

Introducing a formal structure for retiring partners to transfer back some of the most valuable skills and knowledge is a priority that any law firm should start working on. One of the first and easiest steps to do is to give all experienced partners the role of mentor, preferably not through a rigid program, but rather by providing them with the skills and abilities to be effective mentors.

TOP TIP

Best practice for client succession

- Develop an environment where transitions – both client succession and retirement – are considered normal parts of partnership that are neither threatening nor taboo, but rather warrant careful attention.
- Identify likely transition points early on and start planning partners' exits 10 years in advance.
- Equip senior members of the firm with mentoring skills and assign them a formal role of mentor so that they can pass on their extensive knowledge.
- Create mechanisms to hold partners accountable for building effective succession plans into their account and then following through on those plans.

Ideally, they would have held this role throughout their years as partner, but it is essential to hold them accountable for doing so during their last five years at the firm. This has the benefit of not only retaining some of their experience and skills in the firm, but also giving the partners a responsibility and role which will ease some of the transitional difficulties that leaving a firm creates for them.

CASE STUDY

Case study 1

White & Case has instituted an innovative program to proactively address its partners' transitions. Starting 10 years before a partner reaches typical retirement age, the firm begins a series of formal conversations aimed at helping the partner to think about their post-firm career. This dialogue not only prompts the necessary self-reflection, but also allows the individual to start taking steps towards reaching their objectives.

Few lawyers, for example, understand how much advance planning it takes to prepare for a non-executive director role, but experienced professional counselors can help with this positioning. Furthermore, knowledge of the partner's intentions helps White & Case to plan for how to transition client work smoothly, effectively, and proactively.

One inventive step that White & Case has taken is the creation of a client council, where a group of senior partners act as an advisory board for lead client partners. The lead partners develop a detailed client plan and are then accountable to the council for how they are delivering against the plan.

According to White & Case's chairman Hugh Verrier, "the client council is not just authorizing the lead partners to build and broaden the team serving clients, it acts also as a mechanism to monitor and help. The members give the benefit of experience, thoughts, advice. And, to give the process some teeth, the council also give input on compensation for the lead partners."

If the council feels like there are succession issues within the key client program, it will intervene to guide the transition. It actually has the power to change the lead partners, although this option has rarely been used. Instead, the council works with the lead client partners to encourage them to promote a proactive, smooth succession. Although still in its formative stages, the program has so far been successful by combining advice and accountability.

Case study 2

Another law firm that has introduced a similar transition program actually begins much earlier. Starting just five years after an individual makes partner, the firm offers access to a coaching program that helps each lawyer to think about their career in more holistic terms. From then on, each partner has a refresh meeting with their coach every five years until they decide that retirement is within the coming 10 years, at which point coaching meetings happen more frequently.

A leader in that firm described how starting the program early in each partner's career eliminates any stigma associated with it. It's considered a normal, healthy part of partnership, rather than a process designed to manage out underperforming older lawyers. The leader also noted that, although the coach's sessions with partners are confidential, the firm benefits significantly from having lawyers who are more reflective and conscious about their career moves.

Often, the lawyers themselves will approach leaders to discuss their aspirations – say, for a leadership role in the firm, or a desire to temporarily cut back on hours, or to obtain a prominent role in a local non-profit organization.

"The program was designed as a transition program, but the self-awareness and transparency generated through it benefit the firm throughout a partner's career", commented the firm leader.

3. Practical steps

Unlocking mentoring and collaboration potential in a law firm is amongst the most effective ways to tap in to talent and to win business. It is, however, something that has to be designed carefully and then put into action persuasively in order to produce the expected results.

Not many law firms around the globe have yet managed to overcome some of the difficulties which are created by lawyers' independent nature and to develop cultures which support mentoring and collaboration in the most effective way.

The key components of a successful mentoring culture include:

- People have a common definition and understanding of mentoring;
- The senior management act as role models and are highly committed;
- The performance system recognizes and rewards good mentoring;

- Mentors and mentees have the skills to create productive mentoring relationships;
- Numerous informal mentoring relationships exist at all levels of the firm;
- Lawyers accept the expectation to engage in mentoring activities as mentors and mentees as part of their individual development; and
- Successful associates and partners attribute their success to what they have received from others.

The key components of a successful collaboration culture include:

- Lawyers are aware of the full range of services their firm offers and know enough about how those services add value to clients that they can spot opportunities during their own discussions with clients;
- Lawyers proactively open up discussions with their clients to understand their underlying business concerns ("what keeps you up at night?"), so that they can identify expert colleagues with the required complementary knowledge to serve their clients' most pressing issues;
- Partners contribute sufficient time and energy on clients that are important to the firm, no matter who generated the work;
- Lawyers spend more time thinking about their clients' concerns and perspectives than worrying about who gets credit or other rewards inside their firm; and
- Nobody says "my client", but rather "clients of our firm".

The elements that characterize a mentoring culture and a collaboration culture can be described in slightly different terms, but these characteristics create a unified culture built on trust, responsiveness, and citizenship behaviors. Assessing whether the elements of culture that support mentoring and collaboration are present is not something that firms have been easily able to do until recently. There are, however, tools and approaches that can provide accurate pictures of the types of working relationships that go on in a firm.

Mapping data onto a network diagram, for example, provides an easily discernable first step to understand different types of working relationships in the firm. We created a network diagram from our research showing which partners are approaching others for career-related advice in a specific firm.[6] Individual dots are used to represent each partner and colors identify the different practices. The larger the dot, the more that person is relied upon for advice. The patterns also show which individuals are "connectors" across different practice groups and indicate that some partners are fairly isolated (a danger signal).

Measuring the quality and quantity of mentoring and collaboration that goes on in a firm is a starting point on the journey of building the culture and processes that enable both to happen. A number of boutique consulting firms have sprung up to help firms and companies to conduct this organizational network analysis, which has become a popular technique in some of the world's most prestigious corporations; you might find that your own clients use a similar approach. These data and analytics equip you to understand where the real gaps are, which individuals may be overwhelmed by requests, who is contributing significantly to the firm by helping others, and so on.

The steps that follow that initial stage involve both profound change and methodic measures that can have lasting impact on how lawyers work together. From our research, we have developed a five-stage process to introduce or strengthen a mentoring and collaboration culture in the law firm context (see box: "Five steps to creating a strong culture of mentoring and collaboration").

TOP TIP

Five steps to creating a strong culture of mentoring and collaboration

1. **Assess the quantity and quality** of mentoring and collaboration currently in place at the firm. Use hard data, because perceptions are often biased.
2. **Include trust, citizenship, and responsiveness** as priority shared values of the firm. Role model them from the top and celebrate people who exemplify those values.
3. **Design a strategy** to introduce or strengthen mentoring and collaboration that is aligned with other aspects of the firm's culture and initiatives.
4. **Align/introduce light processes** to shape the behaviors that build a strong and distinctive culture to support the mentoring and collaboration initiatives.
5. **Make everyone accountable** for living up to the firm's values and to the culture (through the performance and remuneration systems, but also through less tangible recognition and rewards for mentoring and collaboration behaviors).

Critical priorities

The law firms that best navigate the competition and adapt to the "new normal" around the world are those which place talent development and client service as their most important priorities. Whereas, in the past, the ability for lawyers to work together across teams, geographical boundaries, and generations was not a critical factor of success, it has now become one of the most significant predictors and factors of business performance, brand recognition, and law firm reputation.

A version of this article appeared in Managing Partner *magazine in September 2015.*

References

1. Normand-Hochman, R. (ed.), *Mentoring and Coaching for Lawyers: Building Partnerships for Business Success*, Globe Law and Business in partnership with the International Bar Association, 2014.
2. Bloomberg BNA, Big Law Business Summit panel discussion: "Origination Credit Days Should End", see bol.bna.com/collaboration-panel-origination-credit-days-should-end/?_ga=1.103873159.683645540.1446130662. See also Hackett, S., "Collaborative culture: The in-house perspective on collaboration in law firms", Managing Partner, July/August 2014.
3. Gardner, H. K., "When Senior Managers Won't Collaborate: Lessons from Professional Service Firms", *Harvard Business Review,* March 2015; and Gardner, H.K., "Why It Pays to Collaborate", *American Lawyer,* March 2015.
4. Reyes, E., "Poor due diligence plagues lateral hire", *The Law Society Gazette*, 14 October 2013; available at: www.lawgazette.co.uk/practice/poor-due-diligence-plagues-lateral-hire/5038135.fullarticle/.
5. Brandon, M., *Lateral Partner Hiring and Integration for Law Firms*, ARK Group, 2013.
6. See Gardner, H. and Normand-Hochman, R., "Make the Most of your Partners' Potential: Foster a Culture to Support Senior Level Mentoring", *PD Quarterly*, NALP, February 2015

Chapter 11: Unlocking value through close collaboration with outside counsel

By Danny Ertel, partner at Vantage Partners

The following chapter explains how in-house legal teams and law firms can uncover valuable ways to work together that deliver real savings over more traditional ways of doing the work. It outlines how law departments and their preferred outside counsel are starting to tackle the real challenges of value and delivery of legal services, and how they are trying to solve them together.

In many organizations, the value of in-house counsel is seen partly as a function of the expertise and capabilities they place at the service of the organization through the relationships they manage with outside counsel. Whether the in-house law department is a large, well-staffed one that relies on outside help sparingly, or is one that sends out significant portions of the overall portfolio of legal work, those relationships are important sources of value. In-house counsel play a critical role in selecting the right firms and lawyers, matching assignments to the right resources, negotiating appropriate fee arrangements, and managing the work even after it has been outsourced.

The last few years have been interesting for in-house counsel as they have sought to manage those outside relationships to ensure their company gets value for money. In-house teams have expanded their capabilities, and demand for outside counsel services has declined (with greater use of technology and outsourcing, and with the realities of the economic downturn), leading to a shift in bargaining power in the economic relationship between in-house and outside counsel. Many law departments have experienced a much greater ability to obtain discounts, impose stricter outside counsel guidelines, and freeze rate increases. But all good things must come to an end.

Bargaining for discounts is largely played out as a model. The drop in demand will only afford in-house counsel additional leverage for so long: law firms have laid off staff and are hiring fewer attorneys;

law schools are seeing a significant drop in applications; and as the economy has picked up, deal volumes (and other kinds of demand) are increasing. Beyond the natural rebalancing of supply and demand, law departments are also realizing that discounted rates can only get you so far in the search for value for money. In a "price x quantity" model, squeezing hourly rates is not enough; to get real improvements in value for money you also have to do something about the hours.[1] Indeed, in some markets, law departments are starting to experience pressure on rates again, with annual increases being sought and obtained by their panel firms.

None of this means that the efforts law departments have made to bring some work back in-house, to consolidate their spend with fewer firms, and to tighten (and enforce) outside counsel guidelines has been for nothing. Concentrating outside counsel expenditures with fewer firms is good for more than just demanding discounts. Becoming a more significant and important client of those firms you do continue to work with affords you the opportunity to ask them to invest in more meaningful exploration of the value they provide and the way they deliver legal services. There is nothing wrong with developing and applying some negotiation leverage; you just want to get some more valuable and lasting changes.

It's not just about the tool, but how you use it

Just as convergence (or consolidation of work with fewer firms) can either be used to gain short term advantage through rate discounts or more strategic change in how outside counsel deliver services, so too can each of the various other tools or levers available to law departments be used. Whether you engage in these efforts to identify and capture potential savings or value improvements on your own or in partnership with your procurement organization, a lot of what you achieve will depend on how you approach the effort.

Alternative fee arrangements: Just a way to shift risk or a means to change how the work is done?

Alternative fee arrangements (AFAs) are gaining traction, as more law departments seek to move away from the billable hour model to some alternative model that moves the risk of inefficiency (and of the uncertainty intrinsic in much legal work) from client to outside counsel. Fixed fees define the total fees to be paid for a defined scope of work, regardless of how many hours are actually required. Caps preserve the billable hour model, but set a limit beyond which outside counsel will not be compensated for additional time spent. Collars define boundaries within which a fixed fee may apply, with counsel and client sharing of the risks above and below those collars. Each of these models creates some incentive for outside counsel to complete the work expeditiously, while providing greater predictability of fees for clients.

Many law departments have adopted these billing models by putting competitive pressure on outside counsel. Whether as part of a panel selection process, or on a matter-by-matter basis, law departments (sometimes with procurement's assistance) are inviting firms to bid on the work with a fixed fee or a cap; when their preferred firm's bid has not been the lowest, some have gone back to them and encouraged them to bid lower still. At the extreme end of this practice are online reverse e-auctions, with firms dropping their bids against other bidders and the clock in an attempt to win work.

There is no question that these competitive mechanisms have saved clients some legal fees. But in my experience, clients have also experienced some significant challenges, partly as a result of how these fees were agreed. Some of these consequences are predictable, a manifestation of the well-known "winner's curse" in some types of auctions: if something is to be auctioned off on the basis of price, and there are multiple uncertainties concerning its value (or in this case, what it will take to get the work done), then the winner in a sealed bid auction is the one who is most optimistic about those uncertainties. But the likelihood that the most optimistic bidder is right, compared to the collective wisdom of the other bidders, is low. Hence the winner overpays (or in this case bids a fee too low for the work ultimately required). When the party running the auction actually needs to work closely with the winner, they can expect a winner who is looking for any opportunity to "claw back" some value. In some cases clients see the winning law firms cutting back on partner time, especially if the matter drags on, or ceding the drafting pen to opposing counsel as they approach or exceed their caps. In others, they seek to recover for activities asserted to have been "outside of scope," undermining the budget certainty that drove the client to seek a cap in the first place.

As demands for AFAs have increased, most law firms have indeed responded by placing many caveats on the scope of work covered by the fee or cap (typically characterized as "assumptions" behind the fee quote) and then using these caveats to reopen the fee discussion when the assumptions were invariably breached. Some clients have countered by limiting the number and nature of the assumptions they will accept in any qualifying bid, piling further strains on the relationship between lawyer and client, and introducing unnecessary adversarial elements as they head off to pursue some complicated transaction or resolve some messy dispute.

The winner's curse problem is just one manifestation of what happens when the attorney-client fee discussion is treated as entirely a zero-sum game, with every bit of gain by the client at the expense of counsel and vice-versa. I have found that some law departments are having success with some less adversarial ways of contracting for services. For example, AFAs that are primarily about shifting the risk of the quantum of effort required to perform the work from client to outside counsel are most acutely zero-sum in the context of any single matter. But as law departments consolidate their work with fewer firms and send a bigger share of their total inventory of work to any one firm, opportunities arise to price work at a portfolio level and spread risk and uncertainty across matters, instead of only shifting from one party to another. A firm that knows that it may come out ahead on some fixed fees in the portfolio is less pressured to find some way to improve its recovery on a particular matter where the effort will exceed their estimate. The client still benefits from the desired fee certainty and overall cost reduction; the firm, with some certainty of its own revenue stream can also choose to make some client-specific investments in standard forms, associate training, or their application of technology, thereby improving their efficiency (and hence their margins on the work).

Effective portfolio pricing requires some investment of time, by both sides, to understand the portfolio and agree on proper boundaries to the kind of work that falls within the pricing arrangement; it requires a fairly collaborative discussion of various options for defining how matters are assigned to the firm and categorized within a more sophisticated pricing model, and then managed for efficiency and effectiveness. In one recent example, the law department of a Fortune 500 life sciences company with a large portfolio of product liability work worked closely with one of their preferred law firms to analyze several years of history working together and came up with a scheme for categorizing cases at matter opening into one of three categories, each with a different fee implication. To support the model, they looked at some ways to manage the volatility of individual matters and came up with a tiered volume structure to help the law firm manage the risk they were taking on. In return, the client got some very attractive pricing and the ability to go back to individual business units, discuss their claim history as a function of the numbers of cases in each category they had experienced over the past five years, and use that to develop a longer term budget.

E-billing, counsel guidelines, and legal project management: Vendor compliance tools or a way to improve communication and collaboration?

Many law departments have implemented an e-billing tool and are requiring outside counsel to submit their invoices electronically, which enables clients to generate different kinds of reports on the data, apply macros to search for breaches of their outside counsel guidelines (e.g. concerning the number of attorneys on a call, or the distinction between "administrative" work and legal practice), and even reject particular charges at the individual time slip level. Under the banner of accountability, some have also started requiring matter budgets and matter plans to be developed at the outset and tracked over time. These tools and techniques have indeed helped law departments get a much better sense of where their company's money is going, and to feel that they can tell their internal clients that they are truly "minding the store".

Rules about what is or is not properly billable and the tools to monitor and enforce those rules do provide for greater accountability. At the same time, they continue to push the law department-outside counsel relationship down an adversarial path, with in-house counsel in the role of auditor or hall monitor, rather than partner in the delivery of quality legal services to the business. "Trust but verify" is a nice motto, but when it turns more into "impose rules and try to catch you breaching them" it can disrupt the trusted advisor relationship that provides real value (if you do not really trust your advisor, how likely are you to follow their advice, especially when it feels difficult to do so?). Instead of poring over hundreds of pages of time reports to find charges to reject, how much more valuable would it be to spend a fraction of that time to plan how a matter will be handled and staffed and what that will cost; to discuss what approach outside counsel expects to take; and agree on how the lawyers and their stakeholders will make choices about how to adapt the approach as they learn more?

In my experience, clients and counsel who start by developing a shared view of the client's priorities for the work, the expected products or outputs of the work (and what is not intended to be in scope), the process they will follow (both to get the work done and to stay in synch), and the people who will be part of the effort, are much more likely to find that the effort was "successful," that it was well worth its cost (clients), and delivered at a reasonable margin (law firms). These "4 Ps" of effective matter management turn out to be relatively simple to remember and to implement, but add just enough structure to a legal project management (LPM) effort to make it more useful than bureaucratic. As a large financial services institution and their main outside litigation counsel recently found, adopting such a process jointly and collaboratively, after discussion of what it was intended to accomplish and how best to implement it, has proven to deliver better results than unilaterally imposed guidelines and procedures backed by a threat not to pay bills. Across a complex bundle of related matters, including both state and federal investigations, institutional customer claims and investor class actions, they were able to turn a fairly contentious, line-by-line review of every invoice into a forward looking monthly planning effort, repurposing a lot of wasted time on both sides.

Legal process outsourcing and other kinds of delegation: A client-led tool for driving cost out or a joint framework for process improvement?

Some law departments have successfully reduced their e-discovery costs by insisting that law firms outsource document review, and perhaps even by insisting they do so to a provider with whom the client has negotiated an attractive rate. There is no question that in comparing the hourly rate of a regular law firm associate to that of an outsourced document reviewer, there is a tremendous saving to be had by outsourcing, even if the less expensive resource is less efficient. And with e-discovery often amounting to 50 percent or more of the total cost of litigation, the potential savings are indeed significant.

That said, the hype may be a bit greater than the reality. It has been a while since the large scale document reviews have been regularly done by law firm associates. Most of those that are not actually outsourced are carried out by temporary or contract attorneys or law firm "discovery attorneys" at a fraction of the hourly rate of a regular law firm associate. Technology is also improving by leaps and bounds, and the discovery rules are adapting to those changes. Over time, the proportion of human effort required for document review will only continue to decline and labor arbitrage will become less relevant.

Treating LPO as something the client requires of the firm may have, however, limited its application to the low-hanging fruit: large scale, largely clerical, document-heavy exercises. In my experience, the new entrants into the legal support market, who bring technology and strong process capabilities, can do much more than just review documents. I have found that in a more collaborative discussion, clients and law firms can define a business or legal problem and uncover even more valuable ways to leverage such capabilities or devise hybrid models that deliver real savings over more traditional ways of doing the work. The Cisco-Orrick arrangement around corporate secretarial services is but one example of what can come from such discussions.[2] In that case, Orrick took over an internal database that tracked all Cisco subsidiaries around the world, documenting their respective signing authority, registration obligations, board resolutions, etc. Orrick moved all of the work to a new software platform, standardized all the work to be carried out by local counsel, moved it to a fixed fee structure, and took over the management of the entire service for Cisco at a significant annual saving. They also proved themselves to be a resourceful, innovative partner, strengthened their relationship with the law department, and developed a new service they could make available to other clients.

Exploring new models, together

While it takes a shift in mindset and some well-structured dialogue, it is not actually that difficult to take a more collaborative approach to transforming the law department-outside counsel relationship. While it is certainly true that either side can start this off, I have found that in practice it is much easier for in-house counsel to take the lead. When law firms propose to clients that they get in a room to explore ways to improve legal service delivery, many clients interpret that as an attempt to cross-sell or otherwise "color outside the lines". But when a client extends a similar invitation to one of its panel firms, I have yet to see outside counsel resist.

From the client side, the key to making a successful shift in approach comes in posing a somewhat different question. Instead of asking "how do we get more from outside counsel for less?", I find that a more useful mindset centers around figuring out how to become a more attractive client, and how to become less expensive to serve. While I know that it has become fashionable, given the broad availability of e-billing data, for law departments to try to determine whether they are getting the absolutely lowest rates that their panel firms give any of their clients, I have yet to understand why being those firms' "least desirable client" is something to strive for. There is no real value in this. The practical reality is, in legal services as in many other supplier relationships, clients often get the providers they deserve. Great law departments get great legal services – their outside counsel bend over backwards for them, staff their best teams on their matters, and they bring their best ideas to them. The key is how to become that most desirable client without simply overpaying for legal services.

That's where the need for a collaborative process comes in. Instead of the usual zero-sum push-and-tug over rates (or even over scope and fees for a particular matter), law departments and their preferred outside counsel are starting to put the real challenges of value and delivery of legal services on the table and trying to solve them together. These value discovery efforts, well understood as a best practice in other strategic supplier relationships, are making their way into the legal function. Client and provider together look at a set of requirements and what it takes to meet them efficiently, so as to provide value to both sides. Figuring out how to recruit, train, and retain the best legal talent need not be only the problem of outside counsel. Successfully addressing the ever-increasing demands and risks of a complex global market while also reducing legal spend should not be only the problem of in-house counsel. Determining how to assign the right resources to the right tasks, what kinds of technology to invest in, how to standardize some tasks while maintaining quality, and how to deliver quality services at a reasonable margin, are all problems that are easier to address when you can look at both sides of the relationship rather than just one.

Value discovery efforts between law departments and outside counsel can take many shapes and forms, but they are typically comprised of several key elements:

Developing initial hypotheses regarding value potential

Prior to starting a time-consuming effort to collect and analyze data, interview stakeholders, streamline processes, etc., it is essential to define a handful of hypotheses about the potential value that is going untapped. Whether this list comes from an external consultant, brainstorming by a small team, a broadly disseminated survey, or some combination of the above, well-formed hypotheses should describe what the opportunity is, what the likely obstacles to achieving it are, and what data or other information sources will be used to test and develop the ideas. These hypotheses can then define (and limit) information gathering efforts and focus the attention of the team facilitating the value exploration. See Table 1 for an example of the hypotheses used recently in such an exercise between a law department and an outside firm with whom they have worked for years.

Hypotheses	Likely barriers to improvement	Ways to test/data to consider
1. There are significant inefficiencies in the staffing process that could be streamlined to reduce "drive-by billers" and the total time billed	• Client delays, counterparty actions, third party (e.g. court) demands create urgent deadlines that require "all hands on deck" • Law firm staff development and utilization smoothing needs	Analysis of distribution of how time is distributed by biller, level of experience of biller, and type of activity
2. Managing fee arrangements on a portfolio basis would help [client] better control costs and create incentives for [outside counsel] to manage matters more efficiently	• Each matter is handled differently by individual in-house attorneys and/ or business units • Perceived need to preserve competition limits ability to commit portfolios of work • Law firm lacks real portfolio tracking/ management capabilities	Review of matters open and closed over last __ years: key parameters, bills, hours, and outcomes
3. The budget fore-casting and adjusting process can be significantly improved to increase forecast accuracy	• Inherent uncertainties in the work • Differences in how we each create and use forecasts	Discussion with staff involved in generating and using forecasts
4. Implementing a two-way performance scorecard and a joint scorecarding process will help both organizations better identify and align on key issues	• Lack of visibility into each other's priorities • Traditional view of outside counsel relationship as largely reactive to client requests for assistance	Interviews with key stake-holders in law department, business units, law firm management, and on client team
5. Significant time and effort is expended repeating work or services that were already performed for other matters	• Each matter handled separately, by different partners at law firm and different clients internally • Lack of effective knowledge management discipline and systems	Review of transactional documents and/or pleadings for similar matters
6. We can shift work being performed from higher rate resources to lower rate resources	• Concerns about quality • Skepticism about savings • Lack of clear task and role definitions	Mapping of key activities for common matter types and consideration of opportuni-ties to standardize (to ease delegation)

Table 1: Illustrative value exploration hypotheses

Testing and analysis

To dig into these hypotheses, a small project team, made up of both law department and outside counsel staff should then undertake the effort to look at the data, analyze it, and draft some initial findings. The "data" in this case may include not only time entries in e-billing or other such systems, but also interviews with stakeholders, information about database usage and coding error rates pulled from e-discovery systems, answers to surveys, and more. The analysis should be aimed at trying to understand whether the hypotheses about value opportunities are valid and what it might take to overcome any identified obstacles to realizing such value.

Working sessions

A somewhat broader group of stakeholders from both the client and the law firm then typically comes together to review the preliminary findings put together by the joint core team. These findings should enable the larger group to understand which premises have been validated or rejected as well as the implications for potential improvements in efficiency, quality, effectiveness, or how client and counsel work together. Some of these improvements may amount to real cost reductions (that save the client money without just taking margin away from the law firm); others will address different sources of value for the client or margin improvement for the law firm, such as greater budget certainty, lawyers who are more in tune with how the client's business operates and whose advice can be more commercial-minded and less disruptive of business operations, more consistent execution of transactions, etc. A robust review and discussion of the preliminary findings typically results in agreement about further work that is necessary to turn good ideas into tangible actions that can be implemented. Table 2 shows an example of a set of work streams agreed at the conclusion of another such working session, with plans for the group to reconvene and finalize commitments on the steps to put into action.

The potential savings and other improvements in any given relationship depend on: the size and nature of the client's spend; the specifics of the type of work the in-house team sends to outside counsel; the number of different practice areas and offices implicated at the law firm; what strides they have already made with regard to making use of technology, outsourcing, and creative pricing models; and how much effort the two have already put into exploring how matters are initiated, planned, budgeted, staffed, and managed. That said, in my experience

Work stream	1	2	3	4	5	6	7	8	9	10	11	12
Discussions with data discovery hosting providers about ways to streamline (and reduce the cost of) the e-discovery repositories												
Counsel to identify priority-access subsets or custodians												
Law department to explore "live" versus off-line access options												
Third-party to generate report of frequency of use by subset												
Proposal with risk analysis												
Development of Early Case Assessment (ECA) tools and protocols for fast-tracking some matters												
Counsel to review templates used with other clients												
Joint team to draft ECA checklist												
Joint team to draft protocols												
Proposal with risk analysis												
Solicitation of specific outsourcing proposals from LPO providers												
Draft requirements												
Identify qualified providers												
Solicit proposals (RFP)												
Evaluate proposals												
Develop recommendation (subject to due diligence if ultimately accepted)												
Standardization of matter management plans and templates												
Counsel to analyze matter types, time spent on key activities, opportunities for delegation												
Law department to analyze near term forecast of work in pipeline												
Joint team to prioritize templates/ standard forms for development												
Joint team to develop change management plans												
Working session II												

Table 2: Illustrative work streams following initial exploration working session

changing the question and the nature of the discussion between law departments and outside counsel makes a huge difference in terms of what specific challenges the two try to resolve and the kinds of solutions they come up with. I have yet to see one of these exercises where the two sides did not come away with a significantly improved value proposition for the relationship and a commitment to expand the scope of what they do together.

This first appeared as Chapter 5 in Roche, H. (ed.), Demonstrating Value in In-House Legal Teams, *ARK Group, 2014.*

References

1. Ertel, D., "Say no to discounts" in *Buying Legal: Procurement Insights and Practice* by Dr. Sylvia Hodges, Ark Group, London, 2012.
2. See Ertel, D. and Gordon, M., "Points of Law: Unbundling Corporate Legal Services to Unlock Value", *Harvard Business Review*, July–August 2012. See: hbr.org/2012/07/points-of-law-unbundling-corporate-legal-services-to-unlock-value/ar/1.

Part 3:
People and talent management

Chapter 12: Getting inclusive about inclusion – A talent management strategy

By Lisa B. Horowitz, founder and principal advisor at Attorney Talent Strategy Group LLC

During the last 10 years, law firms have begun focusing on firm-wide talent management (TM) as an important driver of organizational performance. During this same time period, law firms have also implemented women's initiatives focused on advancing and retaining women. These two initiatives have tended (and still tend) to be siloed – that is, treated separately from each other in terms of activities, leadership, resources, and goals.

Efforts to advance inclusion and gender parity in law firms have stalled. At last measure, women are entering the legal profession and law firms at roughly the same rate as men, but they begin to leave law firms within two years. In 2013, women represented only 17 percent of equity partners in two-tier AmLaw 200 firms, 22 percent of equity partners in one-tier AmLaw 200 firms, and 29 percent of non-equity partners in AmLaw 200 firms.[1] Minority women lawyers occupied only 2 percent of equity partnerships in AmLaw 200 firms.

There is no one cause of this problem. It is, however, apparent that this "siloed" approach has not worked and that law firms are losing rather than leveraging half of their potential talent. It is time for firms to consider a new strategy that intentionally aligns and integrates efforts to advance inclusiveness and embeds them directly into the daily operations and fabric of the firm through their TM functions. This article takes a look at how this can be accomplished.

Talent management in law firms – An overview

With "people" as their major asset, law firms engage in TM on a daily basis. Key TM functions include:

- Talent acquisition;

- Talent development;
- Talent deployment; and
- Performance management.[2]

Talent management is most effective when approached systematically with functions that are:

- Aligned: Integrated with each other and as a whole with the firm's strategic goals and rewards system;
- Dynamic: Adaptable to changing markets and business environments;
- Efficient: Have processes and practices that allow the organization to place the right people with the right skills in the right place at the right time;
- Vital: Have commitment, engagement, and accountability at all levels;
- Measurable: Include articulated measurable criteria for success; and
- Simple and transparent.

Law firms are at different stages of development with respect to their approaches to TM. Some firms have comprehensive, consistent, and aligned systems built upon transparent competencies that serve as a foundation for each TM function. Others use competencies to align their talent development activities but not their talent deployment or performance management efforts. Still other firms take a less systematic approach to TM, focusing largely on training without reference to any articulated competencies or other TM functions.

Incorporating and advancing inclusiveness through each TM function

Regardless of the sophistication and nature of a firm's approach to TM, building inclusiveness into each TM function is possible. Each TM function can serve as a regular and powerful platform for advancing (or delimiting) inclusiveness.

Proactively and strategically using a firm's TM functions and activities to foster inclusiveness facilitates a firm's ability to effectively and efficiently leverage the diverse talents of all its attorneys. This is essential for law firm success in the current legal environment. It follows that advancing inclusivity can and indeed must be a key consideration in the design of a firm's TM functions.

Discussed below are some ways in which inclusiveness can be built into, and effectively advanced through, three critical TM functions: talent development, talent deployment, and performance management.

Building inclusiveness into the talent development function

Attorney talent development is a major TM function. This function may include competencies, training, career planning, career advising, and mentoring.

Competencies

Attorney talent development best starts with the articulation of firm-wide and/or practice area specific competencies – namely core skills and behaviors determined by the firm to be necessary to be a successful attorney. These competencies, once articulated, can serve as a foundation for the creation, integration, and alignment of firm-wide and practice group training, career planning, career advising, and mentoring as well as other TM functions, e.g. talent deployment, performance management, and talent acquisition.

Competencies are often grouped into categories relating to:

1. Substantive knowledge and skills;
2. Attorney management (self and others);
3. Business management (project and financial);
4. Business development; and
5. Leadership.

Where defined, competencies can also be articulated by level of attorney – associate (junior, mid-level, senior) and partner.

Articulating competencies clearly and making them readily available to all attorneys is a valuable means of fostering inclusiveness. It allows all attorneys to know what skills and behaviors need to be demonstrated in order to advance and helps to eliminate much of the ambiguity, discretion, subjectivity, and unintentional bias that accompany systems without them, and that impede the advancement of women.

In addition, inclusiveness can be fostered through the content of the competencies themselves. Requiring attorneys to demonstrate competencies that promote inclusiveness, such as effectively participating in and building diverse teams, communicating across differences, and understanding/addressing "unconscious bias" can go a long way toward promoting inclusiveness.

Training

Training is another powerful attorney talent development tool through which inclusiveness can be advanced. Training can serve to advance inclusiveness both through its substance and through its delivery.

With respect to substance, adding programs to a firm's training curriculum, specifically relating to issues of diversity and inclusiveness, is important. These programs can, at a minimum, create an awareness of the issues impeding inclusiveness, as well as advancing behavioral changes.[3] Topics might include those of unconscious bias, effective communication (across gender, generations, and cultures), building and leading diverse teams, and conducting performance evaluations (see further discussion below).

Training related to diversity and inclusiveness has often been delegated to women's initiatives and diversity committees to arrange and promote. Making these programs an integral part of the firm's talent development curriculum sends an important message that inclusiveness is a priority and responsibility of the firm as a whole, and one that is driven by the firm as a whole and not solely by its WI and diversity committees.

The manner in which training is delivered can further impact inclusiveness. Insuring that male and female attorneys teach substantive programs so that both are viewed as substantive experts and role models is a valuable way to promote and reinforce inclusion. Moreover, engaging the firm's male attorneys in the delivery of diversity training and having them share the benefits of inclusiveness, their commitment to it, and their own experiences developing competencies related to advancing inclusiveness (including an awareness of their own unconscious biases) are all also effective means of enhancing the impact of training.[4] Reinforcing classroom training with individualized coaching both by male and female, internal and external, coaches can also be a very effective and often critical tool.

Career planning and advising/mentoring

A commitment to inclusiveness can be built into a firm's TM system through yet another attorney development activity – the firm's career planning and advising/mentoring activities.

Following the example of their corporate brethren, progressive law firms now require, as an element of their talent development activities, that every attorney have a written individual development plan. This plan helps each attorney to think strategically about their career path and the competencies and experiences needed to succeed. Where a firm has articulated competencies that foster inclusiveness (like the ones discussed above), attorneys can look to these to design their plan, set goals and action steps, monitor progress, and hold themselves accountable. By and in the process of achieving their goals, inclusiveness becomes embedded not only in the attorneys' behavior, but also in the fabric of the firm.

A career plan also serves as a vehicle for attorneys and career advisors/mentors of both genders to work together. Mentor and protégé can use this plan to identify appropriate training and experiential learning opportunities aligned with the attorney's developmental needs, including those related to advancing inclusiveness competencies. Engaging men to advise, mentor, and sponsor women attorneys puts them in a better position to understand the developmental needs of their protégées and to use their influence to facilitate assignments needed for their growth and advancement. Moreover, and not all that surprisingly, research by Catalyst has found that exposing male protégés to women mentors provides men with opportunities to develop an awareness about gender bias – the first step in creating change.[5]

Building inclusiveness into the attorney deployment/ assignment function

Experiential learning is critical to attorney development. As such, the assignments given to attorneys play a critical role in their ability to contribute fully to the success of the firm. Providing meaningful assignments to all attorneys allows all attorneys to develop and allows the firm to leverage all of its talent. Moreover, meaningful assignments create commitment and engagement – both of which are critical to retention, client service, and profitability.

Notwithstanding the foregoing, ensuring that all attorneys – including women and diverse attorneys – have an equal opportunity to receive meaningful assignments is often not a consideration in making assignments and creating teams. There is now convincing research that diverse teams lead to better financial and innovative results.[6] In recognition of this finding, more clients are now demanding diversity on their client teams. Intentionally designing inclusiveness into the talent deployment function/assignment processes of a law firm's TM system has, therefore, become not only a developmental issue, but also a business imperative for law firms.

How is your firm making assignments? Are you seeking to align assignments with the developmental needs of all the members of your team by tracking their individual career goals and performance reviews? Are you, like the managing partner of the leading French firm TAJ,[7] tracking the assignments being given to women and other diverse attorneys to ensure parity? Are you holding your managing attorneys accountable for ensuring that women and diverse attorneys have an equal opportunity to get the "meaty" assignments they need to develop and become full contributors on the diverse teams being demanded by clients? Are you assigning women and diverse attorneys to management and leadership assignments that will help them develop the skills they need to serve in departmental and firm management and leadership positions and as role models for other diverse attorneys?

One way to incorporate inclusiveness into the talent deployment function is to design and implement a deployment/assignment process that aligns assignments with attorney developmental needs, tracks the assignments given to each attorney, and holds partners accountable for insuring that male and female attorneys have equal opportunities to obtain the meaningful developmental assignments needed to become full contributors. Such a process allows the firm to develop and leverage all of its attorneys effectively while meeting client expectations regarding diversity and excellent results.[8]

Building inclusiveness into the performance management function

Performance management involves performance evaluation, promotion, and advancement. In an integrated TM system, performance management practices are closely aligned with the firm's attorney development function (discussed above) and reinforced by the firm's compensation/reward system. The manner in which an attorney's performance is evaluated and they are compensated is critical to fostering diversity and inclusiveness in the firm.

To advance gender parity and inclusiveness, it is essential that a law firm's evaluation, promotion, and advancement criteria be clear and transparent. Tying these criteria to competencies (including the inclusiveness skills and behaviors identified earlier), making them readily available (in print and/or online), and ensuring that inclusiveness competencies are evaluated with the same weight as other more task-based competencies, is also critical.

With respect to the evaluation process in particular, research by the ABA Commission on Women has found that, left unchecked, unintended hidden gender bias exists in law firms – especially in the evaluation process – and that these biases detrimentally impact the professional development, advancement, and retention of women attorneys.[9] To stem these biases and the resulting negative impact on a firm's performance and ability to foster inclusiveness, the ABA Commission on Women set forth a number of steps that law firms can take to promote consistency and objectivity in the evaluation process. These include:

- Developing specific job-related performance competencies;
- Defining the rating scale both quantitatively and qualitatively;
- Training lawyers on the major patterns of gender biases impacting women and the evaluation process and providing best practices for preventing these biases from infecting the evaluation process;[10] and
- Assigning an individual or a committee to review all completed evaluations before they are finalized.

Rewards and compensation are powerful tools for advancing inclusiveness. It is a fundamental tenet of organizational development that what is rewarded is achieved. According to Deloitte, rewards are an investment to be managed rather than a cost to be controlled. As such, rewards should be aligned with business strategies and with the performance that supports the business strategies.[11] To the extent that it is a firm's business strategy to foster and facilitate inclusiveness, rewarding and incentivizing those whose behaviors (TM and others) advance inclusiveness, and penalizing those whose behaviors do not, is essential.

Implementing change – 4 Ms

Implementing change – especially culture change – is never an easy task. Intentionally advancing gender parity and inclusiveness through changes to a firm's TM strategy, functions, and activities will undoubtedly present a challenge. Set forth below are a few suggestions for overcoming this challenge.

Mindset – "Zero sum" to "expand the pie"

What is good for women attorneys is good for law firms as a whole. What a concept! Unfortunately, this is not frequently the law firm "mindset". Too often, gender parity and inclusiveness are viewed with a "zero sum" mindset – namely, a belief that advancing women and diverse attorneys can only be undertaken at the expense of majority attorneys. This mindset is a formidable barrier to advancing inclusiveness and parity, and it must change.

Creating a shift in law firm mindset from that of "zero sum" to "expand the pie" will need to start at the top. Firm leaders must be convinced of the costs they and their firms are incurring by retaining a "zero sum" mindset[12] and the benefits to be gleaned from a shift to an "expand the pie" approach that fosters the development, deployment, and leveraging of all attorney talent (not just half) with a corresponding increase in firm revenues, profit, and compensation for all.

Middle manager buy-in

Successfully building inclusiveness into a firm's TM system will require the buy-in and commitment of firm "middle managers" as well as firm leadership. These middle managers are typically the junior partners who are the "boots on the ground" building and managing teams, making assignments, mentoring, and coaching. Encouraging, supporting, and rewarding their efforts to demonstrate inclusiveness through these activities will go a long way to advance the ball.

Male engagement

According to Catalyst, a leading organization working globally with businesses and professions to build inclusive workplaces, gender initiatives have fallen short of their goals to advance and retain women because they:

1. Focus solely on changing women – from the way they network to the way they lead; and
2. Look to women alone to change the organizational practices that maintain the status quo.[13]

According to Catalyst, to accelerate change, organizations need to stop treating gender equity and inclusion as just a woman's burden and must enable and encourage both women and men to make necessary behavioral changes. To this end, Catalyst provides specific actions men and women can take to work together as allies in changing the organizational norms and structures that perpetuate gender disparities.[14]

Measurement

What gets measured gets achieved. Metrics – both quantitative and qualitative – can be defined to monitor gender parity and inclusivity in law firms. While it may be difficult to quantify immediately the impact on inclusivity of the TM changes described herein, efforts can and should be made from the outset to identify specific criteria to be measured and to begin to monitor them early. As a start, such measurement might include monitoring whether/how each of the suggestions described herein (and others) have been implemented (and if not, why not) and their impact (qualitatively and quantitatively) on the inclusion and advancement of women.[15]

Align and integrate TM and women's initiative efforts

Historically, and still today, efforts to advance gender equity and inclusion in law firms have been the responsibility of women's initiatives. To this end, WI have engaged in a cross-section of extraordinarily valuable activities from policy development, training, and mentoring to providing safe venues for women to raise questions and concerns related to their development and advancement. These activities have been, and continue to be, invaluable. Unfortunately, when undertaken independently from other firm-wide systems, like a firm's TM system, these activities have, too often, tended to be marginalized and underfunded.

Women's initiatives must continue to serve as thought-leaders, change agents, and monitors in the drive for gender parity and inclusiveness. WI and TM efforts must be aligned and integrated – not siloed – and must support and reinforce each other to leverage and maximize the impact of their efforts toward a common, firm-wide goal of inclusion.

Conclusion

Traditional efforts to advance inclusion and gender parity in law firms have stalled. As a result, law firms are losing rather than leveraging the diverse talents of all their attorneys. It is time for a new strategy – one that embeds activities that advance inclusiveness directly into the daily operations and fabric of law firms through essential TM functions – talent development, talent deployment, and performance management.

This first appeared as Chapter 8 in Slater, L. (ed.), Breaking Barriers: Promoting and Retaining Women in the Legal Profession, *ARK Group, 2014.*

References

1. National Association of Women Lawyers, "Report of the Eighth Annual NAWL

National Survey on Retention and Promotion of Women in Law Firms", February 2014, see www.nawl.org/p/bl/et/blogid=10&blogaid=56.
2. Horowitz, L., *Talent Management: Taking Professional Development in Law Firms to the Next Level*, Practice Innovations, January 2010.
3. Catalyst, "Calling All White Men: Can Training Help Create Inclusive Workplaces?", 18 July 2012, see www.catalyst.org/knowledge/calling-all-white-men-can-training-help-create-incluseive-workplaces.
4. Ibid.; see also Catalyst, "Engaging Men In Gender Initiatives: Stacking the Deck for Success", 2009, see www.catalyst.org/knowledge/engaging-men-gender-initiatives-stacking-deck-success.
5. Catalyst, "Engaging Men in Gender Initiatives: What Change Agents Need to Know", 4 May 2009, see www.catalyst.org/knowledge/engaging-men-in-gender-initiatives-what-change-agents-need-to-know.
6. See e.g. Feitler, D., "The Case for Team Diversity Gets Even Better", HBR Blog Network, 27 March 2014, available at blogs.hbr.org/2014/03/the-case-for-team-diversity-gets-even-better; Catalyst, "The Bottom Line: Corporate Performance and Women's Representation on Boards (2004-2008)", 1 March 2011.
7. Wittenberg-Cox, A., "How One Law Firm Maintains Gender Balance", HBR Blog Network, 27 May 2014, see blogs.hbr.org/2014/05/how-one-law-firm-maintains-gender-balance.
8. Ibid.
9. Williams, J., and Pinto, C., Fair Measure: Toward Effective Attorney Evaluations, ABA 2d. ed., 2008.
10. The four major patterns of gender bias discussed in the ABA Report are: (i) maternal wall bias; (ii) double standards; (iii) double bind; and (iv) ambivalent sexism. See Williams, J., and Pinto, C., ABA 2d. ed., 2008.
11. Deloitte Development LLC, "The Chemistry of Talent, Straight Talk Book No. 10", 2008.
12. This "zero sum mindset" negatively impacts law firm compensation systems as well. While this is a topic beyond the scope of this article, for more information on closing the compensation gap between men and women, see Rikleen, L., *Closing the Gap: A Road Map for Achieving Gender Pay Equity in Law Firm Partner Compensation*, ABA Commission on Women in the Profession, 2013.
13. Catalyst, "Engaging Men in Gender Initiatives: What Change Agents Need To Know", 2009.
14. See the entire Catalyst Research Series: Engaging Men in Gender Initiatives.
15. For example, partners and practice group leaders might be asked to address in their annual group reports and self-evaluations specific questions regarding how they and their groups have initiated and supported the efforts of others (e.g. professional development, WI, recruiting) to advance gender parity and inclusiveness through their individual/practice group's talent development, talent deployment, and performance management functions.

Chapter 13: **Compensation systems – Integrating partner incentives with firm goals**

By Arthur G. Greene, principal at Boyer Greene LLC

Partner compensation systems are designed to fairly allocate the profits among the partners based on their individual contributions to the success of the firm. For many successful firms, the compensation process has become more than that. Compensation systems have become powerful management tools that reward actions and behaviors the firm wants to encourage. The challenge is to balance individual partner incentives while successfully promoting the firm's strategic goals in a process that is credible and fair.

More law firms are recognizing that partner compensation and the firm's strategic plan are directly related. They should not be considered separate processes. Integrating partner incentives with the goals of the firm's strategic plan through the use of partner annual plans has become an essential aspect of good management.

Partner annual plans are written documents describing any changes in the partners' intended commitment to the firm in the following year. Annual plans can be developed by each partner in discussion with, and with the approval of, firm management. They represent an excellent method for receiving commitments from partners while at the same time providing each of them with a clear message as to the firm's expectations for their performance during the coming year. When tied to the compensation process, they also provide a clear basis for evaluating whether or not the partner has met the commitments they have made to the firm. A review of a partner's annual plan at the end of the year will disclose clear markers which can support compensation decisions.

The management approach of integrating individual incentives may seem simple enough, but encouraging desired actions and then measuring the contribution of each partner requires a credible system and a fair process. The use of annual plans will make any compensation system more open, fair, and credible.

Achieving an integrated approach

The emerging trend among law firm leaders is to promote the firm's strategic plan by integrating it with incentives in the partner compensation system. Depending on the size of the firm, this process can be managed by either the managing partner or the practice group chairs. The critical components involve integrating the firm's strategic plan, a partner annual plan process, and the partner compensation system.

Strategic plan

A strategic plan will set forth the firm's vision for the future with appropriate goals and objectives, along with an intended timeline. The exercise of creating the strategic plan will require all partners coming together in pursuit of a common mission. The strategic plan then allows leadership to make decisions and allocate resources designed to achieve the goals of the plan, rather than make decisions based on a day-to-day perspective. By integrating the partner annual plans into the process, management can be assured that the partners are coordinated in their effort to achieve the stated goals. The next step, of course, is to reward partners based on their performance in achieving the expectations set out in their annual plans.

Once a strategic plan is in place, the next process is to identify the individual actions critical to achieving the goals of the plan. Perhaps they include:

- Originating new clients;
- Creating new practice areas;
- Expanding the firm's geographical reach;
- Developing new marketing approaches;
- Performing work profitability;
- Delegating work to others;
- Leveraging associates and paralegals;
- Training and mentoring associates;
- Changing aspects of management; and/or
- Providing desired leadership.

Each partner will be positioned differently and each of their specific roles in achieving the firm goals will be different. Management needs to identify the actions or behaviors needed by each partner on an individual basis, so that all the necessary parts of the firm's strategic plan will be covered by one or more of the current partners.

Partner annual plans

Partner annual plans provide management with an ability to work with each partner in order to coordinate individual efforts in the context of the firm's strategic plan. The annual plan is an excellent means of communicating what is required from the firm's perspective and the role each partner needs to play in order to achieve the firm goals.

There are a number of different formats available and many firms tailor their own form to fit the firm's individual circumstances. The following topics would likely be included and each partner would commit to their own individual effort to:

- Enhance their skills;
- Expand their practice;
- Improve their productivity;
- Assist others in improving their practice;
- Advance the goals and objectives of the firm;
- Help with management; and
- Participate in civic and professional matters.

A financial aspect is also critical to each annual plan. Expectations as to billable hours, revenue produced from the files managed, the realization rate for the files managed, and the dollar value of originations would be included. The first draft of the annual plan should be prepared by the individual partners, and then the annual plans would be finalized in a session with the managing partner or practice group leader, during which the needs of the firm would be considered and negotiated into the plan.

Compensation systems

Partner compensation is often discussed in terms of four basic methods. However, the number of variations and/or combinations exceed anyone's ability to categorize or count them. While some law firms start out with the traditional partnership concept of sharing profits equally, this method does not stand the test of time. Equal sharing of profits may be seen in start-up firms, but not in established firms that have grown over time. Other firms may have vestiges of the lock-step system, now out of favor (at least in the United States), where partners move up the compensation ladder in predetermined steps, based on seniority. While many of the larger US firms may have operated with such a system 30 or 40 years ago, nearly all have evolved away from that seniority-based system. Today, most firms have a formula-based system, a subjective-based system, or some combination of the two.

Formula-based systems

A formula-based system, which emphasizes each partner's contribution to revenue production, is more common in small firms. Credit is usually given for originations, managing the client, and performing the work. Formula-based firms tend to have weak management and give limited attention to contributions other than producing revenue. While formula systems can work successfully for a period of time under certain circumstances, they do not promote long range success or the growth of the firm as an institution. As law firms mature, they tend to move away from formula-based systems in favor of a subjective-based system.

Subjective-based systems

A subjective-based compensation system involves prospectively setting the compensation percentage (or points) based on an evaluation of each partner's overall contribution to the firm. The factors to be considered in the process are identified and agreed to in advance. While revenue production numbers are important, they are evaluated subjectively without math being part of the process. In addition to contributions to the production of revenue, other factors that are typically considered include: leadership abilities, management, teamwork, associate training, and community involvement. Advocates of subjective-based systems point out that they promote the success of the firm as a whole, rather than individual successes.

Combination systems

Many law firms end up with combination systems. In some cases these are arrived at by accident, while in other circumstances they represent a thoughtful approach incorporating both subjective factors and objective formula-based incentives. Examples could be endless, but they would include:

- All partners receiving the same base compensation (perhaps representing 60 percent of the overall compensation), then at year-end a formula is applied to allocate the balance of the profits;
- The partner base compensation is set based on their respective contributions to the firm, measured subjectively and paid prospectively, and then at year-end any bonus is paid, based on a retrospective formula; or
- The base compensation is established on a formula, then at year-end a predetermined percentage of the profits is allocated subjectively to those partners who made significant contributions to the success of the firm that are not effectively measured by the formula.

For the purposes of this discussion, the two significant points are:

i Integrating individual incentives and the firm's strategic plan requires that the firm has a subjective system, or a combination system with a substantial subjective component; and

ii The most favored systems for successful and enduring mid-sized and larger firms tend to be subjectively based.

The compensation process should include a review of each partner's performance in achieving the expectations set forth on the prior year's annual plan. Incorporating this into a firm's existing compensation system may take some adjustment to the process. Although the annual plan aspect of the discussion may be subjective in nature, the message is clear: partners are rewarded for their overall contribution to the firm's goals based on expectations set forth in their annual plan.

A point to keep in mind

Protecting the law firm as an institution is the cardinal rule. Simply put, the law firm comes first and decisions need to be made based on what is best for the firm, as opposed to what is best for any individual. The integration of the firm's strategic plan with its partner compensation system reinforces this important concept.

It takes a mix of different talents and skills to serve clients and operate a successful firm. These differing skills may vary in importance and will need to be rewarded based on their relative value to the firm. Be forewarned, those firms with compensation systems focusing predominately on one skill, to the exclusion of others, are not likely to attain the success they might otherwise expect. The annual plans provide an important tool for identifying and managing different contributions.

Accept the fact that the allocation of profits among the partners will cause tension. This tension can be healthy if the partners understand the workings of the compensation system and know how their actions and behaviors will affect their compensation. Obviously, good communication and candid discussions are necessary to developing the level of trust that is critical to managing a successful partner compensation system.

"A rising tide raises all of the boats". In the law firm context, a rising tide means that if the firm does well, each individual will do well. The reverse is not true. Most firms want a compensation system that will incentivize actions and behaviors that will improve the chances of the firm, as a whole, doing well.

Finally, do not overlook the importance of a smooth process for succession. The compensation systems should be designed to reward senior partners for beginning to transfer clients; otherwise there will be a tendency to retain exclusive client control. This is particularly true if one of the firm's unintended consequences of its compensation system incentivizes the senior partner to retain control of the clients in order to support their continuing compensation.

When change is necessary

Many firms have compensation systems that provide the wrong incentives which have a detrimental effect on the firm's effort to promote stability and maximize success. Tension over the compensation system can rise to the level of disrupting the firm's ability to succeed. An unhealthy compensation system tends to promote internal competition among the partners – whose energies should be directed externally. Unfortunately, many partners working under a dysfunctional system become resigned to the fact that the system they know may be better than the risks associated with change.

Whatever the system, it is likely to have been developed by the founder and reflect the early culture of the firm. What may have been an appropriate compensation system in 1980, or in 1950, most likely is not the best system for the firm today. Compensation systems should be reviewed every five years due to changes, both in the marketplace and in the makeup of the firm.

A partner compensation system needs to be re-evaluated if it:

- Is not well understood by the partners;
- Is overly complex;
- Is not considered credible and fair;
- Does not involve open and candid discussions;
- Fails to reward desired actions or behaviors;
- Rewards unwanted behaviors;
- Allows partners to "game" the system;
- Does not advance the firm's strategic plan;
- Puts the success of the individual ahead of the success of the firm;
- Does not promote orderly transitions;
- Creates an unhealthy tension among the partners;
- Causes excessive internal competition;
- Results in disruption; and/or
- Has not been re-evaluated in over five years.

The best process for re-evaluating or changing a compensation system involves open and candid discussions, orchestrated by a committee with diverse interests represented. The best results often come from building from the bottom up, rather than being imposed from the top down. Inclusion is key.

The required ingredients to support change include:

1. Identifying the goals and objectives of the firm in the strategic planning process;
2. Understanding the partner actions and behaviors required to achieve the goals;
3. Aligning the financial reports to reflect the data relevant to managing those goals;
4. Adjusting the partner compensation system to reward contributions to those goals; and
5. Developing partner annual plans that articulate specific individual contributions.

Using the partner compensation system as a management tool does not make partner compensation more complicated or more difficult. On the contrary, if properly structured and implemented, it will improve the partner compensation process, reduce tensions in the partner ranks, incentivize partners, and promote the strategic goals of the firm in an open, fair, and credible process.

This first appeared as Chapter 5 in Roche, H. (ed.), Compensation Design for Law Firms, *ARK Group, 2014.*

Chapter 14: Measuring and managing the performance of your people

By Peter Scott, principal at Peter Scott Consulting, and Richard Wyatt, managing director of Cambridge Blue Square Management

In today's competitive market, any law firm that wants to be successful must ensure that the performance of its people will be actively managed. A firm's people will therefore need to know the key areas in which their performance will be measured, their performance goals pertaining to each area, and how their performance rates in relation to these goals. Ensuring that a firm's people are highly trained, skilled, and motivated should therefore be a critical objective if a firm is to achieve a competitive advantage.

Performance measurement and competitive advantage

Many firms measure and manage partner (and other fee earner) performance by using a Balanced Scorecard model.[1] This implies performance is not only measured in terms of financial contributions by way of fees earned or hours billed, but also in terms of non-billable value-added activities. However, in most law firms, as in any other business, cash flow and profitability are paramount (particularly in challenging economic times) and it is unsurprising that financial performance is often prized and rewarded above all else.

A balanced scorecard approach will, however, focus not only on aspects of financial performance but also on the factors that influence or control financial performance; for example, client relationships, firm growth, and personal development. In particular, the approach to managing people performance needs to be closely aligned with a firm's strategic objectives if competitive advantage is to be secured and maintained.

Competition can be defined as "a process whereby services that people are not prepared to pay for – as well as high cost methods of production, and inefficient organizations – are weeded out and opportunity is given for new services, methods, and organizations to be tried".[2]

Competition in this sense provides a means of discovering the most wanted services and the least costly methods and scales of production. It encourages efficiency and consumer incentives as a means of discovering what, how, and for whom to provide services.

Achieving a competitive advantage in this way should allow a firm to focus more closely on those areas of performance that it will need to manage differently, for example, by:

- Providing clients with services they want and at prices they perceive to be "value for money";
- Managing their cost base in order to be able to price their services at levels that clients will be willing to pay, and at the same time produce sufficient profit to enable the firm not only to survive but also to prosper and develop; and
- Developing their organizations in such a way that leads to efficient client services they are prepared to pay for. The Legal Services Act 2007 in the UK has already laid down one blueprint for this with alternative business structures (ABSs).

Measuring and managing partner performance

As many law firms attempt to measure performance by using a balanced scorecard approach, readers should review the following analysis in order to focus on the real issues in their firms.

1. Key determinants of success

This addresses how a firm regards the key determinants of its success. It is important to view the key determinants of success in a firm from the point of view of the objectives which the firm is attempting to achieve. These objectives are likely to change as a firm's needs change, and are likely to be different for each individual and for each part of a firm.

Identifying how a firm regards its key determinants of success is therefore not only an integral part of helping a firm measure performance, but also an important part of the process of implementing a firm's strategic development.

2. Changing priorities

This is designed to clarify how a firm's priorities have changed over the past three years, and how they may change over the coming three years. For example, it may be that an individual or one part of a firm has been given the task of developing certain new service lines in accordance with a business plan extending over a given timescale. In such a case, success is likely to be initially measured in the case of that individual or part of the firm by reference to raising the firm's profile in the targeted area, increasing market share, and winning new clients. However, over the timescale agreed for developing the new service lines, there is likely to be a shift towards measuring the financial success of the venture by reference to its profitability and cash requirements. Measurement of such matters in this way is then likely to form a basis for decisions as to how a project is further developed or, if brought to an end, if the key determinants for success as applied to that project have not been met.

3. Sustainability of performance

This is important because it relates to measuring the sustainability of performance over reasonable periods of time as opposed to taking a snapshot of performance for a short period. In the past, too many individuals have been promoted to partner on the basis of "one good deal" – a decision that firms regret when that performance is not repeated. This approach also links to performance-based reward so that sustainable performance is measured and rewarded.

4. Performance by whom?

This section is also important because it recognizes that law firms are now quite complex team organizations, that it is often not possible to accurately measure performance by looking at the performance of just one individual, and that it can create difficulties for the development of a firm.

In a firm where, for example, the only measurement method is of personal billings by each individual, not only is evaluation on that basis likely to be inaccurate, but worse, a silo culture is likely to develop, where each individual partner exists as a standalone practice and is only concerned with personal billings. This structure will often lead to a situation where there is no cross-referral of work between partners. Moving to measurement-based team performance as well as individual performance can provide a more balanced evaluation and create a culture more fertile to the cross-referral of work and clients.

5. Contribution

This section is central to a firm's measurement of performance and sets out the possible options by which to measure performance. As mentioned earlier, financial performance is often at the forefront.

This is partly because some aspects of financial performance such as revenue are relatively easy to measure, as opposed to those aspects of performance that are perhaps less tangible. On the other hand profitability, which is arguably a more important measure of financial performance than turnover ("turnover is vanity, profit is sanity!"), can be quite difficult to measure in a way that is likely to satisfy everyone because there are different ways to define profit. Measuring a combination of revenue and profit for individuals and practice groups can provide a more balanced picture.

6. Non-financial contribution?

The performance aspects listed in this section can, depending on a firm's priorities at any given time, constitute some of the most important measures of partner performance but can be difficult to measure and are likely to require a great deal of subjective input on the part of others in a firm.

One of the most interesting examples we have seen of how a firm has tackled the issue of evaluating certain aspects of non-financial performance concerns a large internationally based firm. Each year a small group of partners travel to each office and interview every partner, asking questions that enable them to build a picture of each partner's and each office's performance during the previous year. One of the most important questions they ask is: "Which other partner or partners has passed you the most work during the previous 12 months?"

This is a valuable question because the responses will indicate the flows of work between partners and offices, and identify which partners are not only developing and managing their client relationships well, but more importantly are delegating the actual work to those in the firm best suited and qualified to do the work. That firm values not only great client relationship management but particularly values the sharing of work across the firm. Sharing is then recognized by the way in which the firm's reward structure remunerates those partners who share the work with others.

7. Performance measurement used for which purpose?

This section is designed to identify the purposes for which certain metrics are used. Reward and progression are two of the most common purposes, but increasingly, in difficult economic times and as firms restructure, demotion and removal are purposes for which performance is often evaluated.

Performance viewed from a client perspective

Client needs and satisfaction

One of the main challenges law firms face in maintaining their competitive advantage will be to understand what their clients (including prospective clients) and referrers will require in the future, in terms of "value for money" advice and service delivery.

In the same way, attaining and evaluating client satisfaction is critical in order for a firm to set performance goals for its people, and improve its ability to deliver clients' required advice and service.

Client satisfaction is often said to be the only real test of success for law firms, which face continual judgment from clients in terms of their skills in their core work types, their ability to anticipate and respond to market needs, and the resources they have available to deliver the service sought. The consistent delivery of high quality advice to clients, delivered in the manner clients will be demanding, will place ever increasing pressures on law firms to ensure that all their people are equipped with the skills and abilities to perform to the highest standards.

Capturing client feedback

The primary purpose of capturing client feedback will be to learn how the client thinks a law firm should perform in order to successfully compete. Examples include:

- Providing input into its strategic thinking with a view to expanding what it provides, and the share of business it wins from its current clients;
- Ascertaining how it is perceived by clients, referrers, and the market place;
- Identifying any clear requested improvements or gaps in its capability against what its market needs, both currently and in the future, or against what its competitors are providing;
- Identifying any significant strengths and weaknesses against relevant competitors; and
- Understanding levels of client awareness in relation to current services, and how these may need to change.

Client perception surveys

This line of enquiry of clients in relation to a law firm's performance will often identify performance issues such as:

- Skills and technical expertise;
- Speed of response;
- Fee levels;
- Relationships with individuals;
- Access and approachability;
- Consistent delivery and results;
- Size and depth of capability; and
- Specialisms (and the way in which a specialism is delivered).

When a firm receives feedback relating to any of these issues, it should take urgent steps to analyze the issue and, if required, take whatever remedial action is considered necessary in order to ensure that the firm will be able to provide clients with the service they require and in the manner they require. Too often, partners in firms when confronted with feedback will go into denial and refuse to acknowledge that such feedback is accurate or related to them. Unless those who are managing a firm are prepared to deal with such issues, that firm's competitive position will suffer.

Referrer perception surveys

Gathering information on referrers' perceptions can identify different critical factors. For example:

- Knowing the individual/the personal relationship/having confidence in the individual;
- Expertise/technical ability/good quality advice;
- Track record in an area of work;
- Turnaround time/speed/ability to meet timescales;
- Fit with client;
- Location;
- Reciprocation; and
- Team working.

Again, as with feedback from clients, it should be incumbent on a firm if it is to capture information from those who refer work to it that it take action to remedy the situation and improve its service. Unless this is done, a firm will lose ground to rivals. Critical factors relating to performance that often drive client satisfaction are:

- Meeting deadlines and keeping commitments;
- Ability to offer advice quickly;
- Keeping the client informed of progress;
- Care and attention given to work;
- Ability to communicate advice;
- Billing as expected;
- Providing excellent value;
- Personable and likeable people/rapport with the team;
- Quality of people; and
- Showing an interest in/knowledge of the client's business.

If the findings of such a survey indicate a significant lack of client or referrer satisfaction, then that should be an urgent wake-up call for a law firm to take urgent action if it is to rectify serious existing problems, prevent them from becoming worse, and improve in the future.

Action to be taken in response to feedback

A firm will need to consider what its people should be doing differently/better/more of/less of to drive client satisfaction and ensure the firm's performance is aligned with the needs of clients and the achievement of the firm's objectives.

Once a firm has analyzed the issues and is clear as to the action that will need to be taken, it will need to communicate this to its people so that they are all clear as to their roles and what performance is required of them. Defining what is expected of partners will also provide greater transparency for those seeking to become future partners.

In today's legal markets, it is paramount that firms listen to their clients and referrers, and after careful analysis and evaluation of consequent feedback, act decisively on that feedback. To ignore what clients are saying about a firm's performance cannot be permitted as an option if a firm is to successfully compete against its rivals.

Feedback and appraisal

If performance issues are to be managed well and fairly, it will be incumbent on managers to be open and clear with their people (both partners and others) regarding not only what is required of them, but also to provide them with full and honest feedback on their performance.

Once a firm has identified the skills and behaviors to be valued, measured, and rewarded, a process of feedback and appraisal can be implemented with a view to managing performance. This often takes the form of "downward only" feedback and appraisal whereby a senior person in a law firm appraises a junior person. This will include an appraisal, for example, by a managing partner or head of department of another partner, following completion by that partner of a self-evaluation form covering various attributes.

However, increasingly law firms are using techniques such as "all-round feedback" or 360-degree feedback whereby the process of appraisal is carried out by gathering feedback from peers as well as from both more senior and more junior colleagues or various combinations. A firm might go one step further and include feedback from clients.

Increasingly it is being recognized that it is the people who partners and others within a firm work with and manage who are in the best position to provide feedback on performance.

The views of partners' peers and their staff can be the most valuable feedback and the most effective form of appraisal to enhance performance. In particular, providing all-round or 360-degree feedback can help by:

- Reinforcing what partners are already doing well (receiving this feedback is usually a very positive experience);
- Highlighting changes partners could easily make that would have a positive impact on the performance of others (often, people are blissfully unaware of the negative impact certain aspects of their behavior are having on others);
- Improving performance (the feedback will reinforce what partners are already doing well and will highlight ways in which they could improve);
- Improving the motivation and performance of staff (often even small changes in partners' behavior can make a big impact on staff); and

- Aiding in the retention of good people (who might leave because of perceived "bad behaviors" that could be addressed if only partners were made aware of the impact they are having).

An effective all-round or 360-degree feedback process can be immensely helpful for a firm that is attempting to bring about changes in partner performance and behavior. How should a firm plan a performance appraisal involving 360-degree feedback as part of implementing a process to monitor and manage the performance of its partners? We discuss this in the following section.

Partner involvement

Partner involvement is essential to achieve success, for unless they have had a say in the design of the process, partners are unlikely to be committed to it. Furthermore, partners will have a wealth of knowledge that can help tailor a process ideally suited to the firm. An important contribution partners can make is through helping to clarify what is meant by high performance, recognizing that partners will contribute in different ways.

While fee generation is always likely to be an important factor, it is not the only determinant of success, and indeed, if it were the sole focus of attention, the longer-term success of the firm might suffer. Contributions to the management of the firm, teams, and projects should also be recognized, as should business development and technical contributions.

Involving partners in a constructive discussion to define partner performance criteria with a view to tailoring the appraisal process that best suits the firm and ensures partner commitment is also crucial. This can be achieved by working with partners in a single group or, depending on the size of the partnership, in two or more smaller groups. Partners can be involved in deciding:

- What aspects of performance should be judged;
- Who should be asked – a random selection or a chosen few;
- Whether feedback should be obtained by questionnaire, telephone, or via face-to-face interviews; and
- Whether 360-degree feedback should be incorporated into a partner appraisal process or just used as a one-off development tool.

A tailored process

As well as helping to define high performance, partners should also be involved in tailoring the appraisal and performance management process. Codifying a suitable appraisal process, and taking into account the views expressed by partners ensures a firm has a documented process suited to its needs, and to which its partners are committed. And keep it simple.

Obtaining 360-feedback

Obtaining meaningful and broad-based feedback about performance is crucial. 360-degree perception surveys are an excellent way of doing this and a powerful catalyst for self-development, and are increasingly being used by forward-thinking law firms. Feedback obtained in this way tends to be much more constructive than in traditional downward-only appraisal systems.

By having an external party administer, and using a 360-degree feedback process through a combination of questionnaires and telephone follow-up, respondents can be assured of anonymity, which is essential in order to obtain full and frank feedback.

Using peer group feedback to help managing partners become more effective

Managing partners often reveal that they have a partner or a small group of partners who are "off limits" to any kind of effective management. Understandable as this may be in good times, when times are more difficult, managing partners can come under acute pressure from other partners to deal with problem partners. This can be difficult, particularly in a smaller firm when action to deal with a sensitive issue can appear unfair or threatening and potentially destroy the collegiate culture of a firm.

One way in which we have helped firms to resolve such issues has been working with a managing partner to use peer-group feedback. This can involve discreetly obtaining confidential feedback from fellow partners (sometimes carefully designed as part of a partnership-wide exercise), followed by delivering feedback to the partner(s) concerned in a fair, objective, and non-threatening manner. This feedback process can be a wake-up call for partners who may otherwise be unaware of how they appear to others, and it can pave the way, for example, for follow-up coaching to address any development needs that have been highlighted.

Managing partners in particular have found that this process can be more effective in helping them to achieve their objectives than if they were to try to deal directly with the problem partner(s), when they might be open to accusations of unfairly picking on individuals.

Appraisal meetings

The success of an appraisal process hinges on having a positive and motivational appraisal meeting. Clients often value external and objective input in debriefing and coaching partners to respond positively to the feedback they receive, and to ensure that an actionable development plan emerges.

Monitoring and support

Appraisals are usually an annual event, but they need to be supplemented by supportive monitoring throughout the rest of the year to help partners develop and achieve higher performance.

However, a performance appraisal process based around 360-degree feedback can, if used wrongly, be very damaging. It therefore needs to be handled with care. On the other hand, when used correctly, it can be immensely beneficial.

Performance viewed from a people perspective

In the earlier part of this chapter we suggested that the consistent delivery of high quality advice to clients, delivered in the manner clients will be demanding, will place ever increasing pressures on law firms to ensure that all staff members are equipped with the skills and abilities to perform to the highest standards. Performance management will need to become a mantra by which law firms gain competitive advantage.

However, as well as looking at performance from a client perspective we also need to consider matters from the perspective of a firm's people.

What do our people want?

The ability to attract, retain, and develop key people – i.e. outstanding performers who are strong relationship builders, both internally and externally – should be a primary objective in every firm's strategy. As a consequence, many law firms are already putting in place new strategies to retain their best people and, where there are gaps in their service offering, they are aggressively recruiting from other firms.

What does it take to attract and retain the best people?

In order to design evaluation techniques to help develop strategies to achieve these outcomes, it can be helpful to first consider some of the reasons lawyers leave their current firms. Identifying the issues that evidence seems to suggest will persuade a lawyer to move from their current firm to join a competitor, can help law firms to develop people strategies centered round satisfying their lawyers' aspirations for interesting and rewarding careers, and enhance their attractiveness both to potential recruits and to those already working in the firm. Carefully managed exit interviews can be a particularly revealing source of information for this purpose.

Some of the reasons the "best talent" in firms leaves is set out under the following sub-headings, courtesy of John Grimwade of JDP Limited, an executive search specialist operating in the legal profession. All of the following issues established as reasons for leaving should be capable of being managed to prevent their recurrence.

Feeling valued and fairly rewarded

Law firms should never underestimate the damage that can be caused if their lawyers perceive that the contribution they are making to a firm is not being valued and not being fairly rewarded.

Many law firms advertise their values but fail internally to live by those values. In particular, they fail to match reward to what they say they value. And reward does not always need to be directly financial. Relative reward between partners can also be a very powerful driver of unhappiness if a partner feels they are "worth" more than a colleague.

Absolute reward is, however, important to many. In every legal market there is a threshold of average equity partner profitability. A firm below the threshold is at risk of losing its best people and will find it difficult to attract the best. And, if this leads to unhappy clients, then such a firm will no longer be competitive against its rivals unless urgent action is taken to build profitability.

Moreover, a level of profitability that provides funds for investment in people, training, and technology, while ensuring partners and staff are rewarded competitively for their endeavors, can be a powerful incentive when faced with a decision to move or stay.

Reputation and profile of a firm

Reputation is everything. As we have seen over the past decade with professional firms whose reputations have become tarnished, their major asset – their people – does not stay around for long.

Closely linked with reputation is the profile of a firm in the marketplace. A respected and admired brand that accurately reflects a firm's profile and market position is a strong attraction for lawyers considering a move. On the other hand, if a firm's internal perception is that it is not progressing and compared to its rivals is unsuccessful, this is likely to be a major reason good people will leave. Such a firm is also unlikely to attract good candidates – this group will go to firms that can demo strate they have a vision and are taking effective measures to achieve their goals.

Quality of clients and work

The likelihood is also that law firms with the best reputations and skilled practice groups will have competitive capabilities and sufficient resources to be able to involve their people in the better quality work – often seen as the Holy Grail for many lawyers. A core base of clients who provide a flow of work to all areas and who consistently demonstrate satisfaction with the quality of service they receive, combined with the opportunity to carry out and develop higher quality work in a law firm renowned for such work, is a major reason for lawyers leaving their existing firms to join others.

Defined vision and strategy

A clearly defined vision and strategy which unites a partnership is an important factor. This, combined with a management team that is capable of making and implementing strategic and operational decisions in a way which is consistent with a partnership's objectives can be persuasive criteria when faced with a decision as to whether to move or stay.

People and performance management

Another important aspect of a firm's market profile is the extent and manner in which a firm is seen to be driving performance to consistently provide clients with the levels of advice and service they are (and will increasingly be in the future) demanding.

We use the term "partner underperformance" to mean the inability of partners to consistently deliver high quality advice to clients and delivered in the manner they are demanding. The real cost of partner underperformance goes far beyond direct financial loss. A firm that is prepared to permit its partners to underperform in this sense will cease to be competitive and the effects internally on morale can be damaging, leading to the loss of good partners, usually accompanied by their clients.

We have already discussed the benefits that can accrue from a law firm embarking on a carefully managed all-round (or 360-degree) feedback program from a client perception viewpoint. Using such a feedback technique can in addition aid the retention of good people who might otherwise leave because of perceived "bad behaviors" that can be addressed only if partners are made aware of the impact they are having.

A happy workforce is likely to be a productive one. If partners in law firms were to remember to set an example to:

- Provide honest and objective feedback on performance and under performance;
- Find time to praise work that is done well;
- Act as a coach or mentor and assist others to achieve their objectives;
- Create opportunities for others through delegation; and
- Demonstrate fairness and integrity

then it is likely that law firms would be far more successful in retaining their best talent.

Investment in people

It is often said that a law firm's people are its greatest asset (and they do not come cheaply!). Is it sensible to let competitors acquire a firm's greatest resource at a fraction of the firm's investment cost, and at the risk of losing a portfolio of clients at the same time? Would it not be better for a firm to make greater investment in its people with a view to developing not only a higher performance culture, but also an enriching and challenging working environment? It may assist some firms in their efforts to attract, retain, and develop their key people to also address a number of other issues such as:

- Does each person in the firm have a clear career plan?
- Is there a partner admission process that is not solely based upon the size of a client following or "book of business" and if so, is it adequate for the task at hand?
- Are there specified and transparent partner admission criteria?
- How are potential partners assessed?
- Is there a business case for making this person a partner?

- Are potential partners in any way prepared for this process and the roles they will be required to perform as partners?

Culture

A law firm's culture can be defined as "the way people in a firm behave". A culture centered on achieving client objectives so as to maximize business opportunities, if combined with a cohesive and supportive way of working, would be more attractive to lawyers seeking rewarding careers.

To retain top talent, a firm's culture will need to be focused on creating an environment where the needs, ambitions, and aspirations of its people are viewed as being as important as those of its clients. Keeping a firm's talented people motivated will be the key to a law firm's overall success in the competitive and challenging legal market of the future.

Planning a people strategy that enables a firm to recruit, retain, and develop its people in a way that will build its competitive edge will require the firm to identify its peoples' aspirations, fears, and potential risk areas to the relationship. A law firm can capture and evaluate this information in a number of ways. Ideally, managers should be taking an active interest in the wellbeing of their people on a daily basis, but in reality this rarely happens. It therefore often falls to managers to design metrics to try to capture what its people really think, as a way of managing their aspirations, fears, and problems.

Confidential internal questionnaires

Confidential internal questionnaires can also be critical for evaluating what people in a law firm are thinking about certain issues. The following subheadings are examples of questions put to partners in one law firm together with some of their responses. The variety of views can effectively "get under the skin" of a firm, but also need to be reconciled if a firm is to effectively compete in today's legal markets.

Are you and other partners prepared to change how you work and behave to achieve our agreed goals?

- "Yes – whatever it takes!"
- "'I am more than happy to do what it takes to make this business a success, but sadly I am not sure if this will apply across the board."
- "Yes, but only if the person who manages me understands the constraints of my area of work and does not insist on unworkable ideas."

- "Yes, happy to change if I perceive the change to be well reasoned and based upon some meaningful research, and if there is a sense of fairness."
- "To a certain extent!"
- "Yes, we will need to do this in any event to succeed."
- "This question represents the ideal and I am not prepared to answer it."
- "Yes, I work hard already but would strive to up my game further."
- "Once we have a consensus on structures and profitability, we can work towards that common goal."
- "First, specify the goals!"
- "If I acquire some confidence in what those goals are and that we are following them."

Why do you come to work?

- "To earn money!"
- "Good quality clients; good quality work."
- "I really enjoy this firm and also my work."
- "I enjoy the challenge and the people I work with."
- "To earn a living."
- "To provide for my family."
- "I like the reasonably relaxed working environment."
- "To earn a living, but I also do enjoy it."
- "To provide a quality service to my clients."
- "I come to work because I enjoy the company of the people I work with."
- "To pursue an interesting career and a good income."
- "I enjoy my job; interesting interaction with clients and colleagues."
- "I like work."
- "To help clients."
- "Most days now to earn a crust!"

What do you consider it presently takes to succeed at our firm and are these considerations measured and rewarded?

- "Fees billed by you!"
- "It is all down to KPIs and percentages."
- "Finding, grinding, and minding – but only up to a point."
- "To be reasonably good at the job – only billing is measured."
- "Good client base and business development ability."
- "Being financially motivated – and spin!"
- "Willpower and the ability to motivate yourself – sometimes the occasional 'well done' would not go amiss!"
- "We do not measure partner performance well, nor do we identify strengths and weaknesses."
- "To grow and to lead our people to provide a quality service."
- "Work hard. Largely fees and hours."
- "Loyalty, longevity, character, and a reasonable set of partner behaviors. With the exception of KPIs, we have no performance link at any level."
- "'Partly longevity and proximity to key partners."
- "Have good KPIs. In part yes, but only at the cost of others."
- "There is a focus on financials but there is recognition that business development is also important."
- "A sustained record as a fee earner."
- "Primarily fee earning – it is so easy to measure."
- "Shout louder and be a member of the right department."

Perhaps, some of these responses resonate with readers and their firms. If so, it will be important to analyze what such responses indicate about a firm and its partners and then to decide how to deal with the issues raised, otherwise a firm will not progress towards achieving its competitive goals.

Linking performance to reward

Linking a performance management system to a reward system requires that the process is (and is perceived by partners to be) fair, equitable, and has the effect of appropriately rewarding those that contribute most to a firm's success.

At the outset, it is important to understand that there are a number of matters that should always be considered in relation to a performance-based reward system, including:

- Any change should always be consistent with and advance the goals of the firm;
- Performance-based reward should determine relative contribution of each partner with respect to other partners;
- It should be sustained performance over time that is rewarded; and
- A merit-based system cannot make up for lack of profit.

The success of performance-based reward system depends on two processes:

1. Clarifying performance criteria and agreeing target levels of performance designed to improve the performance of all partners by moving them towards their strengths and away from their weaknesses, and which are closely aligned with, and designed to achieve, a firm's objectives; and
2. The process of assessing actual performance against the criteria and the allocation of partners into, for example, their performance bands. It is crucial that those administering the system have the total trust and confidence of the partners.

Performance criteria

Examples of criteria that cover areas a firm may need to make continuous improvement in, in order to establish a competitive advantage, are explained in the following paragraphs. Every partner will need to make progress/improve/develop to varying degrees in some or all of these areas (depending upon precise roles and changing needs of clients and of the firm) if the firm is to achieve its goals.

Recognition and reward

When a firm establishes criteria by which performance is to be measured, this is as a result of the partners having identified behavior they value as core in the way in which they wish to build their firm, and because they value such behavior, they are prepared to reward that behavior. Performance criteria should ideally cover both short-term profit performance and activities that are an investment in longer-term profitability. Performance criteria can also be set relating to individual performance and group performance, depending upon a firm's objectives. Weighting can also be introduced within each set of performance criteria, for example, criteria for an individual or a group might include a higher emphasis on fee generation than on client development, depending on what it is thought are the highest priorities.

The following criteria are examples of factors that are likely to reflect behavior valued in many law firms and which, if firms are to develop and progress, the partners will wish (and need) to reward fairly. Criteria might be based around the following:

Client service

a. Work

- Technical standards;
- Meeting client needs; and
- Communication/rapport.

b. Management

- Income/profit targets;
- Cash management targets;
- Group planning;
- Service standards; and
- People/teams.

Business development

- Existing client development;
- Cross-selling/co-selling;
- Winning new clients; and
- Marketing the firm's image.

Leadership and management

- Motivating people to perform;
- Delegating effectively; and

- Providing support and direction to people.

Team relationships
- Commitment to the partnership/participation in partnership affairs;
- Personal integrity and relationship – internally and externally; and
- Firm-wide management.

Special projects
- Opening new offices;
- Creating new service lines/sectors;
- Acquisitions and mergers; and
- Pro bono work.

Assessing performance

Any system of performance-related reward needs to be accompanied by a performance review. Such a review process is critical to the effective working of a system because it provides:

- A means by which individual partners can establish goals for the next year;
- A process for communicating to a partner what can be done to raise performance and a process by which a partner can ask for help to do so; and
- A means by which partners understand their rating in profit-sharing and a forum in which this can be discussed.

This chapter does not cover in detail the performance review process as it relates to reward. However, a consistent and effective means of establishing performance standards and then assessing people to those standards needs to be developed. Some firms rely on measurement systems to provide a solid, objective data foundation for their reward system to provide a formulaic system where data is entered and the compensation due automatically calculated. Others use a more subjective approach, where a compensation committee determines the compensation due to a partner based on their judgment of that person's contribution to the firm. Despite the fact that individual ratings are likely to result in some form of points score, the authors do not generally recommend that each score be equated with a precise number of profit shares because performance measurement using a number of criteria cannot usually be that accurate. The application of common-sense discretion by those managing the process usually takes care of the few problems that may emerge.

Independent assessment groups

An independent performance assessment group will also need to be established within a firm. While an independent and objective approach to performance assessment is desirable, those involved in operational management should also usually be involved in the process to provide information about the performance of partners. Transparency, trust, and confidence in those managing the system must be present if a system is to be workable and accepted.

If a law firm in today's legal markets wants to achieve a competitive advantage over its rivals, it will need access to highly trained and high achieving people to enable the firm to outperform its rivals. However, as this chapter has sought to demonstrate, such "high people performance" does not happen on its own. Investment by law firms in their people – as clients constantly require higher levels of service, and more complex expertise – becomes an even greater imperative.

This first appeared as Chapter 5 in Scott, P., and Wyatt, R., Measuring and Reporting for Law Firm Success, *ARK Group, 2013.*

References

1. Kaplan, R.S. & Norton D.P., *The Balanced Scorecard: Translating Strategy into Action*, Harvard Business School Press, 1996.
2. Seldon, A., and Pennance, F.G., *Everyman's Dictionary of Economics*, J. M. Dent & Sons Ltsd, 1965.

Chapter 15:
The future roles of partners and leaders

By Patricia Wheatley Burt, founder of Trafalgar – The People Business

Becoming a partner has traditionally been seen as the pinnacle of career success and, once achieved, something to be clung on to until retirement. While this is still a valid career goal for many lawyers in any country, whether in a traditional partnership or an LLP, it is no longer considered the Holy Grail, and young lawyers are looking at all the available options before deciding which career path they should be pursuing.

Firms need to be clear about options

Law firm leaders need to understand where their particular services fit in to the price/value equation as applied by clients. As George Bull, head of professional practices at Baker Tilly, commented: "This sounds like a marketing point. I suppose it is in part. But it also fundamentally affects the way partners approach their business streams."

"In the case of low price/low value services, client-facing partner content may be slight, the relationship limited but the delivery mechanism has to be very smooth. Leverage will tend to be much higher, services will be delivered with great reliance on systems and the few partners involved will generally be business managers rather than service deliverers.

"For high price/high value services, client-facing partner content, and people contact generally, will be much higher. The service will be much more bespoke. Leverage will be lower and the services more akin to a traditional professional offering."

The opportunity the new structures offer is to re-visit just what is required of the firm's (business) partners, who will in the main be expected to be the leaders. For every firm it ought to be possible to answer the question: "What does it mean to be a partner or leader around here?" That goes for the most senior equity partner as well as the newest junior fixed share partner. In future there will be greater emphasis on how roles are delivered, and remuneration policies will continue to range from pure lockstep/equal profit share in some partnerships through to modified performance-related pay and bonus structures where as much as 90 percent is performance based.

Emphasis in future partner roles

No matter the structure selected, there has been such a shift in the profession that there are now some new basic responsibilities for anyone with senior responsibility – whether called partner, leader, or director – which will include:

- Greater emphasis on financial and commercial competence;
- Focus on genuine client (customer) service met through people, technology, and value for money services as set out in value statements;
- A range of cultures and internal values, clearly reflected in decision-making processes, leadership, and authority;
- Congruent performance management, remuneration, and incentive policies, driven by all of the above; and
- Clarity in non-partnership structures that separates ownership from delivery and enables external investors' involvement in decision-making and strategy.

Being a "clever" lawyer was the peak requirement 10 years ago; now, it could be seen as being "geeky", or an "expensive librarian". The dilemma firms face is that "Recruiting really nice and clever people who frankly would not spot a client, no longer has a place in the larger firms", as one partner commented recently. At the same time, there is evidence of firms seeking to build tiers of partners, accepting that some will never have what it takes to be a leader and are best at being rainmakers.

Today's successful firms acknowledge that leading a knowledge enterprise requires a sound understanding (and some say experience) of the work done at the front line. There are very few successful non-lawyer CEOs who have the same level of authority as lawyer managing partners. And while recognizing that others may be better at managing the firm than the partners can be bruising and challenging for those partners, they have to accept that the best legal technocrats do not necessarily make the best business managers. As a consequence, an increasing number of firms run regular business skills development programs for their emerging and newly appointed partners, although only a few have extended this to include the senior partners. Despite this shift in emphasis, it is unlikely that the most senior leaders in a firm will not have practiced as a lawyer at some point.

"A proprietorial approach and risk-taking attitude is necessary, even if it is not for a partner's immediate personal benefit. They must be able to say 'I can see how this will help the firm and I support it, even though it will cost me (in some way), now'", says Ed Turner, senior partner at Taylor Vintners. "The MP must manage their own profit and loss, and may not be the best lawyers in their field. They may not have direct understanding of all areas of the law under their management. It is their skill as managers that matters, as that is what will move the firm forward longer-term."

Key traits required of leaders

Each partnership structure requires a different style of leadership from the top, with different traits. Any change in structure will have an impact on the culture of the business entity. If there are no changes, i.e. the firm chooses to stay as a partnership or an LLP, other changes may be necessary. The key traits that are currently scarce include:

- A genuine definition of and commitment to the vision, values, and ethics that set the overall tone of the enterprise;
- Sparkling, clear, and admired leadership;
- Appreciation of the complex roles to be undertaken by the equivalent of MPs, SPs, and boards;
- Sophisticated commercial acumen and nous to run the business;
- Adaptability to flex the strategy in response to market forces, accepting risks;
- A sense of nurture for all staff and fellow leaders, high levels of emotional intelligence (EI); and
- Creative thought leadership, open to new ideas.

Definition of and commitment to the firm's vision, values, and ethics

The common values and behaviours and their impact on the delivery of value-added legal services must sit comfortably with all partners and staff. Muddled or cloudy definitions waste time (which is money) and lead to misunderstandings.

Avoid following the example of the international organization that included the following "own goal" on its core values webpage (in very small but readable print) : "These values may not be complied with from time to time." Like shares, they may go up or down.

Defining the values and beliefs of the organization is key to establishing "how" partners and staff will behave. All role definitions have to be seen in the context of values, behaviours, and skills which clients, staff, referrers, and stakeholders can refer to as "the way we do it here". By clearly describing what behaviours are and are not acceptable, it means that everyone knows what to do and expect.

Sparkling, clear, and admired leadership

An overt partnership style must include sparkling definition and communication of the vision to all staff members in a firm, not just the partners. Neil Kinsella, CEO of Slater & Gordon, said partners today should be clear about the overall structure of the firm, dividing roles between:

- Ownership;
- Stewardship and management; and
- Delivery.

Each role must be aligned to the firm's overall strategy, values, and culture. Individuals will have to decide whether they want to embrace future changes and structures. The main partnership roles of the MP, CEO, SP/chairman, heads of departments, and any global role, will be based on competence, rather than seniority or longevity.

When firms adopt a corporate structure, there is a need to create the clear distinction between those partners who are responsible for the overall leadership and direction of the firm and those who are better suited to client-facing roles.

The value of complex non-legal roles

Partnership and operational boards should have clear strategic responsibility and mandated authority to make swift decisions in order to advise shareholders, over and above their vested interest in a particular practice area or office. Clear authority and accountability is also critical to ensure the partner, MP, and/or SP is dedicated and committed to meeting business objectives and targets. Inevitably, this will require firms to have smaller strategic and partnership boards. Non-lawyers are perfectly capable of taking on such roles and, if included, often share/coach others to build their corporate skills.

Specific roles for the MP, SP, and department heads, for example, whether wholly or partially non-fee earning, will become more common. This is not easily achieved in smaller firms or newly established offices (such as those overseas) where the MP has an active responsibility to win work and fee earn, at least initially. Success or failure and end of tenure could result in the MP or SP (as chairman) leaving the business and moving to another firm, which is often the norm in other organizations.

The importance of commercial acumen and financial reporting

Critical to success will be the ability to understand and manage financial information, to determine the specific and overall performance of teams, practice groups, and the firm. Commercial acumen means partners and leaders will be able to genuinely encourage and achieve performance improvement swiftly. Numeracy will become a given, and some cultures and languages lend themselves to this. For example, simply counting in Mandarin requires mental arithmetic.

An adaptable and flexible strategy ensures sustainability

The ability to adapt a firm's strategy quickly in response to market forces is critical. Firms must utilize market intelligence and be prepared to test and experiment with their approach so that the early adopter advantage is achieved.

Nurture staff and fellow leaders using emotional intelligence

To support and develop all practice groups and levels of staff to identify individual skills and talents. Those that excel are retained, while underperformers are let go, all in line with client/sector/services and cultures and demonstrating high levels of emotional intelligence (EI).

Leaders need to be creative thinkers

Creative thinkers gather and respond to market intelligence effectively. Creative leaders, who are prepared to innovate, push boundaries, and take strategic risks, will differentiate the firm. They need to have developed adaptive selling skills, requiring the ability to satisfactorily service clients' needs.

Appealing future roles for partners and leaders

Specific partner roles, as discussed under the following sub-headings, will demand, attract, and encourage specific skills and behaviors of future partners and leaders.

Aspirant partners

Aspirant partners look for commercial opportunities and are qualified lawyers. Emphasis will be on business opportunities, strategic client relationship management, strong, agile numeracy, and business acumen.

Entrepreneurial partners

Entrepreneur lawyers or partners seek innovative opportunities for business growth – for example, developing a web-based service offering. These partners desire "generating profits outside the traditional law firm structure" and are often recognized as a technical expert in their field. More an innovator than a manager, they can be disillusioned by other slow and low risk taking partners.

Transactional partners

Transactional partners are capable transactional lawyers with competent client contact, some supervisory responsibilities, and they may be closer to an employee or inheritor partner. With modest aspirations and no interest in full equity, these partners could be an asset in a commoditized firm as they are less keen to be a director and are capable of managing others in volume teams doing repetitive tasks.

Technical partner/in-house lawyer

These partners have strong technical capabilities as lawyers, with no interest in partnership or management, but have an eye on career kudos and often opt for in-house roles such as "of counsel". These partners prefer roles where there is no requirement for time recording, chasing financial metrics, or getting involved with commercial activities. Rather, these partners and lawyers are more comfortable working in a firm that focuses on purchasing other law firms' services. This could include roles such as the company secretary, or as the in-house lawyer for a football club, dealing with a range of corporate and personal work, with emphasis on just the one client.

Head of legal, public sector

Similar to technical partners and in-house lawyers, this role involves choosing to work in the public sector and/or with government bodies, which are often considered more secure than private practice. Public sector work is perceived by some to have less emphasis on business management, a greater focus on team work, no need to time record (in the main), and a possible career succession.

Flex-time partner

Flex-time partners value a balanced work life over partnership. Most firms will allow partners to work part time (often getting five days' input in four). There are stories of partners reducing to four days per week to be told that this resulted in a 40 per cent reduction in profit share at plateau, which is clearly in direct conflict with equality and discrimination. Flexibility requirements can affect men and women at key stages of their career or family cycle (for example, to start a family) or to effect a period of pre-retirement.

Independent, self-employed partner or lawyer

These are lawyers who want to work as self-employed, in a flexible way as per flex-time partners, in what some view as "lifestyle" or virtual firms. Keystone Law (UK), for example, has a central administrative office with some 130 lawyers around the UK, operating independently and in small teams. There is greater choice for when, how, and whom to work for, although this presupposes a strong client following and high level of technical competence. As independents, they enjoy working with other lawyers or on their own, but do not want "any hassle with risk, compliance with regulations – so need it taken care of by some central resource". Axiom and Riverview Law are other examples of these firms offering 24/7 access to legal advice with choice on both sides.

"Leadership then lawyer" partners

These lawyers focus on a specific and interesting area, which may be more commercial in its delivery. They may choose to join one of the commercial/commoditized vehicles, such as the UK-based Co-operative

Legal Services (CLS). These partners progress their careers along the management chain, having scope to progress beyond the legal department into other areas of the enterprise. This provides more corporate opportunities for these partners.

Using competency frameworks and Balanced Scorecards

There are a number of internal and external factors that make up the whole of a partner's role, whether as an MP, head of department, or as a partner in a small team. Most firms can manage the tangible, financial measures of a partner's performance – i.e. the "what". These measures are essential, but it is equally important to manage the "how" or softer skills – i.e. to measure how each partner behaves and interacts with clients to drive profitability. Defining the required behaviors as sets of competencies across both internal and external areas of responsibility makes the standards and expectations clear and brings the role to life. The following examples help to illustrate this point:

- A partner who is 120 percent over target on fee income, yet their team is underutilized – i.e. resources have not been used effectively, the partner has not delegated or managed their work; hence, the overall profitability of the work completed is reduced;
- A partner who is excellent at winning client work, but useless at managing the billing and cash collection process is not profitable, as debtor days will start to reduce the profitability of the transaction; and
- If a partner has to keep re-recruiting lawyers and staff because their attitude and behavior towards others is intolerable, the lost opportunity costs of underperforming staff (due to de-motivation) as well as recruitment costs will erode the profitability of the team over a three- to nine-month period.

Firms often divide sets of performance competencies into groups of internal and external activities, such as relationships and administration, doing the work, etc. To reiterate, most firms set out descriptions as follows:

- Internal:
  - Technical expertise, finance, risk, quality, and administration; and
  - Partnership, business management, and team-player (staff and peers).

- External:
  - Relationships with clients, sectors, referrers, and stakeholders; and
  - Business development, profile, and brand awareness of the whole firm.

Application of competencies

Competencies are designed so that even the most junior member of staff can see what they should be doing now, and what would be expected at the most senior levels. The framework can be applied across a number of people and performance management activities, including:

- People and resource planning (and budgeting);
- Recruitment and then selection during/after interviews;
- Establishing development needs for new recruits – based on any gaps identified during the interview process – should form part of the induction program;
- Probationary review after one, three, and six months;
- Regular performance management processes;
- Promotion or career projection;
- Partner selection;
- Capability/underperformance disciplinary actions or grievances;
- Dismissal; and
- Selection for redundancy.

Firms developing global systems based on a Balanced Scorecard or equivalent should consider the cultures of each region and office and not just slavishly apply descriptions of skills and outcomes that simply are not culturally congruent. For example, the eastern culture does not sit comfortably with challenging authority or overt conflict; therefore, awareness of this should be blended into the measures of success. Firms must follow cultural customs and business practices when establishing overseas offices, and partners should be mindful that what works in the US may be counter-cultural in the UK or in Hong Kong.

Role Profile© – A brief outline

With the potential for so many future partner roles, what will be required of each partner could vary hugely. In light of this, the author (Patricia Wheatley Burt) has, over the years, devised a simple summary document called a Role Profile©. This A4 document collates the:

- Technical qualifications and core experience required to do the job;
- The top responsibilities (that would normally be set out in job description);
- The KPIs likely to be relevant for the role, but which can be flexed year-on-year; and
- The competencies most relevant to the role.

An example of the Role Profile document is included at the end of this chapter. It has been completed for a mid-tier firm, although the details need to be personalized. Personalizing this document allows the firm to take advantage of the individual's skills, and to apply them to the firm's best advantage. This document can be used for defining what each leadership role should contain – for example, for the SP, MP, department heads, and so on.

Will future selection processes for leaders exclude elections?

Commentators suggest that where firms introduce a corporate structure, it will require an appointment procedure, rather than elections. Of course, selection processes will develop over the rest of this decade, as the structures evolve, to include how appointments are confirmed. Elections will not be relevant for all structures except for traditional partnerships and some LLPs. Allowing those with a bias to choose a leader will not be possible where ownership and leadership are separated. The future differences will be:

- A selection process that requires an individual to be interviewed against the role profile for the job – i.e. competency-based by trained and competent members of the executive, HR, and maybe external recruiters or head hunters;
- The process will include business presentations;
- Individuals are likely to be put through a battery of psychometric

assessments, predictive behavioral tools, and tested on EI, to help benchmark them and assess team fit;

- More rigorous due diligence and reference processes for candidates, regardless of whether from within or external to the organization; and
- More specific contracts for the role with clear KPIs, objectives, and outcomes, with some linked to bonuses. Tenure will be more akin to that of a corporate executive, so for an agreed period. Also, if the role is terminated early by the firm, there will be penalty clauses for "letting the MP go early", as in any usual commercial executive contract.

Fundamentally, senior leadership roles will be vulnerable to similar vagaries as now (in terms of tenure), but with:

- Greater honesty, transparency, and evidence of success;
- Better valuing of the qualities and expertise being brought to the organization and of the job to be done; and
- With this rigor should come a better appreciation of, and response to, the decision-making process, responsibility, and accountability for success or failure.

These criteria attract people with self-confidence and the ability to develop professional skills, either through experience or gained through academic studies – although that should not be solely relied upon – and stronger self-awareness and awareness of others. Any external investor will be involved on all senior/executive appointments and will have at least one representative from their private equity finance house as part of the selection panel, if not also on the board.

So long as firms keep ownership tied to partnership, electing the partner will remain the sole process, with all its politics, split vote, and divisiveness that has badly ripped apart some firms in recent years. Many such firms now have processes in place, which include candidates submitting a business plan or manifesto setting out the vision and strategic intent for the firm under their stewardship.

Encouraging talent through to promotion

Smart businesses work towards a sound, thorough, and flexible "people plan" which assesses and maps the talent base for each sector or practice area, highlighting who the next tier of partners or leaders are likely to be. This should protect the firm against any unforeseen event. All partners/ staff need to be clear about who is and is not on track for promotion. Honesty about those staff members who will not "make it" enables them to find an alternative job that is better suited to their career path in good time.

Recent trends in laterally hired partners has helped widen the client base, but has also frustrated existing aspirant partners who have found yet another person blocking their way to the next partner step (if that is what they are after). In addition, as a result of mergers or as a condition prior to an acquisition, choices about who should be included in the deal can suddenly mean long-standing partners are no longer required. Often merging firms fail to have rigorous selection processes and the acquirer will naturally prefer to select their own people.

Using assessment (and development) centers for promotion

Using development and then assessment centers to select candidates for promotion brings such firms into line with the banking, finance, and commercial sectors, where this has been a normal approach for 20–30 years. All vacancies will be advertised internally and externally unless there are exceptional sensitivities. These centers are also likely to be run by external providers – the professionals in this specialist area – and avoid any potential conflict of interest for HR and other functional directors (who could be appointing their own bosses) or any bias.

This professional approach to appointments helps senior associates who are currently reliant on the competence (or otherwise) of their mentor for promotional appointments, which may have helped or hindered candidates in the past. In the new order, poor talent spotting or lack of development of key staff will be a mark against a leader, for it will be seen as a failure to create a supportive culture in their team.

If there are too many blocks to promotion for lawyers, or too many decisions made based on arbitrary choices, the growing trend of avoiding partnership or leadership responsibilities will increase. Having worked hard at school and then university, Generation Y (and Z) lawyers are no longer prepared to sacrifice their lives by letting work overtake other priorities in the hope of being rewarded with partnership or some form of shareholding. For an increasing number, being a consistently well paid lawyer is preferable to taking on more loans and risks in joining partnership.

Key take home points

- Emphasis for futures roles for partners and leaders will be on many facets, but mainly financial and commercial competence, intuitiveness, and innovation.
- Being a "clever" lawyer is no longer enough.
- Leadership requires a more proprietary approach and risk-taking attitude, and in the future will have complexity which will be better valued than often the MP or SP are today.
- Soft attributes such as nurturing talent, developing team values, and setting the tone at the top are increasingly recognized as crucial in terms of contributing to the bottom line. These attributes are particularly valued by Generation Y and Generation Z.
- Adaptability will be an essential leadership trait, as will being open minded and capable of testing to get the right answers.
- There will be many types and styles of role for today's partners, ranging from those dedicated to corporate models, through to the pure technocrat.
- Using competency frameworks can complement and bring to life job descriptions and KPIs, but should be culturally congruent.
- Using a Role Profile© to encapsulate all key elements of a role makes it easier to flex KPIs or competencies, based on the needs of the business.
- Future selection processes will not include elections by shareholders and will have greater structure and rigor for all legal service businesses, other than those that stay as partnerships (small) and LLPs.
- Promotion methods will veer towards assessment centers to ensure greater equality and diversity.

This first appeared as Chapter 5 in Wheatley Burt, P., The Role of the Law Firm Partner, 2nd edition, *ARK Group, 2015.*

Role Profile©

Job title: Head of department

Reporting to: Managing partner

Technical qualifications and experience

- Minimum of 10 years post-qualification experience in department
- Knowledge of current law in area of specialism and broad knowledge of specialism of department
- Five years' experience of managing a group
- Management development training
- MBA or similar

Accountabilities

- Develop department plan and deliver business objectives and targets for department
- Agree, manage, and monitor budgets addressing poor performance quickly
- Delegated authority for expenditure up to £50K
- Provide leadership and motivation to all partners and staff in team
- Develop new business/ existing clients, including across teams
- Manage and develop efficient systems for team
- Manage and monitor compliance, risk, and quality for team
- Curate professional ethics and compliance

Key performance indicators

- Profitability of department
- Fee income billed
- £ target: £
- Chargeable hours 1,600v
- Non-chargeable time for management, training, and admin
- Work in progress xxxx days
- Debtor days (team) xxxx days
- (Average profit per legal staff in department) £ /......%
- Staff turnover – absence and sickness cost £___%
- Achievement of whole department targets (graded 1–5)
- Compliance with firm's policies and procedures and professional ethics (Meet minimum competencies)

Competencies

- Relationships
- Leadership and resource management
- Expertise: gained
- Expertise: applied
- Commercial judgment and decisions
- Business development and marketing
- Delivery: making it happen
- Comunication, culture, and values

Chapter 16: Law firm leadership development – The practice group leader path to law firm leadership

By Harry Trueheart, chairman emeritus of Nixon Peabody LLP

It might be said that more has been written about law firm leadership development than has actually been done about it. The knowledge about what is needed is available, but turning that knowledge into embodied skills remains the tough part. We continue to read debates about the full-time leader versus the part-time leader, the unpaid volunteer versus the paid leader, and (the most basic of all) the debate about the value that the partners in law firms are willing to assign to leadership.

While these debates go on, a record is building of those leaders that have succeeded and those that have failed. Fairly viewed, that record makes the case for skilled leadership increasingly clear and is motivating well-managed firms to put in place leadership development programs. The better programs start leadership training at an early stage of the lawyer's career, focusing first on matter management and leading ad hoc teams that work on matters, teaching fundamental business skills, and then adding additional skills training as lawyers become partners and partners become leaders.

My premise for this chapter is that one of the crucial later steps in developing successful law firm leaders, and good choices for a firm's next managing partner, is to develop a cadre of successful practice group leaders. These practice group leaders will have had a variety of lesser leadership experiences and on-going training before they are selected for these roles. I will focus on the practice group leader's role and their developmental potential.

Practice group leadership roles, correctly defined to parallel how the firm should operate, have the most impact on firm success and are the best final training ground for leading the whole firm. The experience and related training and coaching that group leaders get should translate to improved firm performance and be scalable to the managing partner role. To be a good training ground, a practice group should be analogous to a strategic business unit, and its leader needs to have a key role in running that business. This is a distinctly different role than the predominantly administrative one that many practice group leaders fill.

Today, practice group leadership is an ideal training ground for future senior leadership roles. In many law firms, practice groups are larger and further flung even than the firm itself was only a few years ago. Practice groups are in fact becoming "lines of business" for the firm, with the need to develop skills, satisfy clients, develop new products, market, and sell. The groups now need to recruit and manage large numbers of staff, to develop talent, and to handle most of the other things a fair-sized business or law firm needs to do.

Plan for practice group leadership development

The first step in planning leadership development is to ask what a successful practice group or law firm needs. From that list you can build a list of skills your leaders need, and from that list you can formulate a leadership development plan. Here are a few suggestions for what a practice group or firm needs:

- A good business strategy;
- A plan to implement the strategy;
- Excellent people who are aligned with the strategy and plan, and are enthusiastic about working on them;
- Flexibility and adaptability to adjust to a turbulent market;
- A commitment to extraordinary service;
- Professional and financial discipline and accountability; and
- A team-oriented culture.

The needed skills

The next question is what skills should a leader have to help the group meet those needs? While skills may vary depending on the nature of the practice group, I suggest the following essential list:

- A high degree of emotional intelligence;
- Organizational skills;
- The ability to lead the development of a strategy and a plan;

- The ability to use the strategy and the plan as a guide to all of the smaller, immediate decisions that have to be made;
- A drive to see the plan implemented and the group succeed;
- An ability to recognize talent, and a desire to develop others and see them succeed;
- The ability to lead change;
- Flexibility and the adaptability to manage in a turbulent market;
- Good communications skills and a dedication to using them;
- An ability to approach difficult conversations effectively;
- The ability to motivate the people in the group or firm;
- Political savvy;
- The ability to manage people at a distance, across a firm's multiple offices;
- Proven success, at some stage, as a practitioner and business developer, though not necessarily at the highest levels;
- A greater commitment to the team than to oneself;
- The trust and respect of one's partners and employees; and
- Resilience.

An effective leader is someone who:

- Can ensure that the group develops a vision, strategy, and goals, and can keep them foremost in everyone's mind;
- Makes integrated business decisions that continuously move the group forward;
- Can be flexible and adaptable to changing markets;
- Makes personnel judgments of all kinds that build a winning team;
- Builds a successful collaborative team that is well integrated in the firm; and
- Ensures that the "trains run on time" in the group.

It should be very clear to the reader that no one individual possesses all these skills to an equal degree. Thus, the most important skill that needs to be on the list is the ability to recognize one's own weaknesses and to supplement them with the skills of others. The most important point is that a leader needs to ensure that the organization gets the job done, and not attempt to do it all him or herself. Knowing how to harness the skills of the group as a whole is essential.

A note about the personal characteristics of lawyers

Understanding the characteristics of both the leaders and followers in law firms is important in formulating a leadership development program within a firm.

The work of Dr Larry Richard and others has highlighted what many of us have long observed: lawyers are, on average, great thinkers and problem solvers. However, we are by nature highly skeptical and less trusting or accepting than those in many other professions. We value autonomy highly, dislike rules and routine, and often prefer the role of individual contributor to that of team member. We are, on average, less sociable than the general public. In the terms of the Myers-Briggs Type Indicator, we are more introverted than extroverted. We have a high sense of urgency and are often impatient, looking for quick solutions and results. We are more likely to be thin-skinned and defensive. And those of us trained in the common law had a heavy indoctrination into the adversarial system – to instinctively believe in conflict and competition rather than cooperation.

A number of years ago, my firm engaged the services of one of the leading corporate leadership development organizations to help us train future leaders of the firm. The program used extensive tools for measuring the personal characteristics of those in the training program. The results closely paralleled those found by Dr Richard a number of years later in a study of a much larger cohort of lawyers.

Not surprisingly, these are traits that, on the whole, do not match those of successful leaders, who tend to be extroverted, team and future-oriented, more emotionally intelligent, and thick-skinned. They accomplish their work through relationships and social networks, and work on a mix of short- and long-term goals. They build and perpetuate teams and institutions. They believe in coordinated action more than "Lone Ranger" tactics.

Lawyering skills that are helpful to leadership roles include:

- Intelligence;
- A capacity for hard work;
- Analytical and problem-solving skills;

- Communication skills;
- Client-relationship skills; and, of course
- Substantive skills in the group's area of practice.

Those skills and traits that are not helpful, in excessive quantities, include:

- Adversarial skills;
- Problem finding;
- A do-it-yourself mentality;
- Personal competitiveness;
- Ego;
- A preference for giving advice rather than making decisions;
- Perfectionism;
- Risk avoidance;
- A lack of organizational skills; and
- An overdeveloped use of confidentiality.

A good, simple test is: does the particular lawyering skill work well at home? If not, it probably will not work well in leading the practice group. Leadership training should include significant efforts to enhance the under-developed skills of lawyers and moderate the over-developed skills.

A note about leadership styles

In addition to skills, much has been written about leadership styles. Here is a quick take on styles that seem to work in law firms – and some that do not suit as the dominant trait. It is important to note that any style can be tempered and supplemented.

In general, the coaching style seems best suited to leading highly motivated, successful professionals. I will omit the usual sports analogies because I am sure they come quickly to mind. The charismatic leader can also be effective, provided the leader has a strong team around them to actually get something done. In a homogeneous and highly motivated practice group, a referee style may be all that is necessary.

Several styles that do not seem to work well, if they define the individual, include the "foreman", the "numbers guy", the "administrator" or "bureaucrat", or the "counter-cultural-ist" – that is, the one who rallies the team by identifying the common enemy, which can be another group, another office, or even the firm itself.

Good leadership development should define a style that is effective within the current culture of the firm and in part trains leaders in that style. The reason for the qualification is that, as the market changes, firm strategies may also change, and firm cultures need to change with these. A change in culture may require a different style of leadership and, with that, different training.

Developing practice group leaders

Job description

Practice group leader positions should have job descriptions. What could the job description of a 21st-century practice group leader look like? The practice group leader should have responsibility for or significant influence over:

- Group strategy;
- Planning and implementation;
- Group revenue and expense budgets;
- New business intake and pricing;
- Associate and paralegal hiring and utilization;
- Associate promotion and termination;
- Marketing and sales budgets;
- Professional standards in the delivery of services;
- Client service standards;
- Loss prevention;
- Training and development;
- Partner recruiting and promotion;
- Partner performance evaluation; and
- Partner compensation and status recommendations.

The job description should also include responsibility for the morale and job satisfaction of the group. These are all factors that will materially affect the success of the group. Of course, the job description needs to match the responsibilities the firm assigns to the groups as a whole. In the end, the job description should read much like the managing partner job description, but scaled to the practice group. The job description needs to be shared within the firm, particularly among the partners, and an effort needs to be made to build consensus around the role and its importance to firm success.

Coaching and training

Coaching is essential in leadership development. The "coach-in-chief" needs to be the firm managing partner. Their oversight and interactions with group leaders will be a major factor in their training. To supplement this, group and individual coaching is employed by some firms to help develop leaders. It is also possible to mix leadership skills training with follow-up coaching on the skills being taught. The model is a good one; however, securing commitment to follow-up is a challenge. There are many "executive" coaches plying their skills, including some with law firm experience. Since coaching is inherently situational, the most effective coaches will understand the law firm context.

Training should be done in a variety of settings. I recommend a mix of intensive off-site training and shorter topical and timely trainings, which, for example, can be mixed into agendas for group leader meetings. My firm has used both with some success. The shorter topical trainings work well with day-to-day issues, while the more intense ones are better suited to training for deeper, longer-term skill development.

Goals, accountability, and developmental evaluation

A significant opportunity for learning and development is an annual evaluation for each leader. In my experience, such a process should include three, equally important elements:

1. A self-evaluation prepared by each leader;
2. An evaluation prepared by the leader's "superior"; and
3. Confidential feedback from those being led.

It is important to recognize that some leaders are much better at "managing up" than "managing down" and that, without this broad feedback, firm leaders are often in the dark as to what is actually going on in the group. The results of these evaluations are best conveyed in a developmental context with the purpose of both encouraging and reinforcing good behaviors and dealing with problematic ones. These reviews can help to focus training on missing experiences or skills that need further development.

Separate in concept from the developmental review is a performance review in which the practice group leader is reviewed against the goals for the leader and the group for the prior year. The predicate for this review is a clear understanding of what those goals were for both the leader and the group.

It is equally important that there be a clear understanding of the expectations for the leader regarding the balance of leadership time and personal practice time, and the results expected in both areas. The concept that "people will do what you pay and not what you say" applies to law firm partners. It is important that leaders clearly understand where the firm stands on this point and are treated fairly. If a firm wants pro bono leadership, that is a choice to be made. But if it wants to pay for effective leadership, the firm will need a system of accountability, evaluation, and reward in which the leaders and the partnership as a whole have a reasonable degree of confidence. There are few things that undermine commitment to effective leadership more than confusion about its value to the firm.

The crucial role of the managing partner

The way in which the firm's managing partner manages and deals with practice group leaders is crucial to their successful training. Consider these questions. Does the managing partner:

- Appropriately delegate operating decisions to the group leaders?
- Seek input from those leaders on decisions that impact the group's success?
- Listen to that input?
- Work through the practice group leaders, or around them?
- Plan for and oversee the development of practice group leaders?
- Take the time to coach, rather than just direct, the practice group leaders?

An important responsibility of the managing partner is to build and maintain a strong leadership team. That should be a goal for which the managing partner is accountable to the firm. In other words, accountability at the top for effective leadership development is important to achieving successful results.

Conclusion

Law firms have an easy time understanding that on-the-job training, coaching, formal training, accountability, and reward are part of developing successful practicing partners. It should not be surprising that the same approach can work in developing effective law firm leaders.

This first appeared as Chapter 3 in Slater, L. (ed.), Leadership in Law Firms: An Expert Guide, *ARK Group, 2014.*

Chapter 17:
When firm leaders transition

By Patrick McKenna, author, lecturer, strategist, and advisor to the leaders of premier law firms

Leadership transitions can be a messy ordeal, or they can be carefully orchestrated to progress the best interests of your firm. I wanted to set out here some of the best practices and potential pitfalls that both outgoing and incoming firm leaders need to be sensitive to.

When you are the outgoing leader

The outgoing leader has a number of responsibilities to the firm, to the unbiased selection of his or her successor, and to the transition process.

First

When you have decided (or it has been decided for you by the terms of your tenure) that it is time to step down, the proper course of action would be to assist your firm's executive committee/board in the formation of a nominating committee, but do not involve yourself as a member of that committee or suggest any candidates for consideration by the committee.

Some hold to the belief that the current firm leader should select their successor and that has undoubtedly worked for a very few firms, most notably Jones Day, for decades. The countervailing argument is that selecting your replacement is likely to have you selecting someone that is just like you, which may not be what your firm needs at this stage in its evolution.

When you're handed the keys to the kingdom from a successful predecessor who groomed you for the job, there's a temptation to play the Great One's "mini-me". In some ways, you feel indebted to this firm leader who gave you the opportunity, and you feel obliged to try to carry on in the same style. But that defeats the purpose of the succession. When partners see a new leader who looks exactly like the old one, they may be lulled into thinking the old managing partner has simply been cloned, which in turn encourages a mindset less than receptive to innovation and independent initiatives.

Handpicked leaders can also be reluctant to take the firm in a new direction because, after all, the existing approach worked. That too can be a mistake as it reinforces the old model which, even if effective in the past, sends the message that there is really only one way to get things done.

In any effective leadership selection process, before you can begin discussing the "who", your executive committee/ board must agree on the strategic direction of your firm in light of trends and discontinuities that your firm may be facing in the future. It follows that if the members of your executive committee cannot agree on a strategic direction, they will have even greater difficulty agreeing on the requisite capabilities of their next firm leader. Therefore, in any leadership succession process, you need to pay particular attention to defining the criteria for selecting your next firm leader based on future performance requirements. To go beyond generalities, the board has to identify the very specific effect it wants the next firm leader to have on the firm's business, and to define the skills that it will take to accomplish that.

Second

One common delusion every departing leader may hold is that they are indispensable, or at least that the firm will stumble without them.

Every one of us who has ever held a leadership position may maintain some secret fantasy of one day announcing our plans to resign, and then leaving office amidst tears, a standing ovation from partners and staff, and general consternation about the future. Here is how one firm leader expressed it, somewhat tongue-in-cheek:

> *"You should know: I was 'indispensable' even though the firm has not 'stumbled' under my successor's leadership; that I don't like it one bit but the firm is 'thriving' without me; that I have been very positive about my successor and his new leadership team – and believe me it has not been easy! I never agree with the probably hundreds of my partners that constantly complain about the new leadership team and want me to start a coup... 'Can't you tell? I have moved on!'"*

The bittersweet reality is that your firm will survive and even thrive without you. You should therefore compose a realistic story to tell people, in a positive way, why you are stepping down and to convey your excitement about your next adventure and the firm's future.

Third

The leadership transition period is a good time to finally deal with annoying operational problems or troublesome personalities so that the new leader can come in and immediately begin to address the more important, strategic issues.

Conferring with your successor and, with their concurrence, confronting these often sensitive and sometimes messy situations now, is one of the best gifts you can give your replacement – a clean slate from which to work.

Fourth

Think about what information you would want if you yourself were now about to embark on this new leadership position.

As the incumbent, you typically know more about the firm and its operating nuances than anyone else. Much of that information, or at least how to find it, is stored in your head. Think about how you might codify and share everything you wish you had known when you first took office.

Fifth

To assure the success of the new leader, you should under no circumstances speak with anyone at the firm about his or her performance.

Being perceived as negative or unsupportive only reflects poorly on you. You must also not allow anyone to say, "Well that's not how we handled things when you were the managing partner." That is disloyalty, and you must take issue with it. It may be gracious of partners to acknowledge your good work, but your focus should be on supporting and cultivating the strengths of the new leader.

In a recent discussion with a soon-to-retire firm leader, I discussed a number of substantive issues he needed to discuss with his successor, including how he needed to handle communications with his various partners after he passed on the baton. Here is the script he prepared for himself to communicate to his successor:

"I'll always be here to help you, but you should expect that some of our beloved partners are probably going to go around you and come to me whenever you make an unpopular decision. And, if you are doing your job as our new firm leader, as I know you will, this is guaranteed to happen. I want you to be confident that I am not going to respond, in any way, to any complaints, so don't let the prospect of my responding, impact your decision-making. Even if you choose to fire someone who has worked closely with me for many years, you should proceed to take that action. And rest assured that if I don't agree with some course of action or observe you doing something contrary to the way I did it, I would not go to any partner to voice my feelings. This is now your firm to lead and you may call upon me should you ever feel the need for a sounding board."

Finally

The best advice I can frankly give any leader leaving office is to simply let go. And "letting go" means not sitting on the executive committee/board, not moving from managing partner to firm chair, and not being involved in any way in the leadership of the firm.

Never mind all those lovely things they said about you at your retirement dinner. You are now a beloved part of the firm's history. The firm must learn to live without you, so the sooner you get out of the way, the sooner they can get down to business.

When you are the incoming leader

Few new firm leaders are as prepared as we, or they, might wish. As one expressed it:

> *"New firm leaders mistakenly believe that because they have served as a practice group manager, as an office head, or on the firm's executive committee they have the necessary background for taking on the role of leading the entire firm... Not even close!"*

First

Most professionals really do dramatically underestimate the scope and responsibility of managing an entire firm. One thing we should insist on is that the firm leader has a detailed job description. That description must get widely circulated throughout the firm so that everybody gets a true sense of what the job entails. One thorough description that we examined encompassed dozens of bullet points of responsibility.

I often tease new firm leaders by asking them what they could possibly have been thinking when they took on such a huge role. For all the burdens they are willing to shoulder, their willingness to do so is often disparaged. Many partners see management as pure overhead, as drudgery that does not really reflect on the professionalism that defines a lawyer, and does not generate revenue like practicing law actually does.

Meanwhile, partners at most firms often bristle at any suggestion that they can or ought to be "led". Firm leaders feel they are sacrificing themselves for the betterment of the firm, and should be appropriately appreciated. The partners think of you as "serving at their pleasure"; they are allowing you to hold the leadership title, so you should be beholden to them!

Thus, one of the common mistake that new firm leaders often make is thinking this appointment is about you, when it's all about them. As you begin your new role, it is quite seductive to take to heart all of the wonderful best wishes, congratulations, and accolades you will inevitably receive. You will only succeed when you recognize the truth: you may be the firm's leader, but your partners don't work for you. You now work for them, and they have just become your most important client.

Second

Many of these same professionals underestimate the time that is going to be required of them to really do this job. I recall the Citibank/HBR 2014 "Client Advisory" report that provided a commentary under the title: "The Leadership Challenge". According to the report:

> *"One development which gives us concern is that some of the newer breed of leaders continue to maintain busy, full-time practices. In this scenario, their clients' needs are likely to take priority, to the detriment of the management of the firm. If we could see any change, it would be that firms recognize that to be effective, the firm leader is best performed as a full-time role."*

Indeed, the biggest issue I hear about from new leaders is always the amount of time it takes to do the job. Many of them are not full-time managing partners, so they struggle with trying to maintain some balance between the time needed to manage the firm and the time required to maintain some modest personal practice.

Here's a tip: create a "stop doing list". Take a look at your desk. If you're like most hard-charging leaders, you've got a well-articulated to-do list. We've all been told that leaders make things happen – and that's true. But it's also true that great leaders distinguish themselves by their unyielding discipline to stop doing anything and everything that doesn't fit.

Third

Any new firm leader needs to get a clear sense of their partners' expectations.

Coming into this job you are a professional with a great internal reputation. It is therefore anticipated that you will create momentum quickly and deliver results. Expectations are high and you do not want to disappoint, and that concern over not disappointing will therefore have you mistakenly entering the fray with a given strategy in mind.

New leaders believe that their successful track record, combined with their mandate, guarantees the support of the partnership. They focus attention on the technical aspects of implementing their strategy, wrongly assuming that a critical mass of support is in place. The higher the expectations, the more they believe that everyone is behind them, and the more likely they are to assume that they are on the right track. As a result, they act first and ask questions later. In their rush to make their mark, the new leader can neglect to take sufficient time to learn important information, and to more wisely gauge what I call your partners' "appetite for change".

As a new leader, it's understandable that you will feel that you already have the information you need about how people think and feel. After all, you have been a partner in the firm for many years and may have even served on the executive committee/board prior to accepting this mandate. But how much do you really know? It is all too easy to step on people's toes and, as a result, abort even the most promising agenda. As a new leader, you must use your time, ideally before your actual transition, to gain significant information that will refine and maybe redefine your strategic agenda going forward. In most situations, your initial concern should *not* be to hit the ground running, but to hit the ground *listening*.

The lesson: As early as possible, you must get input from your people on what they see as the preferable direction. Conduct one-on-one interview sessions with your partners (and other professionals in the firm), asking each one the same questions to get their insights, solicit their advice, and see what themes emerge. Clarify what they want to see you "shake up", and what they want to see you "preserve". It is wise to have people see that you are genuinely engaged and willing to listen before you say the first word about where you think the firm needs to go.

Fourth

As a new leader, you are being observed under a microscope. Your decisions, how you make them, whom you consult with, are all viewed very carefully; likewise, everything you say, and the signals you send. You will be barraged with phone calls and emails, questions, requests, and advice.

You have to be especially careful how your relationships are perceived.

If you are coming to the top leadership position after stints as a practice or industry group head, or if you reside in some foreign office, you will likely be perceived as maintaining obvious loyalties to established friends. Once you are identified as being on "one side" of an issue, it becomes even more difficult to solicit disinterested perspectives.

You may need to make time to transform some relationships. Good leaders customize relationships with each individual on their radar screens. And don't forget to inform people about how best to work with you. As you take charge, you will be working with an established team with established work patterns and habits. It is important to them to learn how you like to operate:

- How do you prefer to receive information – in person, by phone, in writing?
- Is your door open or do you prefer that people arrange appointments?
- Do you have any pet peeves that people should know about?
- How do you feel about being called at home?
- Help those who report to you learn how to work with you.

Fifth

Based on what you've been hearing from your interviews with fellow partners, settle on a few major priorities. You can't fix everything at once or do everything you want to do, so you need to make some strategic choices. Here is where you begin to align your firm around a shared direction for the future.

And, within your first 100 days, you need to target a few early wins. Momentum counts and nothing succeeds like success. Pick some problem your firm has not been able to address and figure out a way to fix it quickly. That's how you make some progress and ensure perceptions of a successful transition.

One firm leader began her term with an initiative wherein a number of the professionals and staff throughout the firm collaborated together in small task forces to identify the firm's "sacred cows" – those things that were being done internally that made no sense, frustrated clients, and hampered good service delivery. She then set about having these same task forces kill the sacred cows by proposing ways to effectively eliminate the past procedures, change behaviors, and adopt new approaches. Don't ignore the power of accomplishing a small win. Listen, look around, and find some small but significant change that you can bring about.

Finally

Contrary to what some business literature suggests, real leaders don't worry about legacies. They care instead about the long-term competitive vitality of their firms. If you are focused on fashioning a legacy, you will be remembered as… the individual who was focused on fashioning a legacy!

This first appeared as Appendix F in McKenna, P.J., The Changing of the Guard: Selecting Your Next Firm Leader, *ARK Group, 2015.*

Chapter 18:
What Gen Y wants – How law firms can get the best from the new power generation

By Sarah Sladek, CEO of XYZ University

Generation Y. Millennials. Echo boomers. Trophy generation. Regardless of how you refer to them, organizations worldwide are really perplexed by the generation of young adults now moving into the majority of the workforce, consumer spending, and voting power. Dismissed as "entitled", "attention-deficient", and incapable of interpersonal communication, leaders often lament the fact that this generation is difficult to understand and impossible to engage. Few have taken the extra step to truly seek to understand what motivates and inspires this generation.

Generation Y (1982–1995) has come of age during a time of economic recession, digital innovation, and political revolution, and they are the first generation to come of age in the post-Industrial Era. All too often, we refer to this era as being purely driven by technology, but that's not the case at all.

Generation Y are a product of their environment and they have been shaped by entirely new skillsets, opinions, and values. They won't go back to base on anything because they don't know the Old World; they are settlers of the New World. It may seem like they are always steering us away from traditions, when in fact they are steering us towards what's relevant and meaningful in this New World.

Here's a glance into four of the trends that shaped Generation Y, and what each means for the future of law firms.

Recessionistas

For starters, Gen Y's buying behaviors are unique. Their arrival has confounded many retailers because they are well-informed consumers who walk into stores knowing a great deal about the product; thrifty consumers who tend to reuse and recycle; and investment consumers willing to pay more for quality and trendy brands.

As such, this generation has been dubbed "Recessionistas" – informed shoppers who stick to tight budgets while still managing to stay trendy and cultured. For Ys, it's the trifecta of quality, popularity, and price that drives sales. However, Ys will make the occassional concession if two out of three of their criteria are met. For example, Gen Y invests in Apple iPhones because they are renowned for high quality and because they are popular. Plus, there is a substantial return on the investment – you can organize your entire life on an iPhone.

The Recessionistas are selective consumers and they are likely to "shop" for their employment opportunities in the same way. They will concern themselves with your firm's quality (are there ample opportunities here to further my career?), popularity (is the firm reputable, well known, and a leader in its industry?), and return on investment (does this opportunity offer a significant return on investment for my time and effort?).

Migrators

Generation Y is literally migrating away from the interests and behaviors of their predecessors and the influences of their childhood. The following "migrations" are great indicators to the types of value propositions that will motivate and appeal to Generation Y.

1. Safety to adventure

Generation Y has grown up in the safest environment in human history. They are, in fact, the most protected, supervised, provided for generation in history. However, as young adults, this over-protected generation is now migrating from safety to adventure. They seek frequent opportunities to travel, and dangerous and exciting sports activities like skydiving, rock climbing, and bungee jumping. The equivalent of this trend in the work environment is innovation and a willingness to take risks and revise traditions.

This generation wants an opportunity to break the mold and try new things, and they want their organizations to be cutting-edge, or at least to appreciate a cutting-edge mindset. Too much resistance to innovation, technology, or change will put your law firm in the safe zone, the very place Ys are trying to escape.

2. Isolated to connected

While Gen Y children were raised in a safe environment, it also produced an isolated and disconnected environment. As children they rarely had the freedom to roam beyond the front yard, and their social lives were determined by the quality of friends on the same street, together with the nature of their scheduled social interactions beyond their neighborhood.

As young adults, Generation Y wants to be more connected and less isolated. They manifest this desire in their full-on embrace of social media and their desire to live in places where they can be around others – including the densest, most active areas of cities.

Law firms can fulfill their desire for connectivity through communication and by providing ways for employees to interact with one another. The lack of positive relationships is the number one reason Gen Y employees will leave an employer. They crave opportunities to learn from others, work collaboratively on projects, and to feel like they are part of a community.

3. Inconvenient to convenient

Convenience is another word for time, and Generation Y has a low tolerance for spending time on things that *waste* time. To Gen Y, a car is no longer a convenience if it means a 20-minute trip to buy a quart of milk. This generation has grown up with the world at their fingertips, able to communicate within seconds around the world via technology. As such, they are programmed to get things instantly. Convenience really matters to Generation Y, and should be a priority consideration when interacting with this generation.

You have one, maybe two, chances with Generation Y before you burn the bridge. You have to make it easy to find information on the law firm, its people, achievements, and opportunities. The more information this generation can access, the easier you make the whole engagement process, and the more likely it is that you will engage this generation.

Clearly, Ys are informed, selective consumers (Recessionistas) and they are drawn to innovation, connectivity, and convenience (Migrators). They research every company they come into contact with, and they will do the same with your law firm.

Digital Natives

Generation Y is the first generation to have never known life without technology. We all know this to be true, but do we really comprehend what that means? It means this generation prefers to never be more than, literally, a few feet away from a technology device. It means this generation values access to technology more than dating. It means this generation considers access to technology a basic need, valuing it as much as freedom and oxygen on basic needs assessments.

Generation Y cannot fathom a life without technology because they have never known life without it. Simply put, if your law firm is not using technology in every aspect of the way it does business and interacts with employees, it is alienating this generation and completely irrelevant to them.

Digital Natives is a term used to describe Generation Y – the generation born into the digital technology era. The Digital Natives are emerging as the world's dominant demographic, while the generations that came of age during the analogue age – the Digital Immigrants – are getting smaller. As Digital Natives, Generation Y are more reliant on technology, more comfortable using technology, and tend to be among the first to try new technologies. The typical Gen Y owns multiple tech devices and constantly multitasks across these platforms.

As social creatures who have been networked and been encouraged to collaborate their entire lives, Generation Y loves being part of the global conversation that social media affords. As much as the baby boomers and other Digital Immigrants might want to ignore the glut of 'tweets' and 'likes' in the cloud, and dislike that Ys are actively sharing their selfies and opinions, social media must not be underestimated in its far-reaching capabilities.

The rapid pace at which Gen Ys share and distribute information with each other makes it all the more important for employers to engage employees in meaningful interactions that make them truly empowered participants, whether that means sharing photos, asking questions, or posting interesting news.

Trophy Kids

Parenting and teaching styles changed substantially in the 1990s, and Gen Ys were lavishly praised, and often received trophies, for their successes or contributions to avoid damaging their self-esteem. In fact, this generation was treated so delicately that many schoolteachers stopped grading papers and tests in harsh-looking red ink.

Their baby boomer parents aspired for the corner office and title of president and CEO, and they raised their children to do the same, placing a high premium on success, including academic accolades, philanthropy, sports, and other extracurricular activities. Generation Y was dubbed the "trophy generation" because they have always been rewarded for participation and not achievement. Not surprisingly, a generation raised receiving "trophies" just for showing up expect a significant return on investment from their employers and any other place where they spend their time. In the workplace, these "trophies" come in the form of feedback, attention, guidance, and opportunity – all of which are relationship-based.

It is difficult to foster an emotional commitment to your law firm and its mission when any of the following hurdles stand in the way.

1. Distrust

During the past 40 years, trust in each other and many institutions has been dropping steadily. These years were marked by events that furthered distrust – like junk bonds, Monica Lewinsky, Enron, Catholic Church sex scandals, September 11, and the Iraq War. Gen Ys have come of age during the worst recession in 70 years, graduated with insurmountable amounts of debt, and they have been raised in a media-saturated world observing in great detail the nation's leaders lie and fail to deliver on their promises. As a result, Gen Ys don't readily trust. You have to earn their trust. So, be transparent and avoid keeping all of your board's meetings and decisions private. And if you commit to doing something, do it. No excuses.

2. Hierarchy

Generation Y employees want to feel like a part of the community from day one, rather than this being something they have to work hard at achieving by "paying their dues", figuratively or literally. Law firms are notorious for fostering a "good ol' boys club" culture based on who you know and what you have achieved. If you are holding your young employees back simply because they have not been practicing for more than 20 years, you are in essence telling them that they are just a number, simply paying their dues, and taking up a seat. Remember, this generation was told by their parents that they can do anything they set their minds to. Holding them back from that potential will confuse, frustrate, and alienate Generation Y.

3. Minimal ROI

In the past, it was enough to provide great benefits and a partner opportunity. That era is long gone. This generation has access to more information, contacts, products, services, and education than any other generation. They have always been rewarded for participation, they are the most entrepreneurial generation in history, and also the most supervised generation. Needless to say, this generation is going to expect great things in return for their time and resources, depending on an emotional commitment to both the law firm and the firm's mission.

Generation Y won't be content just to have a transactional relationship with your law firm simply for the sake of being affiliated and part of your community; to the "trophy kids", the return on investment has to be great, and it starts with a meaningful relationship.

Change isn't easy. It also isn't optional.

This year, Generation Y becomes the majority of the workforce. This generation's move into power is already spurring shifts, but we are nowhere near the end. In fact, we are likely to see a great global redistribution of economic and social power in the near future, as power moves away from traditional institutions that have failed to deliver progress and towards the organization whose leaders understand and act on the big trends shaping our future. In other words, the phrase "change or die" is more accurate than ever before.

Take a cue from the New York police experiment. In the 1990s, the New York Police Commissioner made his top brass – including himself – ride the subways day and night, to understand why frightened New Yorkers had come to call it the "electric sewer". The point is, you can advocate for change until you're blue in the face, but lecturing doesn't always work.

The purpose of this chapter is to help you learn more about Generation Y, but you really need to know Y for yourself to know why they are not engaging with your law firm. In the next 30 days, look for ways to get the decision makers to experience the harsh realities that make change necessary. Start by bringing the partners face to face with students and young professionals.

Challenge the partners to hold 30 conversations with 30 people who are from Generation Y – ages 20–33 – and ask each Y the following questions:

- What organizations do you admire and why?
- What are your greatest professional challenges?
- If you could create an ideal employee experience, what would it be like?
- What one word would you use to describe success?

Document the conversations on a spreadsheet and, at the end of 30 days, the stakeholders meet to share their findings and ascertain the best path for going forward. This is the best way to familiarize leaders with the future majority and start the relationship-building process. To succeed in the future, leaders must be able to see the law firm through the eyes of a Gen Y.

I think the ancient philosopher, Lao Tzu, said it best: "If you do not change direction, you may end up where you are heading." Do you simply wish for change to happen, or is your firm being intentional about making it happen? I hope, for the sake of your law firm, it's the latter. Because if you know anything about Generation Y, you know change is needed – and time is running out.

This first appeared as Chapter 3 in Slater, L. (ed.), Generation Shift: Recruiting, Managing, and Retaining the Millennial Lawyer, *ARK Group, 2015.*

Part 4:
Finance and pricing

Chapter 19: Establishing appropriate cash and lockup profiles for teams and departments

By Barry Wilkinson, senior partner at Wilkinson Read LLP

There is a difference between setting performance indicators and key results objectives at firm-wide level and at departmental or product level. In the interests of prudent balance sheet management, it may be appropriate to say, for example, that the firm overall targets a lockup level of 120 days. At a departmental level, this is inappropriate. This target may be far too much, or it may be far too little. In the case of residential conveyancing, a lockup level of four months would be excessive. In the case of clinical negligence, where cases can last for years, it would be hopelessly unachievable. So, targets and objectives need to be set at a level which is appropriate to the kind of work being undertaken, and the terms on which it can be completed and billed.

The Practice Profit Pipeline

In order to establish appropriate targets for any kind of work, it is necessary to understand the working capital aspect of that work in one of two ways. Working capital is often explained in terms of a cycle but, for these purposes, I have found that the concept of the Practice Profit Pipeline is more readily understood by partners, fee earners, and most other staff in the law firm.

The Practice Profit Pipeline starts from the premise that there are five stages in the process of adding value in a law firm. They are:

- Get a client;
- Get instructions from the client;
- Do the work;
- Bill; and
- Collect.

For the purposes of cash management, the pipeline starts from the receipt of instructions. The pipeline can be displayed graphically with the length of the pipeline indicating time elapsed. It can therefore be observed that residential conveyancing should typically have a pipeline length of three months, commercial property transactions typically a little longer, and litigation can have very long pipelines and, as a subset, personal injury and clinical negligence can be even longer. From the point of view of target setting, it is reasonable to assume that at any point in time, matters on average will be half-way through the pipeline and therefore an overall target can be set as half the multiple of the monthly capacity of the department (hour x rate, or matters x price), or the average time elapsed, from instruction to bill (in months).

The value of lockup can be reduced in three ways: by more efficient billing, by interim billing, and by funding arrangements (or a combination of the above). In business-to-business transactions, unless there is good reason to do otherwise, interim billing should be the norm and the standard period of interim billing can determine the lockup target.

The value of the pipeline as a concept can be illustrated by looking at the case of family/divorce ancillary relief work. These cases can run for some time and it has historically been the view that an attorney would only collect their cash at the point where the main family assets (often the house) were sold. Historically, this acted as a disincentive to fee earners to actually do the billing, especially as tax would be payable on bills. The next development was for bills to be raised, but little effort was put into the collection process until the asset was sold. All this accomplished was to move the value of lockup from work in progress (WIP) to debtors – it did not actually do anything to improve the cash flow or shorten the pipeline. More recently, firms have taken to introducing the client to bank/funding arrangements whereby bills can be raised and the lender would lend against the value of the asset. In these circumstances, it actually becomes worthwhile to the firm to interim bill. Thus, while the pipeline provides the starting point, it needs to be overlaid by consideration of terms and conditions, adherence to billing practices, and access to funding arrangements.

Work type	Standard instruction to completion	Disbursements	Interim billing	Payment terms	Maximum payment period before recovery/ cessation of work
Residential conveyancing	3 months	On deposit only	No	On completion	7 days
Family – divorce	12 months	On deposit only	Yes – every 2 months	1 month	2 months
Employment – employer	6 months	Monthly account	Yes – every 2 months	2 month	2 months
Employment – employee	6 months	On deposit only	Yes – every 2 months	1 month	1 month

Note: These examples are clearly neither exhaustive nor definitive. They illustrate the use of time elapsed as a key measure in distinguishing (and controlling) acceptable lockup from the unacceptable.

Table 1: Sample standards

The concept of standards

When is a target not a target? The answer is when it is a standard. One of the most important aspects of managing law firm performance, client satisfaction, as well as cash flow, is the management of time elapsed. It is possible to break down the pipeline into a series of steps and to identify, for each kind of work, how long each of those steps should reasonably take and to incorporate this as a standard. For example, a firm may say in its terms and conditions that it will raise interim bills every 60 days. It is then incumbent upon the partners/fee earners to review their files every 60 days and raise the appropriate bills. Internally, this could be expressed as a target. However, there is a tendency for targets to be considered as aspirational and, provided that they are achieved on average, for that to be considered good enough. But averages incorporate individual items which are both better and worse than the level set. So there will be some items which do not conform.

While there are some kinds of firm – for example those which are high-volume, low-value transaction processors – where the concept of targets is very well embedded, the use of the term "standards" is preferable for fee-earning professionals. In this context, it should not be said that the target is to bill every 60 days, but that the *standard* is to bill every 60 days. This is not simply a matter of semantics because it impacts on the way in which performance is quantitatively managed.

If there is a concept of standards, there is also then a concept of exceptions, i.e. those items which have not conformed to the standard. If management is then orientated to the elimination of exceptions, a situation can be reached whereby every transaction proceeds at the standard level or better – and by doing so, the average achieved performance can actually be reduced to a quicker level than the standard! This has a direct influence on cash flow.

It is up to every firm to set its own standards in accordance with the work types and client types with which they are dealing. If the firm wants to improve its cash flow and its business performance generally, then it should start by reviewing its operating standards throughout the pipeline and identify areas where time elapsed can be reduced. Wherever possible, firms should also look not so much at departments but at work types, and make use of detailed work type coding on the IT system.

Experience has shown that most firms look to set cash flow and lockup targets by department but even by sub-coding items as, for example, road traffic accidents, it would still not always be possible to identify the relevant cash flows. Setting the target lockup also requires an understanding of the business strategy involved in the department. If, for example, a target level of lockup of one year or less was set for a personal injury department, it would mean that the firm would probably seek to pass on catastrophic work. However, assuming that the number of catastrophic claims was relatively few, it becomes statistically relatively straightforward to identify the whole of the personal injury pipeline. This should be a question of taking the volume of each type of case, multiplying by the average value, multiplying by the average length of pipeline, and working on the statistical premise that, on average, matters would be half-way through the pipeline.

Market situation

It has already been said that there should be standards for each kind of work so that, for example, one may look at a typical commercial practice and say that it should have a maximum of two months' WIP and two months' debtors (60 days plus 60 days equals a total lockup of 120 days). Given the state of the market in recent years, there has been a greater emphasis on implementing more stringent procedures for lockup management, particularly including credit control and debt collection so that this should, by itself, drive down the average lockup periods.

Unfortunately, the recession also provided an excuse/reason for many clients to find methods of extending payment – and they prioritized their available cash to pay those suppliers who were most critical to them. This does not always include their lawyers. While the recession may have receded, many clients have maintained their more lax approach. The fact that times are tough should not be used as an excuse for firms to compromise on their collection and recovery standards. In fact, the converse is true; it should be used as a reason for enforcing internal disciplines more strongly.

The issue of mix

One of the reasons for reviewing lockup profiles on a work type basis and managing accordingly is that changes in the mix of business can have a substantial effect on the cash collection and lockup profiles. In the UK, for example, many firms have had an "endowment" of rapid turnover, short pipeline property work – whether in the residential or commercial sectors. These matters were often payable on completion, and in many cases, the transactions progressed very rapidly. The financial recession and consequent decline of transactional property work not only hit the short term cash flow of firms, but it has also fundamentally changed the profile and mix – by removing the quick turnover, short lockup property work and the average lockup periods for the firm as a whole have extended, and this has merely highlighted in many firms the lack of discipline in managing lockup in other kinds of work. This leads into other questions, including balancing the work portfolio and looking at the relevant funding structures.

Client mix

One of the least considered areas in lockup profiling is that of client profiling. For example, there may be repeat clients who would expect to be billed on a regular (monthly) basis. By including the client profiles in the team's lockup profiles it is possible to achieve lower levels of lockup.

Specific exceptions

There are, however, some kinds of work where the firm has little opportunity to proactively manage the process. There are also specific markets where prompt payment is the exception – for example, those firms dealing with Italian business are aware of payment practices being very slow!

Targets

Target setting is an area of much debate. In our consultancy work, we have used a number of approaches over the years, and in the course of recent research, we have encountered more variety than we would have expected.

Targets for lockup

The first point in this context has been to establish whether firms set lockup targets at all. The vast majority of firms set targets for chargeable hours; most set targets for bills raised. Until recently, only a minority of firms actually set formal lockup targets and few fee earners take the lockup target as seriously as the billing or chargeable hours targets. Many rightly see that the partners' focus is on fees, not cash, and when forced to choose, they opt for tradition. For most staff the ultimate question is: "Will missing this target cost me my job/bonus?" This is rarely the case with lockup targets. This has been a surprise and has not necessarily been related directly to the size of firm, although financial disciplines in larger firms have been generally stronger than in the medium sized ones.

Work in progress, debtors, or both?

The second question on which there has been an almost even split in our research is whether the targets should be set for lockup as a whole, or separately for WIP, debtors, and disbursements. As a result of the research, our opinion has hardened. The best way is to set separate targets for WIP and debtors – the most compelling arguments being:

- By putting the emphasis on minimizing WIP, all of the issues become visible – and you cannot manage something unless you can see it. Visibility is much greater once something has been billed, both internally and to the clients;
- The second reason for targeting WIP and debtors separately is supported by the belief that in many large clients, the accounts payable function (the converse of credit control) is the least resourced, with the least qualified staff in the accounting functions.

> This is not thought to be an accident – one respondent describes the behavior of some major clients' accounts payable process as being "institutionally incompetent". This summarizes the client response as: "We do not want to not pay you; it's just that we are not very good at pushing payments through the system."

With funding still tight, the incentive for clients to be incompetent, slower in paying, and for finding ever-more excuses for deferring the process will only multiply. Therefore, getting the value of the transaction into the visible domain – by billing it – means that the overall process will be quicker. Individual targets should thus be set, work-type by work-type, based on the number of days of work outstanding. With a very important rider: The value of exceptions to the departmental standards will be monitored and strict limits will be placed on the proportion which is allowed to operate outside the standard set, both for debtors and WIP.

This first appeared as Chapter 3 in Wilkinson, B., Cash Flow Management for Law Firms, 2nd edition, *ARK Group, 2014.*

Chapter 20:
Practical strategies for improving cash flow – Partners and communication

By Barry Wilkinson, senior partner at Wilkinson Read LLP

There are many reasons for the repeated underperformance of law firms in their cash management, and the lack of sophistication of financial management techniques and the comparative backwardness of financial/cash management in law firms has been addressed elsewhere. So, there are plenty of opportunities to make improvement through changing processes, and they will, in most circumstances, produce significant return on effort. However, technique and process are very much secondary to the will and commitment of the partners. Simple techniques, implemented consistently and with determination by a united partnership, will achieve excellent results and the levels of lockup will permit very low borrowings and a degree of financial freedom and freedom of action that will be denied to other firms.

Sophisticated techniques implemented against a backdrop of disunited, recalcitrant partners will achieve some results, but not so much as a united partnership, and they may not prove to be sustainable as the entrepreneurial creativity of the partners will find ways of overcoming the carefully designed processes of the management board and finance function. It is therefore absolutely crucial that the "soft" issues are addressed at the outset and are treated as fundamental to the project in itself.

As human resources professionals say: "Do not change what they do; change how they think". Lawyers are highly intelligent and usually strong-minded people. They do not like to be told what to do. So, the benefits of high-quality, consistent, and systematic cash management need to be sold to them, and they have to become largely willing buyers of the concept.

The "free rider" problem

The market is tough and some firms are struggling. Most partners, in most firms, will want to do everything reasonable to protect their drawings and standard of living. This is only natural. Most partners will agree that the firm has to adapt to the changed circumstances and that, therefore, some change within the firm will be necessary. Many partners would also prefer that everyone else in the firm changed and that they were allowed to continue in broadly the same way as before. Although similar to most other people, partners do not object to change per se, they object to being changed. One of the benefits of being a partner in most firms is that there is a considerable freedom of action to conduct a practice within a practice and, in many firms, however detailed the partnership agreement, the operational practices can vary significantly at a detailed level. This means that many initiatives in partnerships fail because of the "free rider" problem. This can be best expressed as "there are 50 partners in this partnership and so if I do not 100 percent commit to this initiative, it will still succeed if the other 49 do".

There are two problems with this. One is that if there is not a cast iron commitment on behalf of all partners, the likelihood that only one is not committed is very slim. In fact, the other 49 could have reservations and therefore the initiative will fall flat on its face. In practice, there will be a spectrum. However, the effect goes further than this because partners are looked up to by all the other fee earners and staff, and they take their lead not from what the partners say, but from what they do. So, if the partners decide to ignore an initiative or a directive, many of the other fee earners and staff will do the same, and the partners can hardly object if their staff follow their example. This issue, therefore, needs to be recognized upfront and a means of overcoming it must be found.

A range of attributes

There is good news here. Everything in life is relative and, in tough times, some of the adjustments that firms have to make can be very painful. By and large, improving cash flow management is not particularly painful – it may just be an irritant. Therefore, a cash management program can be sold to the partners partly on the basis that it is the best of an unpalatable set of alternatives.

It used to be the case that a law firm could succeed by having very good lawyers. Increasingly however, other than the few niche pockets, legal expertise has become a necessary but not sufficient condition for a prosperous practice. The prosperous practice needs to be good at three things: lawyer, manager, and rainmaker. We have used a simple diagnostic technique with law firm partners for a number of years and asked them to rate their abilities (both themselves and their firm) for each of those three attributes on a scale from 1 to 10. Almost invariably, the self-appraisal of legal skills will be at least 8 out of 10 (the exceptions being the more entrepreneurial, business-oriented lawyers who really do run successful firms). On the same scale, rainmaking abilities among individual partners can vary from 1 to 10, but so long as the firm has enough high performing rainmakers, it can succeed. Very rarely indeed do we see firms who rate their managerial standard as high as their legal standard. This is not surprising. Historically, the consequences of a modest performance in management, particularly cash management, have not been terribly serious. If a firm was inherently profitable and bringing in business, it could always borrow more money from the bank, and therefore they have adopted the perfectly reasonable posture that their cash management has been as good as it needed to be. If 5 out of 10 was good enough to keep the banks happy and to keep the drawings flowing, then 5 out of 10 would be the standard aspired to.

The new standards

The world has changed. The required standard of performance – even for survival, never mind for prosperity – is much higher than it used to be, and it is rising even further. The time will come when law firms need to be as good in their business management (including sales and marketing, as well as cash management) as they are in their technical expertise. A rating of 8 out of 10 in cash management may become a practical necessity for the flow of drawings to continue into the medium-term future.

Therefore, a cash management program needs to be "sold" to the partners on the basis that it is part of the firm achieving a consistently high standard of performance across all of its activities, not only their technical abilities. Generally speaking, the concept of professional standards has a positive connotation with most professionals; the concept of extending the culture of professionalism across the whole of the firm's activity is hard to criticize if properly presented.

Preparation

If partners are to be persuaded to willingly undertake a cash management program, the preparation and subsequent selling process need to be carefully thought through.

Scale of the problem

The first step is to establish the scale of the potential problem. The easiest way to do this is to do a cash flow projection on the basis that the firm continues broadly as it is and that no particular improvements are anticipated other than the success of existing initiatives and business programs – and the success of these should be factored in relative to the success of similar past initiatives. If this is done over a three to five year forecast timeframe, probably 12 months in detail and subsequent years in outline, the capital requirements and drawings limitations can be reasonably quantified. This identifies the scale of the potential problem.

Sources of opportunity

The next step is to do a very rapid, even subjective, assessment of the current state of play. There may be several underlying reasons why cash management may not be as good as it needs to be. A simple way to identify the underlying issues is to apply a traffic light system. Green is good enough; yellow is not particularly good, but not a major problem; and red is a major issue.

Scale of opportunity

The next step is to do a simple Pipeline Performance Report extract by department highlighting all WIP and debtors and disbursements which are over, say, 60 days old.

Using the Pipeline Performance Report, estimate what the levels of lockup could reasonably be expected to be if the firm actively managed its cash and lockup. A very simple rule of thumb for this would be to halve the level of overdue lockup.

Then estimate what impact this would have on the medium term capital requirement. This should give sufficient information in the first instance to explain to partners both the scale of the problem and the scale of the opportunity. At this point, the issue of "how" has not been addressed.

Sounding out lenders

It is also worth at this point having an informal discussion with the bank and seeking to establish what their current lending criteria for lawyers are. Preface this discussion with a comment such as: "We are doing an exercise looking into the future to see what our capital requirements are likely to be over the next three to five years and, before I get the partners to commit to any sort of specific programs, I thought it would be useful for me to be able to tell them what is the bank's view in the current market."

This will impress the bank. Communication is the biggest single bugbear that banks have about their law firm clients. Secondly, they will feel comforted that the firm is at least taking a positive and pro-active look at the future, even though at this point you have not actually committed to do anything. This also strengthens the finance director/managing partner's hand in putting proposals to the partners because you have already sounded out the bank as to what are the acceptable parameters and therefore what restrictions the partners will have to accept.

Alternatives

The next step is to do a series of "what-if" alternative projections based on potential scenarios which may develop – lockup reductions, recapitalization, changes to drawing profiles, changes to the work-type portfolio etc. From this you should be able to identify a top-10 list of changes which are worth implementing, based either on their ease and simplicity and/or the extent of their potential pay-off.

The "reason why"

Change does not happen without a "reason why". Human beings run a simple calculation through their head; if the consequences of inaction are less than the costs and disruption of taking action and making change, change will not happen – "it is not worth it to me". This calculation causes problems in corporate entities. It causes far bigger problems in partnerships because every partner will be doing the same calculation from their own individual perspective. While in larger firms it may not be possible to get the calculation to have a positive balance for every single partner, it has to be worthwhile for the firm as a whole and the most senior, productive, and influential partners. Those who will see a significantly negative balance need to have their objections and concerns addressed and minimized.

The first step

The first step in establishing the "reason why" is a very simple if time-consuming one. Talk to the partners individually. Partners may have concerns of their own, whether or not they have already expressed them, and it is important to get them on board by empathizing with their concerns, finding out what their views are, and explaining that some formal analysis is being done and a range of options is being considered which will help to address whatever their particular concerns happen to be. This does not only involve talking to them, but also listening to them carefully and getting their thoughts, ideas, and their input. Let them understand that their ideas are being taken very seriously; there is a great deal of evidence in the field of change management that people are far more ready to accept change if they feel that they have been involved, however peripherally, in the development of the changes.

In the case of lawyers, there is particularly good reason for listening to them. While they may not be sophisticated financial managers, they are very intelligent people, often with very incisive minds and some very good ideas may actually be gathered from them to put into the melting pot.

It is also worth taking the time to ask them what kind of changes would be "a step too far", and even floating some red herrings and saying "one suggestion that has been made is..." and gauging the response. It is commonplace that in a partnership, politics can regularly outweigh economics. Even in tough times, when economics usually triumphs over politics, it cannot be expected that every suggestion, however apparently financially sensible, will be acceptable to the partners and the partnership.

Enlisting support

Key individuals

At this point, if the work so far has been done by the head of finance, the task is to get the managing partner and senior partner on board. There are three main financial tools at one's disposal to start with: the cash flow projections on unchanged assumptions (which identifies the scale of the problem); the Pipeline Performance Report (which identifies the scale of opportunities); and some what-if projections (which highlight some potential routes forward).

This must be talked through with the managing partner and senior partner, and their thoughts, ideas, and input should be obtained in order to make any necessary tweaks to the information gained so far. A key part of the discussion with the most senior people is to identify what they think are likely to be the main objections which will be put forward and the main stumbling blocks to action. This may seem a counter-intuitive thing to do but, as any sales trainer will say, overcoming objections is part of the sales process, and anticipating objections is a useful preliminary to this. From earlier discussions with friendly partners, there will already be an idea of the "steps too far". These should be explicitly raised with the senior and managing partners to gauge their reaction.

Force field analysis

At this point, if there are more than a handful of partners in the firm it is worth doing a simple "force field analysis', as in Figure 1.

There are two main steps to this analysis. First, it involves taking a piece of paper and drawing a line down the middle. This represents a neutral position. To the left, a scale of negative sentiment must be created, and to the right a scale of positive sentiment. The first step then is to try to position each of the key decision makers as to where they are likely to sit on the scale of sentiment: will they be broadly in favor, extremely in favor, or to some degree negative? If the proposals have any real merit, it is reasonable to expect that a majority of the partnership decision makers will be on the positive side of the scale. If not, there is a real problem. The next step is to individually identify all of those who are to the left of center, i.e. in the negative spectrum. An assessment is then required not only on the extent of likely objections, but what actions may need to be taken, even what concessions may need to be made to get the most important people into the positive zone. There may be some people who are irredeemably in the negative zone, and if they are likely to act as major obstructions to the cash management program, which will be fundamental to the future of the firm, then the managing partner and senior partner have to consider how to address those individuals. This is not necessarily territory for the finance manager.

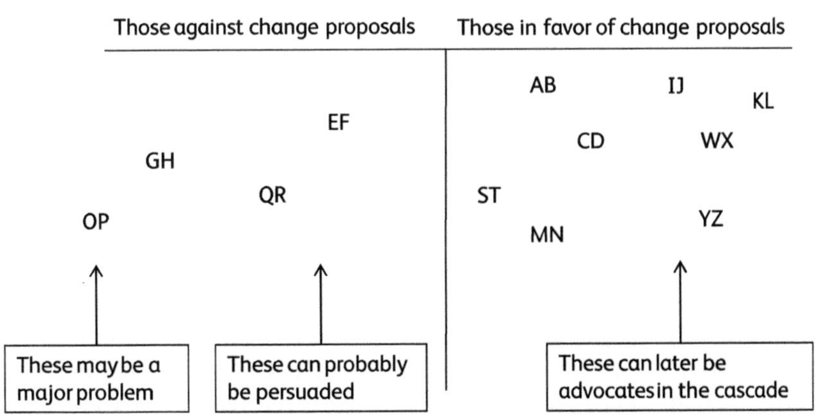

Figure 1: Force field analysis

Consider options

At this stage, it is also worth pursuing the range of acceptable levels of capital requirement with the managing partner and senior partner and to consider ways in which these might be met, other than a straight lockup reduction program. It may be that this is the point where a review of work type portfolios may need to be unde taken. Again, it is perfectly valid for the finance team to identify the cash impacts of the taking on of new work types or the demise of existing work types, but it is best to avoid the politics of it.

Dependent upon the structure of the firm, it may well be necessary to go through a repeat of the managing partner/senior partner process with the management board. There will doubtless be iterations, but if the first soundings have been done effectively there should not be fundamental change.

The wider partnership

The next step is to get the partners on board. This will almost certainly require a partners' meeting, and quite probably a single-issue meeting. There will need to be a presentation to the partners in general, and at the very least this should be a joint presentation by the managing partner and the head of finance.

Partners would not normally expect the managing partner to be a financial technician, but the core of the subject is not about financial technique. It is about preparing commercially sensible responses to the market situation. However evangelical the finance director may feel about the subject of cash management, this is not the time for evangelism. The proposals should be presented as "responding to the market" and to the changed circumstances, and particularly the changing nature of relationships with banks and providers of finance.

Presentation and communication

The presentation should be carefully constructed and rehearsed. The focus should be on clear communication, avoiding clutter. There will be some partners who will want to question the calculations as to future cash flow assumptions, but this is not a question of whether you can do arithmetic. This is about winning hearts and minds. If, as is very likely, the implications of doing nothing are adverse, then the costs of doing nothing should be clearly spelled out. There is a natural inertia in the partnership decision-making process and this has to be overcome, so it is necessary to be explicit. It is also very useful to have a list of at least 10 actions and changes which may need to be made. In our experience, it has been very rare for any partnership to accept all 10 recommendations. One should not be surprised if the partners add one or two additional recommendations of their own. It is again worth exploring likely anticipated objections from elsewhere in the firm. These could be expressed by proxy – "I am not objecting, but I can see some of the fee earners would have a problem with…". If the answers are not ready, it must be undertaken to come back with a suitable response that will overcome any significant issues.

Commitment and process

There will be some partners who want to focus attention on the process changes rather than the issue of commitment. Great pains must be taken to explain the limitations of process alone – this will not come as a great surprise to most of them. Many partners are entrepreneurs and entrepreneurs generally have little regard for process. The free rider issue must therefore be pointed out, as must the need for all partners to commit to applying the agreed policies on a consistent basis. It may never happen, but it needs to be explicit.

Program leadership

It is then necessary to move into some of the specifics of the program. The program will need a figurehead, and this should almost always be the managing partner. It is remarkable how often staff respond to what they see as the managing partner's biggest issue. It may be that the managing partner is "program sponsor" and that the finance director is the program manager. It is worth establishing the authority vested in the finance director to carry out the agreed program activities.

It is best to have the practical elements of a cash management program which primarily includes reducing lockup separately, by actions to reduce WIP and debtors – disbursements tend to be an afterthought.

Dependent on the structure of the firm, it may be worth having one partner overseeing the WIP reduction and either a separate partner or the finance director overseeing the debtor reduction program. It will be worth having a simple progress reporting regime which focuses on the level of lockup as per the example in Table 1. It is probably best for the finance director to work primarily through the heads of department/equity partners to achieve the requisite response in each department or practice group rather than be seen to be the driver of the program. Lawyers respond best to other lawyers. In larger firms, the responsibility for ensuring that salaried partners and other fee earners perform

	Work in progress				Debtors				Disbursements		
Date	3 months and under	4–12 months	Over 12 months	Total WIP	3 months and under	4–12 months	Over 12 months	Total WIP	Total disbursement	Total lockup	End of week overdraft
Week 1	£5,397	£6,685	£3,656	£15,738	£4,809	£2,246	£2,097	£9,152	£1,053	£25,943	£8,625
Week 2	£5,182	£6,662	£3,468	£15,313	£4,985	£2,123	£2,090	£9,199	£1,054	£25,565	£8,707
Week 3	£4,967	£6,640	£3,280	£14,887	£4,801	£2,078	£2,081	£8,960	£1,055	£24,902	£8,469
Week 4	£5,148	£6,457	£3,217	£14,822	£4,832	£2,292	£2,005	£9,130	£1,056	£25,008	£8,638
Week 5	£5,389	£6,369	£3,056	£14,814	£4,194	£2,237	£1,963	£8,395	£1,057	£24,265	£7,903
Week 6	£5,333	£6,270	£3,036	£14,639	£3,972	£1,984	£1,968	£7,925	£1,058	£23,622	£7,433
Week 7	£5,731	£6,163	£2,823	£14,716	£3,835	£1,994	£1,949	£7,778	£1,059	£23,554	£7,287
Movement since start of project	£333	-£523	-£833	-£1,022	-£973	-£252	-£148	-£1,373	£6	-£2,390	-£1,338

Table 1: A simple progress reporting regime

as required should rest with the equity partner/head of department – a form of cascade process is needed. Partners' time is scarce, however important the issue, and so there should be a simple "summary and exception" reporting format which allows the program management group to keep tabs on progress and address any issues as they arise. Regular minuted meetings may be needed for a short while, but certainly for no longer than the project phase is in operation.

Other actions

Part of the rationale for undertaking an active program of lockup reduction and cash management is to minimize the need for more unpleasant changes in response to market circumstances. Such changes could include reducing the drawings regime, introducing additional partner capital, and making changes to the portfolio of work type, potentially shedding whole teams or departments. Dependent upon the severity of the firm's position, it may be best to defer consideration of these matters until the lockup reduction program has had the opportunity to have its early impact.

Many managing partners would, however, take the opposite view that the opportunities to make the sort of change which is desirable but politically unpalatable only come along rarely. And when such opportunities do come along, they have to be taken with both hands. So it may be that changes to product portfolio, drawings, capital structures, etc. are incorporated at the same time in any case. This is the time to establish whether any alternative methods of funding the capital requirement are needed.

Documentation

It is also imperative that the resource implications of the project part of the cash management program are made explicit and understood, particularly if these involve secondments or specific allocations of fee earner time to cash raising. Lack of resource almost certainly will lead to lack of result. Obviously, at a partners' meeting to agree such fundamental changes as have been described, full minutes will be taken. However, one very useful suggestion is that one of the outputs of the meeting should be a form of supplement to the partnership agreement, addressing the issues of lockup and cash management, which should be agreed and countersigned by all of the partners. This will serve to reduce misunderstandings and make it easier to counter the free rider problem as and when it emerges – as it almost inevitably will.

Preparing to implement

A rapid start

With luck, the presentation will have been a success and partners will be keen to get moving and implement the lockup reduction, doubtless relieved that far more difficult changes can be (largely) avoided. The firm should be in a position to start some simple actions which focus on billing and collection very rapidly. These need not wait for any formal process changes, although all should be advised that these will follow.

Initial communication

The most important thing to do is to get the managing partner to write to everyone in the firm, explaining about the lockup reduction/ cash management program. This includes support staff, obviously including the finance team who will be intimately involved, but also secretaries and others. It should be possible to craft a suitably positive message which says: "We are responding to the market conditions by taking a set of positive actions which will help to safeguard our future prosperity and minimize the need for more painful actions. We need everybody to be on board and all of the partners have agreed to sign an undertaking to keep to the new arrangements." Staff are adults and need to be treated as such, and most of them will find some positive messages in that kind of communication. By going public (within the firm) about such a program, you will also start to create a degree of upward pressure, whereby secretaries can then be enlisted to look for opportunities to bill outstanding matters or have a conversation with the client's secretary about any outstanding bills. Getting everyone involved in the process, even if only to a limited extent, can pay great dividends.

First actions

There are two absolutely key documents in the next step. They are the aged debtor report and its sister, the aged WIP report (available on most but not all practice management systems). In time, it will be possible to modify the report outputs from the main IT system, possibly downloading them into Excel and presenting them in a user-friendly format. In the short term, and in order to maintain momentum, every fee earner should receive, preferably via their head of department, a copy of the aged debtor report which shows matters outstanding with two columns appended, generally to the right-hand side, asking two very pointed questions:

- Why has this not been paid?
- When will it be paid?

There should be a covering email for each fee earner which says that these questions should be answered for all matters over 60 days old, and of an outstanding value greater than a threshold. Obviously, the threshold will depend on the size of firm and the nature of work, but it should be sufficient to cover Pareto's 80 percent of the outstanding overdue value. The email should ask for the document to be completed and returned to the head of department/departmental champion within a week. Two further points should be made very clear: first, that the preferred response next week is that the matter has been paid already; and second, that these matters will be revisited a fortnight later to see if commitments and promises have been kept. These follow-ups should be adhered to. The effectiveness of the follow-up process can be extremely surprising.

An almost identical process should be followed on the aged WIP, with two variations:

- There should be an additional question: "What is this WIP really worth?" Work in progress systems have a habit, in firms large and small, of not being entirely accurate; and
- The timing questions should be: "When will the matter be billed?" and "When will it be collected?"

The same rules about materiality apply, and the same rules about follow-up process also apply. The above process and formats have some very clear attributes:

- They are extremely quick and effective and require little or no changes for immediate implementation;
- The results belie the simplicity. They are always good, and occasionally staggering; and
- It is cumbersome, low-tech, and administratively inconvenient.
- The benefits far outweigh the negatives, but it is sensible to automate and systemize the documentation and improve the designs as quickly as the IT department can act.

The role of finance

One of the key features of the process described above to quickly address aged debtors and WIP is that it should be treated as a cascade from the managing partner, through heads of department/practice group leaders and on to other fee earners. Finance should not be seen as leaders in this process. They should be providing administrative support, advice, resolution of queries and, if needs be, coordinating and collating documents and producing notes for follow-up. They should very clearly be portrayed as supporting the partners, not driving the firm into actions on their own account.

Process and training

It may well occur that one of the outputs from the partners' meeting is a change to the business processes such as to the billing and collection processes. It may even be that they are defined for the first time.

It will be a job for the finance team to document the new processes, to draft any new information formats, any new chasing letters or scripts, and to arrange for these to be produced from the IT systems. It will also be necessary to follow up the managing partner and head of department initiatives by briefing and training fee earners and secretaries accordingly.

While there may be some changes to the billing processes, most of the changes are likely to appear in the credit control, collection, and recovery processes. This will involve communicating with clients and asking for money. Whether this is to be done by partners, fee earners, secretaries, or accounts/credit control staff, it needs to be done professionally and consistently, and in a way that will not antagonize the client. It should not be assumed that any of these individuals is automatically capable of holding successful cash-producing dialogue. Basic training and identification of traps for the unwary is a very worthwhile modest investment.

The process will now be underway. Results will emerge with some surprises, including some pleasant surprises amongst them. However, before long there will also be problems emerging. There will be difficult clients; there will be debts; and, more particularly, WIP which quite clearly need to be written-down or written-off. This needs to be faced up to and appropriate action taken as a result. At least the improving cash flow will mean that the write-offs can more easily be accommodated.

Empathy and support

However, different partners will have different experiences and will come up against different stumbling blocks. This is the point at which the finance director's ability to communicate with the partners and empathize with their difficulties is most crucial. The mindset of the finance team as a whole needs to be that of helpers and facilitators. Often in law firms, the task of the finance team is to monitor compliance and to act as policemen. This is entirely inappropriate for this kind of program. If that means that the furniture needs to be rearranged, and the helpful part of the finance team separated from the policemen, so be it. Partners and fee earners should be in no doubt that the finance function is trying to help them to flush cash through their practice pipeline and into the bank. Wherever possible, the emphasis must be on what can be done, how things can be resolved, rather than on what cannot be done.

Inevitably, the finance director's time will become overstretched at this point, and so they should do their own Pareto analysis and identify where the highest value is likely to result from the use of their time – this may be in the biggest fee-earning areas, or it may be in those with the highest-value clients, but more likely it will be in those areas where there are the biggest blockages in the pipeline and where obstructions need to be overcome – not always external.

It is important that empathy exists, that the partners are supported, and that constructive solutions are found. The rule is to spend time where there is the biggest opportunity, and not to get dragged into trivial or lesser problems.

Tracking mechanism

There needs to be a simple tracking mechanism to show progress, probably on a weekly basis, on lockup levels, debtors, WIP, and disbursements. The high-level, firm-wide information should be available very quickly and should be issued via the managing partner so that everyone in the firm knows that he is keeping a personal eye on progress, certainly for the first few weeks. It is probably also worth, in the major high-value teams/departments, having progress reports prepared for them to use in their team meetings.

In general, it is best to maintain a positive tone to the program and to celebrate successes. However, the carrot alone will not do the job and a policy of "naming and shaming" by published exception reports will be needed. Publication should certainly extend to all partners. Reports should show the value of WIP and debtors over the standard (say 60 days) by department/practice group and, in addition, it is worth having, for partners' circulation, a league table showing the highest problem debtors – again, those which are over the standard level.

One of the most important elements in achieving real results is to create and harness a degree of peer pressure. Several respondents when surveyed felt that this was the most telling element in the successes achieved in their firm. Managing partners and finance directors tended to underplay their own contribution and give the credit to some of the hungrier entrepreneurial partners who have taken cash management on board as a key part of their role. In order to achieve this, there needs to be a process of publication, followed by a semi-public "comply or explain" process.

Managing exceptions

It is likely that the positive measures outlined earlier will produce a significant improvement in results. However, it would be fanciful to believe that success will be achieved in all areas, and exceptions should be anticipated, and preparations made to act accordingly. It would be unreasonable to expect immediate success in all areas, hence the need for progress tracking, but as soon as it becomes apparent that a particular partner/team is making little tangible effort to improve cash flow there should be clear unequivocal warnings from the top, and there should be a sequence of sanctions to be used if improvement is not forthcoming.

Sanctions

Most firms who have successfully employed a sanctions regime appear to have linked the payment of prior years' undrawn profits to the achievement of lockup objectives by individual partners. Others go a step further and withhold the current year's drawings. There is a clear division of opinion on this subject. In many firms, it is felt that the threat of withholding drawings only has to be carried out once for it to be effective, and not solely with the individual partner affected.

Communications

There is a counter-view, expressed by the former managing partner of a top 20 firm, that withholding drawings is a pointless exercise for those partners who have made so much money over recent years that the drawings are trivial, and that if they do not want to comply they will simply ignore the requests anyway. This view also states that the use of sanctions such as this can in fact be counter-productive and, by focusing only on one measure, it can divert attention from the primary purpose of the firm, which is to create billings and profit, and that penalizing slow collectors rather than under-billers is iniquitous. Those large firms that have been most successful in achieving low levels of lockup with this program have used the stick very sparingly, but have put great emphasis on one-to-one communication from both managing partner and finance director to the partners concerned, as well as making extensive use of peer group pressure and the spreading of best practice across the firm. Whether or not sanctions can be avoided, it is important to keep publishing successes in order to keep people motivated.

As if the finance director were not already busy enough, the research interviews we carried out reiterated a very important point: There is no substitute for the finance director and managing partner being seen out of their offices and involved in the action. This can mean attending departmental meetings, listening to issues and complaints, and coming face to face with the immediate problems. It can also mean visiting major clients. Major clients produce the most money, and finance directors do understand each other's problems and can generally be minded to work to find a mutually acceptable solution.

The finance director is also the person who is in the position to see the results of activity across the firm, to see where things are working best and where they can be improved. They can, and should, encourage cross-fertilization and best practice across the firm.

There are two other points which sadly appear difficult for many finance functions. There has already been mention that communication is not seen to be finance directors' great strength ordinarily, but two behavioral surveys have demonstrated that people respond to stimuli.

The first is that people always respond better if you explain why something is needed. The second, even more basic but maybe no more surprising, is that people respond to the words "thank you". Learning to say thank you should be part of the finance director's armory.

Training

There are several ways of increasing the understanding of partners and fee earners as to why cash management is important. One of those is to ensure that everybody involved has an element of basic financial training. At the top level this should include "finance for the non-financial manager". The middle levels should certainly include an element of credit control and conversational training on how to ask for the cash, and we have found that the concept of the Practice Profit Pipeline, with its allusions to leakages, blockages, etc., can be understood by staff at all levels, from secretary to managing partner. In the course of the research interviews we undertook recently, one managing partner of a top 200 firm said: "If every partner in this firm had had the 'finance for the non-financial manager' training that I had a few years ago, we would be twice as profitable and have far more money in the bank".

The key differentiator

Far more time and attention has been devoted in this chapter to the "soft areas" of financial understanding – partner motivation, training, commitment, peer pressure, etc. – than would have been expected at the start of the research. However, without exception, those respondents interviewed who had clearly enjoyed considerable success in their cash management were at great pains to stress that these soft elements were in fact the indispensable cornerstones of their success. In contrast, those who had plainly been less successful either omitted to mention the subject or gave it the most cursory of responses. So, if a firm is looking to achieve long-term, sustainable, healthy cash flow – and then regular, on-time profit distributions to the partners – getting the partners on-side and ensuring constant communication is a critical part of the strategy. It will take time, and time is scarce, but the payback will be worth it.

This first appeared as Chapter 8 in Wilkinson, B., Cash Flow Management for Law Firms, 2nd edition, *ARK Group, 2014.*

Chapter 21:
Alternatives to the billable hour

By Patrick J. Lamb, co-founder of Valorem Law Group LLC

We need common nomenclature

Everyone connected with the legal profession understands the concept of hourly billing. It's so simple a child in grade school can understand it. Work for an hour and your firm will be paid so many dollars. Work for two hours and your firm will be paid twice as much. No attempt is made to determine whether anything of value occurred during the hour. You could be sick and your mind might be elsewhere, or you could be fully engaged and have a creative spark that generates a flash that saves the client millions. What is produced in each hour could (and almost always does) vary widely. How much you are paid for the hour does not change a cent. Value is tied only to time, not to what you produce or the result you obtain. The simplicity is alluring.

So, isn't an "alternative fee" a fee that is anything other than hourly rates? If only it were that simple. Lawyers, it turns out, have a special genius for word games. Most law firms have "standard" hourly rates. These are the rates that firms typically charge for matters on which the firm is engaged. Some clients demand discounts from these hourly rates; sometimes, firms accommodate these requests. Indeed, as the economy worsened, discounts were asked for and given far more frequently.

But firms don't like to say that they give discounts. It sounds so unseemly, so, well, second tier. The answer to this Hobson's choice? Play a word game. Characterize these discounted hourly rates as "alternative fees".

Other firms choose to offer "blended" hourly rates for certain engagements. Instead of the senior partner charging $600 per hour and others charging less down to the youngest associate charging $300 per hour, the firms would charge all lawyers at $425 per hour. Voilà! More "alternative fees". And as inquiries from media and clients increased, firms were only too happy to trumpet their experience with alternative fees. A classic example of turning lemons into lemonade!

But marketing skill aside, variations on standard hourly billing are not "alternative fees". At its core, the hourly billing model is cost-plus pricing. Hourly rates have the firm's profit margin built in. For every hour worked, the firm's profit increases. The incentive is to work more hours, not fewer. The incentive is to increase the cost because more cost means more profit. Discounting hourly rates or blending them does not change their inherent nature. If your firm gets paid more for each increment of time you work, you are working on an hourly rate model.

The notion of more time, and the incentive to bill more time to increase profit, is at the core of the hourly rate model. It is a quintessential zero sum game. The alternative to that model is something that does not create an incentive to work more in order to increase profit. The incentive has to be on the lawyer or firm to decrease the cost of production in order to increase profit. There is a nearly limitless variety of alternative fees that satisfy this broad definition. One's imagination is the only constraint.

Before we start talking about specific fee structures, let's return to the discussion of nomenclature. The description of fees as alternative has such a bad sound about it. In writing about the green energy movement, multi Pulitzer Prize winning author Tom Friedman wrote:[1]

> *"In the world of ideas, to name something is to own it. If you can name an issue, you can own the issue. One thing that always struck me about the term 'green' was the degree to which, for so many years, it was defined by its opponents – by the people who wanted to disparage it. And they defined it as 'liberal', 'tree-hugging', 'sissy', 'girlie-man', 'unpatriotic', 'vaguely French'."*

Friedman is right and the same idea applies here. Alternative sounds so counter-cultural, like a 1970s hippie movement in San Francisco, some lifestyle no-one in the mainstream wants to emulate. It certainly does not sound corporate. Alternative fees, or alternative fee arrangements, simply does not cut the terminology mustard.

I believe the essential characteristics of the fees that stand in contrast to hourly fees are:

1. The fee must align with the economic interests of the client and the lawyer;

2. The fee must create a financial incentive for the lawyer to reduce cost, not increase it; and
3. The fee structure must create incentives to accomplish a specific, identifiable client objective.

These are the same characteristics that we would use to define value delivered to a client. Hence, I believe the term that should be applied to non-hourly fees is "value fees". Value fees identify what the client receives, just as hourly fees describe what the client receives. Value fees is a term that is simple, as is hourly fees. Value fees stand in contrast to hourly fees. In the game theory vernacular, value fees are non-zero sum situations, ones where both sides can gain. And, in the Friedman sense, value fees also sounds more corporate and less counter-cultural.

Others have different categories. In its discussion with its members, the General Counsel Roundtable has used these categories:

1. **Flat fee** – A specified sum paid for a specific matter. The fee can be paid in one sum or paid monthly or in connection with certain benchmarks in a matter;
2. **Fixed fee** – Akin to a flat fee, but paid for a larger portfolio of work. A specified sum for all work in a certain area, or some other defined portfolio of work;
3. **Risk sharing** – Outside counsel agrees to a flat fee for a matter, but the fee is adjusted up or down based on the outcome;
4. **Performance-based bonus** – This is much like the risk-sharing structure, but with only an upward adjustment possible;
5. **Capped fees** – A limit on total fees for a given matter;
6. **Volume discounts** – Lower hourly rates based on amount of work; and
7. **Blended rates** – A single, uniform rate charged regardless of what lawyer performs the work.

Of course, volume discounts and blended rates are not really alternatives. They merely alter the rate to be applied to the hours worked, without changing the incentive structure. In these, more hours rather than fewer remains the incentive, and the General Counsel Roundtable's own data show that these are among the least effective in reducing spend on outside lawyers. These hourly variations are not discussed here.

So let's start by describing the basic categories of value fees. There are endless variations, but only three broad categories. They are:

1. **Fixed fees** – Fees where a specified sum is paid for a specified amount of work. These are referred to frequently as flat fees, fixed fees, portfolio fees, or something akin to these. As we will discuss, there are numerous variations to this concept;
2. **Contingency fees** – Fees where the amount paid to the lawyer is tied directly to the outcome, whether as a contingency or reverse contingency; and
3. **Modified hourly fees** – Modified hourly arrangement that adds features that create the economic alignment and interest in reducing cost of production. There are, so far as I have encountered, only two approaches that achieve these objectives.

Within these categories, there are multiple variations. Before we spend a few moments looking at the positives and negatives of each category, as well as the variations, it is important to examine the point of any fee structure.

Fee structures are an incentive to behavior

That may be the most important sentence in this book. When a lawyer and client agree on a fee structure, the lawyer has an incentive to behave in a certain way. As we have discussed, the incentive with the hourly rate fee structure is for the lawyer to bill more hours. Thus, the following behaviors are incentivized:

- Larger teams;
- More work, not less;
- Settle late, not early; and
- Keep as much work with the firm without regard to need or value.

We have been using the billable hour model for so long and it is so pervasive that many have not given any real thought to other behaviors that could be incentivized. Here are some examples:

- **Budget certainty** – More important now than ever;
- **Cash-flow control**;

- **Reduced cycle time** – Generally considered the largest driver of total fees;
- **Results** – Many are willing to pay more for wins than losses;
- **Personnel availability** – Sometimes, the client wants to be sure it will always have access to a specific lawyer or team;
- **Save internal review time and effort** – No-hassle billing allows inside counsel to focus on adding real value to the corporate operation rather than spending time policing outside counsel bills;
- **Risk sharing** – Business people in particular love the idea of lawyers investing in the outcome; and
- **Incentives to lower costs**, whether on legal spend alone or the total of indemnity and fees.

In addition to these general behaviors, there can be business-specific or matter-specific objectives. For example, if an employee leaves with trade secrets and time is of the essence, getting a result in hours rather than weeks has great value and could be identified as an objective to be rewarded. In every case, clients need to figure out what behaviors and outcomes they want to incentivize, and then work with their lawyer to develop a fee structure that rewards these behaviors or outcomes, and penalizes failure to achieve them.

For most clients and most cases, the objectives generally are:

- Lowest possible legal cost; and
- Acceptable economic resolution.

Not surprisingly, businesses implicitly or expressly recognize that they are not in the business of litigating lawsuits and want to minimize the distraction associated with claims. There obviously are lawsuits that are more important, where other behaviors are important. But these two key outcomes will guide our discussion.

Fixed fees

Sometimes called flat fees, there are countless variations of fixed fees. Some have tried to use flat fees to describe payment of a specified sum for a single case and fixed fees to describe payment of a specified sum for a larger group of cases. The distinction is, frankly, not terribly meaningful. The key element of the fixed fee, whether applied to a case, part of a case, or many cases, is that it gives budget certainty and creates huge incentives for the outside lawyer to reduce the cost of production. In its most basic form, these are the two attributes of this fee structure.

Compared with hourly rate incentives noted above, fixed fees incentivize very different behavior, as can be seen in Table 1.

Hourly rate behaviors	Fixed fee behaviors
Larger teams	Smaller teams
More work, not less	Less work, not more
Settle late, not early	Settle as early as possible
Keep work in the firm	Use cheapest resource

Table 1: Fixed fees incentivize different behavior

Both fixed fees and hourly rate structures are indifferent to outcome. In fact, the only fee structure that inherently incentivizes good outcomes is the contingency fee. But as noted, there are many variations on the basic fee structures that modify the behaviors incentivized.

What's the most effective way to incentivize the outcome? As with anything else, pay for it. That notion seems antithetical to many, but it is a business norm. When a company is buying widgets, it only pays for the widgets if they meet the buyer's specifications. So before the buyer purchases the widgets, it provides the manufacturer with a set of performance or other specifications. The manufacturer either agrees to them or the parties negotiate a different measure of performance. Why should lawyers, both inside and outside, be immune from this common negotiation?

Of course, the answer is that they should not. Inside and outside lawyers should discuss the desired outcome at the beginning of a matter. Too often, what happens is that a complaint is e-mailed and lawyers start working without the first clue as to what the client desires in the way of an outcome. One approach that creates substantial incentives for great results is shown in Figure 1.

As indicated, however, a basic fixed fee only creates the budget certainty. A modification is needed to create the incentive for great results, as shown in Figure 2.

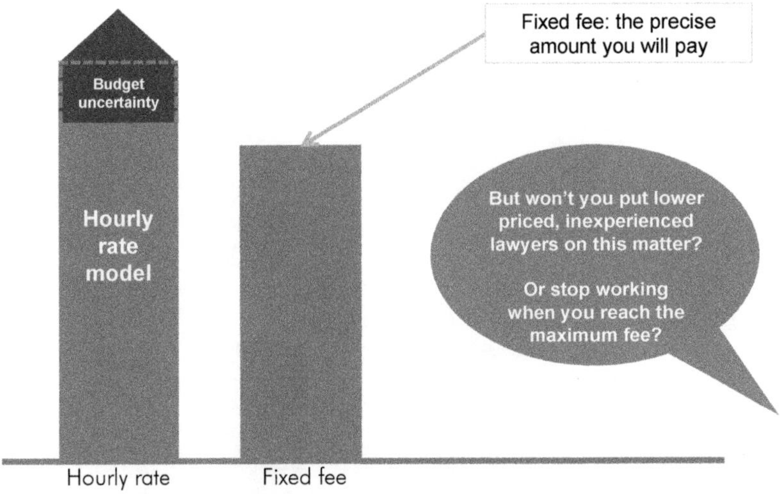

Figure 1: How do you obtain certainty?

A portion of the monthly fee is held back pending the outcome. You might think that the amount held back is not that important, but it is. The bucket is like an account earning compound interest at ten percent. It grows.

The amount "at risk" grows every month. It doesn't take long before the amount the outside lawyer could be paid or lose is quite substantial relative to the monthly payment. This is the amount that creates the incentive for the lawyer to put their best team on the matter and to aggressively pursue the result desired by the client.

The key attribute to this fee structure is that the client determines whether to pay the amount in the bucket at the end of the matter, after the result is known and the client can assess the value of the service provided by the law firm. It is possible to create certain benchmarks for payment or to leave the matter entirely in the hands of the client.

To this point, nothing has been said about flat fees and the amount a client will pay. As noted, one of the incentives clients have is to obtain the lowest possible cost. There is nothing inherent in this fee structure that results in lower total fees. The essential theory of this fee structure is that because it creates huge incentives for outside lawyers to be efficient and try to shorten the time to resolution, there will be a reduction in the cost of production and that some of those savings will be passed on to the client.

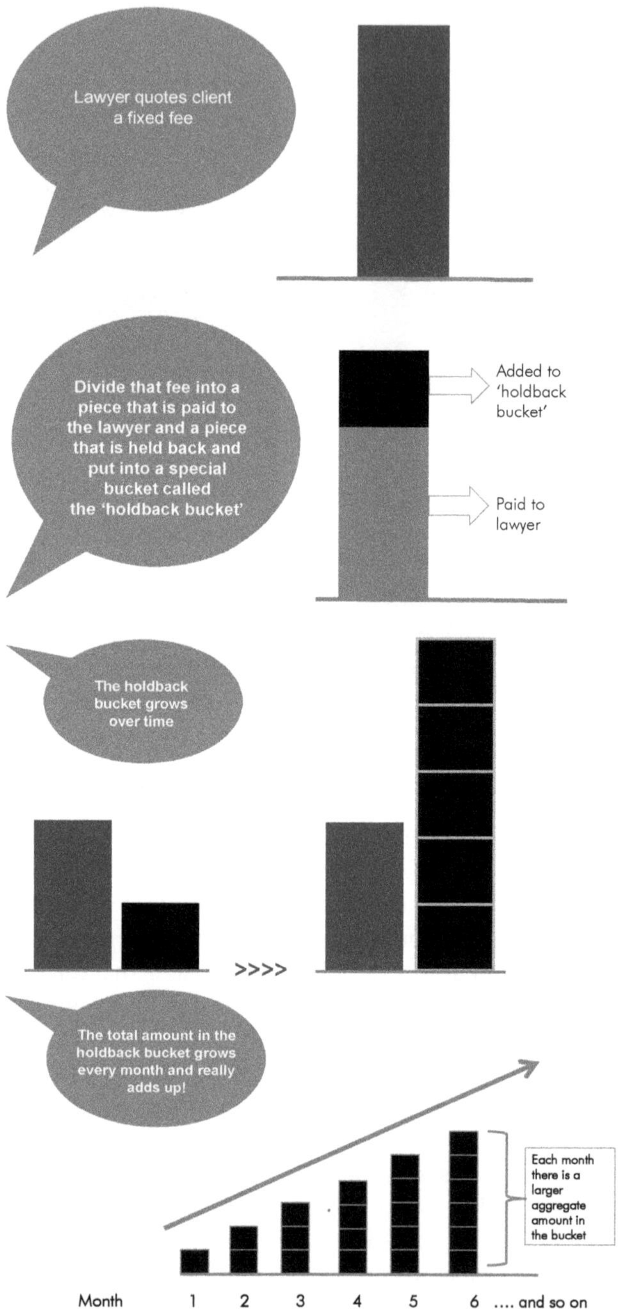

Figure 2: How the holdback bucket works

Variations and incentives

This same "holdback bucket" approach works on a portfolio of matters. The incentives are the same and the ability to quote lower fees is even higher. Look at this in the context of a simple example. Let's say that a client has a portfolio of single plaintiff employment cases. Historically, these cases have cost between $20,000 and $120,000 to litigate, but the average cost has been $50,000 (this data can be either the client's or the firm's – same analysis). If you were bidding on a single case, you would naturally bid in a way that protected you from the possibility that this case was not average, but instead was one of the ones that might be at the high end. You're likely to bid in the range of $75,000. But if you get a group of cases, the odds are that while one or two will cost more than the average, others will cost less and the group of cases will come near the average cost. A greater volume of work allows the firm to spread the risk associated with any one case across a group of cases, thus marginalizing the price risk.

The criteria for evaluating performance on a group of cases can be case by case or across the portfolio. We have one client where one of the key metrics is the settlement average of a certain type of case. Having said that, the other metrics could certainly override this one so that our performance is judged on a wide range of factors.

Another variation on a flat fee is a segmented flat fee. In this variation, a case is broken down into segments and a fee is set for each piece. For example, one segment might be initial investigation and pleadings, followed by segments for written discovery, depositions, expert discovery, and ending with trial preparation and trial. Typically, clients ask for this approach when they are looking to gain the benefit of lower price for earlier resolution since, in theory at least, this would lead to a lower total payment. Hence, if the client thinks the suit is likely to resolve early and they want to try something different, this is the natural default. The other reason for approaching cases this way is when people do not want to invest the time in planning out the case. "There are too many variables", or "This is so complex", or "We don't know what the other side is going to do", are the kinds of things being said if complexity is the issue.

The flat fee by segment does not create an incentive to shorten the case since payment is made at the end of the segment. At most, if the lawyer is paid at the front end, it may increase the incentive to resolve a case at the beginning of a segment before the time is invested. But there is nowhere near the incentive to resolve early that there is under the entire case flat fee.

So when is the fixed fee appropriate? Always, but with this caveat: clients should require their lawyers to have "skin in the game",[2] meaning an economic interest in obtaining an outcome or result defined by the client as a desirable one. Why? Incentives and disincentives provide the answer. As mentioned, one of the most commonly identified failings of the traditional fixed-fee arrangement is that it creates incentives for the law firm to use the youngest and cheapest resource available in order to minimize the cost (thereby effectively increasing the profit margin and the work) or, in circumstances where a firm's work reaches the maximum level allowed, that the firms will simply stop doing needed work thereby reducing the quality of the result obtained. The easiest and most straightforward answer is to not remove outcome from the criteria by which a fee is paid. That means a law firm is forced to have skin in the game – that is, risk that it will not be paid as much for a lesser result than it will be for a greater result. Firms will use experienced lawyers rather than inexperienced ones because experienced lawyers are much more likely to be able to obtain the desired outcome.

In addition to a very highly motivated lawyer, clients obtain a much more thorough and accurate assessment of the quality of the case at the outset since firms will be reluctant to make investments in poor cases. Under the traditional hourly arrangement or even under a traditional fixed-fee arrangement, the firm has no incentive to identify the failings in the case and not take the work. But if a firm is forced to look at a case as an investment of its resources and not just the client's, a firm will make informed investment decisions. If the firm rejects a case because of the likelihood of losing, that sends their client a strong message about the quality of the case.

Dave Bohrer of San Jose's Confluence Law Partners quotes Neal Rubin, Cisco's litigation manager, in a recent article: "While firms are not equally risk positive or averse, a firm's willingness to accept risk provides a useful litmus test that can help instruct the client whether it has realistically assessed the strength of its case. The straight billable hour model provides no such feedback."[3]

The final value from the skin in the game approach is that it ensures that the firm will remain committed to the case through to the outcome. The firm cannot lose interest without losing its investment. If it turns out that the case develops unexpectedly and the prospects appear dim, hourly rate lawyers have no incentive to front this sooner rather than later. When you have an investment in the case, problems are fronted very quickly – if you are going to have to accept a bad outcome, better to do it sooner rather than later.

Another variation is a flat monthly fee payable for however long the case remains active. This approach limits the incentive to push as hard for early resolution, but that obstacle can be overcome by creating a specified incentive. For example, if the case resolves within a year, you will get a bonus $50,000, or some number that is appropriate to create the desired incentive. Another option is for the monthly fee to decline over time as an incentive to push the case forward earlier. There is an unlimited number of variations on the fixed fee theme. It is by far the most common value fee.

Contingency fees

Contingency fees are well known from their widespread use in personal injury cases. Plaintiffs' lawyers agree to take on a case in exchange for recovering their expenses and one third (or some other percentage) of the remaining recovery. In recent years, it has become more common to see corporations use contingency fees.

When are they appropriate? The natural tendency is to say anytime there is a recovery to be had. But that answer really misses the mark. Contingency fees are a good tool when cash is tight or there is not enough money in the budget to bring a meritorious claim. But aside from those rare circumstances, both clients and outside counsel would be wise to look at contingency fee agreements as an investment decision. Examples will help illustrate the analysis.

Example A

A client has a $10 million claim. The claim looks to be solid and the damages are solid. The client estimates it has an 80 percent chance of recovering the $10 million. If it does, the law firm working for a 30 percent contingency will recover $3 million and the company will recover $7 million. The case is likely to take two years to reach resolution. The estimate for actual fees if the matter is handled on a non-contingent basis is $1.4 million. Thus, the client's decision is whether the risk of paying $1.4 million and getting nothing – a 20 percent risk – is worth an 80 percent chance of paying an extra $1.6 million to the lawyers. As the risk of not recovering goes up, the value of proceeding on a contingency goes up as well. But as the risk of not recovering goes up, the firm's interest in handling the case on a contingency goes down.

Example B

The client has a $100 million claim. The client and its counsel estimate the claim has a 50 percent chance of prevailing if the case is handled as it normally would be. The firm believes it can improve that estimate if it devotes extraordinary resources to the case, but it is prepared to do so only if it sees potential for a "mega-recovery". That is, it would not be worth it to the firm to expand and devote exceptional resources to the matter for regular hourly rates. But if it stands to recover $30 million, the firm is prepared to make that investment. What options does the client have?

The point, hopefully, is clear. There is an overlay of investment decision that must be factored into the analysis regarding contingency fees. What does it mean to a client if firms will not take a matter on a contingency? It means that the case is not a good investment for the firm. If it is not a good investment for the firm, why is it a good investment for the client? Likewise, if firms are jumping at a case, it is because they see it as a good investment for them. If it is, why would it not also be a good investment for the client, meaning investing fees and taking the contingent premium for itself?

In the corporate world, there is also the overlay of "whose money is it?". If a case is being pursued, against what business unit will fees be charged, and is there some reason why that unit may not want to invest in a case, or, on the other hand, why they would not want to see a large piece of the recovery go to the lawyers? It is important to be sensitive to the budget and accounting issues.

As with most things involving value fees, contingency fees do not need to be all or nothing. It is possible to combine fixed fees and contingency fees. The client would pay a lower fixed monthly payment (or some other payment frequency) to the law firm, which would then take some reduction in its contingent recovery, maybe from 30 percent to 12 percent. In this circumstance, the potential contingent recovery plays the same role vis-à-vis the incentives as the holdback bucket.

Finally, there is no reason contingency fees need to be used only when there is an affirmative recovery to be had. If a client is looking at a $100 million claim, firms are now starting to work on a "reverse contingency" by taking a percentage of the amount saved. Obviously, the percentages are staggered so that modest savings are rewarded very little but material savings are handsomely rewarded.

In any contingency fee, the potential upside to the lawyers is a huge incentive to do whatever it takes to win, to devote whatever resources and lawyer talent is required. At the same time, because of the risk of loss and the desire to maximize profit (revenue received minus cost to produce revenue), there is strong incentive to avoid spending money needlessly, and thus a strong incentive to control costs. As with the fixed-fee arrangements, this fee structure forces lawyers to look at their costs as investments, and only those that provide a sufficient return are made.

Modified hourly arrangements

The idea of hourly arrangements as value fees sounds like an oxymoron and, to an extent, it is. But a few leading thinkers have developed systems using hourly rates that appear to shift the incentives lawyers operate under and align the economic interests of the law firm and the client. There are three that seem to fit the bill.

The Alliance Counsel Engagement System

The Alliance Counsel Engagement System (ACES®) was developed by Jeffrey Carr, the iconoclastic general counsel of FMC Technologies. More than a decade ago, Carr developed this model based on the way-ahead of-his-time notion that, as a client, he did not want to buy hours. The foundation of the model is matter budgets, which are required for every matter and have to be signed off by inside counsel. The budgets cover both portions of the case and time period because the company budgets by time, not by phase of litigation. Lawyers are paid 80 percent of what they bill so long as they are under budget. If the budget is exceeded, lawyers are paid 20 percent for any excess. The unpaid portion goes into a bucket. The bucket or a portion of the bucket is surrendered for a poor result, or the entirety or a multiple of the bucket is paid out depending on the positive result achieved. The system creates incentives for rapid resolution, so that lawyers bill fewer total hours but are paid higher net rates. The other feature of the system that qualifies it as a value fee tool is that it does not matter what rates lawyers charge or how many people are assigned to the case. It does assume, reasonably I believe, that a firm's partners would balk at extended payments of 20 percent, so that even though you could raise rates and assign multiple people, there is a significant economic penalty that the firm would face (being paid only 20 percent of the over budget amounts) and the risk of sacrificing a significant portion of the-bucket at the conclusion of the matter.

The other very important feature of the ACES system is that it creates a level of financial discipline few lawyers have ever experienced. Litigation becomes numbers driven, including use of decision trees to evaluate cases and make buy-sell decisions.

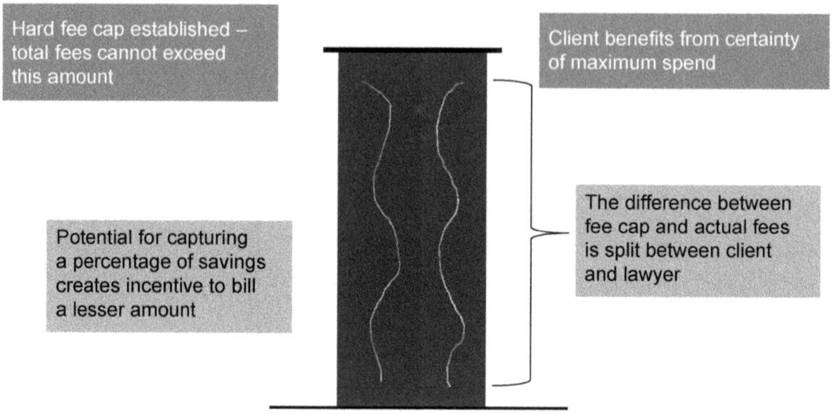

Figure 3: 'Hard cap' hourly rate

Caps, with a twist

This was a nifty concept I first heard about from Jeffrey Novak, the general counsel of AOL Paid Services and assistant general counsel of AOL, Inc. Novak took an area and created a fee cap. He then offered to share the delta between that cap and the amount the firm actually spent. The illustration he offered (I have no idea if these numbers are real or not) was that spend in one area had been averaging $3 million. He created a cap of $2 million, which allowed him to immediately recognize the savings. The firm then spent $1 million, which allowed the firm to gain its share of the $1 million saved and allowed Novak to save AOL's percentage share of that million dollars. This model is illustrated in Figure 3.

The incentives for a law firm to reduce spend here are obvious. But unlike the results-based fixed-fee structure discussed previously, this structure does not create any incentive to achieve results. Thus, it falls on the in-house lawyer using this model to police work quality and results. The other flaw in the system is that (and I am guessing here) it causes headaches for inside counsel as they realize how much they have been overpaying. When I asked Novak about this, he said you definitely have to commit to "looking forward".

Risk collars

Risk collars shift some risk to lawyers. As such, they do not create

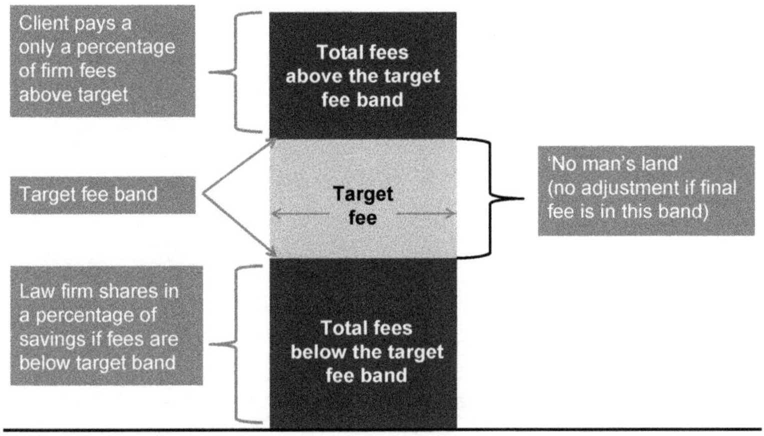

Figure 4: 'Risk bonding' fee model

material incentives to control costs, but they do create some incentive to do so, which makes this approach better than a standard hourly approach. Here's how it works.

There is target fee number and a band on either side of that number. If the law firm's fee falls in that band, also called "no man's land", there is no adjustment to the fee. If the firm's fees fall below the lower portion of the target band, the firm gets a portion of the savings. On the flip side, if the firm exceeds the upper end of the target band, it receives a percentage of the portion of its fees over the band, typically a percentage in the range of 40–50 percent, to avoid creating any incentive for runaway fees – see Figure 4.

This approach is the equivalent of an insurance company buying reinsurance or a homeowner buying an umbrella policy. The firm receives protection for a material overspend, which might be based on bad estimating on the front end, and also has an incentive to try to keep costs below the bottom of the fee band. As with the caps-with-a-twist approach, this model creates incentives to do less work but without the corresponding incentive to obtain results. That incentive somehow has to be created for engagements where results matter, or it will fall to the inside lawyer overseeing the matter to police the results.

This first appeared as Chapter 3 in Lamb, P.J., Alternative Fee Arrangements: Value Fees and the Changing Legal Market, *ARK Group, 2010.*

References

1. Friedman, T., "The Power of Green", *New York Times Magazine*, 15 April 2007.
2. Phrase coined by American investor, industrialist and philanthropist Warren Buffett.
3. Bohrer, D., "Trolling for Efficiency", *Daily Journal* (San Francisco and Los Angeles editions), 24 June 2009.

Chapter 22:
Developing the right pricing model based on data

By Toby Brown, chief practice officer at Akin Gump Strauss Hauer & Feld LLP, and Vincent Cordo, global sourcing officer at Shell

Know exactly what clients want

Increased responsiveness to client needs, added value, and aggressive discounts are the industry norm. In any form of service industry there is an array of pricing menu models to offer. Effective and practical pricing aligned with matter management delivers a profitable solution that works for the client and the law firm. A simplified approach that focuses on how to achieve this will result in an adopted program that makes sense to the business while making lives a bit easier.

Most firms would traditionally raise rates each year in various ranges. In recent years, firms are doing well with 3.5 percent increase and, in most cases, lock in rates for two year periods forgoing these increases. This is not really a pricing model that works. Developing proposals that are a good faith effort to partner with a client to craft a unique means of ensuring quality, consistency, and cost predictability to the legal portfolio is crucial; it exhibits the intent to establish a long-term relationship.

Today's purchasers are developing metrics to have a better understanding of procuring legal providers. Having the ability to make well-reasoned decisions and protect the business involves balancing all factors involved in a matter. This means having more information at the firm's disposal to ask better questions and select the best price and quality. Whenever there is a need for ongoing services such as legal work, clients want to ensure to "lock" the renewal of the prices for these services. The best time to negotiate price is during this time of negotiation.

Pricing efforts always influence the bottom-line for both clients and the law firm. From a client perspective, they have the greatest leverage at the time of contracting – this is the time for them to protect themselves against excessive price increases and to negotiate all of the hidden and future costs. However, from a law firm perspective, this is the time, if necessary, to state the case for budget increases due to outliers and task-based billing reports – based on facts. The "facts" part of this stage is crucial, as providing all of the relevant information to the client is important and will help if firms need to approach the difficult subject of price increases.

Law firms should consider including a CPI Clause (consumer price index) in the information provided to clients. A CPI is defined as "a measure that examines the weighted average of prices of a basket of consumer goods and services, such as transportation, food and medical care. The CPI is calculated by taking price changes for each item in the predetermined basket of goods and averaging them; the goods are weighted according to their importance. Changes in CPI are used to assess price changes associated with the cost of living".[1] It can also sometimes be referred to as "headline inflation". The following is an excerpt from a fixed fee that includes a CPI clause:

> *"Material changes in the scope of work*
> *We must develop the fixed fee and related assumptions based upon the facts and circumstances as they exist presently. Leveraging your legal project management and pricing resources, the law firm would bring these items to the client as soon as possible. In addition, it is possible that the economic market that exists today will change over the course of this X year agreement. In the event that material changes have occurred or the economic market has changed drastically (i.e. an increase or decrease in the CPI Index beyond 3% annually), in the spirit of cooperation, we mutually agree to reopen the discussion on the fixed fee level. This provision provides for flexibility to revisit the fixed fee in good faith to ensure fairness."*

Should firms create their own AFAs?

Law firms are always seeking key differentiators and attempt to create their own variants on AFAs. However, this is not the best way for them to spend their efforts. All firms have preferences based on the types of matters they handle and what they know works best within their organizations, and most clients will also drive the direction that the firm takes in most, if not all, cases. However, the main questions that must be asked are: "What do the firm's existing clients want and what works best for them?" and "What does this prospective client need and what can win this bid?" In answering these, firms must recognize that there are only so many choices and "best price" routes available. Firms should incorporate real testimony on examples of what the firm has priced and how it managed matters in the past into their bids. To ensure value to clients, lawyer experience and who can manage a matter well will determine who is best suited for the job.

Many in-house legal service procurement directors say the same thing. Each firm says they offer LPM and value services. However, it is by showing how it has delivered in the past, through testimony and ratings, that a firm can really differentiate itself. A firm can be somewhat creative with pricing in some cases to align with clients' unique needs; however, the delivery and ability to report on the "real" metrics are the true differentiator.

Clients value the following concepts:

- Transparency;
- Communication (reporting and dashboards);
- Competitive pricing and testimony;
- Predictability/projections;
- Strategy;
- Value services – For example, firms can have a lot of tools and clients appreciate when firms work with them to set up their own systems such as SharePoint or matter profile systems;
- Efficiency – Business process improvement, offering the same services for less money;
- Project (or matter) management; and
- Training – Not just legal training, but business training also (e.g. contracts "abstract" training for business users or Six Sigma training).

We know this sounds good. While these concepts are great promotional responses, they are not easy to execute and it takes hard work to implement. Let's take a look at how they are achieved. Alternative fee arrangements, value pricing, and most importantly, proper legal project management (matter management), play major roles in the solution. Law firms are leveraging task-based billing to manage matters using task codes in a task-based billing approach – on both the transactional and litigation front. Many would argue that ABA codes are not transactional friendly. The suggested solution is to create the firm's own codes that make sense to the budget. To do this, it is essential to work with internal teams in IT and billing to reverse map the codes so they do not impact on e-billing.

Thorough examination of metrics such as historical revenues, "outliers", and costs is required to accurately forecast the fees of future matters. This internal due diligence is continually incorporated into AFA approaches and philosophies and must be appropriately reported on. Legal project managers should continuously examine all aspects of this service delivery (which spans across industry groups, practice groups, and regions) to understand and implement best practices and align them with client needs and goals. The pricing director should spend a lot of time on how they dashboard, report, and communicate these metrics; and not everyone needs to see all of them. They should pay careful attention to the end use of the information they are sharing and consider their needs, interpretation of, and the uses they will make of the data. Why is this important? If all of the metrics are available but they cannot be properly communicated at the right time to the right audience in a real-time and swift fashion, then they are worthless.

Leverage strategic pricing and legal project management processes, together with advanced reporting, dashboarding, an extranet solution, in addition to finance, and time entry tools to accomplish this.

It is one thing to understand pricing options, but another to leverage the appropriate pricing option that fits the needs of both the client and the firm. First, the firm needs to designate a seasoned resource that can and will run the pricing process. Pricing directors are the new resource in the legal market and they work with the lawyers and finance teams, helping to map the appropriate pricing structures. If no such person exists in the firm, then it needs a pricing and LPM specialist. Many variables, as well as knowledge management, must be considered while assessing the type of proposal or opportunity response the firm will choose. Among the factors the firm may need help with are operational costs, utilization, realization, and in some cases, special leadership approvals. Then, the firm must consider tracking these factors for future needs; it is a full-time job.

It is essential to take advantage of the resources available to help while building this model. Strategic leadership with this role cannot be taken lightly. It should not be delegated off to someone in marketing, for example. Tracking this information is extremely important so that the firm can not only standardize processes, but more importantly, track, report on, and train the lawyers (through testimony) on what works best and why.

This can all go badly if the matter is not properly managed to coincide with the budget. When bidding, lawyers can get their "opportunity blinders on" and forget about the rest of the pipeline management or future budget impact on business. Therefore, someone is needed to measure progress against what the firm committed to and how the client is communicated to throughout the life cycle of the matter. One of the best ways to track matters is through advanced budgeting coupled with task-based billing and real-time reporting. Leveraging task codes mapped to the tasks within a matter's budget is the only way to track this kind of detail. The benefits are astronomical and, if done correctly, the firm can systematically find out what type of AFA works best, and it can gain more control on what is marked up and down, based on the firm's own experience in handling similar matters. It is not possible to get this kind of information from sending out firm-wide emails or using generic templates – or anywhere else for that matter.

It is possible to put this into perspective by referring to an example of taking a current agreement with the client based on dated rates, and showing how to pitch new pricing over a two year term. Listed in the next section is an example of a proposed hourly rate for the two-year term.

Context

The current agreement with the client is based on 2013 rates; however, as in real situations, a number of time keepers have exceptions (promotions, joined the firm post-2012, other anomalies etc.).

Table 1 shows an example of 2013 average rates billed to the client (by sample segments often set out by the client), along with "fill in the blank" proposed new rates.

Proposed rate assumptions

Table 1 represents an approximate X percent increase in rates. When a firm is proposing an increase, it may need to note factors to justify the increase, such as:

- Rates were held since year 20##;
- Rates will increase effective from 1/1/NEWYEAR (depending on the time of year the firm is working on this, it should take into consideration that a majority of these requests come into the firm in the fourth quarter and it should factor in its financial impact accordingly by prorating increases);
- A multi-year lock, so realization and profitability will be diluted several percent each year;

- Aggressive volume discounts can be offered (see further below); or
- Consider negotiating some type of CPI protection clause.

	2013 rate		Proposed 2 year rate		Realization
	Rate	Hours worked	Rate	Increase over 2013	
20–25 years					
10–20 years					
5–10 years					
7+ years					
3–7 years					
0–3 years					
			Average		

Table 1: Sample rate chart

Proposed volume discounts

Context

See Table 2 for recent fee billing and realization history.

	Fees	Billing
Year	Billed	Realization
2013 (to date)	75,000	60%
2012	85,000	70%
2011	95,000	80%

Table 2: Fee billing and realization history

Volume discount assumptions – Based on spend

Note that this can also be based on matter count as well as other criteria. Based on recent billing history, the total needs to reflect the firm's actionable/reasonable breakpoint and should include any AFAs in the annual billings figures for volume discount calculations – but AFAs will not be subject to additional spend rebates.

The firm can, and should, be creative here by adding a volume discount chart that maps out the schedule of discounting based on spend. It is also possible to base this on matter count. The point is to be creative and base it on the client's needs.

Would service level models work in legal? There are many approaches in other businesses that are used for expansion. What would the "pro sales blue chip sales resource do"? Regardless of what model or models are selected that work best for the firm, it needs to track how it affects profitability.

Rebate across all practice areas		
Annual billings		
From	To	Spend rebate %
$ 00	$ 500,000	0
$ 500,001	$ 700,000	3%
$ 700,001	$ 1,000,000	5%
$ 1,000,001	$ 1,500,000	7%
$ 1,500,001+	$	10%

Table 3: Volume discounts

A pricing model based on the firm's tacit data

To develop the right pricing model based on the firm's tacit data is a great place to start. This does not mean, however, that one template will work everywhere.

There always seem to be two types of models within a law firm: one being the firm starting point model; and the other is specific to the client that would need financial impact analysis and firm leadership approval. Pricing directors have been thrust into the position of helping their firms to understand and ultimately adapt to:

- Key business trends affecting associates;
- The firm's individual financial performance;
- Client and matter profitability;
- Client relationship support;
- Alternative fee arrangements and secondments; and
- Revenue and sales pipeline management is an inevitable future for

the directors who understand how to support lawyers in a sales support capacity.

The firm needs to work with a range of clients on the basis of an appropriate fee for the value or satisfaction that is actually delivered to the business from the work the firm is asked to carry out. It is necessary to regularly provide clients with annual fixed and capped fees in many areas in which the scope of the engagement is reasonably predictable, recognizing the objective to contain lawyer fees in connection with all types of matters. This role needs to integrate with the client and legal team to be creative with any opportunity. Lawyers must expect that the director will also support them by building a relationship with the other sides of the business – this is a huge factor in this role.

Listed below are some examples of how a pricing director and their team can do this:

- **Opportunities/RFPs:**

  Assist in responding to RFPs for matters involving discounts, AFAs, and other value-based pricing or for hourly matters that request information on legal project management, value add services, secondee offering, contingency fee, or legal process improvement. The pricing team needs to provide financial data and information, and assist in coordinating with the legal and marketing teams to complete the RFP response.

- **Pricing proposals:**

  Create pricing proposals tailored to meet each client's needs. Pricing proposals can include rate lock for a certain term, or a budget and project plan and other detailed information including competitive rate or task code intelligence, historic pricing analysis for similar matters, profitability, and risk.

- **Intake process, budget, process mapping, and matter work plan development:**

  Owning the intake process; profiling the matters appropriately. At the conclusion of the intake process, the team should configure the applications lawyers use to create work product, record time, track expenses, and collaborate. Implement metrics on the finance system and develop an internal budget and process map or work plan identifying firm expenses and staffing requirements for the entirety of the engagement, evaluate options for adjusting the budget to meet a desired price or profitability point, and to accommodate changes in scope.

- **Historic matter information and statistical analysis:**

  Providing historic information and analysis regarding how the firm has priced matters with similar attributes in the past, how those matters were staffed, the realization and profitability for those matters, and the firm can also provide additional qualitative information that may assist with determining the potential risks and rewards of pricing a new matter in a similar approach.

- **Client value and revenue support:**

  Helping lawyers with business activities and processes that help business development and the firm to run effectively, efficiently, and in support of strategies and objectives. Assisting in a client-facing sales support fashion. The set of activities include:

  - Onsite pitch support;
  - Client or practice strategy: Design, planning, and execution;
  - Measurement of results: Reporting, analytics, and revenue pipeline data;
  - Bidding, budget, client volume, portfolio management;
  - Technology and tools, including CRM;
  - Matter profiling;
  - Training and win/loss communication;
  - Practice and industry design and optimization;
  - Relationship management; and
  - Lead generation/procurement programs.

  The client value and pricing teams are often the liaisons for procurement to other parts of the law firm such as KM, finance, marketing, and IT. They also represent the needs of the lawyers in meetings and cross-functional projects.

- **Revenue cycle management**:

  Taking steps to ensure that the firm is getting paid for the work executed in a timely fashion. The revenue cycle starts when the engagement begins. This role can help in improving efficiency in collections.

- **Engagement letter/opportunity response pricing language:**

  Every engagement letter or opportunity response should fully delineate the terms of the engagement and include a detailed scope of work and assumptions, as well as an escape clause which explains what happens in the event that the scope of work changes. The pricing and LPM team should assist in drafting detailed pricing engagement letter language in order to increase firm realization and profitability and to reduce fee disputes, write-downs, and write-offs. Further, once the matter is in place, the LPM team will be versed on what to track; helping with more efficient tracking of missing time and management of all other aspects of the engagement.

- **Competitive intelligence:**

  Providing information and analysis on what other firms have charged for comparable work, the level and type of staffing they used, as well as the structure of their fee arrangements is essential. In addition, working with clients' pricing teams to understand what was previously charged for other work and what price is right for them is key.

- **Task code implementation and mapping:**

  After a matter is underway, leveraging the LPM team can help with establishing matter specific task codes to assist with matter management and for the purpose of creating a database of historic pricing information.

- **Reporting and dashboarding:**

  Provide customized matter management dashboards and reports measuring the budget, task, and work plan performance on a real-time basis, and monitor profitability in order to assist the firm's lawyers with matter management, staffing, and to ensure it is handled in the most efficient and cost-effective way possible.

- **Matter management:**

  Have a committed LPM team that is involved in managing matters from start to completion. In addition to assisting with task code implementation and providing matter management reporting, the LPM team should facilitate regular legal team and client portfolio meetings to review financial metrics and progress, discuss potential road blocks and changes in the original assumptions and scope of work, and manage and plan upcoming tasks.

- **Knowledge management:**

  Having a disciplined approach to knowledge management (KM) by making the best use of knowledge. Focusing on tools and processes such as acquiring, creating, and sharing knowledge and the cultural and technical foundations that support them based on:

  - People – How to increase the ability of the firm to influence clients with their knowledge;
  - Processes – The approach varies from client to client;
  - Technology – It needs to be chosen only after all the requirements of a knowledge management initiative have been established;
  - Culture – The biggest enabler of success; and
  - Structure – The business processes and organizational structures that facilitate knowledge sharing.

- **Education and training:**

  Create and provide firm and client presentations on issues such as maintaining profitability on matters, e-billing setup, matter profiling, metrics, legal project management techniques, and delivering client value and cost-efficiency. In this challenging economic climate, in-house legal counsel face a variety of challenges in managing and controlling workload and legal spend and they are under increasing pressure to improve value and efficiency and improve legal processes. The LPM team could partner with firm lawyers and in-house legal departments to come up with creative ways to increase cost-effectiveness and value and to provide training and consultation to respond to their needs.

- **Technology:**

  Leverage the firm and client tools that can assist with matter/portfolio management. For example, managing matter profiling systems, extranet sites for an individual matter or portfolio of matters. Provide the client with the ability to access real-time matter management financial reporting, the documents associated with a matter or portfolio of matters, and an updated process map or matter work plan that establishes the time frames, tasks, and the status of completion of those tasks and the legal team members responsible. This assists the client in keeping track of how each matter is progressing in relation to the matter work plan and budget.

This first appeared as Chapter 5 in Brown, T., and Cordo, V., Law Firm Pricing: Strategies, Roles, and Responsibilities, *ARK Group, 2013.*

Reference

1. See: www.investopedia.com/terms/c/consumerpriceindex.asp.

Part 5:
Optimization and technology

Chapter 23:
The challenge to optimize

By V. Mary Abraham, co-founder of Broadli Inc

Since 2008 law firms around the world have taken measures to respond to the upheaval in the legal market. As demand for legal services declined, firms focused on reducing costs as much as possible. Initially, some saw these cuts as temporary measures to be put in place until the storm clouds lifted. Others seized on the economic pressures as a welcome opportunity to trim the fat. Nearly six years later, however, it is clear that the bad weather is here to stay. Furthermore, many firms have cut to the bone and now have to rethink the scope of the services they reasonably can provide.

From the client's perspective, the one thing a lawyer must deliver to a client is excellent legal advice on a schedule and at a price the client finds acceptable. All other services provided by the lawyer and their firm are for convenience alone. It is completely reasonable for a client to expect that any service outside the core function of delivering legal advice will be provided at the best price the market offers – whether the provider is a law firm or a third-party vendor. Law firms that wish to provide more than bare legal advice must match or beat what is available in the wider market.

From the perspective of the law firm, things look a little different. Many firms have traditionally tried to offer one-stop shopping to clients. And, even if the service offered did not match the best the open market had to offer, there was a perceived convenience for the client when the law firm simply handled the additional services.

From the perspective of the lawyers of the firm, things get even more interesting. Here we see the lawyer's need to provide excellent client service and how that drives the lawyer to ensure that all the component services are within the control of the lawyer or their firm. To enable this approach, firms found themselves hiring personnel who were able to provide these additional services. This allowed the lawyer to produce work on incredibly short deadlines without worrying overmuch about the constraints imposed by an outside vendor.

Things are changing now. To begin with, clients are no longer always willing to accept higher prices in exchange for the proffered convenience. In fact, clients are embracing the disaggregation of legal services if it means that they can contain costs without reducing the quality of service. Accordingly, clients are pushing law firms to either meet what the market can provide or act as a general contractor to assemble a team of law firm and third-party providers who can collectively serve the client in a seamless fashion at a better price. In some cases, in-house counsel are assuming the role of general contractor and, with the help of a procurement office, are creating their own roster of preferred providers of services ranging from e-discovery review to contract analysis and drafting.

In this context, the work of each law firm support function must be examined under a microscope. How does that support function relate to the core services the client seeks? To what extent does the quality and price of the products and services offered by that support function compare favorably with that available in the open market?

In addition to optimizing support functions for the benefit of clients, there is the task of optimizing these functions for the health and continued prosperity of the firm. From this perspective, firm managers need to ask to what extent each support function enables the firm to meet its strategic goals, and whether the support function has the appropriate array of staff and technology to rise to the challenge. Finally, there are the tough but necessary questions relating to how the capabilities of these functions (and especially their staff) are changing and improving in order to enable the firm in turn to improve its client offerings and economic position.

Why optimize?

To optimize a system or process is to make it as functional and effective as it can be. This requires a sense of what is possible and a commitment to take the action necessary to get as close to the goal of optimization as one can.

While optimization is undoubtedly a laudable goal, it is still worth asking the question: why optimize? Until now, having processes that are good enough may have been enough for some law firm managers and their firms. In fact, for some, achieving a good enough standard may take the combined effort of a department's staff as currently constituted.

Further, given the dislocation and anxiety of the legal market since 2008, staff may lack the inner resources necessary to imagine a better way of doing things, much less do the work required to transform that vision into reality. This means that unless a manager deliberately makes changes to working processes or personnel, the department may not have the wherewithal to achieve optimization.

Before 2008, the existing processes did not seem to get in the way of many firms achieving economic success. The generally accepted view was that what they were doing was working, so why change? All they needed to do was more of the same. In short, firms made money, hired more staff, reached for more comprehensive levels of service delivery, and did not scrutinize too closely exactly what it took to work this way.

As we have learned since 2008, however, this steady increase in profits masked some fundamentally inefficient systems. Once the mask was removed, some firms learned to their everlasting dismay just how far from optimized their support functions really were. The results were sadly predictable: heightened employee review processes, layoffs, and hiring freezes.

The first rounds of cost cutting may have made the bankers to law firms happy, but they put serious stress on the people who were left behind. The remaining staff now faced the task of maintaining traditional service levels despite reduced headcount. No matter how heroic the staff, usually it is not possible for one person to do the work of two or three, so some things necessarily are left undone. If those omitted tasks were superfluous, then the firm is in the happy position of improved efficiency. However, eliminating staff without first examining the logic and efficacy of the underlying work processes in which they were engaged means that the shortfalls in work that inevitably occur when people are trying to "do more with less" can lead to instability in those processes. Without a properly re-engineered work process coupled with a "right-sized" work force, those things left undone are likely to be random, inconvenient, and occasionally deeply problematic.

If things were not bad enough for law firms, the fallout from the financial crisis of 2008 led some clients to be much more vocal about their expectations of their outside counsel. Suddenly it became clear that the frenetic pre-crash activity had not always entirely pleased the clients for whose benefit the firms claimed to be working. Now some clients were demanding that their outside counsel run their firms with the same kinds of business disciplines that governed the clients themselves. Above all, clients were looking for transparency and predictability with respect to the pricing of legal services. To meet these client expectations, firms now find that they have to move beyond simply discounting services to actually re-examining all parts of the firm to ensure they contribute to an efficient organization capable of meeting these client expectations.

This is where optimization steps into the picture.

How to optimize

The path to optimization emerges from a series of strategic decisions. Before taking those decisions, a senior manager committed to optimizing a support function must answer some tough questions:

1. Does your firm management provide sufficient clarity of vision and direction so that you as a senior manager can articulate what constitutes an optimized support function within the context of your firm and its strategic plan?
2. Are you aware of the approach of optimized support functions in your firm or other firms?
3. Are you offering the right array of products and services given current client expectations and market conditions?
4. Do you have a realistic departmental plan to achieve optimization?
5. Do you have the right people?
6. Do you have appropriate technology?
7. Do you, your team, and firm management have the requisite political will to optimize your support function?

(If the answer to several of these questions is no, you will need to consider carefully whether optimization inside your firm is realistically within reach. Further, you should consider whether the better approach is to outsource some or all of your department's functions in order to provide the right mix of products and services at the right price.)

Envisioning and articulating what constitutes an optimized support function may be one of the most important responsibilities of a senior manager. As with many things, however, not all senior managers are created equal and some may not be up to the task. This is due, in part, to the fact that not all of them have been taught to see properly. What does this mean? People tend to see what they know or what makes sense given their frame of reference, and it takes guidance, self-awareness, and intentional action to overcome this cognitive bias. How does selective perception manifest itself among law firm senior managers? For example, until fairly recently it was quite usual for firms to promote from within their own ranks in order to fill senior management positions. The result was a group of senior managers who had deep institutional knowledge, along with deeply ingrained ways of doing things. Furthermore, unless they were active in professional networks, they may not have had any detailed sense of whether or how things were done differently in other firms or other industries. Given the relatively narrow ambit of their experience and limited access to alternative models, it would have been difficult for them to envision other approaches to the work they did. In this context, optimizing the support function they managed would likely be beyond reach.

So how can a senior manager committed to optimization bring that goal within reach? It is hard to achieve that which you cannot see. Therefore, the first task is to broaden your vision. There are several ways to do this, but it begins with seeking out examples of optimized performance in your own firm and then in other firms. Further, given the insularity and conservatism of the legal industry, it would be wise to seek out examples from other industries. Once you begin looking outside the legal industry you will realize quite rapidly that there are useful ideas you can beg, borrow, or steal that are considered commonplace outside the legal industry, but are still viewed as innovative or radical inside our industry. Here lies opportunity.

Optimizing inputs and outputs is another key challenge for a senior manager. Beginning with the end in mind, is the support function in question providing the products and services that are most highly valued by the firm's clients? Have these offerings been validated recently by the client? And are these products and services being offered in a manner and at a price that the client finds acceptable?

This focus on the client is more than a matter of paying lip service. It represents a significant shift from a firm oriented towards its owners to a firm oriented towards its clients. In other words, this approach can (and should) cause the entire firm to think differently about what it does. As new models of legal service providers emerge, we are getting a clearer picture of how things can be done differently in order to deliver products and services the client values and is willing to purchase. And, we are getting a clearer picture of how far from optimized some law firms are.

Once you know what you have to deliver, the next task is to design and staff the underlying work processes in such a manner as to ensure that you provide your chosen products and services as efficiently as possible. This is hard work. It requires painstaking effort to physically map every step involved in each work process. Addleshaw Goddard in the UK reported in 2013 that they are well on their way to creating process maps of key legal processes.[1] In the United States, Lisa Damon (Seyfarth Shaw's head of SeyfarthLean) told the audience at an Ark legal KM conference that "Seyfarth loves to process map. We create process maps for anything that moves within the firm."[2] But it is the rare firm that can make the claim that Karl Chapman (chief executive of Riverview Law) made at the Reinvent Law NYC 2014 conference when he said that his firm had mapped all of their processes. For him, this was the natural outgrowth of the fact that Riverview Law had the DNA of a professional outsourcer rather than the DNA of a traditional law firm.[3]

In the 21st century, optimization most likely will involve technology and, possibly, some form of automation. Unfortunately, there are few law firms that are known for their cutting-edge technology. In fact, one senior IT manager went so far as to call the legal industry "a technology backwater". If this seems extreme, consider how Andrew Chamberlain (head of client delivery at Addleshaw Goddard) described the typical law firm approach to technology:

> *"The legal market is traditionally conservative, and driven by short term returns. It is a market which has never undergone the continuous transformation which just about every sector of the economy has had to go through. It is a market which has typically significantly under-invested in technology – so much so that the big technology providers have largely not bothered to target the market with sector specific solutions."*[4]

To be clear, optimization is not just another euphemism for "implementing more expensive technology". It is, in fact, possible to get closer to an optimized level by engaging in systematic business improvement efforts. However, at some point it will be advisable or necessary to use technology to relieve some of the burden on your staff. Mark Chandler (general counsel of Cisco) told the audience at the Reinvent Law NYC 2014 conference that his staff tries to focus 80 percent of their time and effort on work that gives Cisco a competitive advantage in the market. As for the remaining 20 percent of routine work that does not yield a competitive advantage, they try to automate as much of that as possible. This requires technology.[5]

Once you know where you want to go, it would be wise to create a road map. This plan will help guide the daily, weekly, and monthly choices your support function makes when allocating time, energy, and attention. This plan will provide a framework for decision and action until your department has reached its goal.

The final, and perhaps most challenging, piece of the puzzle is the matter of political will. The senior managers I interviewed who seemed to have led their departments closest to optimization exhibited a strong determination to improve in material ways the quality and impact of their team. There is a great deal a single manager armed with political will can accomplish. However, when that same manager acts in concert with other senior managers of the firm, then that firm has an opportunity to leap to an even higher level of performance. The opposite also is true. A firm led by managers who lack the political will to do the hard work required to change will find that maintaining the status quo will become the new goal, not optimization.

What does optimization look like?

What does optimization look like? I put this question to a number of senior managers. Their answers were surprisingly similar in many respects. That said, the differences they mentioned were striking and often were the by-product of a singular firm culture, the particular responsibilities of their support function, or the personal convictions of the manager in question. To amplify this, I will discuss first some of the common points that emerged from the interviews.

An optimized support function has the following traits:

- It understands its highest value to the firm.
- It maintains an ambitious balance between strategic and operational focus:
    - Its systems and work processes reduce the risk of emergencies, while enabling rapid response when required.
    - It invests in longer-term projects that help the firm gain and keep its competitive edge.
    - It is able to see opportunities and capitalize upon them, even in the face of constraints.

- Its emphasis on knowledge sharing and collaboration gives it influence and impact across the firm.
- It encourages a high degree of knowledge sharing.
- Its preferred approach is working collaboratively rather than creating and defending silos.
- Its drive for efficiency and collaboration means that it eschews efforts to build fiefdoms or administrative strongholds.
- Its personnel are T-shaped.
- It has healthy managers and staff.

CASE STUDY

Highest value to the firm

Doug Doerfler is CFO of Stinson Leonard Street LLP, a firm formed in 2014 by the merger of Stinson Morrison Hecker and Leonard, Street and Deinard – two of the leading full-service law firms in the Midwest. When I interviewed him in 2013, he was CFO of Stinson Morrison Hecker and deeply engaged in the challenge of delivering the highest value to the firm. The information reported below is based on his experience at Stinson Morrison.

If you want to have a real and positive impact on a firm, ask in what way your support function affects the profitability of your law firm and then set out to improve that. When Doug Doerfler asked himself that question several years ago, the answer was very clear: the finance department he managed would have the greatest positive impact on the firm's profitability by shortening the billing cycle. In other words, reducing the time it takes to issue bills and then collect those bills. Having reached that conclusion, he undertook a detailed study as to what delayed the billing cycle at his firm and then set out systematically to remove or reduce each of those delays.

The first and most obvious delay was the time spent simply preparing and issuing bills. While each firm has its variants, the broad outlines of the process are similar: ensuring all the time and expenses relating to a matter have been submitted for the relevant month; creating a pro forma bill for partner review and action; and preparing a draft bill that reflects the inevitable adjustments (i.e. reassigning improperly billed time, writing down or writing off properly billed time, etc.); editing descriptions of the work done; preparing and issuing a final bill. Before this process is completed, days (if not weeks) can go by. Since a firm cannot collect on a bill until it has been received by the client, Doerfler and his team focused on reducing as much as possible the time it takes to get from the end of any given month to the time at which the bill is delivered to a client. At the time Doug and I spoke, his team consistently issued bills by the 10th day of every month.

Doerfler reports that when he tells colleagues in other firms that his team meets this 10-day goal consistently, they usually ask him how large an army of billing personnel he has at his disposal. His answer is eight. To be clear, that is eight employees out of a department of 30 people. (As noted above, Doerfler spoke to me before his firm's merger was announced. These numbers reflect the department's size at the time of our conversation.)

How is it possible to achieve this goal? The secret is in how his staff is deployed. At the beginning of every month, 26 of the 30 members of the department focus on the bills, not just the eight members of the billing function. Working together, the 26 ensure their deadline of the 10th is always met. Among other things, this means that members of the finance department, rather than a billing partner's secretary, handle all the editing of the bills (in consultation with the relevant lawyers). This reduces the hand-off time, waiting time, and turnaround time. In short, the finance department has assumed most of the burden of preparing the bills in order to speed the issuance time.

What does it take to pull off a team effort like this every month? To begin with, it requires a team. Since teams are created rather than born, this requires leadership, shared vision, and team members who are willing to roll up their sleeves to do the windows. It requires an understanding by all concerned of the benefits to the firm of optimizing the billing process. Finally, it requires deliberate practice so that staff who normally work outside the billing group are trained and able to assume the work of the billing group during those crucial first 10 days of the month.

The payback for this effort is that by optimizing the billing process, they have found a way to reliably deliver positive results in their area of greatest immediate impact. This is the benefit of focusing on highest value.

Strategic versus operational focus

Every support function has chores it must do on a regular basis. These are the tasks that allow the computing network to remain operational, the marketing events to occur, the facility to be heated or cooled as appropriate, the library resources to remain in circulation, the model documents to be updated, etc. In the course of my interviews, I asked every senior manager how they divided their time between strategic and operational work. Their answers were illuminating. Some of the managers admitted that they spent most of their time on operational matters. Frequently, they were managers in smaller firms or managers whose staff had been heavily hit by layoffs, retirements, or hiring freezes. Managers in firms of all sizes acknowledged that when their function was understaffed, they and their senior reports had to pick up the slack. In this context, the focus often was on "keeping the lights on" rather than on more future-facing activities such as engaging in research and development activities that might open up new opportunities for the department and the firm.

Several managers interviewed said that they could not always control the allocation of their time between strategic and operational matters. In an emergency, they had to focus on operational matters. In periods of calm, they tried to focus on strategic issues. At first blush, this did not seem unreasonable. In fact, it could be considered the norm for many in a client services industry. However, this approach held their strategic efforts hostage to whatever emergency happened to crop up on a day-to-day basis. Over time, it is likely that this approach would tilt the bulk of their efforts towards operational rather than towards strategic.

In contrast, there were a few exceptional managers I interviewed who designed their department in such a way as to maximize their ability to focus on strategic matters, while ensuring that the lights stayed on. Loretta Auer (CIO of Fish Richardson) is one of these managers. In August 2011, she was awarded the Leadership Award at the International Legal Technology Association's (ILTA) Distinguished Peer Awards Dinner. This award is given to an individual who "leads transformational and innovative change, collaborates with other leaders, and cultivates new leaders within their organization".[6]

When I put the strategic versus operational challenge to Loretta Auer, her response was refreshingly clear. As the CIO, she needed to be able to focus on strategic matters. Therefore, it was critical that her team handle operational issues in such a way as to prevent the urgent from inappropriately trumping the important. To achieve this goal, her first priority was to ensure the reliability of the IT infrastructure. As she put it: "You need to have a rock-solid operation. You should not make penny-wise pound-foolish economies with the infrastructure." To that end, she has hired a highly qualified infrastructure team that regularly identifies and carefully examines every single point of failure in their infrastructure. For each point of failure, they ensure that it is secure and that they have built in the requisite workarounds and redundancy. On top of this, they keep abreast of the constant changes in infrastructure technology and standards. According to Auer, IT infrastructure changes sufficiently frequently that no firm can safely assume that they can simply "fix it and forget it". Rather, it takes constant vigilance and care by a smart and capable team.

Thanks to the excellence of her infrastructure team, Auer is able to devote time, energy, and resources to development projects. A press release announcing the 2011 Leadership Award she received highlights some of the projects that have been possible because of the way she has tilted her department towards strategic work:

> *"Loretta was recognized for her creativity and vision in helping our firm to compete successfully in a continually transforming environment. Loretta has championed initiatives to improve firm wide administrative systems and staff productivity through our Best Practices and Re-Engineering/Transformation programs that will enable us to maintain/gain a competitive advantage in many areas of our practice. She has mentored and developed an information technology management staff that has accomplished projects using the best examples of emerging technologies and development platforms in the legal industry, including Net-based reporting applications, SharePoint, Windows 7, Office 2010 and e-discovery."*[7]

One final note: another very pragmatic CIO told me that she spends 90 percent of her time on strategic matters. She has learned that if she gets too involved in the operational details, she becomes an obstacle or a bottleneck because she has so many competing demands on her time. Accordingly, she hires excellent managers for operational matters and lets them do their job. She focuses on providing them with strategic direction and political cover.

Knowledge sharing and collaboration

In this age of plentiful information, it is not always easy to find the information you need. If law firm personnel worked on an assembly line, there would be little mystery regarding how they spent their time each workday. A law firm, however, relies on knowledge workers rather than factory workers. And these knowledge workers tend to be in offices (often behind closed doors) or in cubicles (often wearing earphones). As a result, it can be challenging for a casual observer to actually know what a colleague is working on.

Senior managers who are focused on optimization realize that poor knowledge sharing within a support function creates friction in the system. It is like a tax on every work process and interaction. What is the nature of this tax? It is the value of time wasted looking for information. It is the cost of missed opportunity due to delayed action. It is the price of frustration when personnel know that they are forced to reinvent the wheel unnecessarily.

Unfortunately, there are several barriers to knowledge sharing within an organization. Morten T. Hansen noted four main barriers that block knowledge sharing and collaboration:

- "Not-invented-here: People are not willing to seek input from others outside their unit.
- Hoarding: People are not willing to provide information and help others when asked.
- Search problems: People are not able to find information and people easily.
- Transfer problems: People are not able to transfer complicated knowledge from one unit to another."[8]

The challenge for senior managers is to diagnose properly which of the four barriers are present in their department and then prescribe actions that will reduce these barriers and help bring about the desired knowledge-sharing behavior.[9]

While it is possible to dictate that staff members report all their activities through time records or other reporting mechanisms, this effort runs the risk of increasing the information overload without meaningfully improving knowledge sharing. Certainly lawyers have long had a love-hate relationship with their hourly billing reports. Is there any reason to believe that other law firm personnel would produce more informative (or more timely) reports?

Rather than trying to force knowledge sharing across all activities, some senior managers have targeted high-value activities and mandated a measure of knowledge sharing for those activities. For example, Shirley Crow (CIO of Farella Braun + Martel LLP) asks her staff to document all key processes and procedures on a wiki. In addition, her team does a lot of cross-training within the department so that they never have to delay service while waiting for someone to return from a vacation.

Another way of fostering knowledge sharing is to create cross-functional teams. Doug Doerfler does this in his department when he creates teams to work on specific strategic projects. Through these cross-functional teams staff members come to appreciate the expertise and understand the perspectives of colleagues who work in other parts of the department. In addition, by working together and getting to know each other, they lay the groundwork for future collaboration and knowledge sharing. Finally, he makes these teams short-term and project-specific. When the project is completed, team members are assigned to other project teams. By this method, he is constantly mixing and blending his staff, thereby facilitating much better knowledge sharing and collaboration.

Morten Hansen makes another specific recommendation for organizations that want to foster better knowledge sharing and collaboration: cultivate T-shaped personnel. What does it mean to be T-shaped? The T-shaped person has deep competence in their area of expertise and can deliver results there (this is the vertical part of the T). The T-shaped person also has the ability to reach across and work with personnel in other units or with other expertise (the horizontal part). By being able to work vertically and horizontally, T-shaped staff are aware of resources and needs outside their own silos, are willing to request input from others (thereby overcoming the not-invented-here barrier), and they are able to assist others (thereby reducing the hoarding barrier).

By encouraging staff to leave their silos, share their knowledge, and collaborate, it is possible to reduce the friction in the system. If done correctly, this fosters teamwork and gives staff a sense of purpose and fulfillment in their work. All of these are hallmarks of an optimized support function.

Healthy managers and staff

It is impossible to have an optimized support function without an optimized staff. This raises some important questions: How can a senior manager create an environment in which staff members want to do their best work? How can a senior manager keep staff members engaged and productive? And what behaviors must a senior manager model and encourage in order to create an optimized staff?

The rot starts from the top. If the managers of support functions do not themselves have a healthy approach to work, then it is unlikely that their subordinates will. As one senior manager interviewed put it, "unless you are healthy, it is hard to run a healthy department". And this requires more than mere physical health. It requires a focus on the humans, not just the headcount in your department. For him, it means creating an environment that "makes people want to come to work every day". He does this by investing in the people who work for him:

"I cultivate very open, supportive and nurturing relationships with my managers." He also tries to remain extremely accessible to everyone in the department. He talks to individual staff members directly and they know that they can come to him directly. By modeling this behavior, he hopes that they will replicate those relationships with the people who work with them. In addition, he does not tolerate relationships among his team that are marked by unexpressed tension. He has learned that, if left unchecked, these relationships can have a toxic effect on others. To counteract this, he tackles problems early by taking people aside and talking out the issues.

A commitment to health involves empathy and flexibility on the part of the manager. In addition to understanding what work needs to be completed by members of their team, a manager needs to understand the individual context of each team member. Another senior manager described an esteemed colleague at another firm as a person who "invests heavily in understanding her people and the pressures that are going on their lives. She gives them appropriate time to deal with crises and family concerns." And this is where it pays to be nimble. Sometimes the individual context of a team member will make a nontraditional schedule necessary. Or, perhaps, that employee might need to work from home or bring a child to work in an emergency. Several senior managers I talked to said that, in light of constrained resources since 2008, it has become especially important to provide additional flexibility to staff members who are trying heroically to balance additional pressures at work with ongoing pressures in other parts of their lives. These managers also acknowledged that their HR colleagues were not always as enthusiastic about these flexible arrangements.

The commitment to health extends to finding and maintaining healthy approaches to work. At Lathrop & Gage LLP, their IT department allows staff members to unplug for three to five hours at a time so that they can be single-focused on a specific project. It relieves them of the fatigue of interruption. A staff member must arrange these unplugged hours in advance with her manager to ensure that there is always someone else available who can cover critical system support, and to be sure they focus on high-priority tasks during the unplugged hours. The IT department strives to allow engineers to do this at least twice each week – especially during heavy project season (e.g. a rollout or a desktop upgrade). This arrangement has proven to be a highly productive, highly effective way of moving projects forward and giving staff professional satisfaction.

Finally, we end where we began. Any senior manager who wants to lead an optimized support function must have a clear-eyed view of themself. As one interviewee put it: "Throw yourself into therapy, work through your stuff and develop sound personal insight into yourself and your motivations (especially the unconscious motivations)". Managers have a disproportionate impact on the work environment of their subordinates, so managers owe it to themselves and their colleagues to strive for health.

This first appeared as Chapter 1 in Abraham, V. M., Optimizing Law Firm Support Functions, *ARK Group, 2014.*

References

1. Chamberlain, A., "Becoming a different legal business", *The Lawyer* [online], 2013. Available at: www.thelawyer.com/news-and-analysis/opinion/becoming-a-different-legal-business/3006257.article.
2. Abraham, V.M., "Seyfarth's Success Story", *Above and Beyond KM* [Blog], 31 October 2011. Available at: aboveandbeyondkm.com/2011/10/seyfarths-success-story-ark.html.
3. Abraham, V.M., "Reinvent Law NYC 2014 in the Rearview Mirror", *Above and Beyond KM*, 10 February 2014. Available at: aboveandbeyondkm.com/2014/02/reinvent-law-nyc-2014-in-the-rearview-mirror.html.
4. Chamberlain, A., "Becoming a different legal business", *The Lawyer*, [online] 2013. Available at: www.thelawyer.com/news-and-analysis/opinion/becoming-a-different-legal-business/3006257.article.
5. Abraham, V.M., "Reinvent Law NYC 2014 in the Rearview Mirror", *Above and Beyond KM*, 10 February 2014. Available at: aboveandbeyondkm.com/2014/02/reinvent-law-nyc-2014-in-the-rearview-mirror.html.
6. Fish & Richardson, "Loretta Auer, Fish's CIO, wins the 'Leadership Award' at the International Legal Technology Association's Distinguished Peer Awards" [Press Release], 26 August 2011. Available at: www.fr.com/ILTA-LeadershipAward/.
7. Ibid.
8. Hansen, M.T., *Collaboration: How leaders avoid the traps, create unity, and reap big results*, Harvard Business Press, 2009.
9. For further guidance, see Hansen, 2009.

Chapter 24: An introduction to Lean and Six Sigma

By Catherine Alman MacDonagh, CEO and founder of the Legal Lean Sigma Institute

What is process improvement?

Let's start with the basics. What exactly is "process improvement"? Most people can identify when there are "issues" with a process. Far fewer can thoughtfully respond to the questions:

- How would you decide which problems are the most important to solve?
- How will you know when you have succeeded in improving a process?

Process improvement (sometimes called legal process improvement or LPI) provides a framework and tools to answer these two critical questions. It is the systematic practice of first analyzing a process to understand how it is *currently* carried out, then searching for issues, problems, and opportunities in the process and prioritizing them. Once prioritized, tools and techniques are employed to solve priority problems or to capture significant opportunities. Finally, the new process must be controlled so that it delivers the anticipated benefits.

A "process" is a describable, repeatable sequence of activities that generates an outcome; as such, to a process improvement practitioner, nearly everything qualifies as a process, from the mundane routines of everyday life (like making coffee or tea) to incredibly complex processes involving multiple operations, people, organizations, and so forth (such as class action law suits). In the words of W. Edwards Deming, who was known as the Father of the Quality Revolution, and was responsible for the first application of statistical quality control principles to a non-manufacturing environment, "If you can't describe what you are doing as a process, you don't know what you are doing."

Already, based on my experience, I anticipate that there are readers who are unconvinced (and may be bristling with the notion) that the legal work they do can be considered or distilled to "a process". One of the things I often hear from clients is that "we don't have a process for that". However, the reality is that if you are doing a particular kind of work right now, you have a process – albeit one that may radically differ from matter to matter, client to client, lawyer to lawyer, or office to office. Moreover, we consider processes to be the way that law firms create and deliver value to their clients. Thus, we recognize that processes embody the knowledge of the law firm, department, practice group, or team. In short, our processes are the way we do and deliver our work. Ideally, they are the best way we have learned or know how to do something – they are our best practices. As such, a great process can create a competitive advantage for a law firm.

What is legal project management?

There is a direct connection between process improvement and project management (also called legal project management or LPM). Consider this: what is the benefit of having the ability to manage projects very well if our underlying process is not the best it can be? Conversely, what is the value of having an excellent process that is not being managed well?

Process improvement helps us determine the best way to carry out a certain kind of work to achieve efficiency, excellent quality of work and service, high probability of successful outcomes, and predictability. When we do develop the capacity to do process improvement work, we can employ project management skills to select the best processes, tools, and skills to be able to carry out our ideal process every time.

Essentially, project management is a role and set of skills that ensure that, for a particular engagement, we review and select the right processes and then apply them appropriately to each particular matter. Then, project management involves actively managing schedules, staff, and deliverables to deliver high quality work on time and under budget to achieve specific goals.

Timothy B. Corcoran, principle of the Corcoran Consulting Group and adjunct faculty and affiliated consultant of the Legal Lean Sigma Institute, defines project management as "the process and activity of planning, organizing, motivating, and controlling resources, procedures and protocols". So, even project management may be considered a process.

Corcoran explains the six steps of project management as follows:

1. Define objective (what constitutes a win for the client?).
2. Define scope and constraints, e.g. budget, timeline.
3. Establish the project plan. (Identify standard, variable, and volatile tasks; establish task timelines and budgets. What is on the "critical path"? What resources are necessary, *including a project manager*?)
4. Execute the plan (track efforts, time, budget, results).
5. Continuously monitor performance, change management (including regular communication and establishing a continuous "feedback loop").
6. Review and improve. (Learning organizations focus on improvement over time.)

Where to start?

Many firms ask: "in which discipline should we invest and engage first, process improvement or project management?" The simple answer is that there is no one "right way" to begin. That stated, my bias is for firms to learn both at once; this is why the Legal Lean Sigma Institute developed the only certification courses that combine Lean, Six Sigma, and project management. My next best suggestion is to engage in process improvement first, so that a firm begins to improve processes and simultaneously to develop project management skills. After that, the firm can train project managers and others using optimized processes.

Whether your firm begins with process improvement or project management, eventually, both must be employed for the firm to fully realize the benefits of either one. We are able to attain a multiplier effect when we combine process improvement and project management: we have better, more standardized processes that are well controlled in order to achieve a high level of performance.

Processes always exist to serve a client. Accordingly, we measure both the process performance and efficiency. Processes have a characteristic performance level, usually called process capability, that describes how well the process meets client expectations (which means, obviously, that we need to understand the client's expectations as well). Additionally, we learn about process resource requirements, sometimes called process efficiency, which refers to the resources (time, people, equipment, money) required to carry out the process. There are many dimensions along which a process may be measured. Moreover, a process may perform quite well in some dimensions and poorly in others.

Ronald L. Burdge points out the value of measuring client satisfaction: "The legal profession frequently proclaims it is dedicated to providing legal services in a way that satisfies... But if we do not measure the quality of that service, then can we really say that we are able to provide excellent legal representation? If you don't know that you are doing good work, can you really be sure you are? If what you value is a satisfied client, then you must determine how to satisfy a client – and you will not really be able to know that until you understand how to gauge client satisfaction in the first place."

What are Lean and Six Sigma?

Now that we have process basics covered, we can delve into Lean and Six Sigma. Lean is about simplifying processes. With Lean, we simplify processes, reduce the number of steps, maximize process speed, and greatly improve productivity – we focus on doing the right things and eliminating waste in processes. In this way, we ensure that we maximize resource efficiency. Six Sigma is focused on reducing and controlling variation. Put together, Lean Sigma is about deciding the best way to do something and then always doing those things correctly.

In short, the two disciplines are about establishing the right things to do (Lean) and then doing those things right (Six Sigma). While it used to be the case that practitioners of each might have argued that their way was better, now they are considered complementary and used together. Some use the term Lean Six Sigma, others use Lean Sigma, which is actually an example of Lean in action, since it eliminates "six" as a superfluous word. That said, both terms are correct and are used interchangeably.

Lean concepts have been applied for centuries, but a major development in this line of thinking occurred in the Japanese automobile industry in the middle of the 20th century:

> *"As Kiichiro Toyoda, Taiichi Ohno, and others at Toyota looked at this situation [of the automobile manufacturing process] in the 1930s, and more intensely just after World War II, it occurred to them that a series of simple innovations might make it more possible to provide both continuity in process flow and a wide variety in product offerings... and invented the Toyota Production System.*
> *This system in essence shifted the focus of the manufacturing engineer from individual machines and their utilization, to the flow of the product through the total process. Toyota concluded that by*

right-sizing machines for the actual volume needed, introducing self-monitoring machines to ensure quality, lining the machines up in process sequence, pioneering quick setups so each machine could make small volumes of many part numbers, and having each process step notify the previous step of its current needs for materials, it would be possible to obtain low cost, high variety, high quality, and very rapid throughput times to respond to changing customer desires. Also, information management could be made much simpler and more accurate."[1]

How do we translate process improvement to a legal context?

One of our challenges is to translate the concepts of process improvement so that they make sense in a legal context. After all, law firms are not manufacturing automobiles or silicon wafers. There is a great deal of variation: each firm, practice group, lawyer, client, jurisdiction, matter, case, set of facts, judge, opposing counsel, and so on, is different. So how can we ensure that the desire to eliminate something in a process does not replace the exercise of good judgment or constrain our ability to do something that is in the best interests of the firm and its client?

This translation of these concepts from the manufacturing world to the legal space is why Legal Lean Sigma® was created. The use of Lean and Six Sigma in law is simple on a conceptual level but not always easy in the application. We have found that it has always been easiest for candidates in our certification courses to understand how to use process improvement in relation to business processes such as timekeeping, client intake, or conflicts. Initially, it can be more of a stretch to think about how these concepts might be applied to legal work since there can often be quite a bit of variation in terms of how lawyers like to do and deliver particular kinds of work.

However, if we consider that every service offered, whether it is litigation or transactional work, contains a series of repeatable, describable steps – even if there is variation in each one – then each one is a process. Accordingly, in each service offering, there are abundant opportunities to apply Lean concepts and tools to make the process simpler and faster.

CASE STUDY

The application of Lean concepts to a service company

In an October 2003 Harvard Business Review *article entitled "The Lean Service Machine", Cynthia Karen Swank related how a service company was able to apply lessons learned from manufacturing. The article is particularly relevant, considering that many large law firms have grown through mergers, acquisitions, and combinations. Moreover, most firms have identified service as a key strategy for differentiation, just like Jefferson Pilot Financial, as Swank describes:*

"Jefferson Pilot Financial was typical of many US service companies at the end of the 1990s. After making four acquisitions that more than tripled its size, the full-service life insurance and annuities company was searching for new ways to grow in a fiercely competitive business [environment]. Rising customer expectations had led to a proliferation of new insurance products as well as an increase in product complexity and costs. At the same time, specialized niche players touting lower premiums and faster handling of policies were forcing full-service insurance providers to both improve service and reduce costs.

The top managers of Jefferson Pilot Financial (JPF) recognized that the company needed to differentiate itself in the eyes of its customers, the independent life-insurance advisers who sell and service policies... It identified superior service to them as a key ingredient of that strategy.

To determine where improved service would have the greatest impact, JPF undertook an in-depth analysis of the operations... The study unearthed considerable variation in the quality of existing services... It was clear that management could significantly increase revenue by improving operations. Indeed, the company estimated that it could increase the paid annualized premium for its Premier Partners by 10% to 15% if it could issue all policies within three weeks of receiving the applications, offer periodic application status reports, simplify the submission process, and reduce errors to 1%.

JPF believed that its business could benefit from lean production because its operations involved the processing of an almost tangible 'service product'. Like an automobile on the assembly line, an insurance policy goes through a series of processes, from initial application to underwriting, or risk assessment, to policy issuance. With each step, value is added to the work in progress – just as a car gets doors or a coat of paint.

In late 2000, on the advice of a consulting firm, JPF appointed a five-person 'lean team' to reengineer the New Business operations according to the principles of lean production. The team included the assistant vice president of New Business administration and a special project manager who reported directly to the senior vice president overseeing New Business operations. They were supported by three lean-production experts from the consulting firm. Thus the team combined in-depth knowledge of JPF's processes with an understanding of lean-production principles.

The initiative has delivered impressive results. The company halved the average time from receipt of a Premier Partner application to issuance of a policy, reduced labor costs by 26%, and trimmed the rate of reissues due to errors by 40%... These outcomes contributed to a remarkable 60% increase in new annualized life premiums in the company's core individual-life-insurance business in just two years. Similar results are being recorded in other departments as the company rolls out the new systems across the whole organization."

If we replace key terms in this case with legal examples, the applicability of Lean to law firms becomes more obvious: Law Firm A was typical of many similarly situated firms. After making four acquisitions that more than tripled its size, the full-service law firm was searching for new ways to grow in a fiercely competitive business environment. Rising client expectations had led to a proliferation of service offerings as well as an increase in service delivery complexity and costs. At the same time, specialized niche players touting lower premiums and faster handling of legal services, such as document review, were forcing full-service law firms to both improve service and reduce costs.

The executive committee of Law Firm A recognized that the firm needed to differentiate itself in the eyes of its clients, prospects, and referral sources. Law Firm A identified providing superior service to them as a key ingredient of that strategy.

It was clear that the firm could significantly increase revenue by improving operations. Indeed, the firm estimated that it could increase the profits per partner by 10-15 percent if it could speed up the delivery of legal work to the most utilized services of its key clients within three weeks of receiving the request for work, offer periodic status and budget reports, simplify the intake process, and reduce errors to 1 percent.

Using Lean thinking to eliminate waste

Lean thinking relentlessly searches for and then reduces and even eliminates eight kinds of waste:

1. Defects and all related waste, including inspection, testing, and correction – Examples of defects include missing a filing deadline, incomplete forms, bad drafting, data entry errors, and omissions;
2. Overproduction – Examples include starting work before clearing conflicts, printing too many hard copies, and drafting a ten-page memo when only a one-page summary was requested;
3. Waiting – Examples include awaiting responses from clients, employees, or opposing counsel, starting a call or meeting late due to late arrivals, waiting for technology such as boot up/restart times;
4. Excess capacity – For example, not using the lowest cost resources such as clients, paralegals, and assistants that are capable of doing tasks, when partners are doing associate-level work, or over-staffing a matter;
5. Transportation (this type of waste refers to things moving as opposed to people moving, which is considered "motion") – Examples include moving files from one place to another and sending hard-copies rather than emails;
6. Inventory – Examples include work in process (WIP), unread email, marketing materials (such as collateral, brochures, and promotional items, or event materials);
7. Motion (which refers to people moving as opposed to things) – Examples include people spending extra time getting from one place to the next due to travel or poor office layout, delivering files rather than mailing/emailing them, extra keystrokes/clicks to find documents; and
8. Extra processing steps – Examples include conducting too much research or double and triple checking (e.g. approvals of expenses without any real review).

Waste is present in virtually every process. In their Lean management guide, "Lean for Legal Staff – The 7 Hidden Wastes", legal services consultants and trainers Levantar give examples of how work in progress (WIP) is created through waste: "One department found that 40% of in the inputs (paperwork and forms) it received from clients contained errors or omissions. To correct these, the legal staff had to call the clients; we know from our work in call centres that only 1 in 3 outbound calls is successful… Imagine therefore that for every 100 matters being processed there were 180 activities generated."[2]

Using Six Sigma to reduce variation

Lean is better when we add Six Sigma, which is focused on reducing process variation to reduce errors and defects. Our concentration is on understanding relationships between many variables. Those include the relationships between inputs and outputs, the key factors that affect outcomes, and the "best way" to do something (i.e. how can we increase our probability of a positive outcome). We question how carefully a process needs to be controlled in order to give the results desired by the client, and ask what are the benefits of consistency and standardization?

While Lean is focused on resource efficiency, with Six Sigma, our focus is on process capability and alignment with requirements. Process capability is what your process can deliver. Therefore, with Six Sigma, we want a capable process that is aligned with requirements. When we reduce and control variation so that we are doing things right, we create a very capable process.

A Six Sigma process is one where there are only 3.4 defects per million opportunities (DPMO). We define "opportunity" as any chance not to meet the required specifications. This standard makes perfect sense in the context of a manufacturing environment where Six Sigma was originally developed (first at Motorola, in the early 1980s, and later at other companies such as AlliedSignal, Boeing, or General Electric, where it was famously championed by former CEO Jack Welch).

Sigma	Defects per million opportunities
1	691,462
2	308,538
3	66,807
4	6,210
5	233
6	3.4

Figure 1: DPMO in Six Sigma processes

The art and science of legal process improvement

At its core, Six Sigma revolves around a few key concepts. The first is "critical to quality", which are the attributes that are most important to the client(s). A "defect" is any failure to deliver what the client wants. We must always keep in mind that variation is what our clients experience, what they see and feel; clients want to be pleased, not surprised, so it is important to have "stable operations", which ensure that we have consistent, predictable processes to improve what the client sees and feels.

NovusLaw offers document review, management, and analysis for lawyers. They offer a stunning case study on the applicability of Six Sigma to the document review process and also serve as an example of an industry driver and innovator:

"Six Sigma is what we use to eliminate defects as we measure and analyze our work processes. Typically, undocumented processes will yield 20,000–60,000 defects per million opportunities. Six Sigma is designed to get that down to fewer than 4/million. On our most recent document review we performed at Five Sigma, or approximately 200 defects per million. By the way, that's about 200 times better than the average in the legal industry today."[3]

This type of work used to be routinely performed by law firms. Now, law firms may do very well to partner with an outsourced provider who can deliver greater predictability and much higher quality work at a predictable price.

Not every step or part of every process should be standardized or controlled as tightly as another step in the same process – this is why legal process improvement is both art and science. There may be plenty of steps that require us to allow for a lot of latitude as we need to build in room for variation based on the lawyer's experience and knowledge. Other steps require little to no judgment and are therefore good candidates for controlling variation. Every case or matter does not need to be approached as though we had never done this kind of work before; this is not efficient and it also actively contradicts what we say to our clients, prospects, and referral sources about the benefits of working with lawyers who have great experience.

The foundation of process improvement is to describe (map) the process. Then, we measure the process. Each process has a characteristic performance level and characteristic resource requirements. The process performance (also called process capability) describes how well the process meets client expectations, while the process resource requirements (also called process efficiency) refers to the resources (time, people, equipment, and costs) required to carry out the process. There are many dimensions along which a process can be measured; a process can perform well in some dimensions and poorly in others.

Lean is used to understand process efficiency and Six Sigma helps us to understand process capability and align the process with requirements. Thus, we now use Lean Sigma (or Lean Six Sigma) for they are complementary and, used together, offer the most relevant and effective approach to employing process improvement in the legal industry. There is no question that opportunities for improvements in law firms are everywhere. When we employ the thinking of Lean Sigma we cannot help but see many chances to make things better in our processes for both the client and our firm – *with no tradeoffs*.

There are some who find it difficult to see the process behind the art of doing and delivering legal work. However, whatever kind of work a lawyer or firm is currently doing, it most certainly involves a process – it may not be a good one, but there are steps that are being followed each time.

Five principles of process improvement

Lean Sigma is both a methodology and a toolkit. The methodology consists of investigating a process and improving it by using a set of five principles in a particular sequence:

1. Specify value in the eyes of the client: We use the client's perspective to evaluate whether an activity is value-adding (activities that work to create a feature or attribute the client is willing to pay for) or non-value-adding (activities that take time and resources, but do not create additional value for the client). All non-value-added activities are priority candidates for elimination or minimization.
2. Reduce waste and variation: In addition to minimizing or eliminating the eight kinds of waste, we are also cognizant of the fact that processes are harder to operate and require more resources if they vary. Also, when processes vary, sometimes the results will be outside the client's acceptable range.
3. Make value flow at the pull of the client: When a process has "flow", the steps are linked together so that we move from one value-adding activity directly to another, without stopping or waiting. Non-value-added steps have been eliminated and activities are now very close together. This means that there is no waiting or batching and the process takes the shortest possible time from the beginning to the

end. This short cycle time allows a law firm to be very responsive to the client. The idea of "pull" is that a law firm is able to create value directly in response to actual client demand. Providing exactly what the client wants and acting exactly when the client wants (and at the last possible moment) requires all process steps to be closely coordinated in order to work together seamlessly.

4. Align and empower employees: To successfully and continuously improve processes, the firm must harness the power of great teams. There are teams of grouped individuals, where each member of the team is carrying out separate aspects of a project. There are also teams that act as an extension of the leader. The integrated, true team is able to leverage individual strengths to achieve extraordinary capacity for coordinated action – this is the kind of team we are aiming for not only when we deliver process improvement projects but in the teams delivering client work and service.
5. Continuously improve in pursuit of perfection: Because changes in the business environment are constant and rapid, they create requirements for higher process capabilities and efficiencies. If we do not continuously improve, we lose our ability to compete and function.

Maintaining the client's perspective

Notice that we begin our inquiry into Lean Sigma by using the client's perspective to evaluate whether any activity is value-adding (activities that work to create a feature or attribute the client is willing to pay for) or non-value-adding (activities that take time and resources, but do not create additional value for the client). Non-value-added activities are priority candidates for elimination or minimization. Of course, we do not just indiscriminately cut anything or anyone from a process. In fact, there are many occasions where we actually need more people/resources to make a process efficient. Moreover, just because value is not clear to the client, that does not necessary mean that the step should be eliminated; it is an opportunity to have a discussion about why something is necessary, advisable, or important to do from the lawyer's perspective. Even after discussion, the client might not find the activity valuable – this is an even greater reason to be highly efficient.

For any of your processes, consider:

- What is the value of the process in the eyes of the client?

- How do you establish this (or how would you find out)?
- What do you do that your clients might not consider valuable?
- What waste is there in the process?
- What are the effects of variation in your processes on your firm and on your clients?

Lean Sigma is the methodology and toolkit that provides a way to explore and answer these key questions.

This first appeared as Chapter 1 in Alman MacDonagh, C., Lean Six Sigma for Law Firms, *ARK Group, 2014.*

References

1. Lean Enterprise Institute; see www.lean.org/WhatsLean/History.cfm.
2. First published in March 2012 and most recently updated in February 2013; see www.levantar.co.uk/index.php/lean-consulting-training-strategy-reviews/lean-management-process-improvement-free-lean-guide-to.
3. Adam Smith, Esq. LLC, "Conversation with Ray Bayley of NovusLaw"; see www.adamsmithesq.com/2008/06/a_conversation_with_ray_b.

Chapter 25: Technology

By Chris Bull, founding director of Kingsmead Square, and David Bason, owner of Just You Ltd

So, exactly what era are we in? What will our great-great-grandchildren name this age? The Digital Age? The Technical Era? The Microsoft Age? The Apple Era? What is clear is that the periods we are trying to label are getting smaller and the pace of change has showed no signs of slowing down.

The advance of technology has been meteoric and we are now seeing things which we only ever dreamed of, or read about in sci-fi novels, or saw on Star Trek only a few years ago! We now have at our fingertips more processing capacity than that used to put a man on the moon.

Access to huge volumes of information is now free (or perceived to be free) and technology facilitates this.

Information businesses such as law firms need to identify exactly where the value of this access to information is in order to survive. Technology will affect business decisions, both strategic and operational. In this chapter, we look at both.

In the past we have experienced one disruptive technology at a time, for example telephones or the mass-produced automobile. Today, we are experiencing three of them simultaneously.

- The move to the cloud and the outsourcing of platforms;
- Mobile access anytime; and
- Social media.

Any business, law firm or not, that does not embrace these new technologies will be left behind, driven so far down the value chain that they cease to exist at all. This is particularly so for any information- or knowledge-driven business, such as law firms. The changes in how lawyers have changed in using technology within the last 30 years are demonstrated in our interview with Gary Assim of Shoosmiths.

Interview: Gary Assim – Head of Retail and Intellectual Property Group Leader, Shoosmiths.

Gary started his law degree in 1984, and then worked as an intern at Natwest before spending 10 years at Travers Smith. He moved to Shoosmiths and has been partner there for the last 14 years. He kindly agreed to provide his opinion on law firms in the digital age.

Do you consider yourself a technophile or technophobe?

I would call myself Mr Gadget Man! I have been an Apple disciple since I could afford it. I have owned the entire range of Apple products. To quote one of Shoosmith's values, I am always *How has technology changed the way you work?*

When I first started at Travers Smith in 1988, we used Telex. We would amend client documents by instructing my secretary of the changes, and she would use a typewriter to retype the entire document or use correction fluid on the hard copy. Drafts would then be sent to customers in the post. The turnaround time was a number of weeks. Now we expect to turnaround documents in hours... or sometimes faster than that! Documents are reviewed and amended online or using a tablet and then sent back to the client. We can even construct and amend documents with clients using online collaboration tools.

What are your predictions for the future of law firms?

We have seen a continued shake up in the legal sector, with several mergers and a number of high profile failures where law firms have made poor business decisions, including Halliwells, Cobbetts, and Chalinors.

I believe there will be very large firms processing huge volumes of work at a low value on the back of the latest technology and efficient processes. There will always be a need for the Magic Circle firms in the City who focus on major deals. Then there will be a fracturing of the remainder, with a lot of niche firms. In these cases I believe the existing pyramid model of feeding trainees in at the bottom with a partner sitting at the apex is costly and clients will not be prepared to "pay" for trainee lawyers' learning. Technology has made information widely available and lawyers more efficient. There will be a partner supported by one or two assistants who will undertake on-the-job training. There may be a trainee or two. These will be sector- or niche-based, for example, technology. If a client has an issue they will go to a legal expert with experience in the sector or industry, likely to be a small niche firm.

Are clients ready for these changes?

The likely buyer of these services would be the traditional general counsel, trained within a private practice firm, who do not necessarily want to change. It is the younger ones who have been brought up in the internet age who will buy differently. It may take a generation, but it will change.

What do you think of cloud computing?

I went to a presentation where they said the cloud is actually a large number of servers in the middle of the desert! I am sure this technology has its place, but a firm will always want an element of control of its own data.

What does the future bring?

This demand and expectation of always being available and providing a rapid response is very stressful and I have already seen lawyers retiring early or making lifestyle changes. Surprisingly, I have seen first-hand the realization from clients that this expectation is not sustainable in the long term and the understanding that lawyers are human after all and need a break. Checking e-mails on holiday is not always expected; I was on long-term sabbatical and not contacted at all!

I want to get rid of the desktop and move to a hybrid laptop which can become a tablet. I want to be less desk-based and more mobile.

The future is browser-based applications, available wherever and whenever needed and accessible through a consistent interface. I do worry that as we become more dependent on technology what would be the consequence of a critical failure in one of the fundamental technologies such as Microsoft. In the meantime I will embrace the changes and remain Mr Gadget Man! within reach and responsive, which means I need to read e-mails and attachments on my mobile device – which needs to be operational wherever I am throughout the day. My main criteria are a decent-sized screen and a long battery life.

This chapter includes an in-depth review of what we consider to be those areas of technology having the most significant impact on businesses, and law firms in particular. For each area, we will provide an explanation of what it is; what is currently happening; what it means to the business; advice on what to do; and some crystal ball gazing on what the future might bring. Recent research (of more than 2,000 CIOs from across all industry sectors)[1] on innovation investment for 2013 shows that:

- 71 percent see great innovation potential but only 2 percent believe that potential will be fully realized;
- 68 percent will invest more in mobility in 2013 and beyond;
- 58 percent will invest more in the cloud; and
- 50 percent will invest more in collaboration.

Cloud

You see it everywhere these days. Cloud-this, cloud-that. It seems like everyone is urging you to 'go cloud', but what exactly does that mean and is it a good idea?

What is it?

Speaking plainly, putting your data or software "in the cloud" means having it hosted on a remote computer that you access via the internet, rather than storing it on a local computer at your premises. We will breakdown the basic forms, although of course there are other various flavors to consider. There are three types of cloud:

Public cloud

This is most likely provided by a network provider and shared by anyone. General internet connections are part of the public cloud. Systems are hosted on shared infrastructure and are shared by all.

Private cloud

This is a network and system only accessible by the organization. This will be a dedicated provision of the services and would see a dedicated network connecting all the offices to a hosting center where the systems would be housed. The only difference to the traditional ownership model is that it is run by an external network provider and a hosting center provider (it can be the same service provider) who are expert in these types of services.

Hybrid

There are many forms of hybrid cloud, including:

- A dedicated network connected to a dedicated system but in a shared environment;
- A dedicated network connected to a shared system in a shared environment;

- A shared internet connection to a dedicated hosted solution; and
- A shared connection to a shared system.

The number of possibilities means that the buying of these services can be complicated and requires a degree of understanding of both the services being offered and the consequences of adopting each of the types of service. The IT industry is very adept at creating new terminology and acronyms for new services, and these are listed below.

Software as a Service (SaaS)
This is probably the most well-known service, and involves a user subscribing to a shared service, for example, Salesforce. You use the same system as all other subscribers to the service, with your specific data segregated. You have the same functionality as everyone else. Licenses are provided on a subscription basis, and include the ability to stop using the software whenever required. Interestingly, we have seen a number of software providers switch their traditional license model to a subscription model, which they would term as an SaaS model.

Infrastructure as a Service (IaaS)
IaaS is the provision of the main server hardware, storage, and network and security devices required – either shared or dedicated to a customer. This is the most basic cloud service model and infrastructure is provided either physically or, more often than not, virtually. Resources are supplied on demand from a large pool of resources installed in a data center. Cloud users will install the operating system (O/s) and application onto the infrastructure and be responsible for maintaining it. Typically, users are billed on a utility computing basis with the cost reflecting the actual usage.

Platform as a Service (PaaS)
PaaS is the provision of the main server hardware and storage required to run the particular software. This service provides the execution environment, databases, web server, and other development tools necessary to support application development and deployment. Application developers do not have the complexity of buying and managing the underlying hardware and software. Typically, users are billed through a combination of the number of users and the capacity utilized.

Data as a Service (DaaS)

DaaS is the provision of data files including text, images, sound, and video to the customer available over a network. With the increasing adoption of service orientated architecture (SOA), it is easier to access a common repository of data from multiple systems. The ability to separate the data deployed within an application from the software provides the ability to cost just the data element, often on a fixed cost per MB basis.

All of these services are made possible and economically viable through the deployment of virtualization. Virtualization is the technology used to create and provide processing power on virtual servers without the purchase of individual physical servers. If sourced correctly, virtual servers can be provisioned and decommissioned very quickly. This leads to the consumption of processing power according to need – and consequently only paying for what is required. The software that makes all of this possible includes VMWare, Hyper-V, and XEN Server. Let us use an analogy to explain what all of this means.

You need office accommodation for your business. You can buy an office outright, perhaps bigger than immediately required, but if you outgrow this office you will need to buy another one. The other option is, of course, to rent… and virtualization is essentially like renting office space, say within a large building, with the ability to increase or decrease the space rented according to need. You have the ability to put up and take down partition walls reflecting the space required by your actual staff numbers. You benefit from someone else's investment in the larger building.

Considerations

The potential advantages of storing your data or systems on remote servers will generally be enthusiastically touted by the vendors of cloud services. The potential pitfalls tend to be somewhat overlooked. Here are the key considerations that a law practice should weigh up when considering cloud solutions.

Convenience

Using the internet to access your data or systems means that, generally, they are easily accessible from anywhere you have an internet connection. This can be especially useful for lawyers who travel a lot and may need to reference files unexpectedly, or query a practice management system's CRM or matter records. Often the hosting provider will have redundant systems to maintain business continuity.

Simplicity

Because the server with your data or systems is maintained by someone else, your in-house systems have the opportunity to be much simpler. The administration complexities of maintaining an in-house server with its associated backup and business continuity issues may be avoided if the hosting organization can provide these for you. The caveat here is that functional considerations may not allow this simplification and this benefit would be lost (see "Performance").

Cost

There is a general impression that cloud storage is cheap, but this is not necessarily true. Depending on data volumes and other technical considerations, the cost per gigabyte of cloud storage can be as much as or more than the cost of local server storage. Cost alone is unlikely to be a key deciding factor in moving to a cloud solution, though.

Performance

No matter how you cut it, access to files or systems over the internet will always be slower than on your local network. It will also be far more variable with time of day, location, and internet connection type... and if your local internet connection goes down, even if you're sitting in your office, you've just lost access to your crucial data or systems. These risks may require a local server with a replica of the data or systems to maintain business continuity, but this does remove any simplicity benefit of the cloud solution.

Security

The security of your sensitive data will be entirely at the mercy of the systems and practices of the cloud hosting provider, so there is a very strong element of trust involved in your business relationship with them. Is internet access appropriately secure? Who within their company has access to your data? What happens to your data if the company ceases trading? If they are global, do you know in which country the servers hosting your data may be located? In some countries, local laws may allow the government or other entities to get unilateral access to your data if it resides there.

Firms considering cloud solutions need to weigh up these key issues in any assessment of a potential product or provider.

The SaaS supply chain

Recent years have seen a dramatic increase in the use of cloud computing services. The most common form of service provided using the cloud is SaaS, although other members of the cloud family exist, such as infrastructure as a service (IaaS), platform as a service (PaaS), and data as a service (DaaS).

The attraction to SaaS typically stems from the reduction in IT spend, as the customer does not need to make significant capital investments in procuring and maintaining physical services and storage units, since the software and associated data are centrally hosted by the SaaS provider and delivered to the customer via the internet or private cloud.

SaaS is becoming more popular as a delivery mechanism for software solutions. This trend is evidenced in the International Data Corporation Study World Wide SaaS and Cloud Computing Software 2012–2016 Forecast and 2011 Vendor shares, which identifies that the cloud software market reached $22.9 billion in revenue in 2011, and expects growth to $67.3 billion by 2016.[2]

With the potential for making a substantial amount of money from SaaS in mind, it is not surprising that there has been an exponential growth in the number of SaaS providers in recent years. As a logical consequence of the maturity of the services being offered, we are now seeing SaaS providers using shared infrastructure provided by a platform provider who may in turn utilize a platform provider that is in a hosting center used by yet another supplier. (It's a bit like a Russian doll – you open one up only to find another inside.) In July 2012, the European Commission published its opinion on cloud computing.[3] Among other things, it said one of the key risks to customers of cloud computing services is the lack of transparency in the outsourcing supply chain, which features multiple data processors and sub-contractors.

Another significant contributing factor to the rise in SaaS providers is the relatively minimal barriers to entry. It is possible to enter the SaaS market with little more than a bright idea and a sales team, as one or more of the core software or infrastructure service can be, and often are, sub-contracted to third parties such as software development, support, and maintenance and hosting.

Of course, sub-contracting is prevalent in most industries and should not lead to trepidation when dealing with SaaS providers; in fact quite the opposite. The proclivity in the SaaS industry for sub-contracting, often to much larger companies with greater economies of scale, has translated into cheaper costs and, in many cases, a better standard of service than the customer would otherwise have received.

However, an SaaS provider's use of sub-contracting can leave the customer with some interesting challenges from both a legal and practical perspective, and these are worth considering.

First, where the SaaS provider lacks bargaining power with a larger more established sub-contractor, a customer may find their terms of the upstream contract with the SaaS provider are dictated by the downstream sub contract, which may not be compatible with the customer's specific business requirements.

Second, because of the very nature of sub-contracting, the customer does not hold a direct contractual relationship with the sub-contractor, only with the SaaS provider. Therefore, the customer must route any issues with the service provided by the sub-contractor via the SaaS provider. This may lead to delays in resolving performance issues or defects, particularly where the sub-contractor has a "too big to care" attitude or the SaaS provider has a commercial interest in keeping the sub-contractor on side.

Third, the contractual distance between the sub-contractor and the supplier may cause security concerns for the customer – particularly where the sub-contractor is holding data on behalf of the customer, such as a hosting provider – because of the perceived loss of direct control over that data and the inability to audit the sub-contractor in order to verify compliance. Furthermore, if personal data is involved, this may also cause complications under English data protection laws, particularly where the sub-contractor is based outside the European Economic Area.

Finally, if the SaaS provider was suddenly to cease providing the services because of the onset of insolvency or other unforeseen reasons, a customer may find it very difficult or nigh on impossible to take over and maintain continuity of the service where there are multiple sub-contractor relationships to manage.

Practical steps

To minimize the risks associated with sub-contracting in an SaaS environment, we would recommend the following:

- Prior to entering into an SaaS contract, complete comprehensive due diligence on the SaaS provider and how it delivers the solution, particularly regarding any use of sub-contractors. If sub-contractors are used, check thoroughly the extent of the SaaS provider's reliance on this aspect of the service and ease of migrating to a new sub-contractor or "in-housing" in a crisis situation.

- List all approved sub-contractors in the SaaS contract. No changes should be made to this list, or additional sub-contractors added, without the customer's consent.
- Ensure the SaaS provider takes full responsibility under the SaaS contract for all acts or omissions of any permitted sub-contractors.
- If the sub-contractor is processing personal data (particularly outside of the EEA), take specialist data protection advice to ensure compliance under UK data protection laws.
- If a business-critical service, consider obtaining direct agreements with each sub-contractor regarding continuity of service in the event the SaaS provider ceases to exist.

Infrastructure as a Service

IaaS enables customers to consume server, storage, and network infrastructure through a simple unified platform. The service:

- Allows IT to react faster and support business agility through faster delivery of IT solutions;
- Delivers expert infrastructure support from the provider's server, storage, and network teams;
- Allows IT to increase business value by focusing on the applications providing services to the business; and
- Allows IT to manage costs, while replacing capital with operational expenditure.

Using IaaS allows customers to gracefully migrate from traditional physical infrastructure into the cloud without requiring complete re-architecture or rebuild of applications. It is suited to customers who need to supplement on-site infrastructure capacity or meet short-term project requirements, and is already used by customers to deliver primary business critical applications.

When sourcing the service, you need to consider if it is provided through UK-hosted and -managed infrastructure, delivered from ISO27001-accredited data centers. The underlying platforms should be managed to a published service level availability that covers performance, capacity, patching, installation, and upgrades.

Customers can quickly deploy and manage infrastructure through a self-service portal, with the flexibility to meet scale-up and scale-out requirements. Customers can provision infrastructure from pre-built Windows and Linux templates, utilize their own templates, or import virtual machines. The customer controls the CPU, RAM, storage, network, and operating system that make up the infrastructure. Full remote administrative access is provided to servers to add and update applications running on them.

The service is delivered from the heart of the provider's network, allowing customers to provision servers within their WAN or publish to public networks, such as the internet, N3, or Janet.

The future

The move to the cloud appears to have become an unstoppable force. Firms are seeing the benefits in letting experts run their infrastructure and software. Buying into a shared software solution offers value for money and the opportunity for smaller firms to buy into the capability of large expensive systems which otherwise would be cost prohibitive. This is only going to continue.

Nervousness about where and how the data is stored will be allayed by continued refinement of the services and a track record of reliability and security.

Of course, the cloud vendor becomes a critical resource for any company. Choosing the vendor is thus incredibly important, as is devoting enough internal resources to maintain a rich, well-informed relationship with the vendor, so that you're likely to know early if there's something to be concerned about. More time should and will be spent on this relationship.

There will be consolidation in the providers of these services and we are sure there will be some more casualties on the scale of 2e2 (a cloud services provider with a turnover of over £300 million in 2012 and 1,400 staff) as the market matures. The move to a shared environment is becoming more acceptable and the ability to provide server capacity "on demand" is an attractive proposition.

Law firms will be able to consume the services of digital dictation and document management on an as-needed basis, subscribing for only those who need it and when. But how will law firms differentiate themselves as the underlying platform becomes common and consistent? Not surprisingly, differentiation will ultimately come down to the skill and expertise of the lawyers in delivering the service of law!

Social/Collaboration

What is it?

Social or collaboration are the words we use to mean all the facets of sharing information widely. This information can be shared with friends in a controlled manner (on Facebook, for example, you have complete control over who to accept as a friend, and you can select what can be seen), but can also be widely disseminated to anyone who might be interested, for example via shared blogs or via followers on Twitter. We are inextricably moving to a socially-driven society, where more and more information is shared more and more widely.

The growth of social media has been phenomenal and some milestones are listed below.

- 1978 saw the creation of the BBC dial-up service, "CBBS".
- 1995 saw the creation of Geocities.
- Blogger was launched in August 1999, and purchased by Google in 2003.
- LinkedIn started in 2003, and now has 225 million users registered. It is rapidly becoming a respected source for recruitment and business sourcing.
- 2 February 2004 saw the birth of Facebook. It had 5.5 million users by the end of 2005 and as of March 2013 had more than 1.1 billion regular users.
- Twitter was founded in March 2006. It is now delivering in excess of 400 million tweets per day.

As a consequence of the wider distribution of information, more parties can collaborate in the resolution of a problem or the creation of a new product. The power of collaboration is being realized across all industries with the ability to have "expert" input despite location or time frame and especially so in the legal sector, where the intellectual property lawyer can be consulted when required. For the purpose of this chapter we will consider collaboration to be the use of technology to facilitate the inclusion of a wider audience than one person, to develop ideas and concepts, and even to support social movements (for example, flash mobs).

Collaboration is the use of technology such as Webex and Microsoft Lync to share documents and other information in real time and allow multiple users to amend or annotate the information. Use of these programs not only allows documents to be produced and reviewed much more quickly, it also means that geography is not a constraint and contributions can be received from around the world if required. The final result should be of better quality and produced more quickly.

The use of online messaging and blogging allows an individual to post a question or a point of view and then receive multiple opinions in an asynchronous manner. Over a relatively short period of time, a statement can be challenged, refined, remolded, and "attacked" from multiple directions. What better way is there for a lawyer to obtain the learned opinion of the legal community!

Considerations

Sharing and networking are now the norm and Generations X and Y are in the vanguard of exploiting this social technology. Lives are lived more publicly, arguments and conversations are quickly escalated as more and more people join the debate. No longer are we given time to reflect and work out our differences.

Bad experiences can be shared widely and very quickly. However, we can also learn of any remedial or rectification action just as quickly. The story of a well-known American airline ruining a musician's guitar and the song he penned in response has become almost legendary. Businesses are now becoming more adept at handling such situations because, importantly, those working in the consumer space can be driven out of business. Boycotts and crowds organized over the web can spring up rapidly and achieve such levels of publicity that their point of view is forced to the top of any agenda. (Flash mobs, it must be said, are not all bad. The event organized to clean up after the street riots in London in 2012 are a prime example.)

Understanding how a law firm is using and exploiting social media can be an important factor in assessing the culture of that firm. This can be the difference between attracting and retaining top talent and not.

According to a recent survey of law firm technology in the US, 75 percent of respondents indicated that their firms used social media as part of a marketing strategy. Not surprisingly, mid-sized firms also exploited this medium with nearly 14 percent of firms with 100–499 lawyers obtaining new clients using social media.[4]

Yet social media is more than just a marketing tool. Forward-thinking lawyers are now beginning to realize that it has the potential to be a versatile platform for both internal and external communication. And, when combined with the power of increasingly ubiquitous cloud-based platforms and services, the possibilities are endless.

For example, some law firms are using online platforms with built-in social media features to interact with current and potential clients. Some platforms are directly targeted toward the legal field and its client base, while others are used by all types of professionals but facilitate interaction with potential legal clients.

For example, Rightsolicitor.co.uk, lawyerlocator.co.uk, and Mylawyer.co.uk are online sites/businesses designed to connect lawyers with clients. These sites aim to make it easier for legal consumers to search for lawyers using the directory and to ask legal questions, which participating lawyers can then answer. These fora allow lawyers to connect with potential clients by posting public responses to specific requests for legal information. Lawyers can increase their online visibility by showcasing their expertise while simultaneously connecting with legal consumers. Many of these sites use a monthly subscription model. For example, the consumer brand Which? offers a fixed monthly fee to buy into their range of legal services.

Through the use of online automated document production tools, organizations such as Mylawyer.co.uk are able to offer the client the ability to create a draft document (for example, a will) through a series of questions and utilizing a number of standard paragraphs, with a lawyer reviewing the document prior to completion.

In the US, LawPivot (lawpivot.com) also offers a question and answer service. Over 2,000 lawyers have participated on LawPivot and respond to questions asked by legal consumers. Law Pivot launched in August of 2010 and has since answered over 46,000 consumer inquiries, many of which were posted publicly. LawPivot was recently acquired by online legal document service RocketLawyer.

Lawyers are also using social media tools to make themselves immediately available to current or potential clients, either via instant messaging or video chat. So, for example, some lawyers have instant messaging badges available on their websites that their current or potential clients can use to initiate a chat with the lawyer. Other lawyers are using Skype or Google+ Hangouts to hold virtual video meetings with clients. Similarly, LawZam (lawzam.com) is a new web-based service in the US that facilitates live video chat between lawyers and legal consumers seeking to hire a lawyer.

Another way that social media tools are being used by law firms is to facilitate internal communication. There are a number of ways to do this, ranging from using social media platforms developed for businesses in general to using practice management software with built-in communication features created with law firms in mind.

One example of a web-based platform that is not specifically targeted toward law firms but is designed to allow businesses to collaborate online in a company-wide, cloud-based environment is Yammer (yammer.com). Yammer bills itself as a private social network for businesses and allows users to communicate with co-workers in a variety of ways, including via private and public messages. Users can also create collaboration groups wherein they can engage in discussions with co-workers and upload and comment on documents. Meetings and events can also be scheduled using the platform.

There are also cloud-based law practice management platforms developed specifically for lawyers, many of which have built-in communication and collaboration features which mimic the features of social media platforms.

Some of these systems are limited to an internal firm-wide network, while others facilitate both internal communication between law firm employees and external interaction with both clients and others. Platforms that include both internal and external-facing online communication portals allow lawyers to collaborate with other lawyers in the firm and with clients, experts, and anyone else granted access to the platform. The benefit of these types of systems is that they are uniquely tailored to meet the needs of law firms and provide lawyers with the ability to communicate and collaborate in a secure online environment – one that is far more secure than the unencrypted e-mail that most lawyers now use for client communication purposes.

The future

So what does this mean to business and especially to law firms? "Nothing!" we hear the old equity partner nearing retirement shout. "It's just a fad!" But it's not just a fad: the importance of social media will only continue to increase.

Law controls society; without it there would be anarchy. Those entrusted with the delivery of the service of law will continue to be under constant scrutiny and mistakes or damaging opinions will be communicated widely and quickly via social media. Without monitoring social media channels, the first a firm may hear about the negative opinion is when they lose in a competitive situation or a client walks away. To tackle this, we will see the establishment and growth of a function dedicated to protecting the brand and reputation of a law firm. The role of the social (media) observer will take on a whole new form. There are already organizations springing up that can provide these services, but it maybe become intrinsic and core to a law firm.

The technology platforms facilitating this social behavior continue to proliferate and there appears to be no respite in the appetite of individuals for information in the here and now. People will trust their friends or "trusted" sites over law firms and official channels.

Of course, any time lawyers interact online, whether publicly on social media or privately in a secure online environment, ethics come into play. For example, public social media interactions can trigger advertising, solicitation, and confidentiality issues, among others. And lawyers sharing confidential information using online platforms must take steps to ensure that the system they are using is sufficiently secure and protects their clients' confidential information. For that reason, it is important for lawyers to be aware of their ethical obligations when outsourcing confidential client data to third parties and to ensure that they are in full compliance with the rules of their jurisdiction.

That's not to say that lawyers shouldn't learn about and fully embrace the benefits offered by these tools. After all, it's the 21st century and lawyers who fail to learn about and take advantage of emerging technologies run the risk of losing clients to more forward-thinking competitors. Instead, they must understand and learn about the risks, benefits, and ethical obligations and then use these tools wisely and put them to work for their law firm. As a result, productivity levels, and ultimately the bottom line, will increase.

Bring your own Device (BYOD)

What is it?

Bring your own Device (BYOD) is a phrase used to describe the practice of employees supplying their own computer hardware to perform work-related tasks. Common examples include:

- Using personal smartphones to access and manage company e-mail;
- Using home computers to access the corporate network remotely; and
- Using personal laptops and tablets on site to access or present company data.

Much of the benefit from BYOD is linked to developments in mobility and cloud, and it is difficult to separate the main drivers. We will do our best.

Considerations

The flood has already begun. Every day, more employees bring their own smartphones, tablets, and laptops into their offices, hoping to become more productive and add more value to their companies. While IT departments sometimes look at the BYOD revolution with concern over having to support more devices, stopping that flow of new technology could do more harm than good.

A recent study by Forrester Research[5] shows that employees are choosing slightly more than half of all the high-tech tools they use – either buying products themselves or choosing from a list of smartphones, tablets, laptops, and desktop computers approved by their employers. Ignoring desktops means that employees are selecting 85 percent of the devices they are using.

Technology research group Ovum recently found that 15 percent of employees used their devices to access company networks without informing their IT departments, and another 21 percent actively violated anti-BYOD policies, many citing that the motive was to improve personal productivity.[6]

Faced with this flood of new technology, companies can either try to resist the tide by blocking outside devices or they can embrace the trend. Banning employee-chosen technology denies the company cutting-edge tools, generates more work for IT departments, lowers the morale of top-notch (in some people's opinion) employees, and robs companies of the benefits of rapidly falling consumer electronics prices by tying future work to aging hardware and networks.

BYOD early adopters are people who are willing to spend their own money to get more done every day, potentially making them the sorts of employees that companies should cherish. And young people, just entering the workforce, have been raised on a diet of electronic devices and communication. Allowing them to use tools that they've been essentially training on for most of their lives should help companies to get the most out of each new employee.

The big challenge to implementing BYOD is that employee choice leads to a motley group of devices. However, offering secure access to data and solutions to such a wide range of hardware options is easier than it sounds. One of the biggest challenges that mobile computing has created is platform churn. Every time a device manufacturer or operating system appears to be gaining dominance, a new wave of products washes it away.

For example, Gartner Inc. research[7] shows that at the beginning of 2011, Symbian was the No. 2 smartphone operating system, making up about 28 percent of the market. The developers who focused on creating apps for that system spent considerable time and effort building for a dying platform. By the end of 2011, Symbian usage was below 10 percent. In 2013, it was down to 3 percent.

Android, on the other hand, went from about 36 percent market share in early 2011 to a dominant 74 percent share this year, but even now, developers can't simply abandon all other systems and only embrace Android. That market share number includes multiple variations of the open source operating system, so developers can't easily transfer between versions of Android operating system, for example transferring an Android 2.3 app onto an Android 4.2 smartphone.

Predicting where technology is going has always been tricky, and most businesses can point to expensive mistakes when they backed the wrong horse. Effectively embracing BYOD means that:

- You don't have to try to predict what will become the dominant system. With the power of cloud computing, companies should be able to use powerful business solutions that will run equally well on any device.
- By using their own smartphones and computers, employees no longer require your company to purchase as much technology for them to perform their duties.
- Staff can remain more productive for longer when they can access company systems at any time. A recent survey found that mobile workers using BYOD devices average 240 hours (30 days) more productivity each year than those who do not.[8]
- Companies become better at coping with localized disasters by allowing staff to remain productive as they work from home.
- Training costs reduce since staff members are using systems with which they are already familiar.

An employee can use whatever tool they feel most comfortable with. Adopting this approach means employees can choose what best suits their working and learning styles. These new devices can do more than just boost employee productivity. Device agnosticism can become a major source of savings for businesses of any size.

The initial costs savings are clear – £200 phones are much cheaper than £1,000 handheld computers – but the cost benefits multiply when you consider the impact on the entire operation. If an employee loses or breaks a smartphone, a replacement can be ordered online and delivered the next day. With cloud-based backup services, personal settings such as phone numbers and browser bookmarks to services can be replaced within minutes. That easy access to hardware eliminates the need to maintain a costly inventory of replacement devices and parts.

Also, when an employee's personal technology fails, their first call tends to be to the manufacturer or the network service provider that sold them the product, not their company's IT department. That reduction in calls should let companies efficiently prioritize IT workloads, focusing on higher-value work instead of telling users how to reboot.

However it is not all positive.

- Your sensitive company data is stored on employee devices with limited security. If the device is lost or stolen, your data could be compromised.
- Connecting non-work devices to the company network increases the chances of virus and malware affecting company resources and data. (32.8 million Android devices, such as smartphones and tablets were infected with malware last year.)
- Your IT team may be overloaded by requests to support an ever-increasing array of devices, often diverting energies to resolving non-work related issues. This may even include providing remote IT support.
- Fewer than 10 percent of people using personal tablets for work have enabled auto-lock to stop unauthorized persons accessing data.
- Just one quarter of BYOD smartphone users have enabled screen locking.

Considerable cost can be incurred implementing the necessary technology to allow these devices to connect to the network. It may not be possible to connect to some old legacy systems. One should not forget the security risk and the potential for data to be retained on devices.

Employees need to understand the risks and be educated in what precautions they must take to protect the corporate data.

Basically, you must get control of BYOD since there are definite benefits to promoting it within your business. You should consider:

- Creating a BYOD policy to govern employee behavior and set defined boundaries for data access/use.
- Implementing security systems that further lock down access rights to prevent unauthorized data use or theft.
- Encouraging the use of security tools built into BYOD devices such as encryption, screen locking, and remote wipe, should the device be stolen.
- Enforcing any policy you create so that employees take mobile security as seriously as you do.

To encourage and harness the BYOD movement, companies should look to solutions that work equally well on any modern device. Instead of trying to guess which product is going to win the mobile wars, focus on the browser, which is an existing piece of software that lets all employees securely access solutions, regardless of the make or model of the device.

The future

The rise of wearable technology highlights the continuing demand for new personal gadgets and the tremendous pace of change which exists.

The desire of people only wanting to carry one device will not diminish. Fostering the BYOD trend can lead to lower operating costs and reduced headaches for IT departments, and can let companies take advantage of the rapid pace of advancement in consumer computing.

New systems being developed should accommodate multiple end-point devices. Standardized browsers that provide a consistent user interface must be deployed. When a firm is selecting new technology and software, this capability will no longer be a "nice to have" but a critical requirement.

The task of "managing" BYOD will no doubt prove difficult. You can't manage it, but you can't avoid it either. The inexorable clockwork of Moore's Law means that employees may soon have dozens of wearable networked devices, potentially even internal medical devices, each trying to use whatever wireless network it can find.

BYOD is not a policy decision; it is an empirical observation. Attempts to fight it will waste resources and at best delay the inevitable arrival of a steady stream of new devices. All you can do is try to figure out how to deal with the reality of BYOD – most importantly, to secure your systems from hostile agents.

How can a business cope with these twin explosions of options and capabilities? There are really only two choices. One is to hire more and more experts at securing such devices within an enterprise, but such experts are likely to be highly in demand and costly to recruit and retain. The other is to make it someone else's problem. You can, in fact, move almost everything relevant to BYOD and security to the cloud. The effort to securely support each new device type is part of a cloud provider's core business, and they're amortizing those costs across all their customers. With a good, reputable provider, your quality of service is likely to go up, possibly dramatically so.

ERP systems

What is it?

In the beginning, we had manufacturing requirements planning (MRP) and then along came manufacturing resource planning (MRP2). These concepts, and ultimately the systems that facilitated them, had their foundation in the manufacturing of products and how best to manage production: first of all, bringing together the physical components and raw materials, and then realizing that resources such as machine capacity and tool availability were critical to the production process. With that came the further realization that the resources of the enterprise as a whole, including human resource and other support processes, needed to be aligned and planned to facilitate efficient, effective, and ultimately profitable production. The enterprise resource planning (ERP) system was born. Of course there are many more concepts, methodologies, and systems which have been created, each of them in turn attempting to enhance and improve the business, ultimately creating efficient business process and, hopefully, profit!

ERP is a system that brings together and tightly integrates all those systems that support the deployment of resource, in whatever form, within a business. The ERP system provides capability to support manufacturing, warehouse and distribution, finance, sales order processing, HR and payroll, and customer relationship management (CRM). These are provided by one software suite from one supplier, and well known systems include SAP, Oracle, and Microsoft Dynamics. Some have extended beyond the boundaries of the enterprise itself and include online customer ordering and supply chain management.

Traditionally, a law firm runs its business on what has been termed a practice management system (PMS). This system provides the capability to support the finance systems within the business including functionality unique to the legal sector, such as client accounting. This would be supplemented by a number of other solutions, often choosing the "best of breed" products supporting other parts of the business. A number of PMS vendors have now extended their portfolio to include time recording, HR, purchasing, and case management all integrated to the core system. To all intents and purposes they are evolving into an ERP system. (A prime example of this is the market-dominating Thomson Elite with its 3E system.)

Considerations

For many years the legal sector has managed to remain largely immune to the volatile and often extreme market forces experienced by most other business and industry sectors. It has been artificially protected from competition by means of legislation preventing the ownership of law firms by non-lawyers, and seemingly shielded from commercial pressures through a misplaced sense of reverence for the legal profession and its complexity.

Similarly, the players in the legal software market have also been in a comfort zone, having enjoyed immunity from any serious level of competition, particularly from the larger software vendors who have tended to direct their considerable resources at what are perceived to be more lucrative and less demanding markets.

Traditionally, the strategic approach to IT in the legal sector has reflected a number of the characteristics which typify the sector as a whole:

- **Specialism** – Lawyers have long perceived themselves to be different and, consequently, have considered that the systems they use should also be different.
- **Introversion** – Law firms have a reluctance to look beyond their immediate peers as a point of reference and have been slow to recognize and adopt good practice from other industry sectors.
- **Conservatism** – Law firms are reluctant to break the mold or take risks and rarely stray from tried and trusted legal specific solutions.

While the majority of businesses seem to have been actively consolidating the number of systems and vendors in their IT landscape, the legal sector seems content, and in some cases positively exultant, in bucking this trend. Many law firms continue to wrestle with hugely complex IT landscapes, small armies of specialist suppliers, and an integration map.

The legal sector has been amongst the very last to receive the attentions of the large software vendors. Whereas industry specific versions of ERP-based solutions exist for most other sectors, such offerings are relatively new to the legal sector and point-solutions from relatively small software vendors continue to dominate the installed base. This is exemplified in the field of case management, where multiple case management systems cater for the perceived unique requirements of specific practice areas – almost as if an IT landscape needs to be complex in order to support a complex business. All things considered, the legal sector has been living in somewhat of a bubble, but that bubble is set to burst.

There has been a lifecycle of system adoption in the legal sector where, 10–15 years ago, many law firms implemented systems for the very first time or replaced or upgraded their old character-based finance system. These systems are now reaching an age where they are more costly to support with hardware and the relevant people skills required are becoming more difficult or impossible to obtain in the market. More importantly, these systems are not providing the required support to the business or enabling and supporting the flexibility and control required for survival.

There are those firms that have decided, mainly because of the cost (either monetary or disruption), that they will only replace their legacy system should there be a major disaster or pending a merger. Many have remained with the legacy supplier, taking a modernized version or replacing it with the newly created "Legal ERP" system, for example Thomson Reuters with 3E. Some of the big names in software are looking at the legal sector and beginning to flex their muscles. However, they need to establish a foothold in the market with a demonstrable implementation.

A number of firms have decided to take, we would suggest, the more game-changing next steps in the ERP direction, notably Shoosmiths and Baker Mackenzie, who have decided to implement SAP, configured by TCS, to meet the specific requirements of a law firm. We have also seen Simmons & Simmons taking a similar route, creating a legal-configured version of Microsoft Dynamics.

Of course, there needs to be a number of business drivers to make the shift to ERP happen. ERP systems have been built on a financial foundation, so it is no surprise that the dominating drivers would be finance related. Like any commercial business, the success of a law firm depends on how much profit it can make and that profit comes through completing work at a lesser cost than what is charged to clients.

Firms that aspire to manage internal and external resources effectively, comply with multiple regulatory regimes, maintain relationships with large corporate clients, run efficient operations, and have all of the information necessary to monitor business performance, need to have effective integrated IT systems.

The characteristics of the firm as a whole have been adopted by the IT functions of many law firms through a process of osmosis, and collectively represent the key challenge to be addressed by any potential entrant to the legal solution market. Law firms do not necessarily think in terms of processes and process efficiency, but this is changing due to client pressure and the different types of aggressive pricing models that are beginning to appear and it requires a keen focus on process.

In other lower margin areas of commerce, process efficiency has been more a matter of survival than profitability. This has also been the case in those commodity areas of law, including personal injury, conveyancing, and wills, though we are now seeing even the corporate lawyers starting to adopt this approach.

Matter costing – or, in the terms of non-lawyers, job or project costing – has become more complicated and comprehensive over the last few years. No longer is it sufficient to book the chargeable time of the lawyers; now, all contributors to the cost of the matter need to record costs against the matter. The discipline of time recording must be enforced; no longer is it acceptable to account for just five hours a day. This information needs to get better to improve the estimates of matter costing, especially when charging a fixed price.

The trust between lawyer and client is a strong one. Work was often awarded on a relationship basis and if estimates were wrong, the client simply agreed to the increase in charges. Customers are now demanding regular updates on costs, regular invoicing on larger jobs, and are driving for fixed prices. The ability to deliver to client expectations will include regular invoicing, the ability for fixed pricing, up-to-date account information, predictable costs, realistic margins, and forecasts. The integration of systems and real-time availability of that data, offered by ERP systems, leads to more accurate costing of working and an improved understanding of where profit is being made during each month rather than at end of year.

The future

In the same way that deregulation has moved the provision of legal services from the wood-paneled offices of the general counsel to the high street and business park, the provision of IT services to the legal sector will, with a sense of inevitability, take a similar road. It may not be welcome, but it will happen.

The initial setbacks suffered by the ERP pioneers currently making slow but steady headway in the legal sector are purely that – setbacks – and are typical of those experienced when entering other sectors. Law firms by their nature are careful; many are conservative in outlook and prepared to wait until others have been though the bleeding edge of early adoption. Once traction is achieved, there can be a cascade of support as firms then try to catch up quickly. ERP vendors need a number of reference sites in order to gain momentum (the tipping point), and once achieved we are likely to see a rush of adoptions.

In the same way that men continue to wear their worst Hawaiian shirt until it comes back on trend, as the fashion pendulum of IT architecture seemingly swings back in favor of the integration of multiple solutions, it could prove the case that the legal sector has ridden out the consolidation trend. What they may be missing out on as a consequence, though, is the opportunity to learn and benefit from the experiences and travails of other business sectors. A sense of reverence persists as far as the field of law is concerned, and this manifests itself in the all-pervading belief that some of the biggest software vendors do not understand the unique nature of law firms.

There is an inevitable convergence between the debunking of law and the increasing use of IT. Opportunities for efficiency improvements present themselves but often require changes in a law firm's fundamental processes. Those firms with an enlightened management team will be able to embrace these changes, enabling efficiency gains in line with other leading edge businesses in other sectors.

One major vendor is now offering a legal specific variant of its core software suite, whereas another has partnered with an existing legal software vendor. What both approaches have in common is the provision of a solution based on an ERP backbone based on the mainstream offering.

It is unclear as to the best route a law firm should take in providing the technological foundation for the business. However, it is clear that a number of information management core principles sit at the heart of these decisions:

- Once entered into a system, information should then be available wherever required;
- Information should only be entered once;
- Updates are made in real time; and
- Referencing unique entities (for example, customers) should be the same, regardless of the system being used.
- Fundamentally, there should be one view of the law firm business which is unambiguous, consistent, and available to support real-time business decision making. All firms are aiming for the serendipitous "one version of the truth"!

Data warehousing

What is it?

Data warehousing can be considered a spin off from the move to comprehensively integrated disparate solutions and ERP systems. Holding most of your business information in one place leads naturally to the conclusion that it is beneficial to hold all key information in one place.

Not only that, rather than engaging the IT team to write a specific report (and we know how difficult that can be at times), it would be more productive for end users to define and write their reports and enquiries themselves.

A data warehouse, or business information system, will hold the transactional data from the business and will be fed updates, normally overnight, from the transactional system(s). These data will be subdivided into cubes of data which can be more easily analyzed. These tools will also come with an easy-to-use reporting tool designed for end users to select and analyze data to produce information reporting.

Considerations

More businesses are realizing they need to make quicker and more informed decisions. These tools and associated processes and structures are now delivering real benefits to the bottom line.

Many ERP vendors will have a warehouse in their portfolio. Integration to the warehouse comes out of the box and, if the vendor has any marketing nous, will also come with ready-made cubes providing the answers to common questions such as how profitable is an individual customer and, maybe more controversially, which parts of the firm and which individuals are the most profitable.

Those without this luxury have the more complicated and costly task of creating a data model for the business and the multiple interfaces for the various systems so the "one version of the truth" can at least be partly met. Consider how difficult this is when the billing system and the CRM system refer to the same customer via two different customer numbers.

End users are vociferous in their appetite for information and are becoming more demanding for data; more often than not, IT departments are becoming less able to meet this demand. We are now seeing the IT departments create the warehouse, with the end users having flexible and easy-to-use tools to analyze that data. They are able to explore whatever their "what ifs" offer them.

The future

You could term data warehousing as Big Data's little brother. Eventually, the amount of data being analyzed will be on a scale not suitable for the data warehouse tools. In the meantime, we can only see the exploitation of this tool increasing.

The provision of standard data cubes will increase and they will be further refined. Organizations will build on what has gone before and further refine the data sets and analysis. The demand is now for real time or "near" time. Technical practicalities may prevent the information being up to date to the second, but it will be as close as possible. Business decisions will be made in real time, enabling the business to respond to the rapidly changing business environment.

Mobile

What is it?

Mobile is pretty self-explanatory! It is basically the ability to work away from the normal office and for the purpose of this chapter will include home working, working from other locations, and also while on the move.

Mobility relies on being able to access a network which subsequently provides access to the internet. The end devices can be many and varied and include smartphones, tablets, or laptops. Connection is via the telecommunication companies' networks (for example, O2, EE), wifi, and broadband connections.

From a business perspective, the systems being accessed must be open to these connections either through the internet or a virtual private network and be "presentable" to the end device, probably using browser technology.

Considerations

The growth in mobile handsets with the ability to access the internet has been exponential. The investment in coverage by the network providers has been significant, both with 3G and 4G networks, but also with wifi coverage, and there are significant benefits to be had by exploiting and embracing the mobile technology.

Inner-city law firms, especially in London, can utilize the coffee shops and public areas for internet access and reduce the demand for desks and meeting rooms. Service stations have now become a place of contract negotiation and proposal presentation. Follow-up actions are being completed and widely communicated before the end of the meeting.

With the advent of web-enabled systems accessible from outside of the company firewall, an individual can be more mobile. When visiting an office (client or supplier), obtaining access to the internet can be a painful and time-consuming process given the necessary security and controls, not forgetting the demand on the IT team to set up access to "unknown" visitors at very short notice. Businesses have now learned to install "visitor" networks to enable non-employees to have internet access easily and quickly.

The capacity of home broadband has increased exponentially in recent years, resulting in system performance in the home being on par with that in the office. In addition, reliability has improved significantly.

The potential working time of an individual is increasing. No longer is a train journey simply a time for reflection and reading a book or newspaper. It is now an opportunity to catch up on e-mails and collaborate online with colleagues in preparation for the first meeting of the day. This is often seen by lawyers as an opportunity to increase their chargeable time. However, it is also an opportunity to improve the work/life balance by being able to choose when to work. Hotel destinations are now often chosen on the availability of internet access and free wifi.

The future

Mobile technology means that, prior to a meeting with a client or going into court, lawyers can check the latest position and be informed. They can have client information at their fingertips and can respond to customer questions immediately. Those able to do this offer that extra bit of customer service.

Expectations are being set. A lawyer is to be within easy reach, contactable at all times, and have access to all the information necessary. Anything less will be seen as a failure.

Big Data

What is it?

Big Data is the term for a collection of data sets so large and complex that it becomes difficult to process using standard database management tools or traditional data processing applications. The challenges include capture, maintenance, storage, search, sharing, transfer, analysis, and visualization. The trend to larger data sets is due to the additional information derived from analysis of a single large set of related data, as compared to separate smaller sets with the same total amount of data, allowing correlations to be found for anything from spotting business trends and determining the quality of research to preventing diseases, combatting crime, and determining real-time roadway traffic conditions.

The law is mature. During the generations of its existence, it has generated a huge volume of data, most of it in paper-based form. This is now being scanned and digitized, and the access to this data provides law firms with the ability to link legal precedents and to review and analyze patterns of behavior within their firm.

Considerations

As of 2012, limits on the size of data sets that are feasible to process in a reasonable amount of time were on the order of exabytes of data. Scientists regularly encounter limitations due to large data sets in many areas, including meteorology, genomics, connectomics, complex physics simulations, and biological and environmental research. The limitations also affect internet search, finance, and business informatics. Data sets grow in size in part because they are increasingly being gathered by ubiquitous information-sensing mobile devices, aerial sensory technologies (remote sensing), software logs, cameras, microphones, radio-frequency identification readers, and wireless sensor networks. The world's technological per-capita capacity to store information has roughly doubled every 40 months since the 1980s. The challenge for large enterprises is determining who should own Big Data initiatives that straddle the entire organization.

Big Data is difficult to work with using most relational database management systems and desktop statistics and visualization packages, requiring instead massively parallel software running on tens, hundreds, or even thousands of servers. What is considered Big Data varies depending on the capabilities of the organization managing the set, and on the capabilities of the applications that are traditionally used to process and analyze the data set in its domain. For some organizations, facing hundreds of gigabytes of data for the first time may trigger a need to reconsider data management options. For others, it may take tens or hundreds of terabytes before data size becomes a significant consideration.

It has been pointed out that the decisions based on the analysis of Big Data are inevitably informed by the world as it was in the past, or, at best, as it currently is. Fed by a large number of data on past experiences, algorithms can predict future development if the future is similar to the past. If the systems dynamics of the future change, the past can say little about the future. For this, it would be necessary to have a thorough understanding of the systems dynamics, which implies theory. As a response to this critique it has been suggested to combine Big Data approaches with computer simulations such as agent-based models, for example. Those are increasingly getting better at predicting the outcome of social complexities of even unknown future scenarios through computer simulations that are based on a collection of mutually interdependent algorithms.

Privacy advocates are concerned about the threat to privacy represented by increasing storage and integration of personally identifiable information; the scale of the information being stored has resulted in various policy recommendations being released from expert panels to conform practice to expectations of privacy.

The future

In the current age, users have various means of finding solutions to problems they face pertaining to products they use. It ranges from search engines at one end to contact centers at another. One aspect that is common across these systems is that for most of the problems, finding the solution is an interactive process. The questions posed by users are often under-specified, thus having a broad space of possible answers. Therefore, clarification dialogue is often needed to negotiate with the user and to get the exact scope and of the problem. While humans are generally good at it, interactive process is a great challenge for automated systems; however, this may soon change.

Holmes is an interactive problem resolution system that allows users to pose complex questions in near-natural language. It targets questions that need not be factual, but for which a solution may include procedures or a series of steps to be executed. To do this, it mines information from various sources (web forums, technical documents, product manuals, chat transcripts) and engages in an interactive dialogue to solve the users' problems.

Being futurologists

It would be very remiss of us not to look around at technologies and behaviors resulting from technology which may not directly affect the business of law or even the processes of a business at the moment (or ever), but may change the social landscape and people's expectations.

Below is our quick summary of the latest developments in technology, attitudes to technology, and other related areas we believe are interesting.

Google Glass

Google Glass allows users to view information online while on the move (and looking not unlike Elton John). They could be used instead of a tablet in client meetings as they allow the user to retain essential eye contact.

3D printing

3D printing is a game changer for the next decade; it will redefine the rules of design and no one yet knows the knock-on effects this technology will have.

Consumers in power

In the past, companies drove technological change. Now, consumers are driving adoption and feel that technological progress inside most organizations is far too slow.

Buy a service not a gadget

People and companies are getting far more comfortable with not owning the "kit", but buying a service. The cloud will transform the ability of businesses to be agile.

Non-technical

There appears to be a shift towards consumers becoming less technical. People will simply buy what they want and then buy a new one if the first one breaks. This has implications for technology, but is excellent for repeat business.

Video everywhere
Video is a far more persuasive medium than written words. Increasingly, communication will move to video over the next decade. More than 72 hours of video are being uploaded onto YouTube every hour and we are seeing "linear" TV being replaced by "on demand". Why not receive CVs on video?

Always connected
We will soon have nationwide wireless coverage. It is much cheaper for providers to offload demand onto a wifi network rather than going via 4G mobile. A basic service on the nationwide network is likely to be free. Anything needing more bandwidth will be paid for.

Digital divide
This is going to become a bigger and bigger problem because the leading edge of technology users is progressing very fast and the backward users are progressing very slowly. That is a major issue creating a real rift between the haves and have-nots. In some areas, being online is already a prerequisite for completing job and benefit applications.

Internet of things
With a massively expanded list of IP addresses, we are creating an "internet of things", so that everything that has been manufactured will have an IP address. We already have more devices connected to the internet than the world's population.

Gamification
This is the concept of applying game-design thinking to non-game applications to make them more fun and engaging. It can potentially be applied to any industry and almost anything to create fun and engaging experiences converting users into players. Making law fun and engaging might be a challenge, but anything is possible, especially as the younger generations of associates and trainees move up in their careers. A recent poll shows 47 percent of media and entertainment executives believe gamification will become the best way to engage with consumers.[9]

Beyond the digital age

So, where to next? Where will technology take law firms? One thing is certain: there will be further change. Some changes you will be able to forecast; others will appear as if from nowhere to challenge existing conceptions on how things should be.

It is reasonably safe to assume that the traits surrounding consumer behavior will continue to permeate the corporate psyche. We will see the convergence of processes deployed to support both these entities. Expectations of the consumer will continue to increase. The consumer's own knowledge will increase as they research legal points before engaging with lawyers (a bit like self-diagnosing an illness, using information available over the internet, before seeing a doctor) and then expecting the added value of the lawyer to confirm or challenge their thinking.

Clients will want access under their own terms, outside of the normal working day, when they turn to personal matters. The assumption is that the lawyer is mobile. No longer will the excuse "I cannot access your notes until I return to the office" be acceptable.

Customers want the advice/solution service to be bespoke to them. They want to feel unique and valued. Technology and process facilitates that, even in volume situations.

The holy grail of "one version of the truth" will be achieved within an organization as ERP systems or highly integrated solutions become the norm. Equally, Big Data can do this outside of the firm. Probably, it will be the next generation of lawyers who will really break the traditional mold, and the X, Y, and Z generations will get to flex their muscles in leadership positions in law firms. Their insight into their own behavior and expectations will be translated into corporate policy and culture.

This first appeared as Chapter 9 in Bull C., and Bason, D., Law Firms in the Digital Age, *ARK Group, 2013.*

References

1. "Harvey Nash CIO Survey 2013".
2. www.idc.com, doc # 235459, June 2012.
3. See: ec.europe.eu/digital-agenda/en/European-cloud-computing-strategy.
4. American Bar Association (ABA), "Legal Technology Survey", 2013.
5. Forrester Research Inc., "Forresters Forrsights Workforce Employee survey", 2012.
6. "Ovum 2013 multi-market BYOX employee study" at www.ovum.com/research.
7. "Market Share Analysis: Mobile phones worldwide", Gartner.com, 2013.
8. iPass, "Mobile Workforce 2011", at www.ipass.com/mobile-resources-all-survey.
9. "The Social Economy: Unlocking value and productivity through social technologies", McKinsey & Co, 2012.

Chapter 26:
Fusion = innovation – How to align your firm's IT and business strategies

By John Alber, futurist at the International Legal Technology Association

In Act III, scene II of *Hamlet*, Queen Gertrude responds to a question from Hamlet with the famous line "the lady doth protest too much, methinks". The phrase has come to signal exhortations or exclamations so intense as to suggest that their opposite is true.

Convene a group of IT managers anywhere in the world and, within a few minutes, you'll hear adamant pronouncements on the need to align IT strategy with business strategy. That sentiment is so widely espoused within IT circles as to have risen to the status of truism – or, as Queen Gertrude might say, untruism. It is honored more in the breach than in the adherence.

The irony of such pronouncements has not been overlooked. A decade ago, Nicholas Carr, in a seminal *Harvard Business Review* (HBR) article, suggested that IT had become irrelevant in the modern business landscape. It was a necessity, and a staggeringly expensive one at that, but for most businesses it conferred no competitive advantage whatsoever.

The article provoked a storm of protest, with more letters to the editor than any HBR article to date. Carr transformed that debate into the book *Does IT Matter?*[1] The answer to the title's question is left implicit on the cover of the book. But, it is clearly "no, mostly". In Carr's view, for most businesses, IT doesn't matter anymore.

How do you change all that and use your technology investments to secure competitive advantage? Carr himself suggests that IT *can* matter, and even that it *should* matter, given the level of IT investment necessary nowadays.

This chapter discusses three key steps designed to move IT from a back office cost center to an essential component of your firm's business. It is possible; indeed, some law firms have become widely known both inside and outside the law for coupling technology and business strategy to deliver real practice innovations.

It turns out that IT managers have been right all along: IT strategy and business strategy should be closely aligned. When they are, innovation almost always follows and competitive advantage is often on its heels.

Typical decision making

We'll start with what not to do. Much IT decision-making both inside and outside the law is driven by two imperatives, neither of which assures tight alignment of IT strategy with business strategy. We'll call those two imperatives the "ovine imperative" and the "consumerist imperative".

1. The ovine imperative

In ancient practice, a wether goat (sometimes called a bellwether for the bell it wore on its neck) would lead lambs into the abattoir for slaughter. That's an apt and nicely descriptive model for much of the technology decision-making that goes on inside law firms and companies these days.

The first sign of such ovine decision-making is often the question: "What are other firms doing in this area?" If enough "sheep" have trodden the path beforehand, then a purchase or a project is deemed safe enough to undertake.

Indeed, many vendors count on (and in-build their revenue projections on) the bellwether phenomenon. Early adopters are induced to try new products by means of clever incentives in hopes that others will follow the goat. Once enough have gone down the path, even remarkably inept products can survive in the marketplace. Where some have gone, others will follow.

In the legal sector, we see millions spent on moribund technologies year after year. For example, document management applications have been around for decades and, notwithstanding being rebranded as content management systems and then matter management systems, they continue to function in about the same way as they always have. They permit versioning of documents and the addition of some searchable metadata to those documents, but not much else.

That doesn't matter, however. Document management companies are thriving on the ovine imperative alone. Once a firm adopts a document management platform, it becomes an annuity based on a succession of fabulously expensive maintenance contracts and upgrades.

Are any firms more competitive as a consequence of all this? Perhaps those that saved their millions and didn't follow the flock. But, clearly, much of the considerable expenditure on these document management applications has been wasted.

2. The consumerist imperative

Consumerism, a term from the realms of economics and social science, aptly names a second imperative that often drives IT decision-making. Consumerism is the purchasing of goods and services beyond basic needs and often in ever-increasing amounts. Coupled with static budgeting practices, it accounts for much of consumption in the technology sector. The consumerist decision process goes something like this: "I've got a budget, now let's see what I can spend it on."

The technology marketplace operates much like other consumer marketplaces. Technology magazines and trade shows are full of subtle and not-so-subtle messages regarding how to spend IT budgets. Technology vendors do their best to get you to think like this: "If I'm a responsible IT manager, I'll buy an Acme load balancer because it's the right thing to do."

As with the ovine imperative, the need to spend cannot in itself confer competitive advantage. Yet, each year, firms and companies start their IT budgeting processes with what is essentially a shopping list compiled from browsing trade publications and walking trade show aisles. Skillful marketing can pull dozens of firms into a product selection, whereupon the ovine imperative takes over.

We see now in many markets, including legal, a rush into cloud computing. That surge is no more rational, I would assert, than the rush into any popular fashion accessory. In fact, cloud computing is not new. It is, however, rebranded and generating the kind of buzz that prompts lawyers to demand their IT departments "do something" in cloud computing.

Fusing strategies

Three things must change to begin to fuse the firm's IT and business objectives into a common strategy:

1. IT leadership;
2. The IT mandate; and
3. IT governance.

1. IT leadership

When an organization chooses a chief executive, it looks for certain qualities: leadership skills, communication skills, and the ability to envision and then execute that vision, for example.

Many organizations, including law firms, have expanded the chief role far beyond the executive suite. Nowadays it's commonplace for every major department or division inside an organization to have its own chief. In this way, IT departments have acquired chief information officers (CIOs) and chief technology officers (CTOs).

But, we have often excused these new CIOs from the expectations that apply to chief executives. Many CIOs, as a consequence, are CINOs: chiefs in name only. They lack the leadership and management qualities necessary to align IT strategies with the principal business strategies of their firm or company.

The process by which we select these chiefs is often to blame for their lack of fundamental business skills. Many IT departments are led by "super peers": consummate technicians who have risen through the ranks and come to be seen as best of breed by their peers.

However, the skills necessary to assure, say, that local and wide area networks function efficiently and at high availability levels are not necessarily the skills needed to transform business processes and foster innovation. Indeed, one can argue that the conservative outlook and risk aversion needed in an IT infrastructure manager is antithetical to the kind of dynamism and acceptance of risk found in a true business leader. Those conservative traits may also lead "super peer" chiefs into ovine and consumerist decision-making.

So, the first task in aligning IT and business strategy is to look closely at your IT leadership choices and ask a series of questions.

- Is your IT chief a chief technician or a chief executive?
- Does he cultivate other leaders inside the IT organization who are driven not by technology imperatives but by business imperatives?
- Is the IT organization insular and invisible, as it might be if led by a technician, or connected and highly visible in everyday operations?
- Can your technology leaders operate within the upper management strata of your firm as peers to top management, rather than as suppliers?
- Can they embrace the strategic imperatives of the firm in formulating their own plans? Can they understand them?

2. The IT mandate

A second line of inquiry in aligning IT strategy with firm strategy concerns what we ask the IT function to do. The principal and very often only mandate that drives most IT functions is that of "keeping the lights on".

On average, more than 90 percent of IT budgets go to procuring and maintaining basic IT infrastructure: the servers, networks, desktops, laptops, and basic applications that keep operations running from day to day. Very often, 100 percent of the thoughts of IT management are devoted to those tasks. The result is an inherently conservative organization that is consumed with the details of day-to-day operations and useless in seeking out innovations that will help to make the underlying business more profitable or competitive.

If you doubt this, then ask what metrics are used to measure the success of your IT operations. Most often, budget compliance is the only metric that rises to the attention of top management in the firm. When that is true, you are communicating to IT management that "keeping on keeping on" is their only job.

To change all that, begin to measure the impact that technology initiatives have on firm performance – on profitability, profit per partner, or revenue per lawyer. You need not start with measuring the impact of basic IT operations. The nexus between basic operations and profitability is too tenuous (which suggests an IT infrastructure management strategy focused on efficiency). Instead, start with discrete projects.

In my own firm, we have identified the technology-related operations that most impact profitability and now manage and measure them separately from basic IT operations. Furthermore, impact on profitability is an everyday metric for those groups. For example, the tools and techniques our firm uses to manage practice economics grew out of one of those groups. We can now examine the pricing and project management initiatives that use those tools and techniques and determine with some precision their impact on profitability. Being able to point to a positive impact on profitability helps to broaden use of these tools and techniques.

You can change the expectation under which your IT group operates simply by changing what you measure. I suggest you avoid the trap of measuring return on investment, perhaps the most easily manipulated of all project justification devices. Rather, begin to ask IT management to help improve profitability in a discrete area of practice. Given the rise of fixed fees and the need to develop efficiencies in areas of practice previously insulated from that need by the billable hour, there should be ample opportunity to do so. Treat that as the "thin end of the wedge" and try to broaden the impact over time.

3. IT governance

Much has been written about IT governance. Perhaps the most provocative recent discussion of the subject is Peter Hinssen's 2011 book *Business/IT Fusion: How to move beyond alignment and transform IT in your organization.*[2] He urges us to ignore everything that has been said about IT governance.

Conventional wisdom has focused on developing a monitor and control culture for IT. The problem with that approach is that it creates a bureaucratic, compliance-focused culture that is the antithesis of the flexibility and creativity necessary for IT to truly become a participant in the business of the firm.

What is required is a fusion of the strategies of the IT group and the organization. CIOs must become entrepreneurs rather than compliance officers. The success of the IT organization can be measured as much by its degree of connection to the firm as by its impact on profitability.

We can find many good examples of such connections. One of the foremost comes from the consulting world. Accenture is, as you might expect, very focused on key performance metrics. However, when it undertook to transform its learning management technology and culture, it was faced with a unique challenge. How could it take something as prosaic as training and use it to drive profitability? And how could it measure the results?

The tale of how Accenture did that is captured in the book *Return on Learning: Training for high performance at Accenture* by Donald Vanthournout.[3] Accenture managed to reduce its budget for training dramatically, yet at the same time achieve a measurable impact on profitability more than three times its investment.

The secret to Accenture's success was that its learning initiatives program was highly "interleaved" within its management structure. Dozens of business units had a hand in its success and executives from every level of the organization acted as stakeholders for various components of the project. This deep connection philosophy is embodied in its V-Model graphic (see Figure 1).

As is evident from the graphic, the program used sponsors and stakeholders at every level of the organization. The same approach works in other settings, including law firms.

Source of innovation

Once you ensure that your IT organization has appropriately entrepreneurial leadership and a mandate to innovate, don't squash their

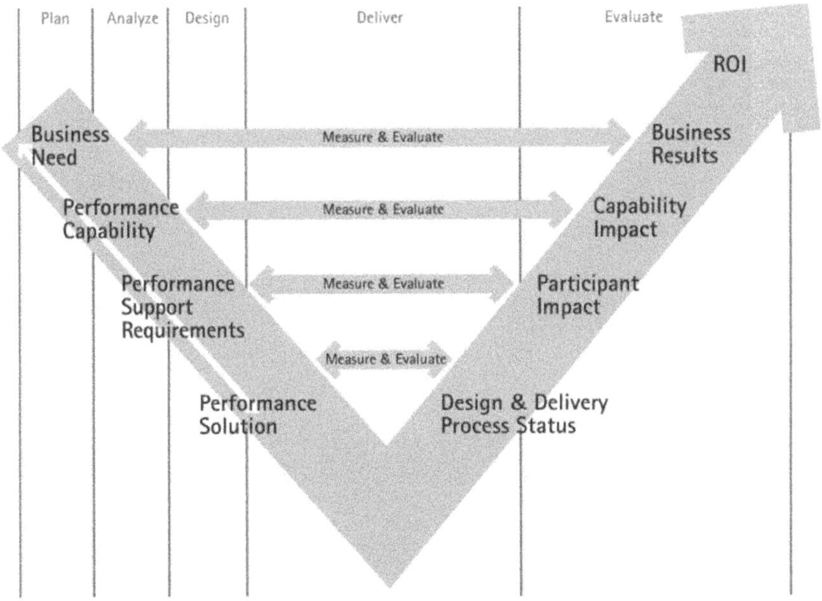

Figure 1: The V model for alignment at all levels, copyright Accenture, 2010

initiative with a compliance-heavy approach to governance. Rather, strive to broaden its degree of connection to critical projects.

Multiply real stakeholders and sponsors and let them interact with the IT group. The more you do that, the more lawyers, managers, and others inside your organization will come to see IT as a source of innovation rather than a source of frustration.

A version of this article appeared in Managing Partner *magazine in April 2013.*

References

1. Carr, Nicholas, G., *Does it matter? Information Technology and the Corrosion of Competitive Advantage*, Harvard Business School Publishing, 2004.
2. Hinssen, P., *Business/IT Fusion: How to move beyond alignment and transform IT in your organization*, Mach Media, Ghent, 2011.
3. Vanthournout, D., et al, *Return on Learning: Training for High Performance at Accenture*, Agate, Chicago, 2006.

Chapter 27:

Projecting success – Get more value out of your law firm's IT investments

By Stephen Brown, IT director at Higgs & Sons

It may seem obvious, but project management is important to the success of all new technology investments. There are many different resources to help us to get things done.

So, why is it that we continue to see negative statistics associated with project management? Two of the most concerning facts I have found are:

1. The average failure rate of projects is between 30 and 70 percent;[1] and
2. Only 2.5 percent of companies complete 100 percent of their projects.[2]

As we all know, there are "lies, damn lies and statistics". While the two above make for interesting reading in isolation, what happens when you apply those statistics to your own firm? To illustrate, let's take the case of an imaginary firm, Acme Law.

Looking at the statistics highlighted above, if Acme Law invests £1 million each year on new programs and projects, it is potentially risking between £300,000 and £700,000 on initiatives that have no chance of success. Even worse, the projects that fail don't just consume budgets – they also divert resources away from other important areas. Based on this scenario, it is easy to see how negative spirals can start to form in organizations where staff morale takes a huge hit as despondency and change fatigue sets in.

Of course, to compound the problem, projects are not always developed singularly. Many law firms will have at least six support divisions and, if each division is estimated to deliver one project per quarter, then that is 24 projects a year. That would result in a project being delivered every two weeks within the firm. Imagine how that impacts on those earlier statistics.

We are all acutely aware that law firms only have a finite number of resources to deliver projects. So the question is: how can we improve on our delivery and the success rate? Allow me to share some experiences which may provide you with some insights in order to help you make changes.

Changing approaches

Communication is vital to the success of any project. To improve the communication between project delivery teams and our wider firm, we reviewed the communication channels and media that were being employed. The review highlighted a number of challenges:

1. Use of different "language"; and
2. Flow of information from the project team to the wider firm, i.e. communicating the *right* message to the *right* individuals at the *right* time.

Once these issues had been identified, we set about making changes to address them. One example was the need to create similarities between a project and a legal matter in terms of the adopted language, methodologies, principles, and structure. We identified areas where we could align the language used between project teams and other staff in order to build a common foundation.

As a result, we found that one of the key areas we could address which required a minimum effort or resources was to rename and restructure the project initiation document (PID). A PID will typically include all of the necessary section documents and plans to successfully deliver a project. However, the term "project initiation" was not one that was particularly familiar to, or featured within, the day-to-day vernacular of our lawyers.

In a legal environment, the client engagement letter would include a similar collection of information as the PID. So, to break down a potential barrier to successful cross-departmental communication, we simply changed the name of the PID to a more widely recognized descriptor – the project engagement letter (PEL).

Although it may appear to be little more than semantics, the change of name enabled all of our departments to recognize the purpose of the document and the expectations arising from it. The PEL (as with its predecessor) includes elements that are familiar to the recipient and requires successful completion of the project.

Included in a PEL are the following fields:

- Project goal – Provide a SMART (specific, measureable, achievable, realistic, and time bound) overview of the project;
- Primary scope – State exactly what has to be achieved as part of this project;
- Secondary scope – State what else might be achieved as part of this project;
- Out of scope – For the avoidance of doubt, the following are out of the scope of this project;
- Project organization – Identify the roles and responsibilities in the project;
- Success criteria – Provide measureable success criteria;
- Communication – Define the communication channels for the project;
- Constraints – List anything that will impact on the success of the project;
- Risks – List anything that might impact on the success of the project;
- Timescales – Provide realistic timescales for the project; and
- Costs – Link back to the business case.

The PEL forms a contract between the delivery team and the recipients of the project, where each party has responsibilities to ensure that any project is embedded into the firm and all of the benefits are realized.

Ensuring success

Think how many projects have been delivered, but then are metaphorically "put on the shelf". To help avoid this, ensure all participants have a clear understanding of what success is in the context of the project (i.e. what is required by the project delivery team and the recipients). Success should not simply be the delivery of the product, but should look beyond that (i.e. the impact of the product on the firm or workforce). Many technologists view success as the "go live" date of the technology, whereas the business views success as when the benefits of working more effectively and efficiently are realized.

The benefits of a project will only be felt if the project is taken to completion – this can be many months after the "go live". Therefore, ensure you revisit the original success criteria and, although there may have been changes to it as the project has developed, it will still provide a good benchmark, especially if the success criteria were well thought out at the beginning.

So, how can project teams enhance their communication during delivery? An important element of any project is the communication plan. A communication plan considers the flow of information from the project-delivering team to all recipients. There is no "standard" communication plan as each one needs to consider the recipient, have a clear purpose, and be alert to the level of awareness.

A delivery team that is living and breathing a project will have a much greater level of enthusiasm, awareness, and interest in the project and in any associated communication. Do not leave your recipients behind – provide background information and explain new concepts, terminology, and procedures carefully. The use of email needs consideration – we all receive too many emails, so consider if your message can be delivered in a different way to capture greater interest?

You could elevate your firm to the top 3 percent of businesses simply by finishing all of the projects you initiate. It sounds easy, but how can you make sure this happens in practice? A rigorous approach to your project portfolio is a good start. Only start projects you know you can finish or that have the right level of buy-in from all potential participants – especially senior management.

A common mistake is to start work too soon, to get the project off the ground as quickly as possible. Of course you want to capitalize on everyone's enthusiasm at the beginning, but starting too soon can prove to be a false economy. Would you be as eager to get on a plane where the required safety checks had been bypassed? Equally, ask why it is acceptable to bypass the checks and balances associated with starting your own project.

At this crucial scoping stage, ask if the project has been fully analyzed. This should include not just the hard elements of the project (i.e. quality of the product being delivered), but have an understanding of all of the soft elements of the project – the social and political implications, for example. To illustrate, here are some questions that may require attention:

1. Does this project have the required sponsorship to succeed?
2. How will my staff respond to the required change to realize the benefits?
3. What processes need to be stopped so that new ones will be embraced?

4. Which "empires" or "ivory towers" need to be removed or restructured to allow the project to flourish?
5. What governance is required to make the project stick?

The first question in that list is possibly the most important you can ask. If this project does not have the required level of sponsorship from the firm, then it has a higher than average chance of failure.

In order to get sponsorship, talk to the senior individuals concerned. Make sure they understand the relationship between the success of the project and the firm's overall aims and objectives. Do not cut corners; continue with this effort until either you have the required sponsorship or consider terminating the project altogether. It is better to call a halt at the early stages before precious time and resources have been invested in a potentially lost cause.

Better outcomes

Delivering programs or projects into a firm is hard work and takes tenacity, but there are ways to give each project a better chance of success (see box: "How to avoid the common causes of project failure").

TOP TIP

How to avoid the common causes of project failure

1. Do not start a program or project without the correct level of sponsorship.
2. Know your starting point.
3. Agree the scope before the project commences.
4. Stick to the agreed scope. Do not be tempted to keep adding to the scope as your knowledge and enthusiasm grows. Remember the project team is consistently moving forwards, which increases the gap in knowledge between the delivery team and its recipients. Furthermore, it is okay to change the scope if it was not right or external factors have changed, but make sure you validate any major changes.
5. Communicate. Have a thorough plan which gives careful consideration to the recipients. Make sure every communication has a clear objective.
6. Ensure every success criteria is measureable. Some criteria might be hard to measure, but they still need to be done.
7. Know your staff and give careful consideration to who needs to be on the project team.

If you do push ahead and a successful outcome is achieved, then it is also important that you communicate that success. Let's not forget the need for celebration and the associated "feel good factor" that ripples through a firm after completion of a successful project. It will also provide the incentive and morale boost to see the other projects through to completion, and be another advantage when you sit down with colleagues to talk about your next "big idea".

References

1. Macdougall, C., "Combatting IT failure rates through IT program executive sponsorship", Project Management Institute, 2014; available at: www.pmi.org/learning/it-failure-rates-executive-sponsorship-1910.
2. Hardy-Vallee, B., "The Cost of Bad Project Management", *Gallup Business Journal*, February 2012; available at: www.gallup.com/businessjournal/152429/cost-bad-project-management.aspx.

A version of this article appeared in Managing Partner *magazine in June 2015.*

Chapter 28:
Robot law

By Chrissie Lightfoot, CEO of EntrepreneurLawyer Limited

In the October 2011 issue of *Managing Partner*, I wrote a feature on the future of artificial intelligence (AI) for law firms, predicting that the use of AI and robots in the legal ecosystem was not far off.[1] I suggested that work carried out by trainees and junior lawyers (aka associates) will be done by AI and robots in the not-too-distant future. Ultimately, I argued, it will be likely that real iCyborg lawyers will evolve who will tap into evolved Watson-type (IBM) AI technology, utilizing either non-invasive or invasive brain computer interfaces (BCI).

Unsurprisingly, and unfortunately, my insights and the article were largely mocked and scoffed. I received a lot of pushback from the majority of readers within the profession via a variety of sources and media at that time, as well as during ensuing years. Nonetheless, those who mattered, the pioneers and game-changers, listened.

Here we are now, four years later, with a blast of AI and robotics advancements throughout the world; and a flurry of new reports, articles, and comments on the tension between the liberalization and exploitation of AI and robotics in society and the law. Such interest even sparked comment from world-renowned physicist Stephen Hawking that AI has the potential to destroy the human race. Elon Musk, the pioneer of digital money, private spaceflight, and electric cars, has voiced similar concerns.

Yes, perhaps. We'd be foolish not to question whether AI is exponentially dangerous, especially with a number of dystopian movies doing the usual scaremongering. But, there is also a plethora of papers and opinions written on 'Helven' – the fast-approaching AI reality of heaven and hell, depending on how you look at it. The term was coined by futurist Gerd Leonhard to explain how "technology is now going inside of us and we are going inside of technology... that's really what AI means – a piece of humanity going inside a machine".

I draw comfort, as you should too, from futurist Ray Kurzweil's recent *Time* magazine feature[2] on how to make AI safe. In the article, he notes, "Ultimately, the most important approach we can take to keep AI safe is to work on our human governance and social institutions. We are already a human-machine civilization. We have the opportunity in the decades ahead to make major strides in addressing the grand challenges of humanity. AI will be the pivotal technology in achieving this progress. We have a moral imperative to realize this promise while controlling the peril. It won't be the first time we've succeeded in doing this."

AI and robotic engineering have already bolted from the R&D labs and been embraced in a multitude of fields, industries, and services. Technology is progressing at an exponential rate, while our ethics, social contracts, and laws remain linear. What is required is new regulation, controls, policies, and robot law if AI is to be "made safe", along with a major consideration of digital ethics.

Leonhard has argued that the power of technology has already surpassed the scope of our ethics. Without a committed focus on digital ethics and robot regulation, we may well be facing an extinction threat from our own inventions.

AI in law

AI and robotics in the legal ecosystem are to be embraced, not resisted, for the new arms race is all about AI. To find a balance between ethics and AI, we must go beyond fear; something lawyers are not usually comfortable with.

Some progress has, however, been made in the deployment of AI in the past year or two in the UK, USA, and beyond, with Allen & Overy employing its first graduate who studied AI. Hodge Jones & Allen has been working with academics from UCL to create software that assesses the merits of personal injury cases. More recently, the possibility of robot lawyers has moved a step closer, with the University of Liverpool in the UK teaming up with Riverview Law in a bid to apply AI to a range of legal tasks.[3]

AI has been applied in the legal ecosystem for some years now. UK legal expenses insurer Das has been using AI for several years to support due diligence on insurance claims. More recently, it has set up a fixed-fee law firm, Das Law, which uses cognitive computing and AI to determine the merits of potential legal claims.

More widely, many lawyers already use voice-activated digital assistants like Siri (iOS), Google Now (Android), and Cortana (Windows) on their smartphones to make calls, send messages, answer queries, and schedule meetings and reminders, among other things. These AI assistants even have a sense of humor built in (with the exception of Google Now).

Process automation and AI is also being used by a range of law firms to enable:

- Integrated analytics;
- Knowledge management;
- Voice mining;
- Client self-service;
- Client relationship management;
- Intelligent documents;
- Expertise systems;
- Collaboration;
- Marketing automation;
- Virtual assistants/e-personal assistants; and
- Intelligent agents (for example, IBM's Watson).

However, AI innovations in the legal space to date are like the Henry Ford conundrum. They provide a "faster horse" solution, instead of completely changing the mode of transport to an automobile. I say this even in light of US law firm Dentons announcing recently that its collaborative innovation platform, NextLaw Labs, has signed a deal with the company, ROSS Intelligence, to develop a legal advisor app (dubbed ROSS), powered by IBM Watson, which is expected to streamline legal research, saving lawyers time and clients money.

ROSS – The world's first AI lawyer

Of course, I agree with Joe Andrew, global chair at Dentons, that this is indeed "an important moment in our profession. Joining the world's largest law firm with the world's leading technology provider (IBM) is just one of the ways that NextLaw Labs is working to transform the legal industry." I also agree completely with Dan Jansen, CEO of NextLaw Labs, that "technology is now and will continue to be a real differentiator in the legal profession." That's a no-brainer.

The potential in companies like ROSS shows how the approach to solving client challenges is changing, and is likely to change even further as technology is increasingly being leveraged to improve the efficiency and effectiveness of legal services. When I heard that Dentons had invested in ROSS, I was not at all surprised by this news. It was foreseeable and inevitable. It's a natural progression with regard to the evolution of the "robot lawyer", and the coming together of brilliant technologies – cognitive computing, cognitive reasoning, AI, and robotics (in due course).

ROSS, hailed as the world's first "AI lawyer" (albeit not yet robot lawyer), is the smart result of a deal between ROSS Intelligence, Apple (using Siri's slick voice capabilities), and IBM (Watson's cognitive computing prowess). It will undoubtedly be a huge boon for lawyers, law firms, and clients. While I am personally excited by this progress, I would warn against describing ROSS as "pure" artificial intelligence, for ROSS isn't really pure AI. It's cognitive computing at its best. ROSS will not be doing the same thing a human does. The evidence-based answer it deploys as a result of its "deep search" will be drawn from a range of possible answers, and the best suited will be presented from an existing data set. AI comes up with something new. This is a faster-horse solution in my book, not a new kind of horse.

Nonetheless, ROSS is first out of the lab, or should I say starter-gate, and Dentons, not unlike Riverview Law in the USA and UK, which is using an element of Watson's cognitive computing for automating legal workflow processes and creating visualized analytics, thereby simplifying workflow, is utilizing what I would describe as the low end of Watson's capabilities (the faster horse).

In time, I predict that ROSS and its competitors will evolve and utilize the high end IBM Watson talent, which tackles complex due diligence legal work (by 2020), and will evolve even farther beyond this (i.e. moving into pure AI). The "lawyer machine" will think for itself without the aid of the lawyer and data sets (by 2030).

AI tipping point

For the time being, I am confident that more US law firms will embrace cognitive computing technologies and AI technologies in due course, such as the ones mentioned here, and eventually combine robotics too, in the not too distant future (by 2020).

Now that an international behemoth like Dentons has launched its intent to use cutting-edge technology (NewTech) in its service delivery, it's only a matter of time until the other "big players" follow suit. Cognizant of the fact that the Magic Circle firms in the UK, with footprints in the USA and beyond, have all been curious as to the potential of IBM Watson, the move by Dentons is a really positive thing, I believe. It will no doubt jolt other Magic Circle and Big Law firms into action too, and thereby kick-start the real AI revolution badly needed in the legal eco-system. Once this tip occurs, I would envisage Big Law moving down the legal vertical, while mid-tier and boutique law firms and new entrants across the globe seriously begin to embrace cognitive computing and AI technologies in order to compete and deploy their legal services in a much smarter, timely, and cost-conscious manner too. Ultimately, the client will benefit.

Riverview's CEO, Karl Chapman, believes IBM Watson "is the holy grail of technology", and predicts that artificial intelligence will change the future of legal work.[4] I agree – sort of – but I would add that what I truly believe will be the holy grail in the legal world will be a technology triad, combining cognitive computing, AI, and robotics. This will ultimately disrupt and thereby change the future of all legal work, incrementally, in time.

I join a chorus of voices, from Bill Gates to the White House, to assume that cognitive computing, AI, and robotics represent an idea that's time has come. The relentless march of industrialization, wearable technology, AI, and robotics will push the boundaries of what it means to be human, social, and a lawyer in the next 30 years. There will be blue-collar and white-collar robot legal staff working alongside "pureblood" human lawyers and "hybrid humans" (NewHuman).

Going forward, pureblood lawyers will need to embrace the rapidly advancing technological evolution (NewTech) and support of NewHumans. For the former, their ultimate success will be based on how well they become SocialHumans by embracing social networking and optimizing their social and human capital during both work and leisure hours.

Need for regulation

We need to address the positive and negative effects of AI and robots in society and the legal world. Advances in AI will inevitably affect legal jobs, the legal role and the effectiveness of the rule of law, and the justice system. Changes to employment law need to be made in preparation for avatars and humanoids (iCyborgs and robots) entering the workplace. Futurist Rohit Talwar predicts that, by 2020, avatars will be mainstream. By 2025, he says, robots will have entered every aspect of human life and will be performing a wide range of functions, from nursing and complex surgery to policing and security, through to manufacturing, retail, and hotel service roles.

By this time, I believe robots will be performing complex legal services too. In the next 25 years, robots will have both cognitive and iterative artificial intelligence. Dentons and Riverview Law are both attempting to capitalize on cognitive intelligence only, at present, because the AI technology with regard to iterative intelligence is not quite there yet. But it soon will be – it's just a matter of years. When it is, the iCyborg lawyer will rise.

When we have avatars, robots, iCyborgs, or humanoids in the workplace, and if a person/non-person has the ability to be injured but repaired and healed very quickly to a potentially better state than before, what does that mean for how we think about damages and what an injury is really worth? If the injury at work is caused by a non-person/avatar/robot, it begs the question "who/what will be liable/accountable for the damages?" Will it be the individual? The avatar is, after all, a copy of the individual, remotely controlled by the individual via BCI. Will vicarious liability come into consideration, and will the individual's employer have recourse to the avatar/robot supplier?

A whole new body of law and regulation will need to be developed to manage the implications of advances in AI and robotics, and law firms will need dedicated practice groups to tackle these and other issues for their clients.

Preparation is key

So, how can law firms prepare for the age of AI and robotics, and how can lawyers future-proof their livelihoods? Steps that can be taken today include:

- Embracing the new breed of consumer/customer/client;
- Being SocialHuman and embracing social networking, relationship building, rainmaking, creativity, intrapreneurialism, and entrepreneurialism;
- Embracing the role that technology and AI can play for lawyers, law firms, and clients – in particular, marketing automation to support SocialHuman activity;
- Embracing the full spectrum of choice and opportunity to provide low-cost commoditized services juxtaposed with high-cost, high-end, intellectually and emotionally intelligent services;

- Being smarter about relationships, marketing, business development, communication, and being social;
- Watching and learning from new market entrants; and
- Creating competitive new practice areas and business offshoots.

Currently, machines have a gift for searching, processing, and analyzing. Humans have a natural talent for being creative and using emotional intelligence – ultimately, being human – something that machines are not capable of, for the time being. Accordingly, lawyers need to be creative about who, what, where, when, why, and how they provide legal services and products in the next five, 10, or 20 years. For example, this means being creative about how you market yourself, how you identify talented lawyers, where and how you work to maximize productivity, and being smart in deploying *who* or *what* to a task best suited for their/its talent.

Accordingly, I would recommend a winning combined-talent formula for legal services for the next five to 20 years, as follows:

- Machine = process, research, analytics, logic, IQ focus
- Human = reason, judgment, creative, EI focus
- Combined talent brilliance of machine and human =
- Increased productivity and increased customer satisfaction =
- Growth and future-proofed organization and individuals.

The dawn of robot law is upon us. Prepare or watch from the sidelines: it's your choice.

This first appeared as Chapter 8 in Slater, L. (ed.), 2020 Vision: The Future of Legal Services, *ARK Group, 2015.*

References

1. Lightfoot, C., "iCyborg lawyers", *Managing Partner*, Vol. 14 Issue 2, October 2011.
2. Kurzweil, R., "Don't fear artificial intelligence", *Time*, 19 December 2014.
3. Manglani, M., 'Riverview Law invests in artificial intelligence research", *Managing Partner*, Vol. 17 Issue 5, February 2015.
4. Manglani, M., "Artificial intelligence to change the future of legal work", January 2015, available at www.managingpartner.com/news/business-strategy/artificial-intelligence-change-future-legal-work.

Chapter 29: The future of law in the age of robot lawyers and blockchain technology

By John Alber, futurist at the International Legal Technology Association

The exponential growth of computing power means that great change is imminent in the legal sector. When we look back on this period in 20 or 30 years' time, I expect we will agree that the most significant metric underlying the transformation of legal practice will have been the cost per unit of processing power. Not profits per partner. Not margin. Not any number of other things we might measure.

Most of the talk about increasing computing power has to do with robot lawyers. Some lawyers imagine machine-learning platforms like IBM Watson taking over large swathes of law practice. Many more lawyers respond to such ideas with disdain. In much the same manner that pilots once said that computers would never be able to land airplanes – that too much subtle human judgment was required – lawyers dismiss the proposition that their judgment can be automated.

Of course, this overlooks the large segments of practice (and the revenue streams attached to them) that have already fallen to automation and process improvement. Think of document review (now very automated), legal research (increasingly automated), and document drafting (in the process of being automated).

Some forward-looking firms are embracing trends like document automation. But, they are imagining that growth in service-sector capabilities will be linear and predictable. Other sectors (such as mobile phones, music, books, and retailing) clearly demonstrate that the digital revolution often yields exponential, unpredictable phenomena.

Blockchain law

How might digitization sweep away traditional law practice? Well, maybe robot lawyers. But, more likely something unanticipated will prove to be the competition – or a hoard of somethings.

Take blockchain technology for example. Blockchains form the infrastructure for digital currencies such as Bitcoin, Qubitcoin, Litecoin, and others. The blockchain is a public ledger of all currency transactions that have ever been executed. It is constantly growing as "completed" blocks are added to it with a new set of recordings.

Blockchains are only possible with substantial processing power and extensive networks (only just possible now, but phenomenally possible later). They form a perfect, publicly available ledger in which to record enforceable obligations.

Here's the thing. Blockchain technology was created not just to support digital currencies, but as the foundation for "smart contracts". These are contracts that are self-enforcing – they don't need page after page of small print, let alone the lawyers who write the small print or the courts that enforce them.

How might this work? Imagine that you've just leased a car. You commit to direct a stream of digital currency to the lessor, and that happens automatically. Should you fail to meet that obligation, there will be no need for lawyers, courts, or even repo men. The car simply will no longer work for you. Indeed, it might drive itself back to the lessor.

Fanciful? Not so much. The first blockchain bond issue by a public company has already taken place. And the creation of that transaction involved more engineers than lawyers. Venture capitalists are funding a legion of smart contract and other blockchain start-ups; some of those will become the Amazons of this sphere.

Response strategies

So, should law firms sharpen up their game and start playing with blockchain tech? I think that's a pointless exercise. Law firms are the antithesis of the sorts of business organizations which are likely to thrive using blockchain power. Law students are negatively selected for entrepreneurship and they are trained to be problem finders rather than problem solvers; to cap that off, law firm partnerships reinforce risk aversion.

But, law firms do still generate extraordinary margins. The smarter firms in BigLaw will invest some of that cash in acquisitions and start-ups that take advantage of blockchain and other emerging technologies. I expect some of those to outgrow and outlive their parents – to Accenture their Arthur Andersens.

And what of other firms? Their best hope for survival depends upon the ruthless excision of inefficiency. The profit model of many firms today is founded on inefficiency in the sense that much revenue is derived from manually doing what can easily be automated. But, that cannot stand in the face of increasingly abundant and inexpensive machine intelligence.

Will all of this lead to the extinction of law practice? Probably not. There will still be the law and the need for expertise in dealing with it. But, at what scale? Will law firms survive in the same manner that some harness makers still survive the passing of the horse and buggy age – as curiosities in a small, dusty corner of the economy?

What seems certain is that inaction *will* lead to extinction. This is part of a perfectly natural evolution of the legal marketplace: over time, inefficiencies get removed, no matter what. And *something* will survive. Whether we call what remains law firms remains to be seen.

A version of this article appeared in Managing Partner *magazine in October 2015.*

Part 6:

Legal skills and business development

Chapter 30:
Pitch team and planning

By Clare Adshead-Grant, business development consultant at White and Case LLP

Poor planning creates unnecessary work and stress. We all know this. Yet we fail to recognize proposals and bids for what they are: very time-consuming and complex projects. Ultimately, the way you manage the process affects your chances of winning, because the prospect will view the rigor that is applied to organizing the bid process as representative of how the engagement will be managed, if successful.

A detailed project plan prepared at the outset will get the team quickly off the mark and make it clear who needs to be doing what – and by when – throughout the whole process. It is particularly important that the lead partner knows what to do personally, when to have quality time with the team, and when and what to delegate.

Deciding on the pitch team

People buy from people. Throughout the pitch process, the prospect will be asking:

- Do I like them?
- Can I work with them?
- Can they do the job?

Very often, the last question is a given. If the prospect has done their homework, they will already have reduced their list of prospective advisers to those who can do the job. It is, much like a job interview, about personality and fit. These characteristics come through the process in terms of communication style, both written and verbal.

Selection of the team is therefore critical. Consider the following:

- Lead partner: This may not be the person who received the invitation. It should be the person most appropriate to lead the work.
- Other team members: You must make sure that everyone has a defined role; that there are sufficient resources allocated to the anticipated volume of work; and that the balance of the team is correct, not only between technical areas, but also seniority of staff.

There are defined roles within the team, which can be categorized as either client-facing or internal roles.

Client-facing roles

Lead partner

The lead partner's role is to be the team leader and decision maker. Ultimately, all final decisions concerning the pitch are theirs. They are also the main point of contact for the prospect.

Engagement team

The engagement team are central for the production and content of the document and presentation. They may also have an involvement in prospect engagement, but normally at a different level (and perhaps more insightful) than that of the lead partner. The key issues and main substance of the pitch are gained from the engagement team.

Mentor partner

The main role of the mentor partner is to challenge and verify decisions being taken by the pitch team and lead partner. They act as a sounding board and provide independent verification on topics such as fee proposals. One of the key roles that the mentor partner performs is during the presentation rehearsal, where they challenge and prepare the pitch team for cross-examination. Another role is that of feedback liaison. While they have been involved in the pitch and know the background and the process followed, they are independent enough to be viewed as separate and therefore will give unbiased, and therefore valuable, feedback.

Internal roles

Bid manager/BD support

The role of the bid manager or business development support is to oversee the whole process and ensure it hits the right deadlines. They are the liaison person between the front office (fee earner), pitch team, and the logistics team. They help to formulate the messaging and structure of the document and the presentation materials, as well as coordinating the back office support. The bid/BD manager is also normally responsible for generating standard pitch toolkit information, document management, and version control, as well as ultimate quality control of the output. This role is normally the lynch-pin between the fee earners and the back office support.

Back office

Generally, back office staff members provide research at the beginning of the process, and the document and presentation production at the end. They also may perform general administration tasks. The back office function includes copywriting and graphic design people, who focus on the legibility of ideas and the look and feel of the document and presentation. In many firms, the finance function is taking an increasingly prominent role in fee estimates and accuracy of project costs, making the whole profitability of pitches much more accurate.

The pitch planning meeting

Once the ITT/RFP has been circulated to the pitch team, a pitch planning meeting should be held as soon as possible. The pitch team, the business development team, and any other fee-earners who know the potential client or decision-makers should be present. If the client is an existing one, ensure that the relationship team is invited. While it should go without saying, it is imperative that an agenda is set prior to the meeting and distributed to all who will be attending.

Pitch planning meeting agenda

Below is a list of topics that could be included in a typical pitch planning meeting agenda:

- Background to the bid;
- Overview of client and their relationship to the firm;
- Client's requirements and expectations/selection criteria;
- Key market/business issues;
- Competitors – who are they, strengths and weaknesses;
- Key decision makers at the organization;

- Pre-pitch scoping meeting/telephone call;
- The firm's value proposition/pitch strategy/winning strategy (see below);
- Fee strategy;
- Team structure and CVs; and
- Actions and responsibilities.

At the end of the planning meeting, there should be clearly documented actions and responsibilities which should be put into your pitch plan, including deadlines. Once the pitch plan has been filled in, it should be circulated to the bid team. This is particularly important for panel pitches and procurement pitches where a structured plan will be needed to ensure that all deadlines are met.

Summary of pitch opportunity	
Prospect	[Name of prospect]
Opportunity	[Summary of opportunity]
Relationship	[Summary of current relationship]
Fees	[Potential fee]
Competitors	[List of competitors and key strengths and weaknesses]
Strategy/Why would we win?/Why would we lose?	[Summary of strategy and options available]
Key selling messages	[Experience, relationship, overcome key barriers]
Requirements	
Deadline	[Time/date]
Method of delivery	[E-mail, hard copy]
Number of copies	[Hard copy only]
Recipients	[Insert names, address, e-mail of prospects]

Internal logistics	
Agree pitch structure	[List headings, writing responsibilities]
1st draft to be sent	[Date, to whom]
Draft edited and returned	[Date, by whom]
2nd draft	[Date, to whom]
Independent review	[Date, by whom]
Generate typeset document	[Date, by whom]
Finalize	[Date, by whom]
Covering letter/e-mail	[Date, by whom]

Sample Pitch Plan

How to formulate your pitch strategy

Having been through the process and finished your pitch meeting, you will have a very clear idea of where you are stronger than your competitors and where you are weaker. Put these factors into the pitch strategy matrix (Figure 2, overleaf).

From this completed matrix you can formulate the overall messages that you need to shout about (i.e. capitalize on) and those that you need to minimize or formulate a solution for that will negate this in the prospect's mind. For example, a prospect is about to undergo a merger with a company which is headquartered in the UK but has substantial subsidiaries in Germany, Turkey, and Spain. You have offices in the UK, Germany, and Spain, but do not have an office in Turkey – unlike your key competitor who has offices in all countries. You do, however, have stronger industry experience. So, how do you pitch to the prospect in order to win the work? The solution in this case could be to highlight similar industry deals that you have done, which may have included a Turkish element, and how the deal was managed (perhaps using your "best friend" firm in Turkey, who also happens to be the leading player in that market).

However, if in this circumstance you were significantly deficient in one or two areas (e.g. if you didn't have any connections at all in the

Turkish market), then you should revisit your stop/go decision. You should question whether you do indeed have the capabilities to carry out the project to the standards required, particularly given the strength of your competitors to service the project.

	Low control	High control
Plus factors	Capitalize	Leverage
Minus factors	Minimize	Eliminate

Figure 1: The pitch strategy matrix

Ask the prospect

So the planning meeting has taken place, you have a completed project plan, and everyone knows what they are doing, and by when they are doing it. Along the way, you will have made some assumptions about the prospect and the opportunity. The best way to test those assumptions is to ask the prospect. Most people who are running tender processes are open to discussions about the opportunity. They want you to have as much information as possible, so that you can demonstrate to them how closely you match their criteria. It also allows more opportunities for the prospect to judge you and interact with you – getting to know you better and seeing if they actually like you.

Ringing and meeting with the prospect indicates to them that you are interested in the opportunity. Or, to put it another way, what if you didn't do this and all of your competitors did? Suddenly, you have put yourself at a significant disadvantage.

> "The fact that they wanted to meet with us and talk through their take on the pitch was comforting. Not everyone did that."
>
> *Prospect*

The purpose of meeting with or calling the prospect covers several areas including:

- Getting to know the client better;
- Really understanding and focusing on the prospect's needs;
- Helping to tailor the pitch more effectively;
- Demonstrating how you will respond to their requirements and bring value to them;
- Showing commitment to their business, culture, and teams you will be working with; and
- Starting to establish a relationship and rapport with the prospect.

Before you contact the client to set up the meeting/telephone call, ensure you have enough background information about the person and their role in the organization. It will be vital to capture all the discussions that happen. Very often, as the person asking the questions, it is difficult to also write up the answers. Consider involving someone else (e.g. your bid manager), so that the key "takeaways" and learnings from the call or meeting are captured. A meeting note should then be sent to the bid team so that it can be incorporated into the pitch document.

Prospect scoping questions

Before the scoping meeting, consider the following:

- Who will be at the meeting?
- What questions will they ask of you?
- Who are the right people to attend from your side to get your messages across?
- How will you structure the meeting so that everyone has a chance to make an impact?

Note: If a formal RFP has been received, then some of these questions will already have been answered and you should not ask the client to repeat themselves!

CHECK LIST

Process

1. What are the issues surrounding the RFP or why are you reviewing your choice of advisers?
2. How many firms do you use and who are they?
3. How many firms are you inviting to tender for the work? Are you willing to say who they are?
4. What will the process be? What time schedule are you working to?
5. When would you like to receive our document?
6. Why are we on the list? What were the drivers to invite us to pitch for this opportunity?
7. As well as you, who will be making the decision on who will be invited?
8. What are your key selection criteria? We would very much like to work with you… what will it take for us to win?
9. When will you be making a decision?
10. When you talk about innovative fee proposals, what types of fee structures have you used in the past that have been successful?

Business

1. What services are you looking to cover?
2. What do you consider to be your main business challenges?
3. What are the key business needs/issues/requirements going forward?
4. What are your business challenges and objectives for the next one/three/five years?
5. What is your annual [adviser] spend? How is it proportioned presently? Is this likely to change?
6. How do you structure yourself internally? (In-house team, management committee, etc.)
7. How do these relationships work?
8. Who hires [advisers]?
9. Who are the key users?

10. What are the main European/international markets you are focusing on and why? Do you see this changing in the future?
11. What is the size of your in-house team?

Personal

1. Do you have any preference regarding the structure of the teams you work with/key individuals that we should include?
2. How long have you worked here?
3. What has been your experience of external advisers? What has made these relationships work well in the past and what do we need to know to fit in with your long-term plan?
4. What in your job gives you the most stress?

The art of questioning

The key to successful questioning (or interviewing) is knowing what questions to ask, how to phrase them, when to ask them, and when not to ask them. Questioning develops your understanding of what the company or prospect needs so that your service delivery can improve and you can win more or new work.

However, it is very often the case that lawyers assume that they know what the company needs and that they act on those assumptions rather than the facts from the company itself: lawyers are, by their very nature, people who like to give advice and talk. However, people respond much better to those who listen to their answers and then ask follow-up questions – it shows that they are listening to the answers!

Approaches to questioning

General questions

General questions set the scene and help you to understand context. General questions could include, for example, "How are things and what's your view of the market?" or "How is business going?"

Probing questions

Probing questions start with a broad subject (e.g. the general questions mentioned above) and then narrow the focus as you define exactly what the interests are of the person you're talking to.

Issue questions

This type of question draws out the issues that are facing the prospect's business and explore any opportunities or problems that they see. An example issue question could be "What do you see as the key challenges in the coming year?"

Implication questions

Implication questions help your client (or potential client) to see, understand, and articulate the implications of taking or not taking actions. For example, you can say "I've had similar clients who have found that this caused X, Y, and Z. Is that what you have found?"

Need questions

Need questions help people to state their needs explicitly by saying what they have done (or not done). For example, "What are you planning to do about this? Might we be able to help in some way?"

Open style

Focus on asking open questions so that the answer is not just one word. Try to use words such as what, when, who, why, and how. Open questions are useful because they force us to not prejudge what the person is going to say. It also forces active listening in order to follow up and respond to what they have said. It also allows the person with whom you are talking to give their answer in their own words.

The art of questioning – What not to do

Closed questions

If you can answer a question with a single word or a short phrase, it is probably a closed question. If you want a free-flowing conversation, closed questions are not appropriate. However, closed questions can be quite useful in order to establish rapport and get conversation going as they are quick and easy to answer and the questioner keeps control of the conversation.

Being unprepared

If you have not read the documentation or information that you have been sent, it will be obvious to the person to whom you are asking questions – particularly as they are probably the person who put the time and effort into collating the information in the first place. A very bad impression will be formed – one from where it is almost impossible to retrieve your position.

Interrupting

It is rude to interrupt someone when they are answering a question that you have asked them. Interrupting will make the person feel that you're not listening to them. You will appear to be jumping to assumptions about what they were going to say. You may annoy them and will miss valuable insight into exactly what the person was thinking. Let the person answer. If you are tempted to interrupt, then stop yourself and give the person space to talk. Your job is to listen, not talk.

Asking multiple questions

Only ask one question at a time. If you ask three long and complex questions all rolled into one, you will not get the answer that you are after.

Cross-examining

Try to make the conversation as natural as possible, particularly when you are scoping out for a pitch. It is easy to slip into cross-examination mode rather than engaging in open and free-flowing discussion. Just because you have a list of questions, it doesn't that mean that you have to work from the top down to the bottom. Try to allow the conversation to flow while also incorporating the questions that you need to ask. You can always check at the end that you have actually covered everything that is on your agenda.

Just remember: the secret to successful questioning is actually active listening.

Fees

In recent years, the words "innovative fee proposal" have been read with a sinking feeling by the bid team. What does the prospect mean? What is innovative to one person will be positively dull to another. The best idea is to ask the prospect what they mean by innovative, if that is possible.

Fee strategy checklist

The fee strategy checklist is intended to be an internal checklist to make sure that you have considered all areas when formulating your fee strategy and ultimately your fee proposal.

- What is the current fee (from us or others) income?
- What work do we currently do, and at what rates?
- Do we provide any value-added services and can we put a figure on what this is saving them?

- What has the client said about fees in relation to this pitch?
- What are our market rates for similar clients?
- What is our initial thinking on the right fee to win the work? Will it be profitable for us at this level?
- What are our competitors likely to do on fees?
- Are there any innovative ways we can look at fees (e.g. fixed, volume, or success-related)?
- Will doing the work for this prospect give us opportunities to widen the relationship and sell additional services later?
- How important is it for us to win this work?
- Can we test our proposed fee informally with any of the decision-makers?

Examples of fee structures

Fee structures come in all shapes and sizes (see Table 1). Some are more suitable for certain types of projects or work, but less or not suitable for others. It is very important to work out exactly what revenue this will bring into the firm, so that you can work out the profitability. Some firms have some very sophisticated financial software which allows them to work this information out, but you can also do this as a simple, but very effective spreadsheet in Excel.

Model	**Options**
Hourly rate	Benchmark rate % discount on the hourly rate
Daily rate	Daily rate proposed which offers a saving to hourly rate for long-term projects
Blended rate	One hourly rate applied to the total number of hours worked, regardless of seniority of person undertaking the work
Fixed fee	Fixed cost for fixed scope work, regardless of time taken to complete
Capped fee	Maximum payment for a piece of work
Abort fee	Agreed % discount or fixed discount to the bill in the event that it doesn't proceed

Success/incentive fee	% increase to daily rate or fixed % uplift for successful outcomes
Performance-related fee	Agreed KPIs to be applied, where % fees withheld and rewarded at the end of the work depending upon performance
Retainer	Fixed monthly/quarterly fee for on-going/standard pieces of work
Value billing	Fee dependent on work undertaken, i.e. 'vanilla' work at reduced fee, with strategic advice provided at a premium
Volume discounts	By number of deals, work across the firm, panel appointment period
Early payment discount	% discount applied if the client pays early or upfront
Modularized pricing	A variation of the above, in that different parts of the project are charged on a different basis, i.e. use fixed fee for due diligence and abort fee for bidding phase

Table 1: Examples of fee structures

Summary

Below is a quick checklist for stage two of the pitch process.

- Decide on bid team (this should include all people, including those supporting the bidding process);
- Invite bid team to planning meeting;
- After planning meeting, detail a project plan and circulate;
- Arrange a meeting with the prospect;
- Debrief prospect meeting with bid team;
- Arrange fees meeting; and
- Debrief fee meeting to bid team.

This article first appeared as Chapter 3 in Adshead-Grant, C., Pitching to Win, *ARK Group, 2013.*

Chapter 31:
Practical advice on building a social firm

By Guy Alvarez, chief engagement officer, and Joe Lamport, chief strategy officer, at Good2bSocial

In this chapter, we offer some advice to core members of a law firm's management team as they set about the task of building a "social law firm". This advice consists of tips and techniques we have developed throughout our years of experience helping organizations inside and outside the legal industry in their quest to transform themselves into social organizations.

It is important to note that while these tactics have proven helpful to many of our clients, every organization is different. Culture, structure, and other aspects of an organization will have a profound effect on its ability to successfully adopt and deploy a social business strategy. There is no "one size fits all" approach, nor is there a "magic bullet" to accomplish the task without impacting on other aspects of the organization.

Even under the best of circumstances, organizational change is difficult and takes time, effort, and strong leadership in order to succeed. However, it certainly can be achieved. As our experience convinces us, ultimately a social business structure will provide significant benefits for law firms that choose to pursue it. Here are some guidelines to help you go about the process.

Developing a strategic plan

Appointing a social business team

The first critical step in getting started is to assemble a leadership team that will be mandated with the task of developing your firm's strategic plan. The team should be comprised of the chief development officer (CDO) and other key stakeholders, including several practicing attorneys, the firm's executive director, chief marketing officer (CMO), chief knowledge officer (CKO), and chief information officer (CIO), director of practice development, and so on, in order to ensure there is alignment with the strategy and execution across all major departments.

Defining goals and objectives

A threshold question for the social business team is to determine how far along the path of social business evolution the firm has already progressed. If the firm is still in the early stages, then the team's focus should properly be directed toward fostering further experimentation at the practice group or departmental level. If the firm has already passed through an experimental phase, then it is time to move on to develop a more general, firm-wide strategic plan that will include the roll out of an enterprise social network.

The planning process usually starts with an attempt to define the firm's highest-level business goals. These are the ultimate objectives the firm hopes to achieve by reorganizing itself as a social firm: goals such as generating new leads, raising awareness of the firm's brand, improving client service and support, fostering knowledge sharing and collaboration, reducing costs, and enhancing and retaining top talent. It is worthwhile starting out by making up a list and prioritizing the objectives from most to least important. In this way, when questions emerge in the subsequent implementation stages about how resources should be allocated (as they inevitably will), the list of top-priority goals can provide a touchstone for future decision-making.

Discovery

After the team has prioritized the firm's overarching goals and objectives, the next step is to undergo an internal and external discovery process. We particularly recommend starting out by arranging meetings or presentations with companies outside the legal industry that have undergone a successful social business transformation of their own. This can be extremely valuable in a number of ways through exposing members of the firm's social business team to the look and feel of a social business transformation. It is the old "show me, don't tell me" approach, which can give the team a very immediate understanding of what it means to undergo this kind of organizational change and provide best practice lessons.

One way to find companies who may be willing to share their social business transformation experiences is to ask social business software vendors for an introduction to some of their customers. The focus here is on obtaining insight, which is potentially much more valuable than a simple demonstration of product features. This is a chance for your team to hear real world examples of how other organizations have failed or succeeded with their own social business initiatives.

In parallel with this process, it is important for the team to do some market research of its own. You should start by gathering information on how your firm is perceived in the market in relation to its competitors. This will help the team to identify gaps and opportunities in your target market that, in turn, may become key elements in shaping your social strategy and content marketing plans, as described further below. We strongly recommend that the team itself begin to use social media monitoring and listening tools in compiling competitive intelligence. "Thinking social" and beginning to make use of social tools is an important step in making any firm into a more social organization. The team will quickly develop a sense of influencers in your target markets and begin to directly monitor competition as well. It is always helpful to expand the base of people in the firm using these social listening tools through training. Soon enough lawyers in practice groups will be using social tools to investigate and follow interesting trends and developments in their practice areas, which will help to build awareness and participation throughout the firm when it comes around to implementing your strategic plan.

Conducting an internal audit

After completing the discovery process, the next step is to perform an internal social business audit to identify the highest value resources available within the firm and where additional resources might be required. This is an area where consultants typically prove helpful, as the views of an objective outsider can be instrumental in helping the team to attain a more realistic assessment of existing resources and needs.

The audit should focus on three key areas: technology, content, and business processes. An accurate view in each of these areas will prove critical in helping your team to formulate the firm's strategic plan.

- The technology audit requires a careful evaluation of the firm's legacy applications (document management, CRM, time and billing, financial systems, HR systems, KM, website, intranet, and client extranets) in order to determine the necessity of, and degree of difficulty involved in, integrating these legacy systems into the new enterprise social network.

- The content audit needs to assess the current inventory (client alerts, newsletters, social media, blogs, seminars, webinars), as well as the strategy and process for content creation, from conception to approval. It is important to consider the human side of the equation, to evaluate who is currently tasked with content creation, and what additional resources may be necessary in order to increase output levels enough to support the content requirements in a more fully developed social business environment. Methods of content distribution should also be covered by the audit.
- Finally, the business processes audit is an incredibly important piece of the puzzle. The best way to approach this part of the audit is to focus separately on each department and practice area within the firm. Appoint a member of the social business team to work with a representative of each department or practice area to identify and map out the critical business processes in that department; describe each task and dependency involved in the process. This will enable the team to evaluate how each critical business process can be enhanced or improved through the use of social business technologies, or which existing processes may be replaced altogether in a new social business environment.

Creating a strategic plan

Your team is now ready to put together a draft of the firm's strategic plan. This is a critical document: the blueprint to your firm's evolution as a social firm. It expresses a high-level vision (reflecting the major goals and objectives the team identified at the outset), but it also provides a well-developed roadmap for how that vision is going to be achieved. It should not be a highly technical document (although it does include a technology needs assessment) inasmuch as it should be accessible and intelligible to everyone in the firm.

In our experience, the strategic plan for a large organization will typically be between 100 and 150 pages. The general purpose is to chart a course for implementing the long-term goals and objectives. The most important elements it should include are a timeline (with particular attention to identifying which initiatives to tackle first), a detailed description of the resources and budget needed, and the business and technology requirements for implementation. Additionally, a thorough strategic plan should include a communications plan, an adoption plan, training and education, senior leader adoption plan, a deployment schedule, and a set of key performance indicators to measure overall success going forward. We also want to stress the importance of including a content development plan as an integral part of the strategic document. This is sometimes overlooked, but it often emerges as one of the key factors in determining the ultimate outcome of a social business implementation.

With the draft of your strategic plan in hand, it is important to remember that this is a living document that is now ready to be circulated throughout the firm for feedback and comment. It is definitely going to change along the way. A firm has to "think social" and adopt social business practices in order to undertake a social business transformation. The next step in this process is to make the strategic plan a firm-wide document and not just the work-product of the social business team.

Building consensus in the firm

Securing executive sponsorship

As previously mentioned, sponsorship and adoption by executive leadership is crucial to the ultimate success of a social business initiative. So the best place to start building consensus for your strategic plan is at the very top. Hopefully, your team was originally set up with senior leadership in some way represented or directly participating in the planning process, which should make it much easier to get the full leadership on board at this point.

In the course of presenting the plan to senior management, it is important to stress the level of commitment from them that will be necessary in order to ensure success. A strong case needs to be made, highlighting both the immediate and long-term benefits in order to justify committing time and resources to such a substantial undertaking. Firm leaders also have to agree to lead by example. Simply saying they are on-board is not enough. They need to actively participate and encourage others in a proactive manner to become advocates and participants of the social firm strategy.

Winning hearts and minds

Once leadership is on board, it is time to turn your attention to the rest of the firm. It is important to remember that, even though everyone on your social team is now steeped in the idea of a social firm, the concept is still new and strange to everyone else. So presenting the plan throughout the firm is an educational exercise. The plan should be teed up in a way that makes clear the value and potential return on investment of such an endeavor. The plan should not be presented as a fait accompli; people should be encouraged to react and respond, and contribute their own suggestions. Most importantly, the plan needs to be sold to the firm. People throughout the organization need to understand "what is in it for me". The answer may differ from one person to another, but it is critical that everyone takes a direct stake in the success of the venture; otherwise, you will be fighting an uphill battle with user adoption at the implementation stage. Many organizations find it useful to put in place a system that rewards people for their advocacy and involvement.

As part of the campaign to win hearts and minds, the concept of a social firm should be explained in concrete terms so that people understand how it will actually be used in every practice group. Well-constructed business use cases provide a good method of illustration. This is an opportunity to draw on the information collected in the business process audit so you can provide clear-cut explanations about how the new enterprise social network (ESN) will meaningfully change a business process within each and every department and practice group in the firm. Creating business use cases based on new or existing projects or matters is a great way to get started. Try to identify those projects that will best leverage the functionality of social technologies and stand to benefit most from the improved collaboration and communication capabilities.

It definitely helps to approach these internal communications much like an external marketing campaign. Get people excited and interested in the project and what it is designed to accomplish. Once you get underway, make a point of acknowledging effort and celebrating success at every opportunity. Law firms need to continue to communicate well beyond launch, sharing tips and examples of how to be effective and successful.

Identify champions

Not everyone in a department or practice group will be an instant proponent of the firm's social business strategy. It is important to identify key influencers at every level of the organization and convert them into champions. In getting ready to move toward the implementation phase of the project, ideally you should look for champions who will help promote and lead the effort at every level of the organization. Champions do not necessarily need to be social media wizards or technology enthusiasts. Rather, it is better to identify those individuals that are natural influencers: the sort of people who peers usually turn to for help or advice. We discuss further how to get best use out of your champions in the section on plan implementation below.

Rounding out the social team

It is now time to begin filling out the rest of the social business team. In the course of the internal audit and drafting the strategy plan, your team should have identified a number of key positions that need to be filled prior to plan implementation. The specific hiring needs will vary from firm to firm, depending on existing resources and the scope of the implementation effort, but here are some suggestions about the type of personnel and skills we usually find are required to fill out the social team:

1. **Project management:** Perhaps the most important member of the social team is the project manager (or project management team). This individual or set of individuals should be certified and have knowledge of project management processes and tools. The transformation into a social law firm is an incredibly complex project that includes different components and phases. A good project manager should have the skills and temperament to keep the project moving forward, while managing tight deadlines and budgets.
2. **Internal communication:** Finding the right person to manage internal communications over the course of the project is the next critical business function that needs to be addressed. The scale and duration of the project, and maintaining coordination of the various interconnecting parts, puts a premium on the importance of maintaining clear communications throughout the firm, keeping staff and leadership up to date on progress and in sync as new features are rolled out. More than coordinating and informing, the goal of internal communications is to build excitement about the project as well as to generate broad engagement and support.
3. **Technology liaison:** Someone in the IT department with a thorough understanding of the firm's IT infrastructure, legacy systems, and available resources, should be appointed as liaison for the project. As the key tech resource for the social team, the tech liaison's responsibility is to stay in constant communication with the firm's CIO, advising them of project developments, and to coordinate resource requirements from the IT department.
4. **Knowledge liaison:** Similarly, someone in the KM department with intimate familiarity with the firm's knowledge management systems, including client intranets and other knowledge-based tools, should be appointed as KM liaison. This individual should

also be well versed in the firm's taxonomy, have a direct reporting line to the firm's CKO, and should be responsible for keeping the CKO informed at all times of project developments and requirements.

5. **Marketing/business development liaison(s):** Depending on the size and geographical reach of the firm, one or more people should be designated as project liaison for the marketing/business development function with primary responsibility for coordinating the project with legal staff in each of the firm's practice groups, as well as with the marketing and business development departments. Depending on how the firm is organized, these individuals might be part of the marketing, business development, or public relations departments, and should report directly to the firm's CMO or senior business development leaders with responsibility for insuring that the firm's brand, content marketing, and marketing guidelines are consistently applied over the course of the project.
6. **Compliance liaison:** In a corporate setting, a large-scale social business implementation team will typically include a compliance liaison who reports to the company's chief learning officer (CLO) or chief compliance officer. Although large law firms do not typically maintain these internal functions, we nevertheless think it is a good idea to designate a member of the social team as compliance liaison with responsibility for ensuring that the project is compliant with all firm policies and procedures, and to ensure that all parts of the project avoid client conflicts or other situations that could increase the risk and liability of the firm. This person should also have responsibility for coordinating the development of the firm's social media governance policy, as described further below.
7. **HR/talent liaison:** This individual will be a part of the firm's HR department or talent management department. They will have a thorough understanding of firm HR procedures and manuals, as well as deep knowledge of the firm's recruitment and hiring process. Depending on the size of the firm, this individual can also act as a liaison between the project and the firm's professional development department.
8. **Professional development liaison:** This individual should be a part of the firm's professional development department reporting directly to the director of professional development. Their responsibility will be to ensure that any and all training and professional development tasks or requirements are properly met. This liaison

role carries the additional responsibility for the firm-wide training on how and why to use the new social technologies.

9. **Financial liaison:** This individual will ideally be a part of the firm's finance and accounting department, reporting directly to the firm's chief finance officer (CFO) or executive director. The responsibility here is to ensure that the project remains on budget and to keep the firm's CFO or executive director aware of any developments, variations, or requests that may impact timing or cost. This individual must also be able to provide information to the project leaders with regards to the financial systems and procedures that must be considered as the project evolves.
10. **Community manager:** This is a position typically found in large-scale corporate environments but may not be necessary in a law firm with a total headcount under 1,000. A community manager should have prior experience and knowledge of managing an online community (external or internal), possessing the skills and instincts necessary to keep the enterprise social network active and thriving. The basic job is to keep stirring the pot by constantly monitoring the ESN, as well as creating and stimulating the use of communities or groups within the ESN. In order to carry out this function properly, the community manager will typically develop close ties and relationships with champions and other influencers across the firm.

The positions listed above represent our suggestions as to the most important roles that need to be filled as the firm prepares to move toward the implementation phase. A number of these roles will diminish or fall away entirely once the project becomes fully operational, although there may also be additional resources and skills required over time to ensure the ESN continues to perform as intended.

Creating a social media governance policy within your firm

Your strategic plan is all set and your staff is in place. Before you move on to the implementation phase, it is a good idea to address one more preliminary matter: creating your firm's social media governance policy (or updating the already existing policy) to make sure it is comprehensive enough to address the needs of a social law firm. Remember that lawyers are conservative and risk averse by nature, their instincts having been refined in law school and reinforced at work. When it comes to the use of social technologies, both internally and externally, most lawyers are unfamiliar with these new tools, and they are therefore reluctant to use them. In order to combat this fear, law firms need to create effective social governance policies that provide clear guidance about how social media should properly be used. A well-crafted social governance policy will not only reduce firm risk, it can also serve as a tool to educate and promote usage to benefit the entire firm.

You can find many sample social governance policies online. There are short and simple policies and incredibly long and detailed ones. In addition, there are specialized provisions that have been developed that refer to the governance of internal social networks and their use by employees. As you review these samples and begin considering how best to approach governance issues for your firm, we have put together a list of basic tips that should be helpful in tackling this issue:

1. **Keep it simple:** The best social governance policies are those that are simple and easy to understand by all employees. A policy that contains a large amount of fine print or technical jargon, requirements, or restrictions will make be difficult to understand, and employees will either ignore it or refrain from using social technologies altogether. Employees may be afraid of making a mistake that might ultimately lead to disciplinary action – or even cost them their job. For this reason, it is essential for law firms to craft short and concise social governance policies that can be posted near the water cooler or coffee machine where it can be easily seen, understood, and reinforced.
2. **Make it positive:** A common mistake most law firms make is to craft their social governance policy in negative terms: "don't do this" and "don't do that". This approach will only increase the anxiety and fear employees have about using social technologies, and will most likely result in diminished participation and effectiveness. Keep in mind that many lawyers and other professionals have an initial fear of social technologies and remain unsure about the proper usage. Employee adoption of social technologies and processes is the single most important component of achieving a successful social transformation so it is important to avoid creating a social governance policy that scares people away.
3. **Reflect your culture:** A firm's social governance policy should reflect its culture and values, as well as the type of social interactions the firm wants to promote, both internally and externally. The style of the social governance policy should reflect the firm's

philosophy and principles. An effective approach adopted by companies like IBM is to enlist your lawyers' and other employees' help in developing the policy. In the spring of 2005, IBMers used a wiki to create a set of guidelines for all IBMers who wanted to blog. These guidelines aimed to provide helpful, practical advice to protect both IBM bloggers and IBM as an organization. In 2008, and again in 2010, IBM turned to employees to re-examine these guidelines in light of ever-evolving technologies and online social tools to ensure that they remained current to the needs of employees and the company. These efforts have broadened the scope of the existing guidelines to include all forms of social computing. The IBM social media policy has thus evolved to directly reflect the values and culture of the firm's employees.

4. **Refer to other firm policies in the social governance policy:** Firms should avoid overcrowding their social governance policy with too much information. Law firms already have organizational policies in place and these should inform their social governance policies. Matters such as employee conduct and confidentiality clauses should already be covered in a law firm's employee manuals. Firms should stay focused on social issues in their social governance policies.

5. **Do not make it too restrictive:** In the US, the National Labor Relations Board (NLRB) recently issued a memorandum which warns companies that making their social media policy too restrictive could be a violation of federal labor laws. The NLRB memo states that it is unlawful to prohibit workers from posting "confidential" or "non-public" information about the employer. Without further definition, these terms are too vague and could be construed as prohibiting worker discussions about their working conditions, which must be allowed, according to the NLRB. The memo reiterated that employees are allowed to use their personal social media accounts in order to discuss "concerted activity" under Section 7 of the NLRB. Generally speaking, concerted activity refers to "anything between employees" that is related to improving the terms, conditions, and details of their employment. This includes factors like their working conditions and even their wages.

    As a result, law firms, either in the US or in other countries, should be careful to ensure that their social governance policies are not too restrictive, and do not run foul of regulation or law.

6. **Keep it current:** Social technologies continue to evolve in a rapid manner. New networks and tools are continuously being introduced. Video services like Vine and Instagram did not exist a few years ago. With technology changing so rapidly, it is important to periodically review the firm's social governance policy to make sure it adapts as new tools and networks are introduced. We recommend reviewing your social governance policy every six months to make sure it keeps up with the latest technologies, as well as how the firm is using social tools.
7. **Have it reviewed by an expert:** However you put together your governance policy, it is important to get it reviewed by a lawyer with domain expertise before it becomes official. A well-constructed social governance policy should reduce the amount of risk a firm is exposed to when dealing with social technologies. A law firm's social governance policy should address issues such as: confidential information, intellectual property, trade secrets, discrimination, retaliation, bullying, and impersonating others. Again, law firms should consult with an expert before making the policy official.
8. **Include internal use:** As your firm is about to deploy an ESN, it is important to have the policy cover internal usage. Sometimes, a firm will maintain separate policies – one for the use of external social media use and another for internal. In our experience, it is most effective to have a single combined policy.

Integrating social into your business processes

Now your firm is ready to move on to the implementation phase. The strategic plan provides your blueprint, leadership is on board, and the rest of the team is in place. In the remaining sections of this chapter, we provide you with a few further guidelines that will help drive implementation to a successful outcome. As we have mentioned several times already, the key focus now shifts to driving broad-scale adoption and usage. The most successful ESNs are those that get booted up on the desktop first thing in the morning and provide the conduit for most employees' day-to-day business activities – becoming as integral a part of the office environment as the air pumping out of the air conditioning unit. Of course, nowadays that also means making sure that all the content from your ESN will be readily accessible from smart phones and tablets. In fact, most major ESN providers have sophisticated mobile apps available to extend the ESN experience to employees on the road or at home in a seamless fashion.

However, easy and ready access alone does not mean the ESN will be embraced. Alan Lepofsky, an analyst at Constellation Research, recently published a report entitled, "Enterprise Collaboration Software: From Simple Sharing to Purposeful Collaboration".[1] In the report, Lepofksy states that while organizations are starting to adopt social business tools and techniques, "unfortunately, many organizations experience adoption challenges with these new platforms, especially when the tools are not part of the business processes employees use to get their jobs done".

This is why we emphasize the importance of analyzing existing business processes and developing real-world business use cases in the course of putting together your firm's strategic plan. The plan should provide your roadmap for how to embed and deploy social technologies in the course of carrying out the firm's existing business processes. Enterprise social networks and other collaborative tools need to be a part of the everyday work undertaken by lawyers and other professionals at the firm. It is not enough merely to use these platforms as a way to chat during downtime. The features and functionalities inherent in these platforms (to find and share information, connect with clients and colleagues, locate internal experts) should blend in perfectly with the type of work your lawyers and support staff perform every day. Whether that means working on transaction documents, performing research, or communicating with clients, these are all business processes that can be enhanced by the use of social technologies.

One way to facilitate the adoption process is to initially launch several different business use cases before the rest of the firm is on-boarded on to the platform. A firm should identify matters or projects (existing and new) that can take advantage of these new social technologies, and launch these use cases several months before a firm-wide rollout. The benefit of this approach is that, when the firm-wide rollout eventually takes place, there will already be well-established examples of success stories to share and lawyers who can act as guides and champions.

From the very beginning of the roll out, it is important to get into the habit of documenting your firm's successes and failures in using the new ESN. The social team should make a regular habit of speaking with members of the firm as they begin using the platform and take frequent user surveys using the ESN's out-of-the-box polling capabilities. It is particularly useful to focus surveys on documenting how the ESN has changed day-to-day work routines. Ask users whether the ESN has enabled them to save time or work more efficiently with another department. We strongly recommend that you try to secure and document success stories at every opportunity, particularly those instances which illustrate the immediate and practical benefits of the new approach.

Another critical part of ensuring the integration of social technologies into existing business processes is to work with the firm's management committee to make them early and active users. As we have already stressed, executive management needs to lead by example. It is therefore a good idea to make the management committee the focus of one of your early business use cases, to drive leadership's active participation and use of the platform. As you proceed with rolling out the platform throughout the firm, encourage senior management to use the ESN as a primary means of communicating throughout the firm – the efficacy of this approach in driving adoption has been demonstrated time and again in many different environments.

Education and training: Building social advocacy into your firm culture

When it comes to driving adoption and usage of an ESN, nothing is more important than firm-wide education and training. Since the concept of a social law firm will be new to most employees, training should be directed at every level of the organization. As people have very varied learning styles, it is important to develop a program that is sustained and uses various methods to impart knowledge. Some people prefer visually oriented instruction; others like to learn on their own; while others prefer a group environment. Regardless of the method employed, the firm must ensure that all employees understand both how to use the new tools and why it is important for them to do so. Below are some suggestions culled from our experience that can help firms design an effective training program:

- **On-demand videos:** Videos are a great way to communicate difficult concepts or ideas visually. In our experience, videos do a fabulous job of providing examples of how social business tools and processes can enhance an individual's work experience through specific real-life examples or situations.
- **Practice group or department training:** Live training at the group or department level is often a very effective way to get a whole group aligned around the use of new technologies, applied to specific business use cases relevant to the department, which will enhance group collaboration and communication. As much as possible, use actual projects or client matters to start the training process and promote immediate usage.

- **Lunch and learn:** This type of format often proves a useful way to cover specific functionality, such as collaborative authoring or how to use an ESN's internal polling capabilities. It is usually a good idea to schedule these regularly as short, one-hour sessions that can be informal and open to lots of Q&A.
- **One-on-one training:** Individual training sessions will usually prove the most effective in overcoming initial resistance and unfamiliarity with an ESN platform, although it may be impractical to provide this across the entire firm. This is one way that you can put champions and other "super users" to good use by having them lend a hand assisting colleagues who are struggling with the new work environment.
- **Firm retreats or workshops:** Training that takes place during special events or out of office retreats can sometimes prove to be highly effective. Everyone is usually more relaxed and focused so they are apt to be more creative and receptive to new information. It may be even more effective to use the ESN as a way of preparing for the firm retreat, or running a pre-meeting to focus everyone's attention on the upcoming issues to be addressed. Again, this is a way to tie training and education to actual business use cases.
- **Computer-led training:** Some of us prefer to take time on our own to figure things out with the help of a computer. Many of the leading social platforms contain computer-led training modules that enable employees to learn at their own pace, and when they have the time.

Each of these methods has benefits and values associated with it. Our suggestion is to try them all out to see what proves most effective in your firm. Whichever method(s) you decide to emphasize, it is important for the firm to commit to a sustained and continuous program. It is also worth mentioning that in many corporate environments, education and training will be augmented with some kind of incentive scheme that is designed to promote ESN usage and uptake. We realize that the use of direct incentives may not be compatible with other aspects of a law firm's culture. Moreover, how to design such a scheme is beyond the scope of this chapter. In cases where education and training alone are not proving sufficient to spur broad-scale adoption, however, an incentive scheme is certainly another option your firm should consider using.

Developing champions and social evangelists

Another key to driving broad-scale usage of your social business program is to focus your initial efforts on identifying potential champions within the firm. These are individuals with an aptitude or inclination to act as advocates for the project. Every successful social business initiative needs "feet on the streets" – employees who will step up to serve as evangelists, ready to urge participation and bring their colleagues along into the brave new world of the ESN.

The search for social business champions starts by identifying the existing influencers within the firm. These influencers need not be the most technically savvy, nor do they have to be active users of social media. Rather, you should be looking for those people who stand out in the organization as a helpful resource respected by their colleagues: the person in a group or department others are most inclined to turn to for advice or direction. These people are inclined to be "sharers" by nature, taking pride in giving other employees the benefit of their knowledge and experience. Once you start looking, you will find people with these attributes situated throughout the organization, whether working as a mid-level associate, a paralegal, or on the AV staff. Their rank and position does not matter so much as the fact that they are generally well liked, and are valued as helpful and well-informed members of staff.

After identifying your influences, it is time to properly train them and turn them into social business evangelists. This training should have a somewhat different focus from the firm's general training sessions. With these influencers you want to spend some extra time talking about *why* using social technologies is important to the firm's future, and *how* it can improve each user's working life. The goal of this training is to transform the influencers into "power users" of the ESN so that they begin to grasp, in any given situation, the ways in which the social platform can be applied. The "how" is usually easy as most social technologies are not overly difficult to navigate and use. But the "why" is just as critical, and sometimes not as easy to convey.

The firm is asking employees to change their established routines. Since we are all creatures of habit, this can be one of the most difficult things to accomplish in any organization. As most business consultants will advise you, instead of dictating change from above – an approach that almost never works – it is usually much more effective to explain the benefits of change in ways that directly relate to employees and their working lives. As we have already emphasized, ultimately, every employee should be able to answer the question: "what's in it for me?" The answer to that question will usually differ from one person to the next, which is part of what makes explaining the reasons for change hard in the first place.

Training and education on the business value of an ESN should enable people to answer that question easily; this is where influencers can play a critical role. Starting at the team- or work-group level, through day-to-day contact with their colleagues, influencers can help to make the explanation personal. This is often referred to as the "train the trainer" method in which the message of change ripples throughout an organization from an individual or group of employees within a department, work group, or team. If you are successful in finding the right influencers, these champions will do much more than train other employees: they will lead by example and act as evangelists for the social transformation, openly encouraging others to get behind the initiative.

Reverse mentoring senior leaders

When it comes to training and educating senior leaders of the firm, the methods described above may prove less effective. The reason for this is that firm leaders are usually extremely busy, having neither the time nor the patience required to properly understand these new social tools and methodologies. Nonetheless, as we have stressed throughout this report, it is critically important for senior leadership in the firm not only to understand the values derived from a social transformation but also to lead by example.

One approach that has proven successful in a number of organizations is the reverse mentoring method. This works by assigning a younger employee within the firm to work with a senior leader and provide day-to-day instruction on using social tools. This will work best if the younger employee not only has a good understanding of social technologies but also has a pre-existing relationship and common frame of reference with the senior leader, perhaps as a result of being within the same practice group or department.

In addition to reverse mentoring, we also recommend personal training for senior partners that focuses on how an ESN can result in more effective leadership. This is one other area where outside consultants or instructors will prove useful. It is no secret in any organization that leaders can end up feeling isolated from their employees. Enterprise social networks provide leadership with an incredibly powerful tool to reconnect and more directly interact with people throughout the firm by establishing a strong virtual presence. It is a new channel for everyday communication that enables you to speak personally, but at the same time reach the entire organization. Given the transparency of the medium, senior leaders should also be coached on how to use the ESN to develop trust and loyalty, and to promote a common sense of purpose throughout the firm.

Measure and adapt: The never-ending cycle

Brian Solis, a principal at Altimeter Group, wrote a book entitled: *What is the Future of Business: Changing the Way Business Creates Experiences.*[2] It is full of interesting opinions and insights, but one of the most valuable points to be gleaned from the book is Brian's very simple approach to social media marketing: listen, learn, engage, adapt. It emphasizes the notion that the effective use of social media involves a feedback loop process, a constant fine-tuning based on market awareness. An organization uses social media to listen, internalize information gleaned, and then uses this information to improve its approach to the market.

We see this same process as lying at the heart of what makes for a successful social law firm. Once an enterprise social network is in place and functioning as intended, it becomes an operating system for the organization – a means for the firm to carry out each of the four steps Solis identifies. The ultimate goal of a social business platform is to enable the organization to be better attuned, and therefore more nimble in adapting to the rapidly changing marketplace.

As we see the process, however, there is one more critical step that needs to be added to Solis' list. We think the full mantra for a social law firm goes like this: listen, learn, engage, *measure*, adapt. The effective use of a social business platform is all but impossible without developing metrics that enable you to determine what is working and what is not. Without an eye on the metrics, an organization runs the risk of simply chasing its tail or embracing change for change's sake, instead of making steady progress towards its ultimate goals – whether that means increasing lead generation, stimulating more client engagement, or broadening participation throughout the firm. The digital world provides an abundance of data – often an overwhelming amount – that must be captured, digested, and absorbed in order to attain (and demonstrate) success.

Below, we take a close look at each of the five steps that make up the adaptation cycle that lies at the heart of any successful social business implementation:

- **Listen:** This is where it all begins. Listening is the first step a firm should take in developing its social business strategy. The social business team starts by using social media listening and monitoring tools in order to discover what is being said about the firm across the social media landscape. Listening provides fundamental insights into how a firm's clients and prospects view the brand. You can also listen to what is being said about competitors and learn more about the market in general, all of which is critical input in formulating a strategic plan.

  Even after your strategy has been developed and implemented, listening remains a fundamental part of the process by which the firm follows the market and readjusts its course. Furthermore, the ESN provides a powerful tool for firm management to listen more carefully to the organization itself. It is a platform that provides instant and continuous feedback enabling leadership to stay attuned to the views being expressed by employees throughout the firm.

- **Learn:** The journey towards social transformation requires an organization and its employees to learn new ways of working, interacting, and thinking. There are new ground rules and skills to be mastered, a new etiquette for sharing and collaborating. It takes time for employees to learn these new rules of engagement. It also takes time for the firm itself to acquire institutional understanding of what is likely to work in this new environment and the sort of content and strategy that will succeed in engaging an audience online.

  A perfect example of this is the process a new user goes through upon first joining a group on a social network such as LinkedIn. Before posting to the group it is always a good idea to start by listening and learning about the group's etiquette. Some groups do not allow individuals to post updates with links to their blog or website. Others only allow this in the comments section of a post, and only if that link leads to content that adds to the overall value of the discussion. This same learning process is involved at every step along the way as a firm undergoes a social transformation.

- **Engage:** After an initial period of listening and learning, the social firm and its employees begin to direct their energies toward using the social business platform to engage with their audience. Engagement, too, has an internal and external dimension. Deploying the ESN, the social firm hopes to enable greater employee engagement across the firm. The ESN essentially becomes the glue that holds the organization together by promoting and facilitating a deeper sense of personal involvement and coherence at every level.

At the same time, the social firm looks outward and strives to engage with its clients in a deeper and more durable fashion. Here, too, the ESN provides a means to achieve the goal of greater engagement. By creating a dedicated communication channel and shared workspaces, the ESN platform can also bind a social firm more closely to its clients. An initial assignment for a new client that is handled through a shared workspace on the firm's ESN is only a first step in engagement, which can subsequently follow a natural pathway to establishing a more enduring relationship.

In effect, every shared workspace offers the opportunity of deeper engagement by evolving into a permanent platform for continuing interaction and fresh assignments. Engagement is also the major objective of a social law firm's marketing efforts. The basic mission of the social firm's marketing strategy is to achieve deeper and longer-term engagement with its online audience, to build trust and loyalty by following the path from casual visitors to the website, to blog readers and newsletter subscribers, and ultimately for these subscribers to become clients. The social firm uses its ESN and social media presence to achieve deeper engagement across multiple fronts.

- **Measure:** The digital world is awash with data. Once your firm's ESN is up and running, every social action and interaction will leave a measureable trace. A social firm must learn how to harness all this data and convert it into actionable intelligence. Proper measurement provides an objective basis for a social firm to determine what is working and what is not.

  Given the abundance of data, it is important at the outset to figure out the right metrics to capture. The metrics will vary depending on the goals of any particular social initiative, whether management is attempting to introduce a new internal business process, or the marketing department is undertaking a new social media campaign. We typically refer to the metrics relevant to any particular project or endeavor as the key performance indicators (KPIs). In a marketing context, the most important KPIs are reach and engagement, which are generally used to measure the efficacy of any given marketing effort. Over the course of time, a social firm will put in place a wide array of KPIs that it monitors to track its various business objectives and initiatives. For each new initiative, it should become a matter of course to establish a set of KPIs to suit the occasion.

- **Adapt:** Measure and adjust; measure and adjust; measure and adjust. If something is working do more of it. If something is not working, try something new. Be creative! A social firm should be constantly experimenting and fine-tuning what it is doing. In the marketing realm, this means testing new networks and content strategies; internally, this means being open to employee input and innovation; for the practice group, it means finding new ways to collaborate with a client more effectively. Social is a journey, not a destination. It is an endless cycle that requires every firm to constantly adapt in order to be successful.

This first appeared as Chapter 7 in Alvarez, G. and Lamport, J., Outperform the Competition: Business Strategies for the Social Law Firm, *ARK Group 2014.*

References

1. Lepofsky, A., "Enterprise Collaboration Software: From Simple Sharing to Purposeful Collaboration", Constellation Research Inc., 2014.
2. Solis, B., *What is the Future of Business: Changing the Way Business Creates Experiences*, John Wiley & Sons, 2013.

Chapter 32:
How to optimize your LinkedIn profile to get found by your ideal client

By Emily Miller, founder of Marshall Walker, and Kirsten Hodgson, founder of Kaleidoscope Marketing

What you will learn:

- What's important to your clients and how to highlight this in your profile.
- How to use keywords.
- Communicating who you are and what you do well.
- How to highlight expertise by adding other sections to your profile.
- Creating a customized LinkedIn profile URL.
- Contact info – what to include and how to include it.
- Integrating your LinkedIn profile with other social media.
- Using LinkedIn's publishing platform.

So, you have a LinkedIn profile. That's all well and good, but unless you flesh out your profile, it won't stand out and attract your ideal prospects and referrers.

If it's important to your clients, it should stand out

Since we work with many law firms around the globe, it's important for us to know what clients of law firms are looking for in their legal advisors so we can help our clients to position themselves via LinkedIn in a way that attracts prospects. Through numerous interviews with buyers of legal services over the years, we've learned that over 80 percent hire the individual lawyer rather than the firm. This is not to say that the reputation of the firm has no bearing on the purchasing decision; it does come into play, especially when the client has complex issues to address or needs advice related to a niche area. But the key things that clients say they look for are:

1. A lawyer with the right expertise evidenced through:
    i. Past transactions, projects, and/or cases;
    ii. Ability to negotiate and influence decisions;
    iii. Reputation and knowledge of their area of expertise; and
    iv. Level of competence.

2. A lawyer who is the right fit. Clients want to work with lawyers who work well with their team – from a personal stand-point and as a member of the matter/project/case working party.
3. A lawyer who understands their industry sector and their business and who will look after their interests.

How should this inform how you position yourself via your LinkedIn profile to attract your ideal prospects?

LinkedIn allows you to communicate your expertise by:

- Requesting client recommendations;
- Listing your key skills and asking clients to endorse you for these skills if it is permitted in your jurisdiction;
- Providing a few short case studies in your summary or experience sections;
- Adding links to your firm's website, your profile on your firm's website, your practice area's webpage, and/or your (or your firm's) listing in a legal directory such as *Chambers & Partners*;
- Adding your Twitter account (or WeChat account if you do business in Asia);
- Using LinkedIn's publishing platform to publish an article or blog you've written; and
- Adding videos, presentations, images, or other material that help demonstrate your expertise via links or uploaded files.

Although it is difficult to convey via your LinkedIn profile if you are the perfect fit for a client, you can give them a sense of who you are and what you offer so that they are more likely to get in touch to learn more. Sometimes, it might even be a personal interest or volunteering experience you have noted on your profile that gets their attention.

CASE STUDY

We recently worked with a lawyer who supported a well-known charity, and although this had nothing to do with his expertise as a legal professional, we encouraged him to add it to his profile as it helped give visitors a more well-rounded view of him as a person. After adding this to his profile, he received an invitation to connect from the CEO of a company. The lawyer accepted the CEO's invitation to connect (of course!), but he then did something that few people actually do – he immediately sent an email via LinkedIn to the CEO thanking him for his invitation to connect and asking if he could help in any way. The CEO immediately replied saying that he had found our client's profile while searching LinkedIn for a lawyer who could help with a certain legal issue and noticed that he supported the same charity the CEO did so he decided to get in touch! This interchange led to a meeting and then an instruction for the lawyer.

According to Stephen Newton, author of *The Invasion Game: Business Development and Practice Growth of Lawyers*, the "like and trust" ("L+T") component plays a major role in a client's willingness to engage your services. From our own experiences, we know this to be true. So, how can your LinkedIn profile impact your "L+T" factor? The short case study mentioned above is a perfect example of content that affected the CEO's "like" factor. Although trust is something that is built over time, your LinkedIn profile can play a part by communicating your experience and knowledge of a prospect's industry sector. If you know their world and can demonstrate this via your profile, this will give the prospect a level of comfort that may help to set you apart from your competitors. Here are a few suggestions of how to communicate your industry knowledge via LinkedIn:

- Add industry specific whitepapers, videos, articles, podcasts etc. that you or your firm have produced to your profile;
- Include examples of your expertise in an industry sector in the summary section of your profile;
- Add industry specific "projects" to your profile;

- Publish your industry specific blog posts onto your LinkedIn profile via LinkedIn's publishing platform;
- If allowed in your jurisdiction, you could upload a presentation with industry specific testimonials; or
- Link to an industry specific eBook that your firm has produced by adding it to your profile – when people click on this they will be taken to a sign-up page on your website where they can download the content in return for their email address (signing up to your news alerts). You can then keep in touch with them on an ongoing basis.

In short, your profile should communicate:

- Who you are professionally;
- Who you can help;
- How you can help them;
- Examples of how you have helped clients in the past;
- A sense of the kind of person you are; and
- A call to action (what you want a visitor to your profile to do after reading it).

Remember, having a great LinkedIn profile will also reflect well on your firm. Moreover, your firm will benefit by expanding its reach as you and your colleagues strategically expand your networks.

TOP TIP

If you don't have a comprehensive LinkedIn profile you could actually lose work to your competitors. A global professional services firm lost a large piece of work, where they were the incumbent, because their team's LinkedIn profiles were not consistent with the submission.

Use keywords

Keywords play an important role in raising your profile amongst your ideal prospects. LinkedIn's search tool takes keywords (among other things) into account when a prospect searches for a lawyer with your skills. So, if you are a patent attorney, but you have only mentioned that you are a "partner" on your LinkedIn profile, then don't be surprised if you rank very low in search results for the word "patent"!

We suggest that you check your LinkedIn profile now for obvious keywords (such as "patent attorney" in this example). Here's an easy way to check to see how many times a particular keyword is found in your LinkedIn profile: hit the CRTL and the F key on a PC or the COMMAND and F on a Mac. You will see a little window pop up on the page like the one shown in Figure 1. I searched for the word "LinkedIn" (obvious keyword, of course) in my profile and it is listed 71 times! When you create the content for your LinkedIn profile, make sure that your keywords are noted throughout.

Just a word of caution here: don't just repeat a keyword over and over again in your profile to increase your ranking for that particular keyword. If the keyword is in your profile 1,000 times, but the content is boring and repetitive, you will do yourself no favors and will put off any potential clients.

Figure 1: Search for key words on your profile

What keywords and phrases are appropriate for you?

If you are not sure what keywords or phrases would be best for you, have a look at your biography on your firm's website – what keywords or phrases come up time and time again? Is it intellectual property, corporate litigation, family law, lawyer, media, pharmaceuticals etc.?

Another option is to use the Google Adwords Keyword Planner tool.[1] Once you are in your Google Adwords account, you can click on the "Tools" menu, then click on "Keyword Planner". You can then find out which keywords are most used on Google as search terms for your services.

Once you know which keywords or phrases are most commonly used when someone is searching for your services, make sure you sprinkle these words throughout your LinkedIn profile.

An increasing number of people are now using LinkedIn's search facility to find people with a particular skill set so it makes sense to take the time to correctly identify and incorporate your keywords into your profile.

LinkedIn Profile Template

We have produced a LinkedIn profile template to help you put together a well-rounded LinkedIn profile that positions you as the "go-to" expert for your target practice area and ranks highly in LinkedIn searches.

LinkedIn Profile Template

In order to develop a compelling profile that ranks highly in LinkedIn's search results, you can start by answering the questions below:

1. What do you want to be known for?

a. What are the key areas in which you want to practice?

b. Which industry sector(s) do you wish to focus on?

c. Describe your ideal client(s) [e.g. HR managers in the manufacturing sector, or those involved in or affected by the leaky homes crisis, or more broadly those in the construction and infrastructure sectors looking at or involved in projects in New Zealand].

TIP: Use the above information to craft your professional headline, your job title, and the summary section of your profile.

Some good examples of headlines (showing some different styles) include:

- *International arbitrator and strategic adviser on construction, energy, and infrastructure projects*
- *Are you buying, selling, or structuring a business, arranging finance, or do you have a property law need? I can help*

2. What are the most common issues/problems your clients have when they come to you for advice? [Think about the questions they often ask you or the common things you help them to resolve/overcome.]

TIP: Setting out between one and three questions is a good way to begin the summary section of your profile.

3. Why should your ideal clients choose you over your competitors? [Think about your working style, as well as anything that makes you stand out – for example, maybe you have a project management qualification, which provides some benefit to your clients, or you do pro-bono work, or have written a book – always think about how this will benefit your target audience. This also fits well into the summary section.]

4. If you could only include three examples of transactions or cases you've worked on to support your expertise in your area, what would you include? [Look at your website profile for ideas]

   If the examples you want to include are not currently on your website, please set out:

   - Who you acted for (if you can't get client permission, then say "a major player in the construction sector");
   - The nature of the transaction/case;
   - What you did, including any novel issues or noteworthy points (e.g. completed in two days when average time for these types of transactions is three months);
   - The outcome for/benefit to your client.

TIP: This information could sit in your current job description or in the summary section if there is room.

5. What's your Call to Action? [To be inserted at the end of the summary section.]

6. Do you have any articles, presentation slides, videos, or upcoming events you would like to include in your profile that will help to position you?

   [If they have a publicly accessible URL, you can choose "Add link". If not, you will need to select "Upload file". Write next to each file whether you'll need to add it or upload it.]

7. What are your hobbies/interests outside of work?

TIP: Include in the personal interests section and possibly also mention in your summary if there is room.

8. Please list previous positions you've held (ideally at least two) and the dates you were employed there [month/year]

9. Thinking back to your previous roles, please list anything you'd like to point to that will help you position yourself in your chosen area(s) or that will evidence your capabilities. [Don't worry if there is nothing, but if there is something, add it to that job description]

TIP: Insert into previous experience section.

10. Please write down details of your degree (and other relevant qualifications), university, and the dates you attended.

TIP: Add into the education section.

11. Do you have a Twitter account that you use for work purposes? If yes, write down your Twitter handle.

12. Write down your website URL – what will you name it? You may wish to direct people to your firm's website or to a specific page.

13. Do you have a work-related blog? If so, you may want to add it as a link to your summary section.

14. What are the top keywords you want to be found for (up to five)? [You will want to incorporate these in your headline, current job title, summary (if possible), specialties, and skills sections.]

Other sections available on your profile

1. Hobbies

LinkedIn is about people. Including your hobbies is a great way for people to connect with you on a different level, learning more about you.

2. Certifications

Add any certifications which add credibility to your experience.

3. Honors & Awards

Add any kind of public recognition that relates to your current professional goals in this section.

4. Languages

If you speak additional languages, add them here to attract an international audience.

5. Organizations

Publicize professional organizations as well as important local ones that you belong to in this section.

6. Projects

If you have been or are currently working on major industry-related projects, you can showcase them here and even link to them.

7. Publications

List any books or articles you have published.

8. Volunteering experience

Add any volunteering experience you have and select the types of opportunities you're looking for.

9. Test scores

List any you wish to highlight.

10. Courses

List any professional courses you've been on or undertaken.

11. Patents

If you have any, this is the place to list them.

12. Causes you care about

Allows you to highlight causes important to you. Listing these may resonate with some of the people who view your profile.

13. Supported organizations

This is related to causes you care about. It gives you the ability to list any charities or other causes you support either financially or otherwise.

CASE STUDY

Case study

One of our clients, Brad Golchin (an accountant), set up a comprehensive LinkedIn profile, when he first joined the platform, as his online CV. He demonstrates his credibility through his experience, client testimonials (recommendations), content he's uploaded to his profile, and posts he's published to LinkedIn. Brad has had two key successes as a result:

1. He was contacted by a large US corporation who found him on LinkedIn and were interested in the way in which he used the latest technology in his business. They sent their 2IC to New Zealand to talk to him, and subsequently flew him to the US to meet their team and discuss collaborating.
2. He connected on LinkedIn with a board member of a New Zealand charitable trust who viewed his profile and saw his content and his involvement in the not-for-profit sector and recommended to her fellow board members that they move the charitable trust's accounting work to Brad's firm.

Your profile – Step-by-step

Now we will go through each section and walk you through the process of building your profile. Questions 1–5 are really about getting your head around what to communicate in your LinkedIn profile headline, summary, and current position.

Headline

Believe it or not, your headline is one of the most important sections of your LinkedIn profile. When a prospect is searching for a lawyer with expertise in, let's say, corporate law and your profile comes up in the search, the viewer will only be able to see this portion of your LinkedIn profile (if you have a premium LinkedIn account, the viewer will see your past positions as well – for those with a free account, only your current role is shown in searches). If your competitor's profile has "corporate law" in their headline and yours doesn't, the viewer may well click on your competitor's profile first as the words they are looking for are immediately visible.

Another reason why your headline is so important is that, whenever you publish to LinkedIn (using LinkedIn's publishing platform) or post or comment on a group discussion, your headline appears prominently. It is an opportunity to immediately position yourself in the minds of others and to create an association in their minds between you and what you do.

Where can you find your "headline" in your profile? It's right under your name as seen in Figure 2. As you can see, I've added key words such as LinkedIn, Training, and Coach to my profile headline.

Figure 2: Add key words to your profile headline

Your LinkedIn summary

This section is your opportunity to set out who you are and how you help your clients. Use the content you've written using the LinkedIn Profile Template sections 1–5 to create your summary. Don't forget to finish with a call to action – what do you want a prospect to do after viewing your profile? Go to your website and download a whitepaper? Sign up for a newsletter? Or simply get in touch? There is a 2,000 character limit for your summary section.

Highlighting expertise – Adding other sections

You can add additional sections to your LinkedIn profile to highlight your expertise. You will find these additional sections under the top section of your LinkedIn profile. Just click on the "Add" button under a particular section to add it to your profile.

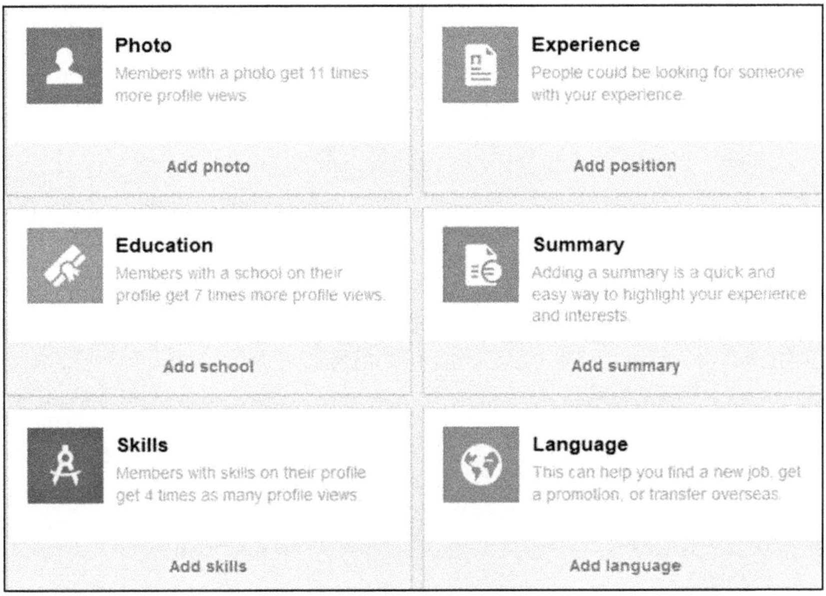

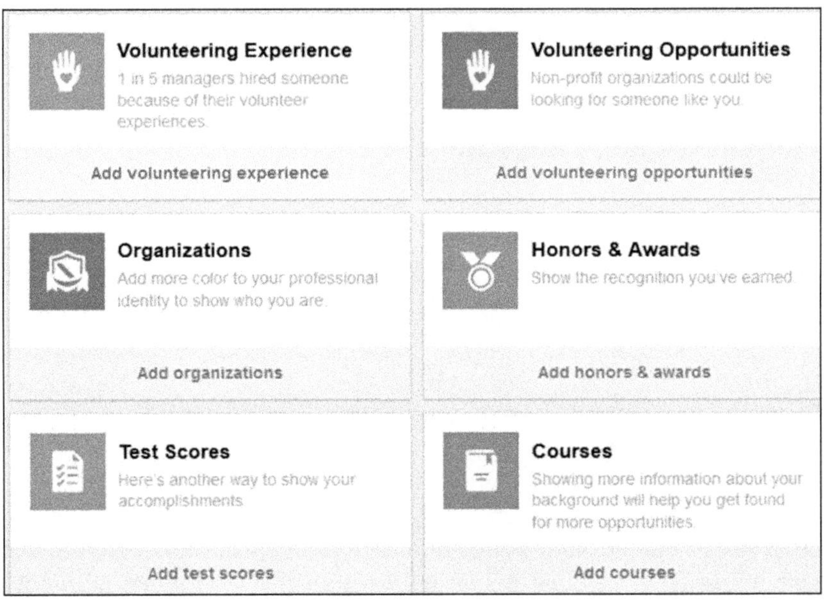

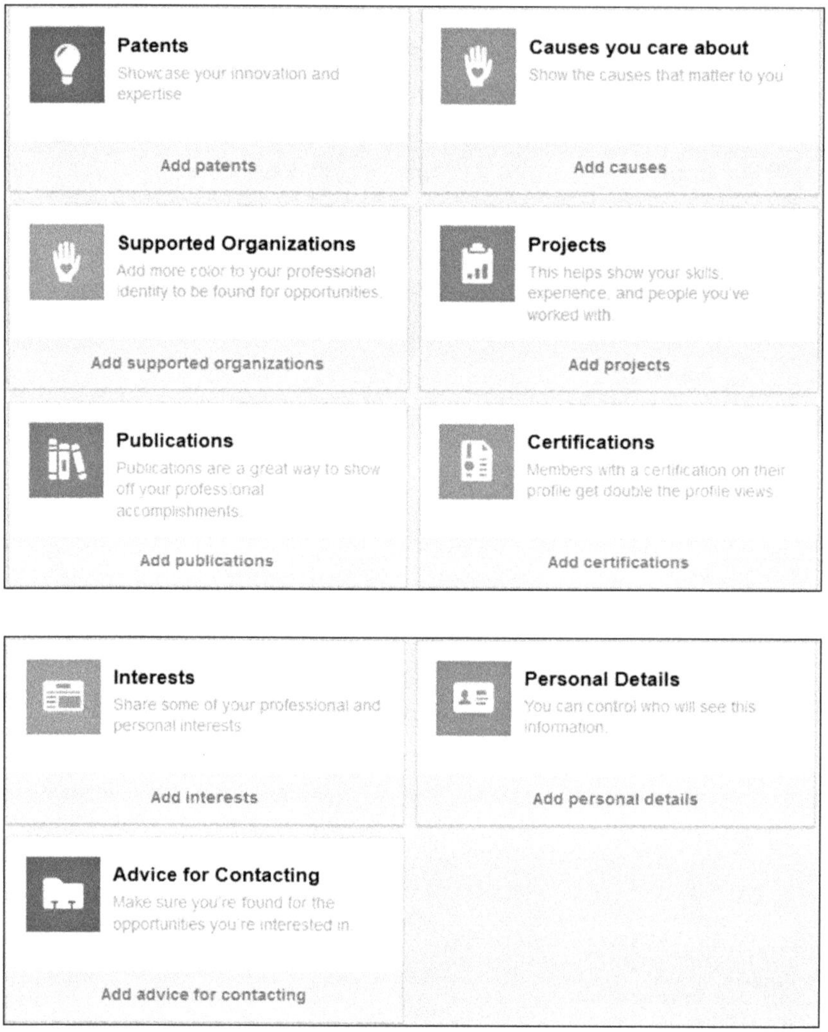

Figure 3: Add additional sections to your profile

Creating a customized LinkedIn profile URL

LinkedIn allows you to create your own unique LinkedIn public profile URL (i.e. website address). Why is this such a good thing? Once you've created your own URL, when anyone searches for you on Google or any other search engine, your public LinkedIn profile will rank higher in the search results. What does this mean? It means that your potential clients will be able to access your LinkedIn profile more easily and find out more about how you can help them. This is especially important if you have a very common name as it means your profile will appear higher up the list than others who share your name – allowing prospects to find you more easily.

You will find your public profile URL directly under the photo area of your LinkedIn profile. Have a look at your profile and see if you have lots of numbers and letters after your name like the profile in Figure 4. If your public profile does look similar, then we recommend that you create your own unique URL.

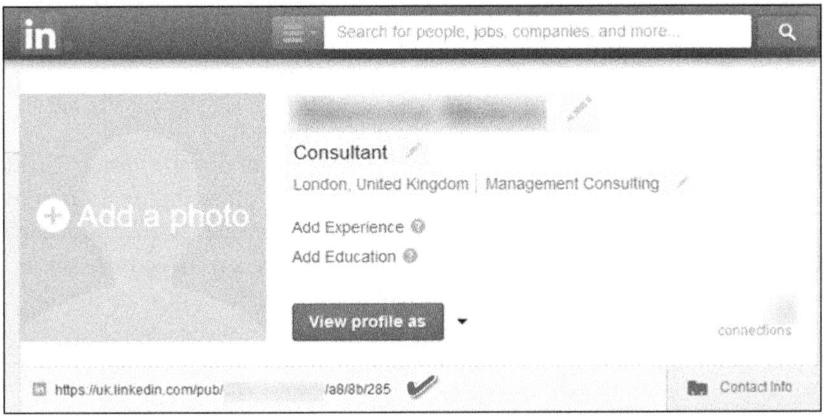

Figure 4: Find your public profile URL

If you hold your cursor right where the tick is in the image above, a little settings icon will appear. Click on this and you will be taken to your LinkedIn public profile page.

Click on the "+ Create your custom URL" link as depicted in Figure 5.

Figure 5: Create a custom URL

Type in your name after the LinkedIn address provided and click on save. You can't use spaces, symbols, or special characters in this URL and it cannot be longer than 30 characters. LinkedIn will let you know if that URL has already been taken by one of the other 380 million users. If your name is already taken, then you may want to choose one of the alternatives LinkedIn will offer you, or you could add a keyword to your name. My name (Emily Miller) is very common, unfortunately, so when I came to create my personal URL, someone else had already taken that name. I got round this by adding a key phrase to my name (i.e. emilymillerlinkedincoach). This also has an added benefit: if "LinkedIn coach" is used as a search term on Google, my LinkedIn profile may appear in the search results.

Contact info – What to include and how to include it

There are two sections in the contact info component of your profile. Click on the "Contact info" icon as seen in Figure 6 to open this section. The top section is only visible to your 1st degree connections (i.e. you have accepted their invitation to connect or they have accepted your invitation to connect) and the lower section is visible to all viewers of your profile.

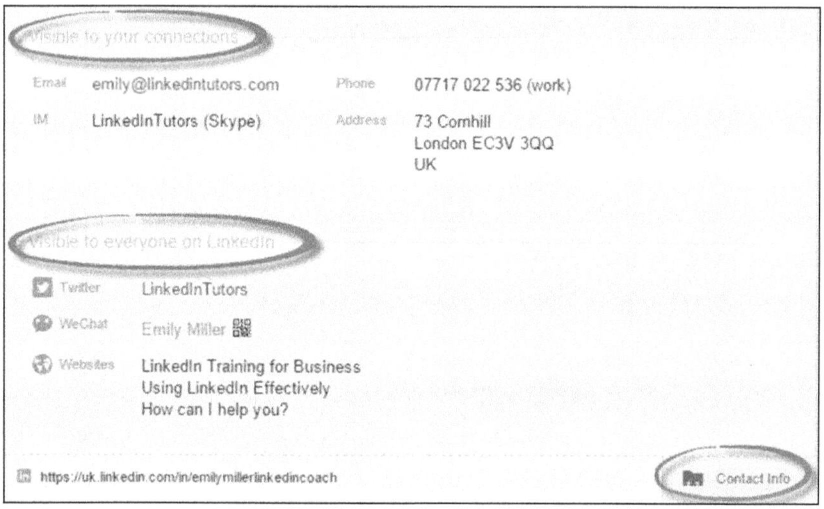

Figure 6: Edit your contact info

The email address you have listed as your "primary" email address will appear in this area. If you plan to use LinkedIn as a tool for engaging with your clients and prospects, we encourage you to set your business email address as your "primary" address. It is good practice to have at least two email addresses attached to your LinkedIn profile – your business email address and your personal email address. This means that you can use either email address as part of the signing-in process. Again, if you plan to use LinkedIn as a client engagement tool, we suggest that you add your firm's main office phone number, your direct number or your mobile, and your address.

LinkedIn gives you the opportunity to link your profile to three different webpages. As we mentioned earlier, these are visible to any visitor viewing your profile. Your firm may want to encourage everyone to add a link to the firm's homepage, a link to the landing page for their practice area, and/or a link to their profiles on the firm website, or blogs etc., or you may want to provide just one website link so it stands out.

Think about the people you want to view your profile – where could you send them that will be of the most value to them? This could be a landing page where they can enter their email address to sign up to your newsletter, or in return for some useful info such as an eBook, whitepaper, or research results. The benefit of this is that you can then market to them on an ongoing basis.

You can customize the name of the website link, although you are only allowed a maximum of 30 characters. You can see in Figure 6 that I have customized the link to our company website to 'LinkedIn Training for Business'. Think about your prospects – what phrase or keywords might encourage them to click through to your website? In order to add website addresses, just click on the little pencil beside "Websites" and the window shown in Figure 7 will appear. Choose "Other" in the

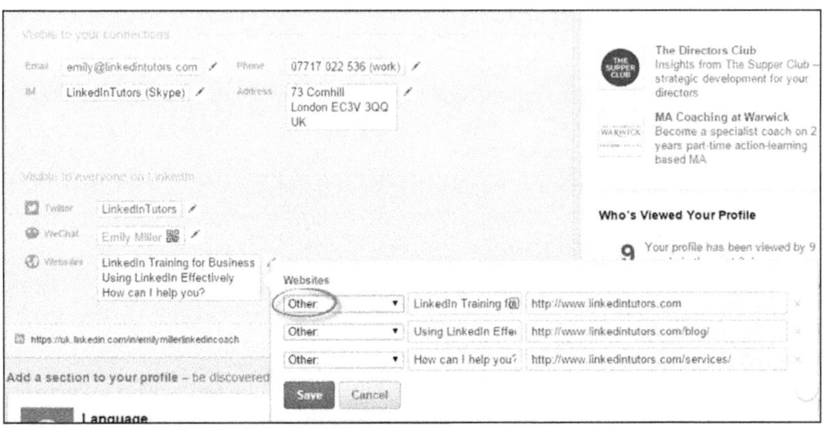

Figure 7: Add and customize website addresses

dropdown menu (instead of the standard "My company" which adds no value to your profile), and then type in the title you want visitors to your profile to see in the next field. Finally, add your website address(es) (including http://).

Advice for contacting

There is a section you can add to your LinkedIn profile called "Advice for contacting". (Have a look at the image in the "Highlighting expertise – Adding other sections" section of this chapter to see where to find it.) Any information you provide in this area can be seen by everyone who views your profile. If you plan to use LinkedIn as a tool to grow your practice, you should at the very least include your firm's phone number. As you can see from the image in Figure 8, I have decided to make it as easy as possible for a potential client to get in touch by providing many ways to do so. If you decide to add your business contact details and then find you are getting lots of spam emails from sales people or recruiters via LinkedIn or via your regular email address, then you could specifically say "These are the types of people I'd like to hear from… If you're a recruiter or sales person, please don't contact me" or something along those lines.

Figure 8: Adding interests gives visitors a more rounded view of who you are

The "Advice for contacting" will appear on your profile in the additional info section. I've added some interests to give visitors to my profile a flavor of the kind of person I am, including a quirky interest (eating twiglets – I love them!). You don't have to add any interests if you don't feel comfortable doing so, but just remember, "people buy people" and this section gives you the ability to share a more holistic view of you as a person.

Kirsten, who listed marathons as an interest, was asked to connect by a barrister she didn't know. She responded (as is good practice) to thank him and to ask him something about his practice. He immediately replied, saying "I see you ran the New York marathon. Me too...". He went on to say that he needed some marketing help and could they have a meeting. He became a client and she asked him why he'd gotten in contact. He replied that he'd searched for legal marketers on LinkedIn and her name had appeared in the search results along with a few others. He'd taken a look at her profile and seen that they shared a common interest, which had prompted him to invite her to connect. Her reply then gave him the push he needed to request a meeting.

There are two key lessons in this example:

1. List your interests; and
2. Respond to *everyone* whose invitation to connect you accept to thank them and to ask them something about their work (this little tactic has resulted in both Kirsten and I generating quite a bit of work!).

Integrating your LinkedIn profile with other social media

Twitter

If you're using Twitter as a business tool, then add it to your LinkedIn profile. Doing so means that when you post a status update via LinkedIn, you can choose to post it on Twitter at the same time. To add your Twitter account, you will need to click on the little pencil icon beside the word "Twitter". You will be taken to your settings page as seen in Figure 9. Just

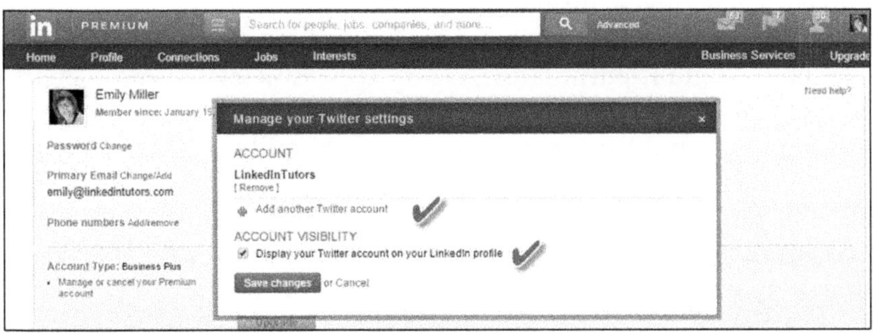

Figure 9: Join up your Twitter and LinkedIn accounts

add your Twitter name, tick the "display your Twitter account on your LinkedIn profile" box, and then save changes.

Once you save changes, you will have to sign in to Twitter and allow LinkedIn to access your Twitter account as seen in Figure 10.

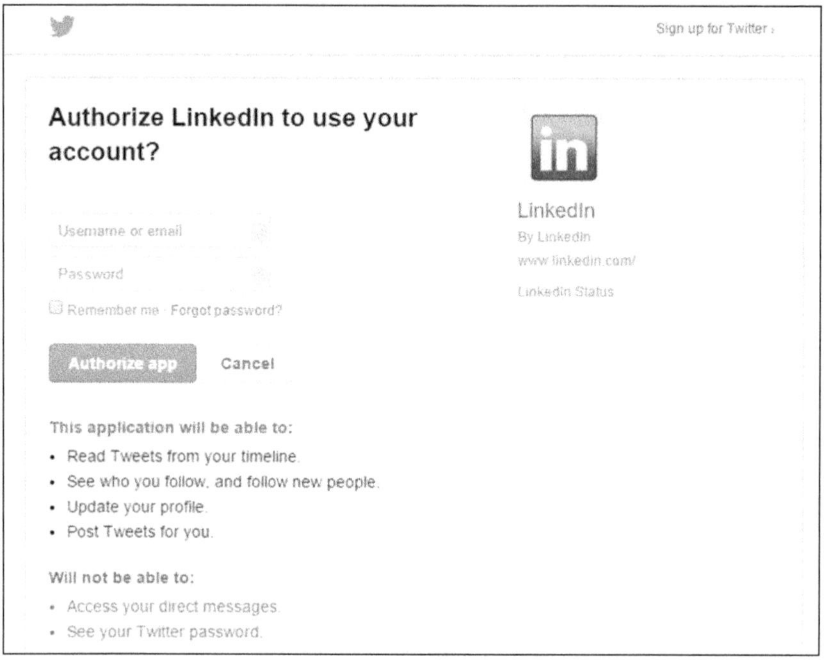

Figure 10: Make sure you log in to Twitter and authorize LinkedIn to use your account

WeChat

LinkedIn has linked up with WeChat,[2] the world's fastest growing social app, so you can now link your LinkedIn profile to WeChat too. WeChat is a multi-purpose messaging app (available on most smartphones) created by the Chinese internet portal company, Tencent. It was launched in 2010 and now has over 600 million users. Although the app is not well known in the UK or in the USA, it is more popular in countries where mobile carriers do not offer unlimited text plans. According to Tencent, the main foreign markets are India, Malaysia, Indonesia, and Singapore, while the majority of users are in China.

Using LinkedIn's publishing platform

Do you blog, or have you produced a report or whitepaper on topics of interest to your target market? Why not repurpose them as long-form posts and add them to your LinkedIn profile using LinkedIn's publishing platform? There are two reasons why doing this is a good idea:

1. Your thought leadership positions you as a "go to" expert – Why not let visitors to your profile see your useful content? Your posts will sit right under the top section of your profile as seen here in Kirsten's profile (Figure 11). This means that your prospects can see them easily and may read them and comment (and get in touch).

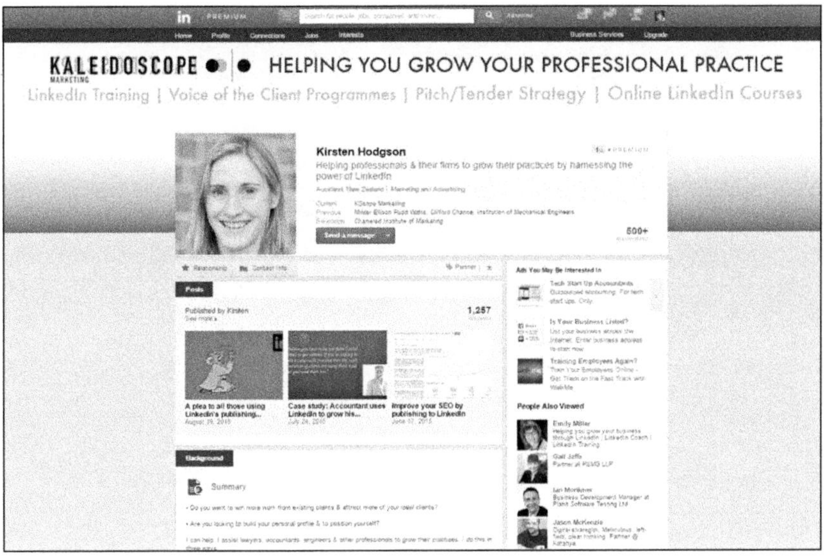

Figure 11: Create long-form posts and add them to your profile to generate interest

2. Search engines (Google etc.) rank content on LinkedIn very highly in searches. This means that your post may rank highly in a search if you have added keywords to the title and the content. This kind of exposure is worth thousands of marketing dollars – why not take advantage of it?

   By way of example, Kirsten wrote a post "How to view people's LinkedIn profiles anonymously" as it was a question lawyers frequently asked her. About two months after publishing it, she noticed the number of views of it had gone through the roof. When she looked at the stats, she noticed almost all of the traffic (6,000 views per week) was from Google. She did a Google search and saw that the post was appearing right near the top of the Google search results when people searched for related terms. She's also noticed a couple of other posts appearing high up in the Google search results – they're getting nowhere near the traction of that one, but they are much more niche focused and are definitely being viewed by those she wishes to reach.

How to publish a long-form post on LinkedIn's publishing platform

Thankfully, the posting process is very straightforward. Go to your "homepage" and click on "Publish a post" (Figure 12).

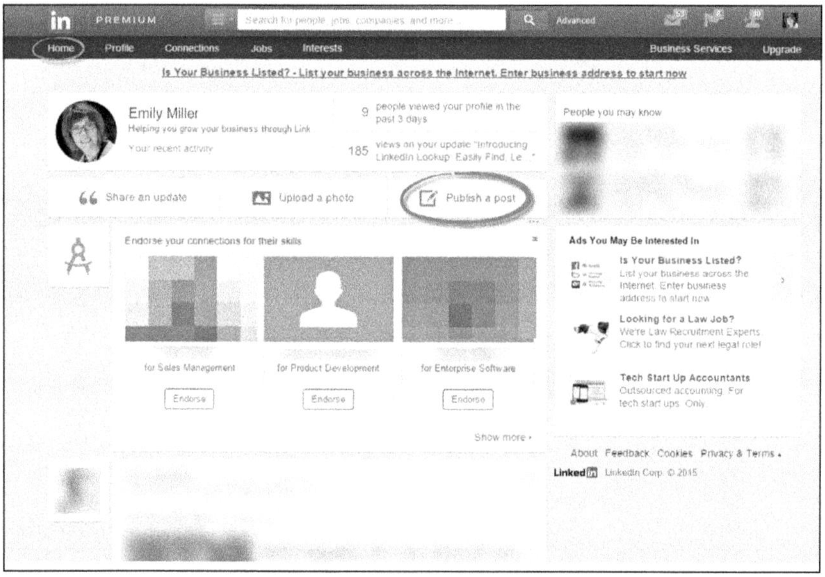

Figure 12: Publish a post

You will then be taken to the post draft page. Add your post title and content. Use the formatting tools to create bullet points, subheadings, etc. You can also include the following in the body of your post by clicking on the relevant icons:

- Images (in JPG, GIF, or PNG format and no larger than 10MB);
- Links to other articles;
- Video;

- Presentations; and
- Documents.

What should you write about and how long should your post be?
Many lawyers ask us about what kind of content they should post on LinkedIn. In nine out of ten cases, our clients already have great content to share. They just haven't added it to their LinkedIn profiles! For those of you who don't have some content you can repurpose, are there common issues your clients face or common questions they ask? If so, then you can assume your prospects have the same issues. Why not write a blog about these issues and give some examples of how you have helped others deal with these?

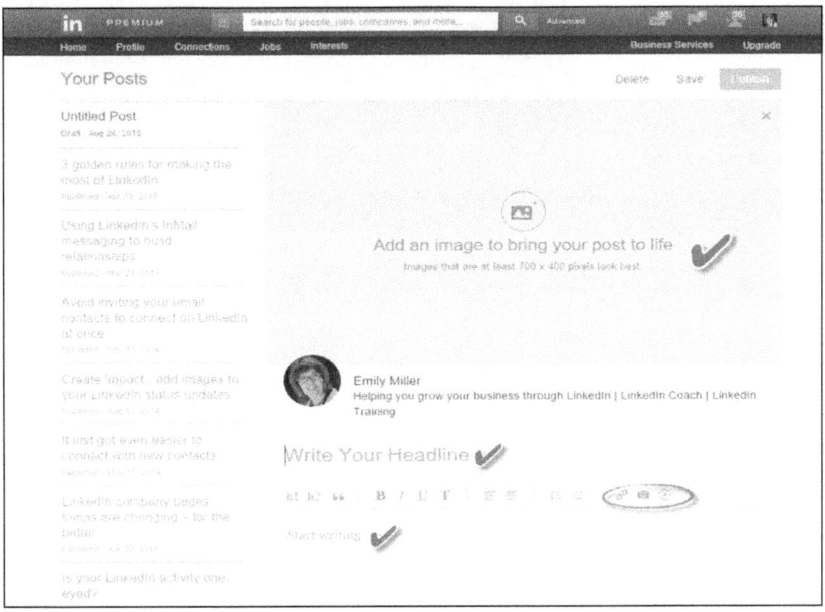

Figure 13: Why not blog about common issues clients ask about?

There is no maximum word count for these long-form posts, but according to LinkedIn, posts with more than three paragraphs get more views, likes, and comments.

It's really important to add an image as it helps your post to stand out. The image looks better if it's 700x400 pixels. You may want to upload the image as it is and see if you need to adjust the pixels. Click on the photo icon to add an image and upload it onto the post. Make sure to credit the owner of the image, if needed, by clicking on the pencil icon noted in Figure 14, and move the image around until you have it positioned the way you want it.

Figure 14: Add an image to help your post stand out

Once you have added the title, content, and the banner image, you can then add three tags to your blog. The tag area is at the bottom of your post draft page. These tags are categories that will help LinkedIn promote your post to members interested in these topics.

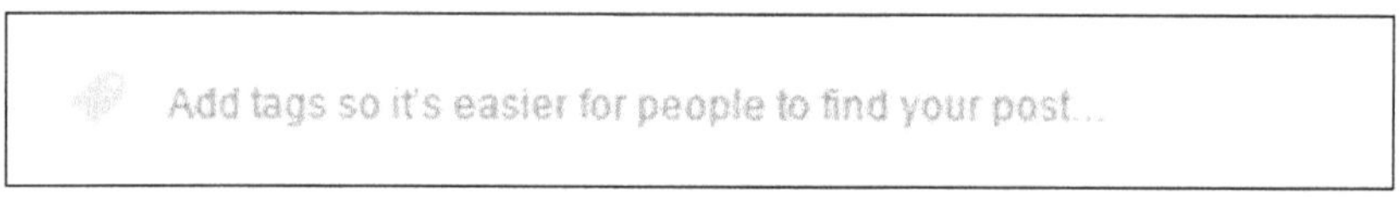

Figure 15: Add tags to help people find your post

To get a good idea of what categories to use, have a look at Pulse, LinkedIn's news channel, by clicking on "Interests" in the main menu, choosing "Pulse", and then clicking on the three lines icon shown in Figure 16 to view the topics (to see more, select "Discover more", scroll down to "Channels", and keep pushing the "See more" button until there are no more channels to see – you may need to press it five or six times). Once you know which channels are appropriate for your post, add them as a tag and then click on the blue "Publish" button found at the top of your post. If you are not quite ready to post it, you can click on "Save" and then publish it later.

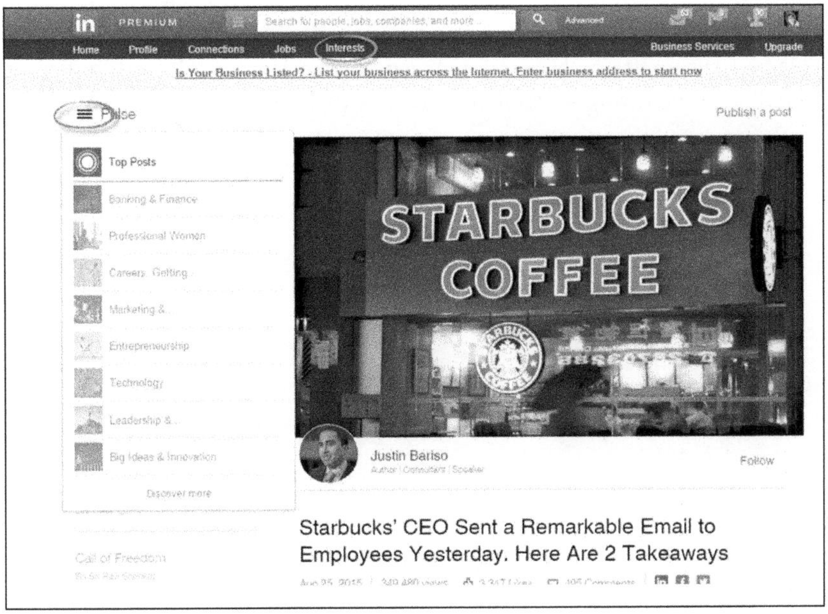

Figure 16: Discover categories that match your post and attract members who are interested in these topics

Action plan:

- Use the LinkedIn profile template to create a profile that attracts clients.
- Highlight your expertise by adding other sections and uploading/ linking content to your profile.
- Create a customized LinkedIn profile URL.
- Include your contact info – make it easy for a client, prospect, or referrer to get in touch.
- Add other social media accounts to your LinkedIn profile.
- Publish your thought leadership pieces via LinkedIn's publishing platform.

Tips:

- Use keywords and phrases throughout your profile.
- Add images to your long-form post to attract readers.
- Add tags to your posts to help LinkedIn to categorize them and to help your target audience to find them.

This first appeared as Chapter 5 in Miller E., and Hodgson, K., LinkedIn for Lawyers: Developing a Profile to Grow Your Practice, *ARK Group, 2015.*

References

1. Go to: https://adwords.google.com. You will need to have a Google account to access this.
2. Visit www.wechat.com.

Chapter 33:
Managing your interview – Essential communication skills

By Geoff Coughlin, co-founder of Emphasis on Skills Ltd

This chapter covers:

- Communication skills – Getting any witness to open up and disclose accurate facts;
- Building rapport – How to build rapport that is as vital as the cognitive interview approach in generating quality facts from your witness;
- Active listening – Really listening actively to your witness will help you control your interview and implement your interview strategy;
- Non-verbal communication skills (NVC) – How your behavior influences witness behavior positively and the amount of information a witness will recall, and verbal communication skills;
- Questioning skills – With a real focus on the use of "open" questions;
- How to use the Interventions and the Assertive Principles;
- Your interview style – The concept of being "supportively neutral";
- Six types of assertiveness, plus three additional techniques – The behaviors you can deploy in any witness interview to generate the full facts and how to challenge assertively differences, discrepancy, or ambiguity;
- Handling emotion in your interview – How to handle emotion in your witnesses and in yourself.

The challenge! Any witness, anytime, anywhere

You do not need me to tell you how challenging witness interviews can be; the challenge is clear – any witness, anytime, and anywhere. A recollection comes to mind…

Once I had just 35 minutes in an airport to interview a significant witness in a maritime litigation matter. The witness was heading out of the country, and this was my client's only opportunity to speak to him face-to-face. There were many reasons for this, suffice to say that there was no other method we could use in what I accept were pretty unusual circumstances. Having agreed to go to a quiet-ish corner of the terminal building, we sat down and I took a minute to set out our challenge, which was to help him to recall in detail the minutes leading up to the specific, day, date, time, and location of the collision. I told him that I wanted to try something and set about getting him to picture himself back on the bridge at the time in question – I just asked him to see it. I was lucky, very lucky, as this technique challenged his memory and what had been recorded in the vessel's log – new information emerged that turned the case.

Remember that I only had about 35 minutes available, I had not met Mr X before, but I still spent the first six minutes or so talking to him, explaining that we had a great opportunity to make a difference here – asking him to carefully look back to the day and date in question. I also tried to be as relaxed as I could be, only bringing out my pad to take some notes just prior to him starting his recall. I also asked him if it was OK for me to record our "conversation" (using that word, rather than anything more formal to help him stay relaxed) and so help my note-taking.

I completely accept that this scenario is about as unwelcome as you could wish for as an interviewer and should be avoided at all costs for obvious reasons. I include it here to acknowledge that the real world can deal you some rough cards sometimes. Equally, even if you have no choice as in my example, you can still achieve much more than you think possible by taking (valuable) time at the start to build rapport – more on this below.

A broad range of communication skills

Getting any witness to open up and disclose accurate facts requires you to draw on a broad range of communication and interpersonal skills to achieve your purpose. Taking time to develop your wider communication and interpersonal skills is essential in my experience in order to stay at the top of your game. It's the same for any professional – from footballers to finance litigators! Sure, some lawyers are highly effective, looking and sounding extremely competent in what they do. It would be wrong, however, to believe that this level of skill and performance comes naturally – it doesn't. It has to be worked at, and we need to learn from experience and be prepared to adapt, change, and develop a range of skills that can be drawn on in any witness interview to enable us to get the best out of our witness.

Aside from relevant technical knowledge, which is a given, here are some of the most important personal skills that we need to have developed to a high standard:

- Building rapport and trust;
- Effective verbal and non-verbal communication;
- Active listening;
- Questioning;
- Assertiveness;
- Influencing or enabling skills to help your witness open up and talk to you; and
- Note-taking.

I want to take some time to look at these and other key skills areas in the context of witness interviewing and how they can be used to good effect. This chapter is not intended to go into all the theory, far from it. It is much more an opportunity to offer practical, helpful hints, tips, and advice in each area that I and others continue to find really helpful.

Building rapport and trust

How can you build rapport that is vital to the cognitive interview approach in generating quality facts and recall from your witness? There are many definitions of rapport, and this is not going to be an exposition of all of them, but at its core, we are talking about *behaving in a way that develops mutual trust, co-operation, and an affinity with your witness.*

In brief, you take some time to consider your witness and where they may be coming from in terms of start point – how do they feel? what's important to them? and so on – because it matters to us to allow some time for our witness to talk about what is important to them. I want to be clear here, I am not talking about a great long discussion that seems irrelevant – many witnesses will resent you for "wasting their time" – no, it's about exercising a heavy dose of empathy, and trying to spot what they need from you in terms of information, reassurance, support, and clarity.

Witnesses will tell you more because you have taken time before and at the start of your interview (in Stage 1 of the cognitive interview model – Creating the right environment) to:

- Answer their questions;

- Deal with their "agenda", issues, and concerns;
- Gain an overview from them;
- Ask how they feel to be talking to you, or how they feel about being here;
- Engage in supportive conversation (social chit-chat) on meeting and greeting (but don't get carried away);
- Consider where and how the interview will take place;
- Make early contact to arrange your telephone interview if that is the only method available; and
- Make contact early on prior to your interview to ask your witness to consider specific points, issued, dates, or events (taking care to agree these with colleagues beforehand if appropriate, and that it is linked to your interview strategy/approach/tactics).

Then, in Stage 2 (the "Explanation phase" in the cognitive interview model), we take the time to:

- Explain what your witness can expect;
- State your aim and purpose;
- Explain your approach, the outline structure you intend to take;
- State clearly what you want your witness to do;
- Ask them to stay focused, to try to concentrate as hard as possible (using appropriate language for each individual); and
- Consider your actions and follow the Rule of 3:
    - Note-taking – Not to be distracted about what you are and are not writing down;
    - Pauses – That there will be pauses, that these are "good news" because they will allow your witness "thinking time", time to think hard about what they have said and to add anything more, more detail. Importantly, that you are not going to fill these pauses, but will move the interview on when it is clear that this is what is needed; and
    - Eye contact – Or lack of it, in fact. You need to be able to start to interpret eye patterns.[1] Are they seeing what you are asking, feeling it, or hearing it? So, it is important to tell your witness not to worry about maintaining or expecting "good" eye-contact and

that just because you are not looking at them, it does not mean that you are not listening – far from it! Explain that you will be listening very hard and making notes so you will not be looking at them very much, but this is fine.

So, as you can see, these two stages of the CI model are all about building rapport and that may seem like it is going to take a long time; in fact, it doesn't.

Trust has to be earned and is the by-product of a strong and healthy communication relationship between interviewer and witness. Being clear about what you can and cannot deliver to your witness from the outset is key, so be clear about what you promise and offer. Real trust is built up over the duration of the interview so that we bring about a situation where our witness talks in detail about anything at all that is relevant. Taking your time with your witness during Stages 1 (Setting the environment) and 2 (Explaining what will happen) and covering each element will set you on the right path, as will avoiding being judgmental of what your witness says. A pattern of listen, note, and gently probe; pause, listen hard again; and ask occasional, well-framed, "open" questions can all dramatically affect the trust that exists between you and your witness.

Let's look at some of the other skills that will help you to get the best out of your witness.

How to listen well

Really listening actively to your witness will help you control your interview and implement your interview strategy. You may have heard of the term "active listening", but what does that mean in practical terms for you as the interviewer? Active listening is defined variously in different contexts. One definition is:

> "*... a communication technique used in counselling, training and conflict resolution, which requires the listener to feed back what they hear to the speaker, by way of re-stating or paraphrasing what they have heard in their own words, to confirm what they have heard and moreover, to confirm the understanding of both parties*".[2]

There are key elements in this definition that can be helpful: feeding back, confirmation, paraphrasing, using the witness's own words, and confirming understanding. Imagine that you have your communication radar turned on – you are listening and watching carefully to see, hear, and feel what your witness means – listening for varied intonation and facial expressions that might add meaning to what you think you have heard.

Some time ago, I came across and developed a grid that shows listening as "ten keys to effective listening" that can be useful to remember when we are interviewing witnesses (see Table 1).

Ten keys to effective listening	The poor listener	The effective listener (interviewer)
1. Find areas of interest	Tunes out dry subjects	Allows the witness some moments (or minutes) to go off-point, giving them time to search in their memory for what you have asked about. Avoid interrupting if possible and allow pauses for facts to emerge naturally
2. Assess content, not delivery	Tunes out if delivery is poor	Assesses content and ignores "poor" communication style/delivery by your witness
3. Hold your fire	Tends to jump in too quickly	Does not interrupt unless it is absolutely necessary – allowing witness to explain fully what they mean
4. Listen for true meaning	Listens only to the words used	Listens for the true meaning by assessing facial expressions and other body language and verbal intonation and exploring these
5. Take efficient notes	Takes intensive notes using only one system	Takes fewer notes and listens harder; makes use of efficient note-taking systems like Mind Mapping, shorthand, and other efficient methods
6. Work at listening	Shows no energy output. Attention is faked	Works hard, exhibits engaging communication skills
7. Resist distractions	Distracted easily, poor planning for interview method	Fights or avoids distractions, tolerates bad habits, knows how to concentrate, tries to arrange face-to-face interview if possible
8. Confront difference and inconsistency	Resists difficult challenges and avoids confronting differences in recollection	Creates opportunities for witness to go over areas again, carefully "setting up" their questions using an "open" question style. Uses pauses to good effect and assertiveness to "notice" difference and inconsistency
9. Keep your mind open	Reacts to emotional words	Interprets "color" words; does not get hung up on them; checks out meaning by asking "open" questions to seek clarity and understanding

10. Think about the facts; it is faster than speech	Tends to daydream with slow speakers; loses concentration and focus	Adopts the 80–20 percent rule – listening for 80 percent of the time, and talking, instructing, explaining, and questioning only 20 percent of the time available – preferably less! Anticipates, mentally summarizes, weighs the evidence, listens between the lines to voice tone

Table 1: Ten keys to effective listening

Non-verbal communication skills (NVC)

You can use your behavior to influence witness behavior positively; equally, NVC can and does adversely affect the behavior and amount of information a witness will recall. There's a good behavioral principle that you can bear in mind and that is "behavior breeds behavior". In other words, the way people behave towards you is directly related to the way you behave towards them.

Table positioning

So, it is worth considering your positioning in face-to-face interviews, for example. Studies and experience show that, when the interviewer sits directly opposite their witness, you build in an element of confrontation that is completely avoidable if you adopt the "90-degree principle" – notice in the diagram in Figure 1, the relative positions of interviewer and their witness.

Although there are clear cultural variations, it is fair to say that aiming for a space of about 18 ins (46 cm) between you and your witness will work well in most situations. What you are trying to do is preserve and respect the "personal space" that most of us have, and which we do not like to let anyone into unless an element of intimacy exists between us. The "18-inch rule" is also useful because it puts just enough space between you and your witness so that they cannot easily see what you are writing – great! The last thing we need is them craning over and looking at everything you write – off-putting for them and also for you because we are becoming an active distraction!

Also notice that, in the example in Figure 1, you as the interviewer are located in a position that will allow you to write using your right hand, take notes, and easily refer to your bundle or other documentation. Simply reverse the witness and interviewer positions if you are left-handed. You can use exactly the same approach whatever shape your table is, but hopefully you get the idea – not to sit directly opposite your witness.

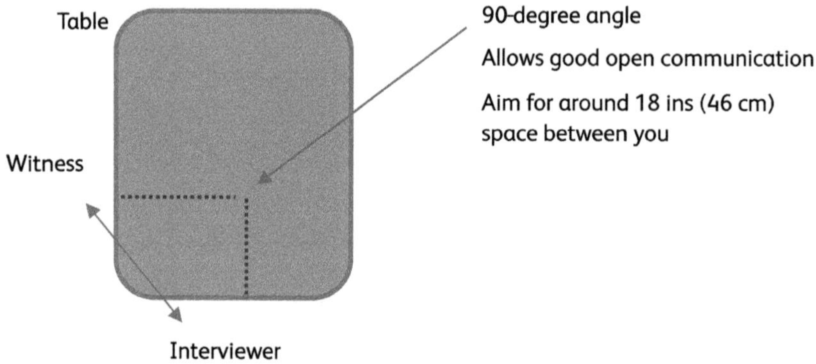

Figure 1: Table positioning

Facial expressions

Small gentle nods and smiles from time to time, less eye-contact than usual because you want to take occasional looks and glances at your witness to see what they are doing with their eyes and interpret their eye patterns. A simple raise of the eyebrows in an encouraging way, maybe with a small nod, can cause your witness to continue, and with practice, you can learn to say a lot less than may have been the case to date; you just need to work at it and train yourself to do something different. Avoid fidgeting and excessive movement. Get comfortable at the start and try to minimize any distraction for your witness – they need to concentrate.

It is better when using the CI approach to use small nods and smiles to help or encourage your witness to continue than to use verbal "word-spacers" ("um", "ah-ha", "yes", "I see" etc.); these are fine in everyday business and social interaction, but simply distract and adversely affect the free flow of witness recollection when used in a CI.

How you dress

Not an easy one to generalize about because there are so many points of view and so many contexts in which witness interviews can take place. As a starting point, I always think about the person who I am going to interview – who are they? where are they? who will be there? etc. – as well as practical considerations given the physical location and so on. I try to think about how the witness is likely to be dressed given all of the above and select something I think will enable me to create the right impression, be taken seriously, and enable me to carry out my role effectively.

Some examples:

- I was interviewing a financial director at his home in Surrey and so I decided to wear a suit but no tie – smart yet not too uncomfortable for me. It "felt" right.
- On another occasion, I had to interview a mother in her home in a medical negligence case and it seemed appropriate not to turn up looking too formal, all suited and booted. I wanted to help her to feel comfortable and relaxed and not overwhelmed by this very formal-looking professional turning up at her door. I just replaced my suit jacket with a smart, yet more casual, navy blue fleece jacket.
- Again, when interviewing a CEO from an NHS Trust a few years ago at his office, I felt that I would have more gravitas and "power'"by dressing in a suit and tie, and I definitely felt that it helped me to perform well.

I have included this small section really just to get you to think about how you dress; it is never something that I take for granted and, as you can see from the above examples, it is important never to just dress the same whatever the interview. Years ago, when I was an instructor at the Metropolitan Police College, Hendon, we had an outstanding personal development consultant, Mike Eales, who did a lot of work with us at that time. He was definitely not someone who would ever be comfortable wearing a suit, yet he exuded calmness, control, and power. He always arrived wearing some kind of sports jacket, shirt, tie, and cords – this was very formal for Mike and he used to call it his "battle dress" because he felt that it gave him power in what was an alien environment to him. Talking to Mike, he said he dressed this way because it helped him perform well and also was respectful to the organization paying for his services – I learned a lot from Mike.

Verbal communication skills

Your use of plain, straightforward language, avoiding exclusive language and jargon, will pay dividends in helping you build effective rapport and be more efficient with the time you have available.

Plain, straightforward language helps to make the task of remembering easier for your witness

When we have studied responses to interviewer questions and looked at the answers a witness gives, it becomes clear that there is a link between the language of the response and the type of question asked. We look more closely at questioning later in this chapter, but it is worth considering the language that you use when you interview your witness.

Part of the problem lies in what your witness understands you to be asking, and what you really mean, or are trying to get at. Witnesses often struggle to concentrate, are easily distracted, look for a memory that is easier to recall/construct rather than try hard to remember exactly what they experienced, and so on. So, there is a need to make sure that the task of remembering is as clear and straightforward as possible. To that end, it should make sense to think carefully before your interview about the questions and areas that you want to know about, and to find a form of words that creates a situation where your witness answers exactly what you want to know.

From all the research and my own experience, it is clear that witnesses can easily get confused by the interviewer, and I have seen this many times in legal interviews. Typically, the interviewer takes so long to actually get around to asking their question – talking and filling in – that by the time their witness is expected to answer, there is usually a pause, followed by a comment like: "... err, sorry, what did you want to know?" Not good!

Avoid over-talking – This closes down your witness

This is again very common and occurs when the interviewer is not fully focused and actively listening to their witness talking; rather, they are thinking about the next thing they want to say, another question, or are too eager to find out more about what is being said. There is a clear link here to the value of pausing after asking your question, but try to remember to stay focused, listen hard, and make notes; look and listen to see where you may need to go next, and where does what you are being told leave you in relation to what you know from other witnesses or documents.

Witnesses quickly pick up on your style and approach, and if they spot that you are looking to say something, they tend to stop talking and look to you to make the next move, when in fact they should be mentally "back in the there and then". They pick up on your non-verbal communication and/or they hear tiny noises from you (you know the ones – immediately before you actually ask a question or make your next contribution). Our task is to learn to be patient at times like these: listening hard, staying quiet, looking for relevant facts to note down, and only really speaking when you need to.

Trying to impress or establish your credibility

It is perfectly possible to establish your credibility through provision of good quality and easy-to-understand material as well as using clear language when giving information to your witnesses and answering their questions. Some lawyers have a way of talking that sounds over-complex, superior even, and when you add to that legal words or jargon that your witness may not understand fully, this is going to have a negative effect on your ability to build effective rapport right from the outset. Sometimes, it can be very useful to perhaps record an interview that you conduct. I use my iPhone and its voice memo facility and the phone just sits next to me. The sole purpose is so that I can listen back to my verbal communication and especially the questions that I ask and look to make improvements and changes next time. Try it and see what you think – you will be amazed at what you hear! For sure, you should let your witness know what you are doing and that its sole purpose is to help you review afterwards what you have done and, in my experience, they are completely fine with it – both witness and interviewer forgetting that the interview is being recorded. It doesn't adversely affect the witness at all. An added bonus here is that you have captured accurately all the information to help prepare your draft soon after your interview in concluded.

Questioning skills – With a real focus on the use of "open" questions and how these can be applied at each stage of the interview

Here, I want to go into the different question types that get asked in witness interviews as well as raise some red flags based on my own experience of watching thousands of lawyers carry out witness interviews over the years. Perhaps the red flags first.

Interrupting with another question – Ask, pause, and wait!

Geiselman and Fisher[3] noted that interviewers typically interrupt their witness after only a few seconds with another question. This has the effect of preventing the full facts from emerging, so we need to learn to think carefully about any questions that we want to ask (preferably beforehand) and deliver them carefully and skillfully at the most appropriate time in the interview. You can make the links, I am sure, with some of the points raised above, and how easy it is to interrupt in your eagerness to get through the interview in the shortest time possible. This is, however, a false economy; many more facts are likely to emerge if you remain quiet after asking a well-worded "open" question that has clear parameters (a start and finish point) for what you want your witness to talk about.

Asking leading questions – Avoid them like the plague!

So, what is a leading question? It is one where you introduce or suggest content that has not been provided by your witness. In my own experience of watching interviews, this is a real problem and one that interviewers fall foul of regularly. Why do you do it? Have a think about this for a few moments and jot some thoughts down, and then consider the effects your leading questions can have on your witness.

Here are some examples of leading questions that I noted when listening to lawyers:

- "What did they look like? About average height, maybe?"
- "'I certainly wouldn't have been very happy about that; I expect you weren't very happy about that either, were you?"

It is interesting, isn't it (he says in a closed, leading way!) that when you look at these questions, they just look and feel wrong. Suggesting content in this way simply contaminates your witness's recollection and should be avoided for that reason alone. We know how witnesses like to be led; they expect it, so we need to manage their expectations when we explain what's going to happen in Stage 2 of the CI approach.

Leading questions in witness interviews lead (or mislead) your witness into taking possibly the easiest route (or way out) by frequently just agreeing with what you are suggesting, or picking one of the "choices" of recall you are suggesting. This is a dangerous situation from a case perspective because the answers you get may not be what your witness actually experienced at all, but simply what they think you want to hear. Evidentially, there are problems too because so much of what is likely to emerge after you ask a leading question may not be accurate. What you end up doing is creating a situation where your witness goes into their recall superficially, quite possibly constructing their reply and you record it as if it is accurate, genuine recall of the events.

What questions should I ask? "Open" questions whenever possible

Ok, so now the red flags are out of the way – what questions should I ask and why? Open questions are highly desirable because they do not contaminate the answer like leading questions do. Additionally, your witness is highly likely to give you a much more expansive and comprehensive answer that allows you time to listen hard to what they say, make notes, and consider where their answer leaves you in terms of what you already know from others and documents.

Here are some examples of decent "open" questions that could be appropriate at different times in a witness interview:

- "Remember when you said that you came into the office and that there were a few people there [three second pause]? Can you just picture being there now [three second pause]? Look around and tell me all about who you see – take your time."
- "You mentioned feeling embarrassed about how he behaved [three second pause]; can I ask you to think carefully about that now [two second pause]? Tell me all about that."
- "You described hearing a loud bang [two second pause]. I really need to know more about that now [two second pause]. Can you take a few moments to describe what you heard in more detail?"

My intention in asking the above questions is to try to generate more detailed recall, much more detailed. By making your question an "open" question and using pauses carefully, you are managing the expectations of your witness to do what you have asked: think carefully, not to rush, and explain fully. The good news for us as interviewers is that witnesses are very good at picking up on what we are asking and expect – if we practice what we preach. In other words, in Stage 2 of the CI model when we explain what will happen, we say that we are not going to interrupt, ask lots of questions, or fill the pauses, and so your first few questions asked are critical in terms of influencing the behavior of your witness – positively or negatively.

It is worth noting here the importance of setting clear parameters when asking your "open" question – a start and a finish point for what you want to know. If you do not set clear parameters, you run a high risk that your witness will seize the opportunity to go off track and wander into irrelevant and unproductive areas. Here is an example of an "open" question that has parameters within which the witness can work:

"You mentioned, James, that this was a Tuesday [pause two seconds]. I'd like you to just think carefully about that day [pause two seconds] and tell me why you think that it was Tuesday? [long pause]"

Hopefully, you can clearly see the parameters here (Tuesday) and the request to focus, at this time, only on "that" day and why the witness thinks that it was a Tuesday. Notice the word "Tuesday" is mentioned twice (the witness has already offered that information).

Multi-headed questions – Avoid these because they confuse your witness

This is where the interviewer asks more than one question at a time, in the same sentence. The problems here are legion, but amongst other things, multi-headed questions:

- Confuse your witness;
- Cause their answers to be shorter because the witness loses focus and clarity about what you are asking; and
- Cause potential conflict evidentially because it is hard to attribute individual answers accurately to specific questions.

Clearly, it should not be our purpose to confuse and mislead our witness, let alone influence their recall. I suggest it is better to find out the full facts and have to deal with any inconsistencies and ambiguity later in the interview than try to influence witness recall to fit the documents we have. This latter point is one that is more common than you may expect, often done with a view to speeding things up, saving cost on interviews, and a belief that you are representing your client's interests in the best way possible. Not so.

Other observations on questioning

On the rare occasions that witnesses are called to give their evidence in court, I have seen first-hand and heard horror stories from lawyers and advocates about witnesses changing their story quite readily, adding or denying "facts" contained in their statements, and many of these problems are caused because the lawyer taking the initial statement did so using inappropriate questioning.

Usefully, research suggests that witnesses that have been interviewed using the CI approach are more reliable and consistent when cross-examined in court; they rarely change their story. I am sure that this is so, not only because of the results of studies and available evidence, but because in a CI the interviewer takes the witness deeper into their memory, generating more in-depth and reliable recollection. Other factors are also likely to play a part in the CI. For example, your witness works hard and concentrates deeply and memory is not just magically recalled; a witness needs to search their memory and try several times (multiple retrievals) to recall what happened. It therefore follows that when we ask good "open" questions, have built effective rapport, and use the CI approach, we will get better results.

Avoid offering choices in your questions – If you do, answers are more likely to generate constructed recall

This is an interesting one and, again, more common than you may think. This situation occurs when the interviewer appears to offer a choice in their question – an "option A or B" scenario. This is how it can look and sound:

> *"You said a few minutes ago that you had a new manager and this was the first time you had seen him – can you please describe him for me? Was he, short, tall, old, or young?"*

Well, what if it was not any of these subjective and leading suggestions? That is the problem. We are contaminating their recall by suggesting and offering a choice – was it this or was it that? This is a very unhelpful thing to do when asking your questions. It is much more effective to think carefully about what it is you want to know and then set up one or more good "open" questions. You need to "set up" your question so that your witness knows exactly what it is that you are asking (the task); they need to search their memory "store" to find the detail that will answer your question.

The brain likes to take the easiest route in many ways, especially when presented with an easy way out! Concentration is hard work; choices make it easier not to think and try so hard and therefore, perhaps predictably, your witness will take the course of least resistance and offer you something that they think will "please you" (after all, you have just suggested what you are looking for!). Or, maybe they just want to be "helpful" and take your lead, doing exactly what you are asking them when you present them with a choice.

Context is everything

Just take a few moments to watch interviews on television and especially those where politicians are interviewed by TV reporters and studio presenters. Multi-headed, leading questions, judgmental tone, and interruptions abound – fine perhaps for TV viewing, amusing sometimes, but wholly inappropriate in a witness interview context. You have to ask yourself: what is my purpose? If it is to confuse, destabilize, evade the "truth", and embarrass, then maybe the TV way is acceptable. On the other hand, if your purpose is to be objective, searching, and open-minded with the intention of establishing the full facts, I suggest the cognitive interview approach has much more to offer.

What do you want to say? How the interventions can help you to say the right thing at the right time

This section is designed to help you with your approach, questioning, and interview style. The material that follows has its roots in the work by John Heron, entitled *Six Category Intervention Analysis*, in which he suggests that there are six main forms of "helping" behaviors or interventions that can be adopted by anyone. In my training, I have spent some time re-working these for use by lawyers and interviewers so that you can consider how you communicate in your witness interview based around your *intention*. It is a way of classifying and grouping the huge range of interventions under six headings, which are six kinds of "purpose" or "intention". It is these intentions which underlie the ultimate choice of what the successful interviewer actually does to express this intention.

These communication skills are in fact used to train lawyers, managers, and leaders, and many others like teachers, trainers, nurses, doctors, dentists, and accountants. They enable the interviewer to make a conscious choice about which type of intervention to use (what to say and do) at any moment in their interview. This can lead to much better rapport and understanding between interviewer and witness.

To recap, then, each of the six behaviors has an "intention" behind it. So that, for example, each time we as an interviewer open our mouth to speak to the witness, it may be our intention to either:

- Offer advice; or

- Give information; or
- Confront issues; or
- Deal with the other person's feelings; or
- Help them to work through their recollection themselves; or
- Offer support.

Interventions

An intervention is an identifiable piece of verbal and/or non-verbal behavior on the part of the interviewer. For example:

- "This is what you should do next..."
- "We have an information booklet that explains how to do this."
- "I notice that you appear to be avoiding that particular issue."
- "How did you feel when that happened?"
- "What do you want the next step to be?"
- "Don't misunderstand me, I can see that it's difficult for you."

It is the skill in choosing the most apt type and manner of intervention that is important. This model deals with six types of such interventions by classifying them under six headings. This gives you the choice of response in order to get the most out of an interaction between you and your witness, so that full information can emerge in a timely manner.

The interventions are divided into two main groups (as shown in Table 2). What follows are some simple examples of questions and statements that I think illustrate each of the interventions and what they could look like if used in a witness interview environment. Try not to read too much into any of them – it is easy to assume or add your own intonation when reading them that could make them sound relevant and appropriate on the one hand, yet quite irrelevant or inappropriate on the other. So just try to notice the wording and intention behind each of the examples.

Advising	
Informing	These three are authoritative
Raising issues	
Feelings	
Learning	These three are facilitative
Supporting	

Table 2: Six types of interventions

Advising

An advising intervention seeks to direct the behavior of another person by demonstration, advice, command, and suggestion, telling, requiring, insisting, or proposing:

- "I think that you should take a few moments to relax and think carefully about what happened..."
- "I would like to send you a draft of your statement within the next week; please read through it carefully..."
- "What I would like you to do is look at this bank statement..."
- "As soon as I receive the email you mentioned, we can talk again on the telephone..."

Informing

An informing intervention seeks to impart knowledge or information to your witness by telling, instructing, and using expertise:

- "What I am going to do now is prepare your draft statement and send it to you..."
- "Other people have certainly found it easier to remember by trying to picture the scene..."
- "I would really like you to draw a diagram of the room – show exactly what and who is in there please, and also add..."

Raising issues

A raising-issues intervention seeks to raise the consciousness of your witness about some limiting attitude or behavior of which they are relatively unaware:

- "I get the impression that you find that hard to talk about?"
- "You seem unhappy about that – what are you thinking about?"
- "It sounds as if you were unsure of what to do next?"

Feelings

A feelings intervention seeks to enable the witness to share and express any negative feelings, fear, or even anger about the situation:

- "You seem very upset – tell me about it?"
- "That's ok, go on, tell me what you said, that's fine [pause]..."
- "You sound pretty angry hearing you now? [pause] What's going on?"
- "You mentioned being worried about speaking to him again – tell me about that worry [pause]..."

Learning

A learning intervention seeks to elicit self-discovery and problem solving in the witness:

- "What are you thinking?"
- "Let me see, is this what you meant when you said..."
- "Have you thought about looking at it from a different point of view?"
- "You said that you wouldn't repeat the error again? How did you deal with this going forward?"
- "What would you like to happen now?"

Supporting

A supporting intervention seeks to offer encouragement, reward (in a communication sense), and appropriate thanks:

- "It was extremely helpful that you sent through the document as I asked..."

- "That's very good, you've remembered a lot about your meeting..."
- "Thanks for calling me back as agreed; because you have done that I think we can proceed..."
- "You've explained that well and what would be really helpful now would be for you to..."

The use of interventions in your everyday work

Over the years, I have found these interventions very helpful when I have reviewed my performance and looked to develop my style going forward. It is important to remember that there is no right or wrong about any of these interventions; it is all about choosing the right intervention for your situation, there and then, at that moment in your interview, making the most appropriate choice of intervention so that you achieve your intention.

In my mind, I think: "What does this witness need from me right now, at this moment?" It could be anything from more information, an explanation, through to me simply staying quiet, listening hard, and then encouraging them to explain or say more if appropriate.

The interventions and your interview style

The interventions need each other in due measure and in an ever-changing ratio to keep your communication co-operative, "open", and professional – although the balance at any one moment may be towards one of these in particular. Reviewing our performance and especially our use of each and balance in using these six interventions can help us gain insights into our interview style. Here are some questions to get you thinking about this:

- Look back at a recent interview that you conducted and write down some specific examples of what you said and did – which specific interventions did you use and when?
- What do you notice about the breakdown and balance of authoritative and facilitative interventions?
- Did you use more of either group? If so, when and why?

I had a conversation with a lawyer about these interventions on a course and he spotted right away that "I do far too much telling – talking really". We discussed the value of being aware of this and then taking a few minutes to review the next few interviews, having discussed some practical strategies like listening more, using pauses to better effect, realizing that his witness interviews are not conversations, but cognitive interviews that use a deliberate and intentional set of actions and protocols.

It is equally inappropriate to use only facilitative interventions. For example, knowledge cannot be drawn out where it does not exist. When it becomes clear, after appropriate attempts to draw it out, that your witness does not know or cannot remember, it is time to move on. Moving on and using an authoritative intervention, such as giving a clear instruction or request to try to remember another issue or topic in more detail, is probably a good decision. The professional skill is to select the intervention most likely to elicit the desired result.

Assertive influencing – Helping your witness open up and talk to you, whatever their circumstances

As you will be aware by now, the "complete interviewer" needs to be able to draw on a range of powerful communication and interpersonal skills, and whether or not you use the cognitive interview approach to interview your witness, you need to be able to adopt an assertive approach and communication style.

Together with my business partner, I have spent many years developing and refining the following set of Assertive Principles that are widely used (or versions of them) when helping lawyers to develop their personal effectiveness in all areas of their work. The principles are a set of assertive behaviors that can be used to great effect when interviewing witnesses and so are worth keeping uppermost in your mind until they become absorbed into your repertoire of normal behavior. They become simply part of what you do, what you can do when communicating with your witness, so that with practice you do not really think about choosing to deploy one or another principle – you just draw on any combination of them at any time when you see that there is a need for it. Much the same thing applies to the six interventions you have seen above; it is awareness and practice of using them that, in time, will make them habitual because you value the intention behind each one of them.

Just before we look at the 11 Assertive Principles, it is worth taking a quick look at what I mean when I talk about 'assertiveness'. Here's my working definition: assertiveness is being able to say clearly and directly what it is you want to say or feel, but not at the expense of the other person. This definition is quite generic in terms of application, but look what is at the heart of it when you apply it to your witness interview. I have carried out exercises on training courses in the past year where I asked lawyers what they believed to be the key assertive behaviors that interviewers should be able to use when interviewing witnesses. Here are some of the responses:

- Appear and sound confident;
- Show that they are knowledgeable;
- Be sensitive;
- Be a good listener;
- Show that they are interested;
- Show empathy when needed;
- Ask great questions in an "open" style;
- Challenge the witness if their story is inconsistent;
- Be supportive in their style;
- Prepared to be patient and wait for the witness to finish; and
- Step in when they go off-track.

These are certainly the main suggestions, and it is good to see the links between what lawyers know they should be doing and believe to be effective and the principles offered below.

The 11 Assertive Principles

1. **Avoid getting into an "enemy position"** – Try to maintain an open channel of communication between you and your witness. What might you need to say and do differently to encourage them to explain more and give additional detail or clarification?
2. **Put yourself behind what you say** – You should look and sound genuine. Expressions, eye contact, and other mannerisms should be consistent with what you are saying.
3. **Be ready for a working compromise** – At least, be prepared to listen to your witness and recognize that they may have a different point of view. You may have a different viewpoint, perhaps based on the bundle of documents before you, but consider the possibility of changing your mind or understanding based on what your witness says and does.

4. **Ask for what you want** – State what it is you need, and be clear and direct. This is especially relevant during Stage 2 of the cognitive interview model (Explaining what will happen). You need to be able to ask your witness to do things like: staying focused, trying hard to concentrate, not to be distracted by you and your note-taking or lack of eye-contact. You need to be prepared to find the words and tone appropriate to your request.
5. **Don't take it personally** – When your witness appears to be being aggressive, or just rude to you, it does not mean that they are necessarily being personal or verbally attacking you. They may feel that they have very good reasons to behave this way – as far as they are concerned. Take a deep breath and listen hard for themes and issues in their delivery (content) that may give clues to what is driving their behavior. Pause. Wait. Usually, the best thing to do is not to jump in or become defensive; just wait. When an opportunity arises and they have calmed down, check out your understanding and avoid making assumptions about their behavior and what may be causing it. Deal with your witness without feeling you have to make them like or approve of you.
6. **Show you understand their point of view** – By echoing part of their last sentence perhaps, or saying something like, "yes, I understand that you were unhappy", or "from what you say, it sounds like you didn't agree?" There is a fine line here in a witness interview context. On one hand, you do not want to show too much "agreement" or encouragement, because research shows that some witnesses can be unduly influenced by this "reward", so keep the nodding and any comments or word-spacers like "yes, yes, I see…", "uh huh", "mmm", "yes, go on…", and so on to a minimum. Small nods and occasional facial expressions that are encouraging work well.
7. **Express your views** – Try to be confident enough to state your point of view. The opportunity to do so can occur when you point out to your witness something that you have noticed, followed by a pause. This has the effect of causing your witness to think carefully about what they have said, and possibly reconsider their approach. I have an example of this when I interviewed a medical consultant against whom there had been an allegation of assault. Initially, he was very reticent and stated that he was not even on duty on the date in question. Prior to the interview, I had secured a copy of the duty state for that day that clearly showed he had signed in at the

beginning of his shift. I presented this to him, without any judgment in my tone, and after quite a while (2 minutes and 17 seconds to be precise – I remember it well!), he said, 'Well if I was there...'. What is interesting, I think, and an example of this Assertive Principle in action in what followed, is that I went on to tell him that I had not seen any report or document anywhere that put his version of events, and more detail emerged.

Later on, I said, "Have you considered how it might look later when you had this opportunity to explain fully what happened from your point of view and you didn't take it?" This example is seriously abbreviated, but just notice the language and opportunities that presented during this example to express my view. I think it felt appropriate at the time to express my view, but also realize that you need to watch your voice and intonation, ensuring that you do not leak any judgment in your tone because this is likely to have a seriously negative effect – closing your witness down.

8. **Avoid being judgmental of your witness** – Try to stay focused on the issues and avoid making personal comments or judgments about what your witness is saying, or indeed about them as a person. This principle is linked to the one above (expressing your views). We have a saying in the development world: *If you think it, you'll leak it!*

   Since being very young, we have all grown up learning about and perfecting our ability to read others' body language. If someone looks confused, there's a pretty good chance they *are* confused; similarly, if they look worried or concerned, they may well be worried or concerned. Of course, there can be other explanations, but the point here is to be careful what you think because it is likely to show out when you talk to your witness. It is surprising how easy it is to fall into this trap. You find yourself thinking, "I really don't believe what this individual is telling me", and (surprise, surprise) they see it written all over your face. Or, you leak some small verbal comment or aside. Should you sense, hear, or feel something that does not sit well or you are struggling to validate or corroborate, just try to listen hard for clues that may give avenues to follow up and probe further. Ask yourself: Why do I think this? What is making me feel this way? And try to follow it up in a non-judgmental way.

9. **When making mistakes, be responsible for them** – The idea here is that honesty is the best path to success. Mistakes in the witness

interview context are really to do with your understanding and interpretation of what your witness is saying. It is easy to mishear or misunderstand what your witness actually means when they use a particular form of words. By listening carefully to your witness, they will usually tell you directly or more subtly whether you have got it right or not. It takes a lot for your witness to come straight out and say to you that they think you have got it wrong, or misunderstood what they have said, a point or detail. In fact, many witnesses will simply agree with what you are saying if it is close to what they think they said – the brain finds it easier!

Practically, I have found it really useful to concentrate when I am summarizing, watching their expressions and behavior because they may well "leak" that they do not completely agree with my version or understanding. It is much more assertive, effective, and efficient to just stop for a moment and check out the accuracy of your understanding:

- "Let me stop there for a moment – you look a little unsure of that?" or
- "Ah, that's not quite right?" or
- "Oh, what exactly did you mean there, when you said..."

10. **Beware of limiting beliefs** – We often do not say something because we fear or have limiting beliefs about what a witness may think about it. I have heard many lawyers say things like: "Oh, I could never say that..." or "They would never answer *that* question...". The reality is so often very different – many witnesses have said a lot more than possibly they should, but because they have been dealt with professionally, in a fair and encouraging way, they go on to give much fuller, factual detail – the medical consultant example outlined above is just one example I have found.

    When using the cognitive interview approach, Stage 2 (the "Explanation phase") is critical because you need to give some clear directions and guidance assertively, and to ensure that you come across as believable and credible. One of the essential directions is to ask your witness to "be back in the there and then – picturing 'X', seeing it now", and so on, and you need to be able to do it well. Early on, there is a danger that you may feel silly, or simply that it would not work. Rest assured, it will work – and with practice, the better you get at it, it just sounds right, and your witness goes straight there, which is very good news because better quality, additional factual recall will emerge.

11. **Keep working on the "relationship"** – The "relationship" in this sense means the mutual respect that exists between the two people communicating – you and your witness. Talking to each other and adopting an assertive approach should ensure that you are able to remain honest and genuine with each other. Inevitably, skills of rapport-building, open and honest communication, adopting a neutral style that is professional, yet friendly and encouraging, will all help.

    This Assertive Principle is important in your repertoire because you value it, much like any of the others. It matters to you to keep your communication flowing, positive, and productive. Inevitably, this means that, from time to time, we have to work hard to stay on the same side (in a communication sense), so you take the time to check out understanding, avoid making assumptions, and summarize your understanding to ensure that your notes, and ultimately your draft (statement) or other record, will accurately reflect exactly what your witness has recalled and remembers.

Your interview style and approach – The concept of being "supportively neutral"

During training days on cognitive interviewing, I do a 20-minute demonstration of Stage 2 (the "Explanation phase") and Stage 3 ("Using the Recall techniques") of a CI where I interview a course participant, usually about a business meeting or something similar that they have had some months earlier. Someone commented when asked to describe my style and approach that it was "supportively neutral". I have to say that I like that description and observation because it embodies what is at the heart of being assertive and remaining consistent and in keeping with the cognitive interview method for witness interviewing.

Pressing the group further to give examples of the behavior that they had seen consistent with being "supportively neutral", the following was given in feedback. They said that I:

- Was confident;
- Did not interrupt;
- Gave rewards from time to time – "thank you" and nods;
- Was encouraging;

- Used pauses well;
- Asked "open" questions; and
- Did not lead or ask leading questions.

So, these are just some simple yet practical examples of adopting a "supportively neutral" style when interviewing a witness. The key things to watch out for are that you do not slip into the common pitfalls. Here is a quick reminder of "four common mistakes" – the things you should not be doing or should try to avoid:

- Asking leading or multi-headed questions;
- Interrupting your witness;
- Distracting them by sitting too close, saying too much, fidgeting; and
- Allowing your witness to go on unchecked if they deviate from your question for extended periods – look to gently bring them back on track when there are pauses.

Six types of assertiveness, plus four additional techniques

The following six types of assertiveness and additional techniques are designed to increase your understanding of the behaviors you can deploy in any witness interview to generate the full facts. This section describes how to challenge assertively differences and discrepancies or ambiguity in what you are being told.

Six types of assertiveness

There are several types of assertiveness and you have looked at this in part already when considering the Assertive Principles. The ability to be assertive and demonstrate this behavior with any witness, at any time, and anywhere is a real strength as an interviewer. The context, individual witness, and any existing relationship amongst other factors will determine which principle may be most appropriate to use at any particular moment in your interview, but for me it is all about having the maximum number of options available to use at any moment.

When you consider the following types of assertiveness, try to remember that using them is absolutely not about trying to catch people out; rather, it is about having the ability to challenge what has been said, perhaps, or to notice difference and ambiguity if that becomes apparent. Remember, too, no judgement in your voice tone when using your chosen form of words (remember the Assertive Principles above). These different types of assertiveness are all about extending your options to create a powerful communication package that is available to you whenever you need it.

Here are the six main types of assertiveness:

1. Basic assertiveness;
2. Negative feelings assertiveness;
3. Empathetic assertiveness;
4. Consequence assertiveness;
5. Discrepancy assertiveness; and
6. Responsive assertiveness.

I will go on to give definitions and examples for each of these assertiveness types, so that you can distinguish between them and also see examples of when each one can be used in a witness interview.

Here are the four further techniques:

1. Fogging;
2. Sticking to it (also called "Repetition" or "Broken record");
3. Saying "No"; and
4. Workable compromise.

We will look at these too!

Basic assertiveness

This is a straightforward statement where you say clearly and directly what it is that you want to say or feel, and not at the expense of your witness. It involves making clear your needs, wants, beliefs, opinions, or feelings about the situation, and any of these has to be appropriate to your situation.

Examples of basic assertiveness are:

- "You have been very clear, giving me some very good detail about that conversation."
- "The next step will be for me to send you your draft statement to carefully read through…"

- "I don't agree with that – there's every chance that you will be able to remember a lot if you can really focus and think as hard as you can..."
- "Please think carefully about what you have just said – what's making you say that?"
- "What I'd really like you to do is take this pad and pen and draw me a plan diagram of the room – what you need to do is..."
- "I think it's very positive that you have given very careful consideration to what you remember..."
- "I did say that we will be finished by 4.30pm and that's exactly what we will do."

Empathetic Assertiveness

This type of assertiveness contains the element of empathy as well as a statement of your needs or wants. By empathy, we mean the ability to put yourself in the other person's position and recognize the feelings, needs, and wants that they may have. As always when trying to show empathy, it has to be really meant and sincere, as well as appropriate. Many interviewers make the mistake of saying things like: "...yes, I know how you feel, awful isn't it?" When the reality is that we simply are not the witness, and so we *do not* know how they feel. However well-intentioned we may be or want to appear, many individuals will hear such statements and comments as insincerity, glib even, on the part of the interviewer, and rapport may suffer to a point where you may end up getting into an "enemy position" (see the Assertive Principles above).

Some examples of Empathetic Assertiveness are:

- "I really appreciate that you don't like talking about being there, but please, take your time and think now about actually being there, in that room etc..."
- "I know you're busy and that it's difficult to give up time that's valuable to you, but can I just explain why your contribution is so important now...?"
- "I recognize that it's difficult to look back to nearly three years ago, but if you think hard about it, remember what it felt like to be there..."
- "I can see that this must be at least the second time you have been through what happened and now I'm asking you to do it again. What I can tell you now is that today is different..."

- "Let me say now that I have never had such a difficult experience, but today is all about being able to remember what happened in great detail… You can do this well, and I'm here to help you…"

As you see from these examples, empathy is different from *sympathy*, although the two are sometimes confused in the context of witness interviews. Sympathy usually involves feeling sorry for someone, and leaves your witness where they were – feeling sorry for themselves. This works against your behaving assertively towards them. For instance: "What a shame you didn't say that at the time. I know you must be feeling very disappointed. Ah well... there we are". By contrast, *empathy* gives due recognition for where people are, and also moves them or you forward: "I do see that you're very disappointed about not discussing in detail the potential risks to the company at that time... I think now is a very good opportunity for you to try to remember what happened again, to think all about what you talked about with the broker".

Discrepancy Assertiveness

By this we mean pointing out the discrepancy between what has previously been said or agreed, and what is actually happening or about to happen. It often concludes with a statement of your needs and wants.

So, for instance:

- "Do you remember when you were telling me all about what was discussed in that conversation [pause]? I notice that you just said 'X' wasn't mentioned. Can you please think carefully about that again now [pause]; what can you remember of it?"
- "You just said that you were not even on duty on that day [pause]. Can you please help me here – this appears to be the duty state for your ward and that date [pause], and this appears to be your name and signature [pause]?"
- "Remember when you were talking about who was in the room – your trainee was sitting to your left [small pause], and the CEO, and FD to your right [pause]? Earlier you thought that there was someone else present [pause]?"
- "Thanks for that – Jack, you say? I don't recall him being mentioned before [pause]…"
- "In this email, I notice that the address at the top appears to relate to a different email account [pause]…"

Negative Feelings Assertiveness

Here you are making a statement that draws the attention of your witness to the undesirable effect their behavior is having on you. So it can contain the following four elements, not necessarily in the order given:

1. **When you…** (an objective description of other's behavior)…

   Example: "…you mention her name, you get very angry and annoyed – you've raised your voice a few times…"

2. **The effects are…** (how that behavior specifically affects you)…

   Example: "…and I then find it hard to follow you – to fully understand what the issue really is…"

3. **I feel…** (a description of your feelings)…

   Example: "…frustrated, because I want to understand the full effect that her behavior had on you, what impact there was…"

4. **I'd like…** (a statement of what you want or prefer – remember the Assertive Principle: ask for what you want)…

   Example: "I'd like you to take a moment, just take a few breaths – it'll help and take your time… please just try to relax now and tell me, tell me slowly again, talk to me about it in detail…"

Example of negative feelings assertiveness are:

- "When you keep jumping in and interrupting, we lose our way and that means we'll take longer – I'm sure neither of us wants that. What you have to say is very important, extremely valuable, and I need to hear it, but I can't talk and listen at the same time. Can I just ask you to hold on, listen hard to what I'm saying – what I'm asking you to do – and then tell me?"
- "I notice that that is the second time you have hinted that you disagree with me? That makes me feel uncomfortable about continuing, what's troubling you?"

Consequence Assertiveness

This informs your witness of the future consequences for them of not changing their behavior. It also includes an opportunity to change that behavior before the consequences occur.

So, for instance:

- "If you continue the way you are, have you considered how it could look later on down the line [pause]? What anyone looking in from outside could make of the fact that you didn't take this opportunity to explain what happened from your point of view [pause]?' We have a very good opportunity here to record exactly what happened from your perspective, to record exactly what you remember and why events unfolded the way they did [pause]. I wouldn't want you to miss this opportunity."
- "I have seen no report or any other documentation setting out your story, your version of what happened – only one side of what's alleged is contained in this pile of papers. I'm keen that you have the opportunity to give your version of what happened."
- "You have given a very full and detailed account of what happened that day and I think I have all that I need. I will go away and turn all these notes into a draft statement for you to read through. Over the next 24 hours, I would like you to still keep thinking about what you have been telling me and jot down on this paper any additional details or anything you remember differently. When can I call you tomorrow to ask what you may have jotted down?"

Responsive Assertiveness
We have listed this one last, not because it is least important, but because it is a rather different animal. The emphasis with this behavior is upon finding out where your witness stands – their needs, wants, opinions, feelings in relation to any matter or issue that you are discussing. This is often achieved by asking questions, but can also be done by statements making it clear that you would like to hear from them.

Examples of both forms are:

- "What are your reservations about going there?"
- "You look confused? Tell me…"
- "How long did it go on for?"
- "What problem does that create for you?"
- "What would you prefer to do?"
- "Sylvia, I'd like to hear exactly what went through your mind when she said that – think back carefully – try to be there now [pause].

Tell me, what's going through your mind?"

- "We have plenty of time, so please think carefully – there you are, sitting in his office [small pause], you said that he came in [small pause], tell me what you see happening next – what happens [pause]?"

Words of warning!

All of the above are small examples that illustrate in a simple way each particular type of assertiveness and, as I mentioned at the start of this section, you should be careful not to read too much into these. It is very easy to change the meaning of any of them simply by changing your intonation, and I am conscious as I write them that you could easily sound patronizing, bullish, or judgmental, and none of these should be your intention – all will have a detrimental effect on the communication flow between you and your witness.

I'm sure you will be aware of just how important your intention is – if it is positive and assertive, consistent with the Assertive Principles, then there is every chance that you will make good progress and be efficient in your task of generating high-quality factual recall from your witness.

On the other hand, being careless or thoughtless when it comes to delivering your question or statement, such as using any of the examples above, is likely to bring the shutters down on your interview. Your witness may begin to feel judged, accused, or criticized – none of which serves any purpose at all if your primary task is information gathering.

Further assertiveness techniques

In addition to the different types of assertiveness we have looked at so far, and of course the Assertive Principles, there are additional techniques that you can use to complement them, and some useful ones are described below.

Fogging

When someone is agitated, on the front foot, and even behaving aggressively, they tend to expect disagreement and charge ahead not listening. Fogging is used to slow them down by an unexpected response. It is a way of side-stepping their issue and still retaining your point of view and integrity by agreeing with some part of what they say. It is called "fogging" because the effect is very like suddenly being faced with a bank of fog when the way appeared to be clear. It is not hard, concrete, or solid; however, because it is so hard to see through or round, it is necessary to hold back a bit and pay attention to what is being encountered.

The word "yes" takes them by surprise and really helps put the brakes on. For example, if your witness said, "Well, that is a pretty stupid question", and you wanted to "fog", you might say, "Yes, I can see that you think that it was a pretty stupid question". You are not agreeing that you *had* asked a stupid question, only that you can see that they believe that.

Fogging gives you time to get things onto a more even keel and can reduce the temperature in a potentially explosive situation. Here's another example of fogging:

- Witness says: "I can't believe it – you're asking me these questions? What about the HR manager? She'd know that, not me!"
- Interviewer, fogging: "Yes, I know it must seem one-sided to you that I am asking you about this [small pause]. You have said that you were there in the meeting with her when Raj was disagreeing and I would like you to please think carefully about what you saw and heard [extended pause]."

Remember, using this technique is not a means of establishing a win/lose situation, but a means of achieving or moving towards a "workable compromise" (see the Assertive Principles) and co-operation. You are not trying to dominate your witness, far from it, but you are trying to retain control of the process by perhaps:

- Sticking to your point;
- Enabling your witness to think again;
- Consider their approach; and
- Move away from being evasive, even.

Assuming that you have a very good reason and purpose for asking this witness about this particular point, then you are trying to find that fine balance between keeping them on side (in a communication sense) and potentially alienating them, yet minimizing "wriggle-room" and allowing them to avoid answering a relevant and appropriate question to which you want an answer.

Sticking to it (Repetition or Broken Record)

This is a very powerful technique and you need to exercise care when deploying it because it can be misunderstood by your witness. You may be seen as being bullish or badgering them, neither of which is your intention. A lawyer once described this technique when used carelessly as the "Jack Russell dog syndrome" – the similarity being one of just not letting go of the issue, point, or question – like a Jack Russell dog that does not let go of your trouser leg!

Stay with your statement/request; state it calmly, firmly until it is received. You could ask the witness to say what they have understood you to have said. Avoid side issues and don't get side-tracked by saying, for example, "Look, what you mean is...." Children are experts in the use of the Broken Record technique and use it very effectively. It is useful to help make sure that you are listened to and that your message is received. Sometimes, when people are actively involved in their own concerns or needs, they pay little attention to what you have to say or to your situation. "Broken Record" makes sure that your message does get through without nagging, bullying, or badgering.

With the Broken Record technique, it is important to keep on repeating the message until it can no longer be ignored or dismissed. It is also important to use some of the same words over again in different sentences. This reinforces the main part of your message and prevents others raising red herrings or diverting you from your central message.

For example, to insistent client contact: "We won't be able to meet up until the 15th, when I am back from leave. I understand it is frustrating for you and I would like to meet sooner, but the hard fact is, I'm not back in the country until the 15th. I can give you some bullet points to think about, some key areas to try to remember before we meet up; what we can't do is have our meeting before the 15th."

Saying "No"

In the context of witness interviewing, this may seem like an odd technique to introduce – the concept of saying "No". In fact, when you start to think about it, there are many occasions when your gut-reaction – intuition – says to you, "No, that's not right", or "No, I don't think that's true or accurate", or "No, I'm not happy with that short reply; I want and need a fuller explanation". So, this particular technique is really all about trying to find a way of challenging the status quo that you are unhappy with or find unacceptable.

In other – for example, business – situations and communication, you may want to adapt what follows or find a "stronger" way of saying "No", but here in the context of witness interviews we need to try to be clear about what we want, what we want to hear, and what we don't.

During a witness interview, I often find it helpful to draw on several of the Assertive Principles and any of the different types of assertive behavior discussed above to achieve my intention at that exact moment. Remember the section above on "What do you want to say?" and the Interventions? By fully understanding what is behind any of these assertive behaviors, we can usually find the right form of words and approach to achieve our purpose.

1. **It's not easy to say "No"**

   Saying "No" can be tremendously difficult for some people. There are many different reasons why interviewers find it so hard. You do not want to offend, or you get taken off guard, or maybe it's that you just like to please others and feel that "No" would be an unwelcome response. Some interviewers are afraid of the aggressive reaction a "No" might provoke. On the other hand, some people are just unthinking or unrealistic about what they are able to deliver. Whatever the reason, a lot of individuals find 'No' impossible.

   When a child first learns to speak, it is interesting that its first word is usually "No". After "mum-mum" or "da-da", "No" is top of the list. Children so much enjoy saying "No" they even say it when they mean "Yes"!

   Think about an occasion when you were interviewing a witness and you found yourself disagreeing with something they had said, even if you just thought it. Now consider why: what lay behind your desire to say "No"? It is important for you to think about why you want to say "No". If you believe it to be the right response, then you should find a way to say it as directly as possible without making excuses and beating about the bush, or giving long-winded explanations. You retain a lot of "personal power" (strength in the way you communicate with your witness, your presence, how you are seen, standing, and credibility) if you can hold firm with your question, request, or response.

   We will look at some specific examples of saying "No" below and I hope that these will be helpful to you in your witness interviews. The key to an assertive "No" is to remember that you have the right to say "No" without guilt. Saying "No", firmly and reasonably, is quite acceptable to most people (and witnesses), and much better than ignoring what you believe. It can be helpful for people to think about the kinds of things they find hard to say "No" to, and also what kind of witnesses (personalities and behaviors your witness might demonstrate) are hard to refuse. Is it trying to stop them going off track because they hardly seem to draw breath? Challenging a witness who keeps giving contradictory information? Or perhaps even prior to the interview itself, taking on a last-minute interview request from a supervisor or partner without any time for preparation? (Rather than perhaps trying to re-schedule). Saying "No" becomes easier with practice and saves a lot of worry and lack of self-respect later. It is worth trying, not least because it builds confidence as you realize you can handle a greater variety of witness and personality types. In addition, you will notice that you are realizing the tangible business benefits that being able to use the cognitive interview approach well will bring you and your firm.

2. Saying "No" and feeling guilty

(a) Limiting beliefs:

- (i) Others can't cope with my refusal – they may feel offended/rejected and remove their good will/co-operation etc.;
- (ii) Others will disapprove of me and I can't handle that; or
- (iii) Others' needs have priority over my own all or most of the time (compassion trap – you always think the witness is "right" or can't be challenged).

(b) Results:

- (i) You say "Yes" and mean "No" (self-betrayal); or
- (ii) You say "No" and feel guilty.

(c) Consequences:

- (i) You end up doing something you don't want to do, like giving in too easily or not probing or challenging (appropriately) what you are told;
- (ii) You disrespect yourself for being "dishonest" – "dishonest" in this context means not true to what you really believe or want to ask;
- (iii) You feel resentful/annoyed/lose your temper etc. Usually this occurs after the interview has concluded – because you know that you didn't follow your intuition;

(iv) You feel that your witness has got one over on you, taken advantage of your good nature, been playing with you, that they have won and you have lost; or

(v) You feel frustrated/powerless etc. – simply that you didn't take full control of your interview and achieve all that you could, perhaps should, have had you made different choices of approach.

3. Saying "No" and feeling OK

(a) Notice your immediate gut reaction – it's often an infallible guide.

(b) If you're unsure, ask for more information, check out your understanding, and pose probing questions – open questions like: "I'm interested that you said... [pause]?" or "Why do you think that [pause]?"

(c) Take responsibility for saying "No" rather than passing the buck or blaming someone else. Example: "I think that there's more you are not saying [small pause]. No, that's not it – talk to me... [extended pause]"

(d) Remember, you are refusing a request, not rejecting the person. People may or may not feel hurt by your refusal. Example: "No, I don't accept that, I'd like you to think very hard and tell me again, but in your own words – take your time..."

(e) A refusal does not have to be heavy, aggressive, or hurtful. Example: "You've said that before, but we both know that's not what you really think, is it?"

(f) Do not hover around out of anxiety, this can result in indecisive immobility. This is very common after making some kind of challenge or intervention that may have felt uncomfortable for your witness. Incorrectly, we look for approval, some kind of reassurance that your witness still "likes" you. Try to avoid this by moving on positively and swiftly after you have listened to and recorded the information you need. I've often heard interviewers saying things like: "Is that OK?" or "Sorry to ask you to do that..." or "How do you feel now?" These responses may be appropriate in some circumstances, of course, but not after you have exposed some information and facts detrimental to your witness, or caught them being evasive, lying perhaps, or simply after they have disclosed facts that they had not declared previously (perhaps in an earlier interview).

(g) Sometimes, it will be appropriate to offer an alternative. Example: "No, I can see that you don't want to go there at the moment, to look at what Jane has said, but we will return to it later – can we agree to that? Let's return towards the end of the interview to that point – agreed?"

(h) Stand firm and people will know where they are with you. Example: "You know that we can't really move on until we've explored that meeting – exactly what was discussed and what the argument was about?"

4. Assertive approach to saying "No"

(a) Making your decision – This is a key element, perhaps the most important element, to being able to challenge and/or say "No" – making the decision. Dithering and indecision are your worst enemies at a time like this. Think about using one of the helpful "holding" questions like: "Tell me more about why you say that [pause]?"

Just by asking one of these types of probing questions, a witness will often reveal more information or take you to a deeper level of understanding about their motivation, or what was behind their actions or behavior.

5. Saying "No" clearly

If you decide to say no, then work out a short statement which will make that message clear. If possible, be prepared to use the word "No" since nothing could be clearer than that. You have some good examples above.

Make your statement an "I" statement, so you take responsibility for the decision. Some examples include: "No, that's not right...", "No I'm not willing/prepared to...", "No, that's not something I want to explore at the moment...", and "The answer's no". It is important that you find the form of words with which you feel most comfortable (given that saying "No" is often uncomfortable anyway). Let your witness know your "decision", what you intend to do or not to do. Use assertive body language to come across as positive, firm, clear, intentional – expressions, adopting an "open" posture, leaning forward slightly, or maintaining eye contact could all be used appropriately, adding to your presence and sense of gravitas.

Handling emotion in your interview

How to handle emotion in your witness

Handling difficult witnesses? No, not really. I've never really been able to accept this as a satisfactory title for working with this key area of witness interviewing. The main concern I have is that already we are starting to "blame" the witness for not performing or behaving in a way that we approve of or are easily able to handle. Certainly, we may have witnesses that we find difficult and challenging; the issue for us as interviewers is finding a way to connect and maintain an open, flowing channel of communication and factual recall.

Going back to the initial work by Geiselman and Fisher, it transpired that it is not the witness who is the "problem" in most cases at all, rather the way the interviewer conducts the interview and their behavior (by asking leading questions, interrupting with more questions, distracting the witness, and so on), and hence the importance and value of adopting the CI approach. In a similar way, we should really focus here on behaviors that can be used to help our witness through the process of recall, even if this is difficult for them.

What if my witness gets upset? What can I do?

Many witnesses get upset, and that is a fact of life in this kind of work. When it happens, it is important not to feel embarrassed or uncomfortable. This is sometimes hard to do – especially the "feeling uncomfortable" part. Initially staying quiet, pausing, and listening hard can be a real help to them. Equally, within a few moments, it is likely to be appropriate to quietly come in with a small supportive comment (see the Interventions above) like:

- "That's ok, no problem [pause]…"; or
- "That's fine, take a moment [pause]…".

Something of this sort can be very beneficial to your witness because it is supportive and also shows that you are able to handle their emotion professionally. Do you have your "emotional first aid kit" to hand? In no way do I intend to be flippant or devalue the really difficult place some witnesses find themselves in when interviewed, but here I am talking about a practical "kit" to help you and them: a box of tissues, water, or other refreshment to hand, a quiet location and careful consideration of your location (e.g. in Stage 1 of the CI Model – Setting the environment) are all important, and any failure here on your part may come home to haunt you.

Be prepared to carry on after a few moments and remember the eye patterns, too – especially when your witness looks down and to your left, their right, as they may well be accessing emotional recollection. So, when your witness looks like they are able to move on, you may want to quietly ask if that's ok? Equally, you may just make the decision to move on, taking your time and care to use a low yet assertive voice and an "open" style of questioning. That could include some good, probing questions that often work well when you re-engage like:

- "Go, on, tell me... [pause]"; or
- "You were saying... [small pause], what are you thinking? [long pause]..."

I feel that what is key here is not to blow your interview – pull out or panic – but to try to stay calm, in control, and think what your witness may need from you at this moment. Support, a few moments to gather themselves, reassurance, information, or simply nothing at all – just a quiet space to sit for a few moments. Sometimes, it is necessary for a witness to become emotional when they recall what happened, and working with it, in a positive, proactive way, can help them access facts that may only ever be recalled if they think and recall emotionally. Equally, I would not be too keen to call for a big break in the interview, perhaps quickly resorting to a re-scheduled date – this can simply postpone the problem, is costly, and is likely to be counter-productive, but is an option that you could consider as a last resort.

What if my witness gets angry or annoyed?[4]

- **Listen hard and stay quiet** – Stop, wait, pause, and listen hard – listen out for themes or a point in what they are saying, even if this feels uncomfortable to listen to. In some respects, your initial reaction is similar to that above for an upset witness – stay calm, quiet, and listen hard. This is a critical part of the initial response – an ability not to exacerbate and inflame the situation. What is important is to try to quickly, yet patiently, listen for what may lie behind or be the cause of this emotion. It can be very frustrating for witnesses to "be back there again" going through their story once more and perhaps talking to a lawyer who (in their mind) does not understand their position at all.

- **Take your time and look for a suitable pause to re-engage** – But not too quickly. They will want and need to have their say, to get "it" off their chest. Having stayed quiet and listened, a useful way to re-engage as soon as you feel they have calmed a little (perhaps a lot!) is to consider saying something like:
  - "Right, I can see that this has really frustrated you, James, and what you seem to be saying is…"; or
  - "James, yes, yes, I can see that must be very frustrating for you – I can see you are angry about 'X' and I want to help you now with that. When you said…[go for the point, the key thing that you believe is the problem or causing their anxiety at that moment]…"

  Thinking about the material you have read above, you could use an "empathetic assertiveness" response such as: "James, I can see exactly how frustrating that must have been in your position, I really get that and what I want to say now is…"
- **Don't interrupt** – A key element of success will come, in situations involving high emotion, from the interviewer not interrupting – this can be fatal in terms of making effective progress. Remember, behavior breeds behavior – the way people behave towards you is directly related to the way you behave towards them, and it is worth remembering this at all times. Keep demonstrating assertive behavior and, in all probability, your witness will eventually moderate their behavior and move to being more assertive and "reasonable" with you.
- **Avoid being defensive** – Remember the Assertive Principles? Avoid being judgmental and do not take it personally. Avoid interrupting and trying to defend your position or what you have said. It may be that your witness is looking for an explanation and justification for why you are asking what you are, but this should really all have been taken care of via an early phone call and/or in Stage 1 (Setting the environment), or finally in the Explanation (Stage 2 of the CI Model).

  A key task is to remain objective and focused on your interview plan, not deciding to go head-to-head with your witness – that is likely only to alienate them and cause a stalemate or withdrawal from full engagement in the process. Notice and listen to your own responses to your witness's behavior – why are you thinking the way you are, and what's behind your reactions to what they are saying? Taking a few discreet long breaths to get oxygenated blood flowing into your brain will help you to think quickly and more clearly (also useful for when you are presenting at a conference or other public speaking).

- **Consequence Assertiveness** – Consider spelling out what is likely to be the outcome of continuing with any behavior, especially with negative behavior such as: the interview will take longer, you won't be able to represent their views properly and fairly, others may read negatively into what they have been saying and doing. The whole point here is to remain assertive, not to judge, but to get things back onto a more positive footing as soon as possible and make progress towards your interview objectives and outcomes (see above for more detail).
- **Don't argue!** – This may sound obvious when you read it here, but it's surprising how often it happens in witness interviews. At the end of the day, if you *want* something different you have to do something different (one of the key presuppositions from Emotional Intelligence – EI). So, for example, your witness does not appear to be listening to you because they keep focusing on some point or other that is uppermost in their mind and they do not answer your question – think about why that may be. Often, it is better to listen hard and try to deal with their "issue" rather than argue or ignore it. When that is cleared, you are likely to start getting answers to your questions and making progress.
- **Fogging** – (See "Further Assertiveness Techniques" described in this chapter.)

Final thoughts

Remember that this is "your" interview, yours in terms of running and controlling it. That means controlling the process using all your skills and knowledge of the CI approach and the underpinning skills identified here, plus any others that are needed. You can control your own behavior, and you can influence how others (your witness) behave towards you by deploying assertiveness in any of its forms and keeping to your interview plan. Take time to review afterwards any occasions in interviews when they have got out of hand or you have had difficulties in managing your witness's behavior, making adjustments, and trying something different until you get the response you are looking for that will move you both forward.

Protecting yourself and colleagues

This is really just an opportunity to consider self-protection and your own personal safety as well as that of any colleague who may be with you. Here are just a few considerations:

- **Let the office, PA, or a colleague know where you are at all times** – This is especially important if interviewing away at the home of a witness.
- **Consider taking a colleague** – Any colleague could do, potentially – maybe a trainee, or other relatively junior member from your firm if they are available. They could always help by taking notes and offer other practical help to justify their attendance (and extra cost).
- **Location** – Home (your office) is likely to be better than away (their home or chosen location) for the location of your interview. You have more control and can set up your environment in the best way to suit you and your witness.
- **What's their mood?** – Consider all contact to date and prior to your interview – and also consider making a confirmation call on the day of your interview to briefly test their mood and attitude to the task ahead.
- **Contingency** – Consider agreeing with a colleague to call you at an agreed time soon after you estimate that your interview will be concluded, just to check that all is well. Remember, if you have any doubts at all about going to interview a witness at their location, don't do it. Consider a neutral venue as a compromise if they seem unwilling or it simply is not practical for them to come to your office.

This first appeared as Chapter 5 in Coughlin, G., Unlocking Memories: Cognitive Interviewing for Lawyers, *ARK Group, 2015.*

References

1. For more information on observing eye patterns in witness interviews, see Coughlin, G., *Unlocking Memories: Cognitive Interviewing for Lawyers*, ARK Group, 2015.
2. Wikipedia: https://en.wikipedia.org/wiki/Active_listening.
3. Fisher, R.P., and Geiselman, R.E., *Memory-Enhancing Techniques for Investigative Interviewing, The Cognitive Interview*, Thomas, Springfield, IL, 1992.
4. A good source of further reading and practical help is: Mulligan, J., *The Personal Management Handbook – How to make the most of your potential*, Sphere, London, 1995 and 1988.

www.ingramcontent.com/pod-product-compliance
Ingram Content Group UK Ltd.
Pitfield, Milton Keynes, MK11 3LW, UK
UKHW021849150926
8657IPUK00005B/168

9 781783 582235